CRUDE DOMINATION

DISLOCATIONS

General Editors: August Carbonella, *Memorial University of Newfoundland*, Don Kalb, *Central European University & University of Utrecht*, Linda Green, *University of Arizona*

The immense dislocations and suffering caused by neoliberal globalization, the retreat of the welfare state in the last decades of the twentieth century, and the heightened military imperialism at the turn of the twenty-first century have raised urgent questions about the temporal and spatial dimensions of power. Through stimulating critical perspectives and new and cross-disciplinary frameworks that reflect recent innovations in the social and human sciences, this series provides a forum for politically engaged, ethnographically informed theoretically incisive responses to these important issues of late modernity.

CRUDE DOMINATION

An Anthropology of Oil

Edited by
Andrea Behrends, Stephen P. Reyna
and Günther Schlee

Berghahn Books
NEW YORK • OXFORD

First published in 2011 by

Berghahn Books

www.berghahnbooks.com

© 2011 Andrea Behrends, Stephen P. Reyna and Günther Schlee

The permission to reproduce the cover image and the production of the
index for this book were both generously funded by the German
Research Foundation (DFG).

Library of Congress Cataloging-in-Publication Data

Crude domination : an anthropology of oil / edited by Andrea Behrends,
Stephen P. Reyna, and Günther Schlee.
    p. cm. -- (Dislocations v.9)
  Includes bibliographical references and index.
  ISBN 978-0-85745-255-9 (hardback : alk. paper) -- ISBN 978-0-85745-256-6
(e-book)
  1. Petroleum industry and trade--Social aspects. 2. Petroleum industry and
trade--Cross-cultural studies. 3. Social responsibility of business. 4. Human
rights and globalization. 5. Culture and globalization. I. Behrends, Andrea.
II. Reyna, Stephen P. III. Schlee, Günther
  HD9560.5.C78 2011
  338.2'7282--dc22

                                                                2011014624

British Library Cataloguing in Publication Data

A catalogue record for this book is available from the British Library

Printed in the United States on acid-free paper

ISBN 978-0-85745-255-9 (hardback)
ISBN 978-0-85745-256-6 (ebook)

CONTENTS

Part III | Latin America

Part IV | Post-socialist Russia

LIST OF FIGURES

PART I

GENERALITIES

Chapter 1

THE CRAZY CURSE AND CRUDE DOMINATION

Towards an Anthroplogy of Oil

Stephen P. Reyna and Andrea Behrends

The oil price is very high, it's crazy. There is no additional supply.
—Pumomo Yusgiantoro, OPEC President (*The Economist*, 2004)

Immanuel Wallerstein wrote of a 'systemic crisis' that he believes within twenty-five to fifty years would produce 'disintegration of our existing historical social system' (1997: 1256). Strong rhetoric from a person dedicated to painstaking investigation of the *longue durée* of the modern world system, and not to histrionics. It might be objected that Wallerstein is to the Left and besides that he is an intellectual and so not a practical person of the world. Consider the practical world of government and journalism. Alan Greenspan, ex-Chairman of the US Federal Reserve, respected elder statesman of US finance and an architect of neo-liberal globalism, has written *The Age of Turbulence: Adventures in a New World* (2007). Here he suggests that it is now a time of instability, a world of turbulence. Naomi Klein, a journalist covering global calamities, has written *The Shock Doctrine: The Rise of Disaster Capitalism* (2007) in which she strips away neo-liberal cloaking rhetoric to reveal contemporary capitalism in shockingly complicit bondage with disaster. So there you have it. Recently, on the Left and Right, academics, statesmen and journalists have been talking of 'systemic crises' in a world of 'turbulence' characterised by 'disaster capitalism'. Why?

Responding to this question brings us to oil. Oil is the key scarce, strategic resource needed for almost all capitalist enterprise (Homer-Dixon 2001; Klare 2002). It is not renewable. One concern of those studying oil has been how to conceptualise its supply. M. King Hubbert suggested in the 1950s that it might be imagined as a bell curve. This meant it would have an ascending slope as output increased; a highest point before decrease set in; and a descending slope, as output decreased. The high point has come to be known as 'Hubbert's Peak'. Hubbert's work allowed yearly projections of what the oil supply bell curve would look like. In 1956 he predicted US oil production would peak around 1970 and decline thereafter. The prediction of production decline after the peak was correct. His simulation methods have been improved and found to be reliable (Deffeyes 2006). Thus, the approach helps answer the question: what years will be those of Hubbert's Peak, after which production subsides? Available evidence suggests that Hubbard's Peak is fast approaching. There are ninety-eight oil-producing countries in the world; sixty-four of these are believed to have passed their geologically imposed production peak; and of those, sixty are in terminal production decline (Strahan 2007). Oil prospecting has turned sour. In 2010 oil production declined by 1,2 million barrels per day, or 1,7 %, the largest decline since 1982 (BP 2010). Peak oil specialists predicted that Hubbert's Peak had occurred, or would occur between 2000 and 2010 (Kunstler 2006). Indeed, Deffeyes has asserted it occurred in 2005 (in Green Car Congress 2006). Consumption of oil, on the other hand, has been predicted to rise 60 per cent between 2003 and 2025 (IAGS 2003). So, oil production declines, very soon, under conditions of rising demand. Its replacement is theoretically possible, though not currently economically or technically feasible.

What will the loss of oil mean? There is a general concurrence that there will be severe and lengthy worldwide depression resultant from shrunken economic activity, high inflation, and rising transportation costs. Furthermore, reduction of petroleum supplies will compromise food production, threatening mass human starvation, because contemporary industrial agriculture is dependent on cheap oil (for fertiliser, herbicides, pesticides and machinery fuel). Additionally, the carbon dioxide released into the atmosphere by the utilisation of fossil fuels is a major cause of global warming. This means that global warming will accompany consumption of the remaining oil supplies 'during the 21st century' and 'could lead to a relatively abrupt lowering of the ocean' temperature due to melting icepacks, which, in turn, could lead to 'harsher winter weather …, sharply reduced soil moisture and more intense winds', leading finally to reduction in 'the human carrying capacity of the Earth's environment' (Schwartz and Randall 2003: 1). It should be noted that the preceding judgement does not come from 'radical' ecologists. Schwartz and Randall work for the US Department of Defense. Under such conditions, according to one observer, 'If the US controls the sources of energy of its rivals – Europe, Japan, China and other nations aspiring to be more independent – they win' (Dayaneni and Wing 2002: 2). Thus, there is a gathering 'turbulence', due to 'systemic crisis' because, as the head of OPEC put it in 2004, there is 'no additional supply' of oil – 'it's crazy'.

One point to draw from the preceding is that in some sense the future of the world depends upon oil and how humans use it. As the past and the present are the *only* predictors of the future, this means to some extent that the fate of humanity depends upon inquiries into how oil affects the dynamics of human social forms. As we shall see below, anthropological inquiry into oil is limited, while that of other social sciences is richer. So the goal of this introduction is to propose a research strategy for anthropological analysis of oil. It will do so by interrogating findings of existing oil literatures, discussing the research implications of the articles that compose the offerings of this book, and finally sketching on the basis of these analyses an anthropology of oil in a turbulent world. This sketch, offered in the third section, will propose a 'crude domination' approach, whose goal is explanation of oil's crazy curse.

The Crazy 'Curse': Current Approaches

The oil literature to be discussed is that in economics, political science and anthropology starting in the 1970s, because it was at this time that the current turbulence began. The turbulence began on a high note. Oil prices boomed in the years following the early 1970s, bringing, according to one oil minister, 'More money than we ever in our wildest dreams thought possible' (in Karl 1997: 3). 'Petro-states', as understood here, are capital-intensive oil exporters with high ratios of oil to total exports; petroleum industry enclaves; and enormous rents or royalties (from oil sales), which accrue directly to the central government. 'Social development' is any sequence of events that leads to beneficent, sustainable economic, social and political change for all segments of a population. The 1970s boom meant that oil rents became enormous. Petro-dollars, people dreamed, would buy petrostates' development. Dream and reality marched down different paths.

Oil turned out to be a development 'curse' (Auty 1993; Ross 1999). Most petro-states found their economic performance worsened in the 1990s (Attiga 1981; Gelb 1988; Karl 1997, 1999). Some 'oil rich' petro-states found themselves 'dirt poor' in the sense that their poor became poorer (Gary and Karl 2003). Michael Ross (2001) found democracy unlikely and authoritarian regimes likely in petro-states. Worse, oil is 'black gold' over which social pirates fiercely compete. So, oil-exporting countries have found themselves operating under conditions of intense internal and external conflict (Kaldor, Karl and Said 2007; Klare 2002). Some of this has been non-violent, involving competition for oil-derived benefits. Much has been violent. There has been international (Peluso and Watts 2001; Vallette et al. 2003) and intra-state warfare (Ross 2002). 'Oil's curse', as understood here, is the triple conjuncture in petro-states of stagnating social development and poverty; high conflict, often violent; and a tendency towards authoritarian regimes.

The preceding suggests a paradox: if money is a condition of development, and it surely is, why do petro-dollars buy petro-curse rather than petro-utopia? Because this paradox is so puzzling – what is supposed to create prosperity makes the reverse – let us recognise that oil producers suffer from a *crazy* curse. Crazy phenomena have an important effect on human welfare, therefore they beg for solution. Accordingly, investigation of oil's crazy curse is the research object of this anthropology of oil. Some major contributions to this literature are considered next.

Resource Curse, Dutch Disease and Greed

Economics, often labelled the dismal science, strengthens this reputation with its handling of oil's crazy curse. Classical economists in the eighteenth and nineteenth centuries first formulated theory relevant to the curse. They observed that Spain and England had marched down vastly different developmental paths – Spain to decline, England to growth. Adam Smith explained this with a theory of resources, which warned of the perils of natural resource rents. 'Rents' or 'royalties' are payments to owners of land for using its various raw materials in the production of goods and services. Economies based on renting natural resources motivate rent-seeking behaviour and not profits from productive activity (Smith 1776). Further, raw material rents were exhaustible and, thus, experienced diminishing returns (Mill 1851). Thus classical theory predicted that economies based upon rent of their raw materials were flawed. Their logic was: rent a lot, and then less and less. It was as if they suffered a 'resource curse'.

The Dutch Disease, based upon studies of contemporary resource booms, seemed to amplify classical theory of rentier economies (Auty 1993). This 'disease' is a body of generalisations concerning 'the sectorial reallocation of productive factors' during a raw material boom' (Gelb 1988: 22). Specifically,

> if the income derived from this is spent rather than saved abroad, the sum of the consequences includes a resource movement effect which draws factors of production out of other activities and into the booming sector, and a spending effect which draws factors of production out of activities producing traded commodities (to be substituted by imports) and into non traded sectors. (ibid.)

'Traded sectors' are those selling export goods. They are usually in industry and agriculture. They suffer. 'Non-traded sectors' are those not involved in export trade, and include services and transportation. These prosper. Oil is a particular resource, so oil's curse is a specific instance of the Dutch Disease in petroleum-based resource booms.

Sachs and Warner believed that the evidence showed the curse to be 'solid fact' (2001: 828). Recently, however, 'solid fact' has appeared less so. Some find the Dutch Disease 'less common' than originally believed (Ross 1999: 305). David and Wright (1997) provided evidence that some resource-based economies actually do well, while others do not. Thus economic evidence suggests: sometimes economic development was hampered by the curse and sometimes it is not.

Recently in economics, stimulated by the work of two economists associated with the World Bank, Paul Collier and Anke Hoeffler, there has come to be an economic explanation of why oil's curse involves so much warfare. Collier's and Hoeffler's approach emphasises greed, asserting on the basis of statistical data from seventy-eight civil conflicts from 1960 up to and including 1999, that 'opportunities are more important in explaining conflict than are motives' (Collier and Hoeffler 2001: 2). Further, abundant resources play a major role in providing opportunities, and greed to control these resources – legally or illegally – provokes and/or maintains wars, most of which are civil strife. This approach to the association of warfare and oil is discussed and critiqued in Andrea Behrends' contribution to this book. Suffice it to say that it has become a major position in the literature of oil and violence attracting support, modification and scepticism (Ballentine and Sherman 2003; Marchal and Messiant 2002; Reno 2004). Let us now turn to political science.

Rent Seeking, Institutional and Patrimonial Theory

Two political science approaches have been significant in the study of oil's curse. The first offers an explanation of petro-states' development difficulties under conditions of rent seeking. The second is more specific to African conditions and emphasises patrimonialism. Karl's seminal investigation of oil booms, *The Paradox of Plenty*, emphasises 'political institutions' (1997: xvi). Her central claim is 'that prior interactions of structure and agency create the institutional legacy that constrains choice down the road' (1997: 10). These legacies are path dependencies. In petro-states high oil rents multiply 'the opportunities for both public authorities and private interests to engage in rent seeking' (1997: 15). 'Rent seeking' occurs when an individual, organisation or firm seeks money by manipulating the political and/or economic environment, rather than by making a profit through either trade or productive enterprise (Krueger 1974). US agriculture is rent seeking when its agents seek subsidies and tariffs to protect its revenues. Rent seeking, according to Karl, in petro-states 'leads to a … marriage between entrepreneurs seeking to link up with the state and public officials seeking to intervene further in the market'; with the unfortunate economic consequence that the state's oil rents go to those adept at manipulating officials and not 'to those engaged in less remunerative but more productive activities' (1997: 57). This is a rent seeking/institutional hypothesis because transformations that lead down the path of development difficulties result from actors altering economic and political institutions to facilitate rent seeking. Oil ministries and companies become institutions that distribute oil rents. Private enterprises become institutions less involved in productive or distributive business than in seeking rents.

African oil is becoming increasingly important to the global economy. Further, African petro-states, as documented by Behrends, Ekholm-Friedman, Reyna and Watts in their contributions to this book, have been especially and violently burdened by oil's curse. A type of patrimonialism, called neo-patrimonialism, may explain this situation (Bayart 1993). Weber (1978) developed the concept of patrimonial states for ancient and medieval polities where the state was regarded as some form of 'private' property of a kin group. Certain political scientists, importantly J.-F. Médard (1992), proposed that a 'neo-patrimonialism' explains postcolonial African states' development woes. This is because institutions of 'public authority' in African states were 'made an object of appropriation by the formal officeholders, functionaries, politicians and military personnel', who based their 'individual ascendancy or family ascendancy on a private usage of the *res publica*' (ibid.: 167). This is a neo-patrimonialism because 'patrimons', officials with the capacity to allocate public assets, act as if the state were their patrimony, even though in contemporary times this is not the case. Patrimons allocate public assets from public institutions to maintain or create loyalty among their rent-seeking clients, kin or friends. Oil rents are public assets. Their vastness in petro-states raises the potential of corruption to new levels. This can produce two possible, not mutually exclusive outcomes. A first outcome is that client enterprises perform poorly because clients lack the qualifications to manage the enterprises. This is well documented for Gabon (Yates 1996). A second outcome is that conflict turns violent, because the patrimon's favouritism to certain rent seekers inflames antagonism among the disfavoured. Let us now consider literature on the anthropology of oil.

The Anthropology of Oil

Roy Rappaport, when President of the American Anthropological Association (1987–1989), urged the discipline to contribute to the formulation of public policy, particularly that concerning the drilling of oil and gas. But to many anthropologists at the time such a concern seemed peripheral. Why do applied anthropology, when there were other, tastier fish to fry; such as those in *Writing Culture* (Clifford and Marcus, 1986) and other fishy, postmodern delicacies? Consequently, today the *New York Times* does not announce triumph after triumph in the anthropological analysis of oil, rather it publicises Pentagon programmes to embed anthropologists in the US Army to support the USA's colonial oil wars in Iraq and Afghanistan (Rohde 2007).

Scrutiny of the literature that does exist reveals some fine studies, informed by anthropology, by those in other disciplines, such as Robert's Vitalis' work on Saudi Arabia (2006). Some applied anthropology did follow Rappaport's suggestion and sought to document the effect of oil on local communities in oil- or gas-producing regions. There have been impact studies, for example, concerning New Guinea (Sagir 2004), Nigeria (Fentiman 1996), the US Gulf coast (McGuire and Gardner 2003), throughout the Arctic north (Degteva 2006; Picou et. al 1992), and Latin America (Pearce 2004; Rival 1997). There are articles where discussion of oil is a detail in a broader canvas; for example, James Ferguson's insightful critique of James Scott's *Seeing Like a State* (Ferguson 2005). Finally, and promising for a richer future, there is research by younger anthropologists who make oil the core of their intellectual practice. However, there are three mature works concerning the anthropology of oil including Suzana Sawyer's *Crude Chronicles: Indigenous Politics, Multinational Oil, and Neoliberalism in Ecuador* (2004), Andrew Apter's *The Pan-African Nation: Oil and the Spectacle of Culture in Nigeria* (2005) and Fernando Coronil's *The Magical State: Nature, Money, and Modernity in Venezuela* (1997). Let us look more closely at these texts, beginning with Sawyer's book.

Ecuador's Amazon jungle is a major supplier of crude oil to the United States. Consequently, the Ecuadorian Amazon has endured the economic, political and environmental consequences of a growing US thirst for petroleum and the policies of neo-liberalism designed to satisfy that thirst. *Crude Chronicles* tells the story of the rise of an organised indigenous movement during the 1990s and its struggles against a US oil company and Ecuadorian neo-liberal policies. *Crude Chronicles* documents the growing sophistication of indigenous politics – utilising marches, demonstrations, occupations and negotiations – as Indians fenced with, undermined and, occasionally, yielded to US Big Oil. Equally, Sawyer follows the complex strategies and discourses that the multinational corporations and the Ecuadorian state deployed as they sought to brook no opposition from their indigenous opponents. Against mounting government attempts to privatise and liberalise the national economy, Suzana Sawyer shows how Ecuadorian neo-liberal reforms led to a crisis of governance, accountability and representation that fuelled one of twentieth-century Latin America's strongest indigenous movements and which ultimately led to the more leftist government that currently governs Ecuador. Crudely put, the heart of Sawyer's analysis is who is going to get how much of the value of the crude and, as such, her ethnography documents conflict between Big Oil, their neo-liberal allies in the Ecuadorian state, and indigenous Amazonians over oil rents.

Pan-African Nation interprets the significance of the Second World Black and African Festival of Arts and Culture (FESTAC) in 1977. This was for Nigeria a Lollapalooza-style cultural extravaganza, as important for what might be termed a Nigerian postmodernity as England's Great Exhibition in the Crystal Palace had been for Anglo-Saxon modernity. *Pan-African Nation* argues that FESTAC forged a new national culture, one reflecting Nigeria's confidence resultant from its oil boom, through its showcasing of masks, dances, images and souvenirs from its different peoples. In the dazzle of its oil boom, FESTAC stood as an 'empire' of cultural signs that included all Black and African cultures within its sovereignty, erasing colonial cultural memories from collective consciousness. But Apter also documents the postcolonial Nigerian political economy in which this cultural 'empire' is found. Here he describes the association of an ethnic clientelism with oil wealth and the rise of a new entrepreneurial elite. This elite struggles for as much of the oil rents as possible using kin and ethnic clients in a distinctively Nigerian version of the patron/client model.

Let us now turn to Coronil's work. *The Magical State* is a minor classic with three analytic concerns. The first is to offer a historical interpretation of Venezuelan state dynamics tossed in the turbulence of oil booms and busts. At the heart of these dynamics was the cultural view that the state, the 'transcendant and unifying agent of the nation' (1997: 4), would act as the guardian of natural wealth, 'sow the soil' with oil wealth, and magically bring about a prosperous and diversified modernity, hence the notion of a 'magical state'. *The Magical State*'s second concern is to present an ethnography of the state during the boom of the 1970s and the bust of the 1980s. The third concern is to interrogate Marx's theory of ground rent, in the context of a Latin American literature on dependency and underdevelopment, in order to contribute to theory of subaltern modernity. The second concern is in many ways the most original. *The Magical State* explores the rise during the boom years of a motor industry, the rise and fall of a tractor factory, and the emergence of a new criminality, involving political assassination. Coronil interviewed the actors in these events, be they government officials, corporate executives or just ordinary folk, and was able to construct their daily lives and lived experience in the 'magical state'. Coronil's contribution to subaltern studies argues that the Venezuelan state is dominant in Venezuela but subaltern in a global system dominated economically, politically and discursively by an 'Occidentalism'. However, each of the three sections reports a similar *telos* for life in the magical state. This *telos* applies both to individuals and groups and has to do with striving to acquire a slice of the oil pie. So oil rents were disributed not so magically throughout the nation, but pragmatically to those whose strategies prevailed in contests over oil rents.

Anthropology, as is illustrated by this work, brings to the investigation of oil's crazy curse three benefits absent in economic and political science approaches, and one concurrence with them. First, absent in the other approaches, is the presentation of the reality of an oil-dominated world from the vantage of everyday, experienced lives. Second, these lives tend to be lived in local settings. Third, there is an expertise in discovering the significance of culture in the crazy curse. However, the anthropologists share with their counterparts in economics and politics recognition that crude realities, i.e., those involving oil, tend to be conflictual, involving a struggle over acquisition of oil rents. Let us offer a summary of these oil literatures.

Five explanations of oil's crazy curse predominate. The economists posit: (1) a resource curse, (2) the Dutch Disease, or (3) Collier and Hoeffler's greed hypothesis; according to political scientists, the crazy curse is explained by (4) rent-seeking/institutional theories or (5) patrimonial theories. These explanations are not necessarily mutually exclusive. The Dutch Disease is an amplification of the resource curse. The greed hypothesis, rent-seeking/institutional and patrimonial approaches might well operate when the resource curse is present. No anthropological account of oil's crazy curse has been as remotely influential as the five preceding positions. However, anthropologists bring to the study of oil concern for human experience, in local settings, in which culture operates. It is time to turn to the contributions of the anthropologists in this book.

The Crazy Curse: Contributors' Approaches

Apart from this introduction there are ten chapters in this volume. One traces the wider implications of oil in a global perspective (Friedman); four investigate Africa (Watts, Behrends, Ekholm-Friedman and Reyna); three Latin America (Gledhill, Schiller and Gustafson); and two post-Soviet

Russia (Khizriyeva/Reyna and Stammler). The rationale for such a choice is that it allows comparison between older, established petro-states (those in Latin America and Russia) and younger, emerging ones (those in Africa). Günther Schlee adds an afterword placing the contributors' comments within a broader context. We begin our discussion in Africa. Michael Watts is a geographer by training, but his African work is so deeply informed by anthropology that it can be included with the anthropologists. Further, his work over the decades has established him as one of the major figures in the social analysis of oil.

His article provides understanding of the current oil insurgency of the Niger Delta in Nigeria. It does this by revealing the full complexity of local, regional and global structures and policies influencing this rebellion. Watts documents a new 'scramble for the prize of African oil'. He explains the insurgency as the result of a particular dynamic exhibited by African petro-states, characterised by a 'descent into violence and ungovernmentality' resulting from a 'vortex of forces linking dispossession, war and energy'. This 'vortex' is the article's focus. It is analysed in six parts. In the first, Watts situates readers in a Panglossian world that is the contemporary Niger Delta. Remember Pangloss was Voltaire's character in *Candide* who promulgated hyperreality as the best of all possible worlds in a world whose actuality was utter horror. In the Niger Delta, Panglossian hyperreality – orderly modernity conjured by politicians, planners and development experts – turns out to be an everyday life 'weirded out' on the steroids of violence, poverty and competing (so, mutually defeating) governmentalities. Such life in the Niger Delta is, as it was in Voltaire's fable, utter horror; except that the Delta is no fable. The remaining sections of Watts' contribution explore the vortex generating this situation. The second section analyses the role in the vortex of recent development policy, a world view dominated by the neo-liberalism of Hayek, the structural adjustment of the World Bank, and the stabilisation policies of the IMF the consequences of which have been further underdevelopment of Africa. The third section details application of this world view in the development of the oil industry throughout the continent. The fourth and fifth sections narrow the analysis of the vortex to Nigeria and the Niger Delta, explaining how two institutional forms – the petro-state and the oil complex – operate in the vortex. The final section adds an 'imperial' force to the vortex, reporting development by the USA and Europe of a military capability to control African oil; especially in the Gulf of Guinea where the Niger Delta is located. Watts concludes his analysis of the vortex of forces operative in the Delta with a rejection of what he terms the 'commodity determinism' of economic explanations of warfare in petro-states. Rather, he suggests that in the Delta 'insurgency emerged from the political struggles over centralised oil rents, a struggle in which party politics, the electoral cycle, inter-generational politics, organised oil theft and the history of ethnic exclusion played constitutive roles'. In effect, Watts accuses the economists of oversimplification. It is not simply the oil that determines the occurrence of violence, it is the complex of institutions, each with their different powers, that forms a vortex with the force to drive actors to violence.

There follows Behrends' article concerning the border zone between two countries – Sudan and Chad. Most of the social science oil literature deals with areas of well established oil production. Understudied are regions where the oil sector has only just begun. Therefore, inclusion of these two countries allows us to strengthen our understanding of the beginnings of petro-states.

Behrends' chapter considers the case of fighting for potential oil when there is no actual oil yet. It does so by explaining the role of regional actors, such as rebel militias; national actors, such as the Sudanese and Chadian governments; and international actors, such as multinational oil companies, the United States, China and the UN. Importantly, Behrends brings individual actors into the analysis; showing their relevance to events involving global processes and, further, that individuals in different structural positions possess varying subjectivities. So for example, local actors fight for reasons quite different from those of regional or national actors. Why they fight is at the heart of her analysis.

She provides a critical reading of the literature dealing with warfare in petro-states. She follows Marchal and Messiant (2002) and Watts (2004) in critiquing the greed position by showing that it does not fit the Darfur case, since it oversimplifies events. Instead, she explains how increasing disintegration, and with it violence, results from problems related to current and the previously existing socio-economic conditions and to power structures involving local, regional and state governance regimes. Thus, oil and violence in Behrends' analysis are explained as part of the dynamics of a complex system structuring power and wealth, whose dynamics are understood to involve on all too frequent occasions the exercise of violence to achieve wealth, even though this wealth is only a possibility in the imagination of gossips.

The final two chapters dealing with Africa are those of Kajsa Ekholm-Friedman and Stephen Reyna, dealing respectively with two ex-colonies in French Equatorial Africa, the Republic of Congo (hereafter Congo-Brazzaville to distinguish it from the other Congo across the river, the Democratic Republic of the Congo, or Congo-Kinshasa) and Chad. The chapters might be read together because both investigate the supernatural in the context of the struggles to dominate oil rents in developing petro-states.

Ekholm-Friedman considers child witches in Congo-Brazzaville; Reyna analyses sorcerers and lionmen in Chad. Further, both articles make these investigations by exploring relationships between objective and subjective realms of Congolese and Chadian social reality.

The objective realms that Ekholm-Friedman analyses are at different, inter-related levels of the political and economic structure. She is especially interested in the alliance between a French transnational oil company (Elf, now Total), Congolese entrepreneurs, and the state in Brazzaville – all desiring oil rents. The subjective realms that she examines are those of Congolese experience as constructed by existing notions of witchcraft, as a result of what happened in the objective realms. Congo-Brazzaville, from independence (1960) up to and throughout the 1990s, witnessed struggles that became civil war involving Elf and various competitors for the control of the central government and its oil rents. This brutal fighting impoverished ordinary Congolese. Then, at the end of the 1990s, child witches were reported in Congo-Brazzaville, Congo-Kinshasa and Angola. This witchcraft is explained in terms of events, resultant from the social disorder, within family and clan, and in terms of ordinary individuals' subjective constructions of these events. Impoverished, violence-dazed parents and elders in family and clan were no longer able to function as parents or clan elders. Under these conditions, some children and juniors accordingly become disoriented and rebelled against their seniors. This rebellion was diagnosed as child witchcraft by the 'pastors'. Finally, witchcraft is subjectively interpreted by impoverished Congolese as a form of magical power; stronger than other powers commanded by the political class and their Western allies, feeding at the trough of oil rents. Such a belief allows the pauperised to imagine that they too have their powers, and to psychologically resist their dominators. Consider next certain rumours of recent nighttime horrors in southern Chad.

In 2003, in the Doba Basin, the oil-producing zone of Chad, there was gossip that certain Chadian Exxon employees were sorcerers and, further, that there were lionmen who were attacking them at night. Reyna seeks to explain this gossip using a critical structural realist theory that explains the constitution of imperial domination in objective and the construction of monsters in subjective realms. The chapter begins by examining two texts: one concerning the just mentioned rumour in the southern Chadian bush, and the other the epic of Beowulf. What could they possibly have in common? For starters both texts are about fear and monsters in imperial systems of domination. But the modes of this domination vary. In *Beowulf* the domination was that of pre-modern empires, and the function of the text might be seen as motivating its aristocratic audience to overcome fear of monsters to become agents fighting for their king, thereby helping to reproduce pre-modern imperial domination. The lionmen/sorcerer rumours take place within a developing petro-state undergoing integration into a modern system of imperial domination. This integration involved constitution of an oil complex in Chad by structural actors – ranging from a consortium of petroleum transnationals led by Exxon, the World Bank and the Chadian state – that allowed most of the capital from Chadian oil revenues to be accumulated by Exxon. Specifically, this chapter proposes that the gossip, resulting from Doba Basin peoples' experiences of the constitution of the oil complex, constructed fear among those sharing the rumours of a particular monster (Exxon sorcerers), creating a desire to oppose them (as do lionmen); thereby helping Doba Basin peoples to distrust modern imperial domination. It is as if the rumour produced anti-Beowulfs in the Chadian bush; agents disposed to resist, not reproduce, imperial domination. The argument advancing this position develops over two stages. First, a theory of the rumour is proposed in critical structural realist terms. Second, this explanation's plausibility is tested by observing whether the events which occurred in Chad from 1995 until 2007 are those predicted by the theory. A conclusion speculates about the role of fear and monsters in other petro-states. Let us now turn to the chapters concerning Latin America.

John Gledhill's contribution analyses three major oil producers in Latin America at the beginning of the third millennium – Mexico, Venezuela and Brazil – by exploring the struggles and alliances between economic elites, political classes and diverse popular forces. Specifically, he considers the effects of a 'persistent imaginary', a popular nationalism, which involves deeply held popular views that there should be national control over oil in order to develop social justice. Gledhill speculates that this imaginary facilitates counter movements to the neo-liberalism fostered by the US colossus to the north.

The chapter shows that the state counts; counts in the sense that how different social actors in the state operate opens up different spaces for social development. A comparison of three South American states functions a bit like a controlled experiment, holding constant geographic region and treating the states' different histories of politics and policy as experiments in social transformation. However, the chapter equally clarifies that just as the state counts so do other actors; especially imperial ones such as the US, whose transnational oil firms organise under what might be termed the empire's neo-liberal imaginary.

A significant amount of Gledhill's analysis documents struggles to capture portions of the oil rents. Whereas in Africa this conflict has tended to be violent, in the countries Gledhill considers it operates relatively peacefully. In part the competition is over acquiring position in institutions that control oil rents. Such institutions have importantly been national oil companies or their associated trade unions. Equally, the struggle has been over determination of policy which regulates how much oil rents should be allocated to what actors under what social conditions. It is here that Gledhill's imaginary is most persistent, impeding efforts to privatise Mexico's oil industry and facilitating Venezuelan and Brazilian labours to build a more multi-polar world.

Naomi Schiller's chapter continues and extends the book's exploration of Venezuela. Her topic is the Venezuela of Hugo Chávez and the struggle to more widely distribute the benefits of oil. But more than this she is concerned to explore how the building of sustainable participatory democracy proceeds in a world of very powerful anti-democratic forces. All four of the commercial television stations in Venezuela are anti-Chávez. However, there is one community television station, Catia TVe, in Caracas, which represents the poor, and supports Chávez. Catia TVe is the object of Schiller's analysis and her aim is to understand how much it contributes to the goal of creating participatory democratic institutions, in part through participating in the politics of oil nationalism. Some might argue that Catia TVe is as much a tool of the Chávez government, just as the commercial media are instruments of the Venezuelan capitalist elite. Schiller shows how such a position over-simplifies the complexities of current political struggles by, among other ways, scrutinising the history of oil-based nationalist ideology.

She explores at different times in Chávez's rule Catia TVe's relations with the central government, with the PDVSA (the state-run oil company), and with the poor of Caracas. She describes how Catia TVe is organised into small, independent producer teams of largely poor neighbourhood residents, given training and equipment by the station, who produce the bulk of its programming. With their mini-DV cameras and broadcasting savvy Catia TVe members had a significant role representing the events of the April 2002 coup attempt against Chávez, especially in documenting the violence committed by the coup plotters against those protesting the coup. The coup's sudden reversal was for Catia TVe's employees a 'transformative moment' when they believed that at last they had contributed to steering Venezuela's destiny. However, Catia TVe is heavily funded by the PDSVA and obliged to televise pro-government propaganda videos, raising the possibility that Catia TVe is a mere appendage of a pro-Chávez PDVSA. Schiller suggests that the situation is more intricate, involving 'reciprocal relations' between the state and grass roots local organisations. The suggestion is useful because it tells us where to look both theoretically and practically. At the level of theory, the fact that relations of domination are 'reciprocal' asks us to conceptualise the nature of that reciprocity.

At the level of practice, the fact of 'reciprocity' between powerful national institutions and less powerful local ones reminds us that power does not invariably flow from the top, dominating the bottom, but that local, participatory institutions can have their influence.

Bret Gustafson's chapter concerns not oil but national gas in Bolivia. Since the election of Evo Morales in 2005, Bolivia, like Venezuela, has sought to move in a more socialist direction, one rejecting the neo-liberal policy advanced by the US and much of the Bolivian capitalist elite. Bolivian gas is located in the Santa Cruz-Tarija Basin in the southeastern part of the country, where there are very considerable gas reserves, equivalent to an estimated four billion barrels of oil. Gustafson's interest is in the conflicts, spawned in part to control distribution of the gas rents, between Bolivian capitalists and their allies, especially in the eastern part of the country, and Morales' central government and its allies in various indigenous and peasant movements. It is important to stress that at present this conflict is of a different order than the grim civil wars found in Africa and, as we shall see, in Chechnya. Rather between 2000 and 2007 Gustafson conservatively counted 115 cases of collective action and relatively small-scale violence involving blockades of roads, ritual displays, protest mobilisations, and occasional attacks upon indigenous and peasant activists. Explanation of these 'multilayered, politically complex conflicts' is Gustafson's object of study.

He accounts for them in terms of 'spatialisation', by which he means 'discourses, practices, and organisational forms through which social actors foreground referents of community, locality, or region and use these to mobilise collective engagements with or against existing relations of power or formal institutional order'. He believes he has found two 'spatialising modes' in these conflicts. The first he calls a *'popular* spatialising mode' and the second an 'elite *autonomist* mode'. The first of these modes 'is a subaltern, provincial, and inter-ethnic form of territorialising practice allied with the nationalist-indigenist political agenda'. The second 'is an urban-centred project tied to agro-industrial elite-backed proposals for regional "autonomy" against the central government'. Gustafson likens the conflict to a 'chess game' where the players in both sides in Bolivian parlance are involved in 'measuring forces' (*midiendo fuerzas*) or 'political arm wrestling' (*pulseta política*). Gustafson's account of this 'arm wrestling' is exceptionally rich and important because it documents the sorts of struggles that occur to dominate distribution of hydrocarbon rents. The game his two different 'spatialising modes' play might be imagined as between complexes of political-economic structures allied and opposed in a competition to determine, among other matters, the mode of domination of hydrocarbon rents in Bolivia. At issue is whether that mode of domination will be more or less progressive.

The final two chapters in this book consider Russia. The chapters dealing with the Russian Federation concern contrasting geographic areas – the far north in the West Siberian case described by Florian Stammler, and the far south in the Chechen case discussed by Khizriyeva and Reyna. Perhaps the most striking contrast between the two regions concerns organised violence. West Siberian oil development has been relatively peaceful; that in Chechnya has been the reverse. The oil and gas deposits of West Siberia form the backbone of the Russian economy, and count today for half of the EU's import of these resources. As a consequence, the region has become more intensely integrated into the Russian and global economies. The exploration and extraction of these deposits since the 1960s has had considerable impacts on residents of those Siberian territories, be they incoming industrial workers or indigenous reindeer pastoralists, hunters and fishermen. However, these impacts have not provoked rebellion as is the case in Chechnya. Stammler, working in part in a Durkheimian tradition with an interest in collective conscience, seeks understanding of this situation.

He analyses the changing nature of industrialisation in Soviet and post-Soviet times and the implications this has on the relations between indigenous people, companies and authorities; using the example of the West Siberian oil and gas province, which is also the home of the world's largest domestic reindeer herds. During the Soviet period, oil-based industrialisation had not only an economic dimension, but was part of a broader socio-political vision where benefits, such as rents, went to collectives rather than individuals. Many local people believed in this project. The Durkheim in Stammler emphasises the role of the Soviet notion of *kollektif* as a 'social glue' that contributed in Soviet times and still contributes in the current conjuncture to the absence of violent conflicts. Further, he argues that a common Soviet and post-Soviet sense of collectivity, emic traditions of social organisation and indigenous leadership, the history of conflict resolution, the presence or absence of international organisations in the region and the role of the national and regional state can explain the relatively peaceful northern Russian hydrocarbon extraction. Finally, he suggests that investigating these sorts of factors with ethnographic fieldwork is a useful way to put an anthropology of mineral resource extraction on a global comparative basis.

Khizriyeva and Reyna offer an interpretation of the function of oil and violence in Chechen history. They investigate the role of domination in reaching this understanding. The major ethnic group in Chechnya is the Vainakhs and it is their struggle with the Russian state in Moscow that forms the special object of analysis. Three periods of Vainakh history with different modes of domination are distinguished: a first era when Chechnya was subjected to the domination of the Russian Empire; a second when it experienced Soviet domination; and a third when it was menaced by the domination of the Russian Federation. During the third period of domination – often described in journalistic terms as a time of oil barons and warlords – the Chechen War developed and with it what we have chosen to term a 'centre/periphery clientelistic network'. This war, like the earlier Caucasian War and the different rebellions of the Soviet era, involves resistance of the Vainakh periphery to a Russian centre. The struggle over domination concerns, among other things, who will get how much of different oil revenues. Further, the clientelistic network is suggested to be a structure that, by integrating the oil industry and a military into a single organisation, gave the Chechen elite a capacity both to produce oil revenues and to fight to hold on to them. Given the existence of these three modes of domination, it seems warranted to assert that the history of Chechnya since 1785 has been, as Lieven put it, 'against … domination'. Finally, it is argued that the evidence of the chapter reveals the existence of a 'Hobbesian elitism', where under conditions of a weakened centre privileged elites struggle against each other in a war of 'all against all' for wealth, often that derived from the oil industry. Why the difference in the histories of violence in Chechnya and West Siberia? A complete answer to this question awaits further study; but one aspect of this study should examine the degree to which the Hobbesian elitism in the former region and the Soviet sense of the *kollektiv* in the latter determined distribution of oil's benefits. Let us now proceed to sketch an anthropology of oil.

Piñatas and Domination: An Anthropological Approach to Investigation of the Crazy Curse

Remember that the anthropology of oil we propose is designed for investigating oil's crazy curse. Let us be clear what we mean by this. The curse is the paradoxical situation where what should bring good, brings bad: oil's fabulous revenues bring the bad of the triple conjuncture to petrostates: stagnating social development and poverty; high conflict, often violent; and a tendency towards authoritarian regimes. It is our contention that the curse, at least in part, can be understood as an aspect of crude domination; and that the concept of domination has not played a central role in the existing social science of oil. So we believe it useful to sketch rudiments of such an approach to oil's curse. This sketch comes in two parts: the first leads to comprehension of what is meant by crude domination; the second offers generalisations that show how the crazy curse may be explained in terms of crude domination. To help readers grasp crude domination, we bring them on a sentimental journey to a birthday long ago where the celebrants played 'Bop the Piñata'. But before going to the party, we accentuate two findings of our review of the social science literature of oil.

A first finding is that it makes sense to speak of a scramble for oil. This finding is warranted by the conclusions of the political and economic perspectives emphasising the war/oil connection, rent seeking and patrimonial politics; the existing anthropology of oil in the work of Apter, Coronil and Sawyer; and all the chapters included in this issue. But we further insist that this struggle is more complex than many scholars imagine; because it includes a swarm of local, regional, national and transnational structural actors. For example, as Watts suggests for Nigeria, there are transnational actors like Chevron and Shell Oil as well as the US military; national actors from the Nigerian central government, like the oil ministry; regional actors from different state governments or insurgent groups like MEND, as well a local actors from different Niger Delta villages. Each of these actors is involved in a scramble in the sense that they are struggling directly, or indirectly, for access to some of the oil rents. In different ways Behrends and Reyna document a similar struggle for Darfur and Chad; while Gledhill does the same for the three Latin American examples. Consequently, accounts of oil's curse need to explain the complexity of the struggle for oil wealth.

A second finding is that while all developing petro-states exhibit the curse, some suffer it more than others, suggesting a hierarchy of damage. For example, if amounts of violence and poverty are taken as curse indicators, Mexico, Brazil, Bolivia and Venezuela are less cursed than Nigeria, Chad and Sudan. Further, it might be observed that there is oil production in one advanced capitalist state (Norway) inclined towards programmes of social welfare. Here the curse appears less than that found in Latin America. So that there appears to be a three-tiered hierarchy of oil's curse in oil-producing states. Level one, 'least cursed', Norway; level two, 'cursed', Latin American developing petro-states; and level three, 'really cursed', African developing states. The preceding suggests that any anthropology of oil needs to explain *both* the struggles for oil rents and the hierarchy of oil's curse. Crude domination will fit the explanatory bill here and a remembrance of birthday parties past explains why.

Crude Domination

One of this introduction's authors, Stephen Reyna, remembers attending a birthday party when he was about eleven years old in the US. Mommy brought you to such festivities in the 1950s in a car with big tail fins. Once there, first you played games. Next, the birthday girl or boy blew out the cake's candles and opened presents. You ate the cake and some ice cream. Then you played for a second time. Finally, mommy came and took you home in the car with big fins. At the game time of this particular party, the birthday boy's mommy announced, 'We are going to play Bop the Piñata'. (The verb 'to bop' means in American slang 'to hit'.) We already knew 'Pin the Tail on the Donkey' and 'Musical Chairs', quite tedious. Bop the Piñata suggested relief from the tedium.

The birthday boy's mommy explained that a piñata was a 'Mexican thing'. She showed it to us and it looked like a pink cardboard donkey. She promised it had lots of candy inside. She also advised it would be hung from the ceiling and we were to 'bop it hard' with special plastic sticks. When it broke we could collect all the candies. The birthday boy's mommy stood on a chair, and hung the piñata. She gave us our plastic sticks, made us stand in a circle under the piñata, counted to three and shouted, 'Go!' We bopped, God, did we bop – the piñata, each other, and sometimes nothing at all. Finally, the piñata broke, candy fell. Everybody jumped for it, pushing and shoving. The birthday boy started crying. He had just stood around, getting mercilessly bopped, coming away with little candy. His mommy, looking like maybe she thought she hadn't organised Bopping the Piñata right, turned pink – like she was going to cry too.

Bopping the Piñata is a useful metaphor for what happens when domination occurs, and we believe that the curse occurring in developing petrostates can be investigated in terms of struggles to regulate domination. Why is this case? Hydrocarbons when sold on the market produce vast rents. This 'black gold' might be imagined as fantastic candy in a piñata. Different social actors, seeking to acquire, or continue acquiring, some of these rents are like the kids at the birthday party bopping for the candy. Their rush to get hold of rents, emphasised by rent-seeking approaches in political science, is a struggle to constitute, or reconstitute, domination. Existing social science approaches, as we have seen, simply do not emphasise understanding of this topic in terms of domination. We do, and in order to understand how this is the case let us present our notion of domination.

Colloquially, 'domination' is what some people make of other people to get a lot of 'candy'. Less colloquially, the understanding we propose is a 'structural/regulation', or more simply, a 'structural' one. Its central explanatory chore is at the structural level and concerns explaining *why, and how, certain groups regulate other groups and, in so doing, acquire social value, like capital*. Structural approaches to domination are concerned with structural level. A 'structural level' is a field of social form including a particular number of individual subjects functioning in particular ways with varying powers over persons and territories.[1] The greater a social form's power, the more people and space it exercises power over, the higher its structural level. 'Regulation' is the managing of what some structural levels do to acquire value for themselves (the dominators), at the expense of other structural levels (the dominated). Regulation takes place within two, connected realms of objective and subjective structures. 'Objective' realms are external to, but inclusive of, subjects. They are of subjects doing things at different structural levels of force and power (Reyna 2001, 2003). Creation of such structures is said to be their 'constitution'; their maintenance or enlargement is that of 'reconstitution'. Domination involves constitution and reconstitution of regulation of value flows such that some structural levels differentially acquire that value. Persisting patterns of value-flow regulation that result in diverse structural levels differentially accumulating value are different 'modes of domination' (MODs). Modes of domination based upon accumulating oil rents are 'oil modes of domination' (OMODs).

Modes of domination vary in degree. The amounts of value flowing to particular structural levels indicate the degree of domination. When most of the value is accumulated by one or two structural levels, e.g., transnational oil firms and national elites, then such a MOD is said to tend towards more 'crude domination'. However, when the value accumulated is shared even-handedly by different structural levels, then such a MOD is said to tend towards more 'equitable domination'.

'Subjective' realms are internal to individuals, i.e., the subjects, and pertain to biological structures involved in experiencing, feeling and knowing objective realms (Reyna 2002). Persons lacking in subjective realms are like players in a game who do not know what to do, such as the birthday boy at his party who just stood around while everybody else bopped the piñata. Formation of subjective realms creates subjects who 'know' how to play their parts in objective structures, like OMODs. Creation of such structures is said to be their 'construction'; maintaining them is their 'reconstruction'. Such construction and reconstruction involves placing within individuals the cultural and authoritative knowledge about how to regulate force resources in particular objective realms. Because such knowledge comes with an emotional impulse it is termed 'cultural or authoritative desire'. Desire is wanting to regulate force resources in some way. Cultural desire is defined by a person's culture. For example, it might be a person's desire to get rich. Authoritative desire is sanctioned by some authority a person has as a member of a group. For example, Exxon employees in Chad had full authority, and hence desire, to negotiate with the Chadian central government the most oil rents possible for Exxon. Domination cannot occur unless the dominators and the dominated desire to do the regulatory work in the different modes of domination. So

oil company executives are constructed to be executives; provincial bu-
reaucrats are constructed to siphon off oil rents; and peasants are constructed to have desires based upon knowing what it means to have others accumulate all the oil wealth. Of course, some dominated people may
experience domination as unpleasant. When this occurs what may be
constructed or reconstructed in their subjectivities is opposition, i.e. resistance, to domination. This embedding of cultural or authoritative desire
in individuals may be said to be the construction and reconstruction of
the subject. 'Crude domination' in this optic refers to the constitution and
reconstitution of OMODs as well as the construction and reconstruction
of subjects who regulate or resist OMODs. It is time now to suggest how
the study of crude domination assists in the study of oil's curse.

Explaining Oil's Crazy Curse

Let us return to the trope of Bopping the Piñata. When oil is discovered it
is as if a gigantic piñata has been found, and everybody wants some of the
candy. 'Everybody' here means different subjects at different structural
levels that might desire a cut of the oil wealth. To begin to analyse the
complexity of the struggle for oil-candy, four types of structural players at
ascending levels of geographic power might be imagined. First, there are
local groups; those in, or near, where oil has been found, whose force resources are such that their powers typically extend over a few communities. Second, there are regional groups. Regions may be provinces within
states. Regional groups are those whose force resources are such that they
have only the power to operate within provinces. Third there are national
groups that have the force resources to have the powers to act throughout
a particular state. Regional and national structural actors often involve
economic or governmental agencies. However, they may involve religious
groups. Fourth, there are transnational groups. These are political, economic or religious groupings with the power to act across international
boundaries. These players are the participants in Bop the Oil Piñata.

Unfortunately, there is only so much oil in the ground, and only so
much can be sold each day, meaning only so much rent can be generated.
The candy that transnational players get is denied to local players. Bop
the Oil Piñata is a contradictory game. Contradiction is defined in terms
of power though this definition is derived from the broad Leninist sense
that contradictions refer to 'mutually exclusive, opposite tendencies in all
phenomena and processes of nature' (Lenin 1958: 357). In social phenomena these 'opposite tendencies' refer to the propensity of groups (players)
to operate so as to acquire power and value from each other. Power is the
ability to do things, and value is the 'candy' which confers power; and it

is understood that the revenues from oil are an especially sweet candy. 'Contradiction' in this optic is the operation of particular structural levels (players) in an articulated system of structures to acquire value and power from other structures (players) in the system. The government and transnational corporations in a petro-state are two players articulated to each other by oil revenue flows. Oil revenue flows are flows of money value (candy), which is easily transformed into power. If, as has frequently occurred since the oil crisis of the 1970s, governments reconstitute OM-ODs by successfully nationalising oil; then more revenues are regulated to flow to the governments, less to the oil companies, and the governments' powers are augmented. Contradictory situations, where large quantities of value flow to player X at the expense of players Y and Z, may be said to be those where X constituted or reconstituted domination over Y and Z. Operations of players to constitute or reconstitute more value and power from other players may be said to be struggles.

A field of contradiction consists of all the structural players struggling for value and power. In the Bop the Oil Piñata game this struggle is above all over portions of the oil rents. Out of this bopping are constituted, and reconstituted, different varieties of regulation of the flow, or non-flow, of hydrocarbon wealth to all the players in contradiction with each other. So investigation of the struggle for domination, how such MODs are constituted and reconstituted, allows investigators to intensively explore the curse's complexities, because such analyses oblige elucidation of the regulatory fate of all the players in the struggle.

We posit that the intensity of conflict in a mode of domination influences the level of curse exhibited by it. The 'intensity' of contradiction is a ratio of the amounts of value flowing to dominators and those dominated in MODs. Contradictions are said to be intense when the percentage of total oil rents going to dominators is high. Contradictions are said to be intensifying when the percentage of total oil rents accruing to dominators is rising. A hypothesis is proposed, termed 'Oil's Crazy Curse' (OCC), which accounts for the relationship between the intensity of contradictions and the severity of the crazy curse. The OCC hypothesis consists of two propositions. The first states:

> *The severity of oil's crazy curse is positively related to the intensity of contradictions in MODs.*

The second proposition accounts for why this positive relationship is found. It states:

> *In OMODs characterised by intense contradiction: (a) too little value flows to the dominated for their development or poverty alleviation; (b) differentials in values sharpen*

conflicts between dominators and dominated, would be dominators, and fallen domina-
tors, often escalating violence; (c) the existence of intense conflict in OMODs produces
authoritarian governance regimes.

Let us now consider how to investigate the hierarchy of different curse-levels. Here the object of analysis is not the actual bopping itself but, once modes of domination have been constituted or reconstituted, the implications of this for the degree of curse. Remember, the birthday boy's mommy regulated the game so that everybody flailed away and dived for the candy at the same time; an aggressive way to do things. But the game could have been managed differently. Mommy could have regulated it so that only one person at a time bopped the piñata. She could have ruled that everybody got the same number of pieces when it finally burst. Comparative analysis of the utilisation of force resources in the regulation of different modes of domination can enhance understanding of how different curse-levels in oil-producing states occur. Underpinning such a comparison is recognition that the more violent the force resources that are utilised, the more cursed is an OMOD. Recourse to utilisation of violent force resources would seem to be in part a function of: (1) the amount of oil rent available to those competing for it in contradictory fields and (2) whether institutions utilising non-violent regulation of oil rent distribution control sufficient force resources to inhibit violent forms of regulation of these rents. In Chad, for example, the amount of oil rents has turned out to be less than certain elite competitors for it imagined. Some of those who feel slighted in this regard have organised armed rebellion to acquire control over the state so as to have the ability to control the state's portion of the oil rents. Further, the central government lacks sufficient force resources – violent or non-violent – to prevent these rebels from fighting for the oil rents (Reyna 2007). Consequently, Chad suffers grievously from oil's curse.

Speculatively, two curse-levels for modes of domination might be distinguished, with one mode having two sub-modes. There is a first mode of domination where the flow of value is in some measure regulated by utilisation of violent force resources; and a second mode where this flow is regulated through operation of political and economic authorities. Nigeria, Chad and Sudan are examples of the first mode; while Latin America and Norway are examples of the second mode, with relatively more of the value flow diverted out of the public sector for the upper classes' use in the Latin American instance, and in that of Norway, relatively more of the value flow remaining in the public sector to benefit a wider range of classes. Investigation of different curse-levels becomes the search for knowledge of why and how different force resources come to regulate value distributions in different modes of domination.

We have been discussing the analysis of OMODs in objective realms. Certainly, there needs to be understanding of what happens to individual actors' subjectivities in MODs. Investigators seeking such knowledge need to discover how individual actors' cultural and authoritative desires are constructed, and reconstructed, in different groups receiving different amounts of oil wealth. We believe that anthropologists are admirably well suited to study the making of the subject. This finishes our sketch of a crude domination approach to oil's crazy curse.

Conclusion

This introduction began with recognition that knowledgeable people from all points of the political compass feared 'systemic crisis' in a world of 'turbulence' plagued by 'disaster capitalism'. By the autumn of 2008 this turbulence had reached damaging levels throughout global finance. But concealed in the turbulence in finance capitalism is a potentially even more destructive crisis: that of oil's crazy curse. We have argued that this curse was part and parcel of struggles to dominate the flow of value produced by oil; that the existing social science literature overlooked the role of domination in oil's curse; and, hence, that an anthropology which analysed the curse as a struggle to dominate oil wealth would be a useful addition to existing approaches. How significant might such a domination approach be for understanding the crisis of the current conjuncture? If oil becomes scarcer, as the peak oil specialists predict; and if the US, with its huge military, continues striving to violently and globally dominate allocation of oil rents; then the conditions for greater conflict will be met, and oil's crazy curse will be petrol thrown on the global systemic crisis made explosive by the USA seeking crude domination.

It might be supposed that by concentrating our theoretical focus upon domination we believe that crude domination is the fate of humanity. Nothing could be further from the truth. However, it does seem to us that currently the struggle for oil is a bit like the struggle for candy at the Bop the Piñata birthday party – pretty unregulated, with powerful structural levels pushing and shoving weaker ones in crude domination games. We hope by focusing on such struggles, just as Marx focused on the struggles of nineteenth century industrial capitalism, to acquire critical knowledge of oil domination games – to better move them in the direction of equitable forms of domination. Finally, we believe that it is anthropology, with its tradition of direct observation of what actually happens, that is in the best position to observe how games of crude domination work and, thus, to imagine their elimination.

Note

1. A 'social form' is any human grouping composed of 'subjects', individuals whose internal worlds have been fitted with cognitive and emotional cultural schema to facilitate operating that social form.

References

Apter, Andrew. 2005. *The Pan-African Nation: Oil and the Spectacle of Culture in Nigeria.* Chicago: University of Chicago Press.

Attiga, Ali. 1981. How Oil Revenues Can Destroy a Country. *Petroleum Intelligence Weekly.* Special Supplement (19 Oct).

Auty, Richard. 1993. *Sustaining Development in Mineral Economies: The Resource Curse Thesis.* London: Routledge.

Ballentine, Karen and Jake Sherman, eds. 2003. *The Political Economy of Armed Conflict: Beyond Greed and Grievance.* Boulder, CO: Lynne Rienner.

Bayart, Jean-François. 1993. *The State in Africa: Politics of the Belly.* Harlow: Longman.

British Petroleum. 2010. Statistical Review of World Energy 2010. http://www.bp.com/productlanding.do?categoryId=6929&contentId=7044622. (last accessed 7 March 2011).

Clifford, James and George E. Marcus. 1986. *Writing Culture: the Poetics and Politics of Ethnography: a School of American Research Advanced Seminar.* Berkeley: University of California Press.

Collier, Paul and Anke Hoeffler. 2001. *Greed and Grievance in Civil War.* Washington, DC: World Bank.

Coronil, Fernando. 1997. *The Magical State: Nature, Money, and Modernity in Venezuela.* Chicago: University of Chicago Press.

David, Stephen R.. 1997. Internal War: Causes and Cures. *World Politics* 49(4): 552–76.

David, Paul A. and Gavin Wright. 1997. Increasing Returns and the Genesis of American Resource Abundance. http://ideas.repec.org/a/oup/indcch/v6y1997i2p203-45.html. (last accessed 7 March 2011).

Dayaneni, Gopal and Bob Wing. 2002. Oil and War. http://www.lysistrataproject.org/oilandwar.htm#OilandWar. (last accessed 7 March 2011).

Deffeyes, Kenneth. 2006. *Beyond Oil: The View from Hubbert's Peak.* New York: Farrar, Straus & Giroux.

Degteva, Anna. 2006. *The Oil Industry and Reindeer Herding: The Problems of Implementing Indigenous Rights in the Nenets Autonomous Okrug, Russia.* Tromsø: Center for Sami Studies, University of Tromsø.

Fentiman, Alicia. 1996. The Anthropology of Oil: The Impact of the Oil Industry on a Fishing Community in the Niger Delta. *Social Justice 23: 87–99.*

Ferguson, James. 2005. Seeing Like a State. *American Anthropologist* 107(3): 377–82.

Gary, Ian and Terry Lynn Karl. 2003. *Bottom of the Barrel: Africa's Oil Boom and the Poor.* Baltimore: Catholic Relief Services.

Gelb, Alan. 1988. *Oil Windfalls: Blessing or Curse?* Oxford: Oxford University Press.

Green Car Congress. 2006. Deffeyes Date: Peak Oil War 16 December 2005. http://www.greencarcongress.com/2006/02/the_deffeyes_da.html. (last accessed 7 March 2011).

Greenspan, Alan. 2007. *The Age of Turbulence: Adventures in a New World.* Harmondsworth: Penguin.

Homer-Dixon, Thomas. 2001. *Environment, Scarcity, and Violence*. Princeton: Princeton University Press.

IAGS. 2003. *The Future of Oil. Washington, DC: Institute for the Analysis of Global Security. http://www.iags.org/futureofoil.html*. (last accessed 7 March 2011).

Kaldor, Mary, Terry Lynn Karl and Yahia Said. 2007. *Oil Wars*. London: Pluto Press.

Karl, Terry Lynn. 1997. *The Paradox of Plenty: Oil Booms and Petro-states*. Berkeley: University of California Press.

———. 1999. The Perils of Petroleum: Reflections on the Paradox of Plenty. *Journal of International Affairs* 53: 23–57.

Klare, Michael. 2002. *Resource Wars*. New York: Owl Books.

Klein, Naomi. 2007. *The Shock Doctrine: The Rise of Disaster Capitalism*. New York: Metropolitan Books.

Krueger, Anne. 1974. The Political Economy of the Rent-seeking Society. *American Economic Review* 64: 291–303.

Kunstler, James. 2006. *The Long Emergency: Surviving the End of Oil, Climate Change, and Other Converging Catastrophes of the 21st Century*. New York: Grove Press.

Lenin, Vladimir Ilyich. 1958. On the Question of Dialectics. *Collected Works vol. XXXVIII*. Moscow: Foreign Language Press.

Marchal, Roland and Christine Messiant. 2002. 'De l'avidité des rebelles. L'Analyse économique de la guerre civile selon Paul Collier. *Critique Internationale* 16: 58–69.

McGuire, Thomas and Andrew Gardner. 2003. Contract Drillers and Causal Histories along the Coast of Mexico. *Human Organization* 62(3): 218–28.

Médard, Jean-François, ed. 1992. *Les Etats d'Afrique noir. Formations, mécanismes, crises*. Paris: Karthala.

Mill, John Stuart. 1851. *A System of Logic, Ratiocinative and Inductive, Being a Connected View of the Principles of Evidence, and the Methods of Scientific Investigation*. London: Parker.

Pearce, Jenny. 2004. *Oil and Armed Conflict in Casanare, Colombia*. Discussion paper. London: Center for the Study of Global Governance.

Peluso, Nancy and Michael Watts. 2001. *Violent Environments*. Ithaca: Cornell University Press.

Picou, J. Steven, Duane A. Gill, C. Dye and E. Curry. 1992. Stress and Disruption in an Alaskan Fishing Community: Initial and Continuing Impacts of the Exxon Valdez Oil Spill. *Industrial Crisis Quarterly* 6(3): 235–57.

Reno, William. 2004. The Empirical Challenge to Economic Analyses of Conflicts. Presented at the SSRC-sponsored conference, The Economic Analysis of Conflict: Problems and Prospects. Washington, DC. 19–20 April.

Reyna, Stephen. 2001. Force, Power and String Being? Max Planck Institute for Social Anthropology Working Papers. *Working Paper # 20*.

———. 2002. *Connections*. New York: Routledge.

———. 2003. Force, Power, and the Problem of Order. *Sociologus* 3(2): 199–223.

———. 2007. The Traveling Model That Would Not Travel: Oil, Empire, and Patrimonialism in Contemporary Chad. *Social Analysis* 51(3): 78–102.

Rival, Laura. 1997. Oil and Sustainable Development in the Latin American Humid Tropics. *Anthropology Today* 13(3): 1–3.

Rohde, David. 2007. Army Enlists Anthropologists in War Zones. *New York Times* 5 Oct. http://www.nytimes.com/2007/10/05/world/asia/05afghan.html. (last accessed 7 March 2011).

Ross, Michael. 1999. The Political Economy of the Resource Curse. *World Politics* 51: 297–322.

———. 2001. Does Oil Hinder Democracy? *World Politics* 53: 325–61.

———. 2002. *Oil, Drugs, and Diamonds: How Do Natural Resources Vary in their Impacts on Civil War? International Peace Academy*. Los Angeles: Department of Political Science, UCLA.

Sachs, Jeffrey and Andrew Warner. 2001. The Curse of Natural Resources. *European Economic Review* 45(4–6): 827–838.

Sagir, Bill. 2004. The Politics of Petroleum Extraction and Royalty Distribution at Lake Kutubu. In *Mining and Indigenous Life-worlds in Australia and Papua New Guinea*, ed. A. Rumsey and J. Weiner. Wantage: Sean Kingston Publishing.

Sawyer, Suzana. 2004. *Crude Chronicles: Indigenous Politics, Multinational Oil, and Neoliberalism in Ecuador*. Durham, NC: Duke University Press.

Schwartz, Peter and Doug Randall. 2003. An Abrupt Climate Change Scenario and Its Implications for United States National Security. www.edf.org/documents/3566_AbruptClimateChange.pdf. (last accessed 7 March 2011).

Smith, Adam. 1776. *An Inquiry Into the Nature and Causes of the Wealth of Nations*. London, New York.

Strahan, David. 2007. http://www.davidstrahan.com/blog/. (last accessed 7 March 2011).

The Economist. 2004. Pumping all they can. http://www.economist.com/node/2986468. (last accessed 7 March 2011).

Vallette, Jim, Steve Kretzman, and Daphne Wysham. 2003. *Crude Vision*. Washington, DC: Institute for Policy Studies, Sustainable Energy and Economy Network.

Vitalis, Robert. 2006. *America's Kingdom: Mythmaking on the Saudi Oil Frontier*. Palo Alto: Stanford University Press.

Wallerstein, Immanuel. 1997. Social Science and the Quest for a Just Society. *American Journal of Sociology* 102: 1241–57.

Watts, Michael. 2004. Resource Curse? *Geopolitics* 9(1): 50–80.

Weber, Max and Walter Garrison Runciman 1978. *Max Weber: Selections in Translation*. Cambridge, New York: Cambridge University Press.

Yates, Douglas. 1996. *The Rentier State in Africa: Oil Rent Dependency and Neo-colonialism in the Republic of Gabon*. Trenton, NJ: Africa World Press.

Chapter 2

OILING THE RACE TO THE BOTTOM

Jonathan Friedman

Silver is said to have been a curse for the Spanish American Empire. This 'silver curse' was obvious to at least one early Spanish commentator:

> although our kingdoms could become the richest in the world for the abundance of gold and silver that have come into them and continue to come from the Indies, they end up as the poorest because they serve as a bridge across which gold and silver pass to other kingdoms that are our enemies. (Cortes in Cipolla 1993: 186)

Silver was a curse because it encouraged a massive increase in demand, driving up prices. This price inflation led to a total blockage of internal manufacturing and agriculture due to cheaper imports; the bloating of bureaucracy; and the not-so-gradual marginalisation/stagnation of the Spanish economy except as a motor of elite consumption. The elites who sat atop this process were unaware that it was undermining Spanish hegemony. For example, one Alfonso Nuñez de Castro exclaimed in 1675,

> Let London manufacture those fabrics of hers to her heart's content; Holland her Chambrays; Florence her cloth; the Indies their beaver and vicuna; Milan her brocades; Italy and Flanders their linens, so long as our capital can enjoy them; the only thing it proves is that all nations train journeymen for Madrid and that Madrid is the queen of Parliaments, for all the world serves her and she serves nobody. (Cipolla 1993: 186)

Silver, gold, oil and other single resources that can have immediate world market monetary value (as opposed, for example, to coal which is largely local and not easily monopolised in global terms) are virtually the oils of the capitalist system in the most general sense. They have peculiar contextual properties. They are like money itself and a source of financial power in the larger world due to their easy convertibility. But they are not money as such. The printing of money and its increasing circulation poses a direct problem for the economy due to its effect on inflation and declining relative value of the state currency. Precious metals, oil and other similar resources are not money and must be converted into money. They can be exported as commodities as well, thus increasing the value of national money since they are a source of capital accumulation. The problem with such commodities is that they can inflate price levels in quantitative terms to such an extent that other forms of production may become uncompetitive on national and international markets. This is because they are sources of wealth that need minimal intervention of manufacturing process, and that thus entail immediate conversion into money and demand which make the country in which they are produced relatively more expensive than competitors. Strategic raw materials, whether they be strategic for the financial sectors or the industrial sectors, share similar properties with respect to their potential effects. They are not necessarily integrated into national or territorial production processes but represent direct sources of wealth that can increase the level of costs of production of everything else within the territory. This relationship is, however, relative, since it is quite normal that territories price themselves out of the larger market due to their relative success in export which in a normal market situation leads to trade surpluses and an increase in value of the territorial currency. This tendency is offset by increases in productivity that lower costs of production thus maintaining the competitiveness of territorial production. In the end what can be suggested is that the territorial control of strategic goods is tendentially deleterious to the territorial economy as a whole, but that this can be regulated. The regulation, a political process, is in turn dependent on the specific strategies in place in particular states at particular times. Oil shares these tendential properties with other lucrative strategic resources, properties that can produce effects similar to simply printing money.

Oil is the major resource of modern industrial production, having largely replaced coal which replaced wood. In each case these resources have been relatively finite or at least have posed the problem of marginally decreasing returns in the long run. This book is a product of the contemporary realisation of another end-in-sight of a resource which has led to increasing concern with the nature of the resource. One might assume that there is a simple relation between the approaching depletion of the resource and its market value. However, this is not necessarily true since there is no clear evidence that the costs of production have risen. The actual price of oil is part of another process of valuation, from spot market to the block politics of Organisation of the Petroleum Exporting Countries (OPEC), it does not necessarily reflect the relative scarcity of the product itself. The geographical location of resources and the functioning of global capitalist accumulation articulate to form a set of variations on the way extraction/appropriation is related to the context within which it occurs. The latter depends in turn on the nature of the political-economic properties of that context. Thus oil production takes different forms in Russia, Norway, the United States, Africa and Latin America.

This collection, while entirely focused on the oil economy, might be said to demonstrate the weakness of a resource determinist approach[1] to oil and violence that has developed in recent years (Karl 1997; Ross 1999) due in part to the obvious situation in certain parts of the world, not least Africa where warlord politics has become directly linked to resource wars. At the same time oil is of course what the struggle is about so the issue remains open in some sense, in the most vulgar sense of the scramble for socially identified scarce resources which is always a potential trigger of violence. The chapters cover Africa, Latin America and Russia, three levels of intensity of the relation between oil and violence dependent on a complex of interrelations between major actors involved in the appropriation process. And the example of Norway and to a lesser extent Siberia is used to argue against the direct causality of oil technology, noting the crucial importance of the social context within which it is implemented.

From this point of view it is not oil production as such that is important but the way it is appropriated and re-deployed within the world economy, the latter determining its effect on the local societies in which the process transpires. This book reveals what an anthropology of oil can accomplish in grasping the nature of the articulation between the appropriation of a particular product and the larger context in which it occurs. In this sense this collection is about the nature of appropriation of strategic resources, the all-important role of state and class structures as they are linked to particular strategies of control and distribution of wealth, and the historical specificity and positioning of the latter within the global system.

Here it is important to note and to decipher the meaning of a specific commodity within its social context. With respect to violence there are plenty of other raw materials that have been the focus of violent competition. In eastern Congo we have a complex of relations between Rwanda and the Republic of Congo which recently has been dominated by the intrusion of the Rwanda-supported conqueror Kabila in the period following the Rwanda massacres in which a large Hutu population of militarised groups fled to eastern Congo and made it a base of operations. While Rwanda supported Kabila's ousting of Mobutu, things are again reversed, with a new figure, Laurent Nkunda, a Tutsi, supported by Rwanda, leading a war against Hutu militias and the Congolese state (Polgreen 2008a). The shift here has been to wars over minerals, not least coltan (columbite-tantalite), a crucial ingredient in electronics components, but the area is full of other valuable minerals. The proliferation of militias is extraordinary and the state's presence is more than weak if continually approaching the horizon. In the newest struggle the local militias have been converted into direct proxies of the RC and Rwanda (New York Times 2008: A5). The liability of alliance-making is obvious, but the intervention, however indirect, of the state is also in evidence in the struggle. If this is a developing situation one might suggest that interstate conflicts may now be returning to prominence. More probable, however, is a continued multi-actor conflict in which states are one among several partners to such situations. The past decade, in any case, has witnessed extreme levels of violence surrounding the competition for control of raw material resources by a translation of increasing regional fragmentation into ethnic gang formation. In Niger, also part of the same fragmenting continent, a battle is unfolding around uranium mining. Niger is the world's fifth largest uranium producer. The uranium is mined in Tuareg territory, and accounts for 70 per cent of the country's export earnings, none of which are returned to the area. The Tuareg rebel movement is concerned with their percentage of the take on uranium rather than any problem with the commodity itself. Here again it is the ethnic divisions, whether or not merely potential, which when mobilised are the foundation of armed conflict (Polgreen 2008b; Spiegel 2008; Tuareg Culture and News 2008).

Thus the relation between violence and oil can be understood as one of an array of conflicts over resources in which a fragmenting political situation accompanied by the linking of fragments in transnational networks leads to a reproduction of violence within the local and regional arenas. It is the fragmentation that is crucial rather than the particular resource at hand. The conflicts will not be realised where resources are directly and strongly controlled by the state. Where the resources are integrated within a functioning national economy, the situation is quite different. In such a situation they are integrated into complex cycles of internal reproduction in which they are dominated by a broader division of labour. While this in itself does not eliminate the 'Dutch Disease', it neutralises it to some extent. Norway is an interesting example insofar as it has largely failed to prevent the disease from spreading except by attempting to dampen liquidity by means of reduced state investment. This is partly the effect of the ideological control exercised by the nation or a 'sovereign people' over its state representatives.

Just as the relation between oil and violence depends on the state context, the relation between oil and other social and economic contradictions depends, likewise, on that context.[2] Our examples with respect to violence demonstrate that it is not oil that leads to violence but that it is rather all exploitable and exportable resources of high value that are articulated to different state structures. It is not oil or other resources that generate conflict as such. The fragmentation of the state into competing sub-units, territorial or nomadic, is the context, one that occurs most clearly in Africa, one that is generated by global systemic considerations and Africa's place in the global arena. The chapters in this volume document the articulation between different social orders producing quite different results. But the differences in themselves are expressive of the contemporary transformations of the global system and not globalisation or the spread of neo-liberalism as such. In fact globalisation and neo-liberal politics are themselves part of this larger transformational process. We begin with the latter and their regional manifestations.

We have witnessed a major global recession or even depression, one that is the result of a global credit crunch leading to a typical liquidity crisis with strong deflationary tendencies. It is also part of a declining US hegemony and the rise of economic power in East and South Asia, a massive shift in capital accumulation that is responsible for the particular nature of the credit crunch itself. The United States, having exported its own capital, has become, for quite some time, a consumer of the imports of the originally exported capital. Europe and Japan have followed suit. Because of this shift the maintenance of economic power in the centre is increasingly problematic. The West increasingly becomes a finance economy in which fictitious capital[3] becomes dominant in a rapid casino-spiral of speculative instruments, especially the various forms of derivatives. The reason for this shift is the declining competitiveness of industrial production in the centres of the world system. While shifts from production to finance are periodic phenomena, when coupled to the longer term cycle of hegemony it produces more significant crises. A hundred years ago the financial sectors became dominant in the capitalist economy in the decline of British hegemony. This was the era of Hilferding's *Das Finanzkapital* (1910), which described something similar to what is happening today in a more amplified way.

The elements of today's process involve political and economic fragmentation. The economic process – involving decentralisation of Western capital accumulation – includes five attributes:

1. Global decentralisation of capital accumulation: multinational and transnational economic forms.
2. Rise and consolidation of new production zones (East/South Asia) and decline of old centres – Western Europe, USA.
3. Financial crises of the state in the West, emergent trade surpluses in selected growth zones.

4. Transition from Fordist to post-Fordist organisation: outsourcing of production and services and concentration of core financial activities to headquarters. Flexible accumulation = flexibilisation of labour and lumpen proletarianisation of large portions of the work force.
5. Formation of global cities in which a concentric model organises the post-Fordist financially dominated economy, with 'Bunker Hills' in the centre surrounded by higher to lower services and a periphery of flexible poverty (Sassen 2000).

This set of processes generates an economic order based on networks of actors linked in unstable hierarchies and partial dependencies, which are loose at the level of interaction insofar as subcontractors can be easily replaced as conditions of profitability change. Thus the export of textile production to peripheries led to a new strategy of sweatshop production in the West based on a combination of legal and illegal immigration. Both tendencies, the export of capital and the import of cheap labour, still exist in a competitive relation. This might appear chaotic at the behavioural level since such situations are labile and may change rapidly and be difficult to chart. But there is an invariant logic involved that dictates the way choices are made and which encompasses the longer term tendencies in terms that can be referred to as a race to the bottom or, following Rosa Luxemburg, the self-cannibalisation of capital (1964 [1915]). Thus the post-Fordist network nature of capitalist accumulation is not the result of neoliberal theory, not the product of a project by Hayek and his acolytes, but a structural phenomenon. Neo-liberalism is not a phenomenon in itself, but the rationale for the double process of fragmentation and networking of a formerly centralised economic process. The logic here is lodged within the transformation of the global system itself and is not the product of a new idea, a new project, even if such projects are contained and resonate within the change. Now I will discuss political fragmentation.

Fragmentation of contemporary political orders includes:

1. Weakening of the Western state as a centralisation/assimilation machine and a resultant decentralisation or devolution of functions. This leads to:
2. The emergence of a state-sponsored multicultural politics, one that begins in the 1960s in the United States (local community control)[4] and in the late 1980s in Europe. It develops into a strong cultural politics from the late 1970s and includes all the fragmented identities that are forged in this period, indigenous, regional, national and immigrant.
3. Crisis of the Soviet imperial state and decentralisation to successor states competing for flows of wealth in the region.

4. Fragmentation of formerly centralised institutions, not least the military, and the formation of military firms in both centre and periphery.
5. Fragmentation of political orders and their re-connection in global networks. Ethnic, religious, gender-based and ecological (animal rights, vegan) orders all become increasingly radicalised and ethnic in character. Subnational and transnational orders link up in this process.

The fragmentation of the political order parallels and articulates with the fragmentation of the economic order. The result is an emergent proliferation of networks of social actors, the latter 'liberated' from a formerly integrated larger complex of units. This leads to a proliferation of what many perceive to be chaos, landscapes that are not homogeneous state territories but points of extraction on a larger map, or export processing zones that are often militarised compounds of concentrated productive/ extractive activity in unstable zones that can pack up and move as soon as the violence becomes a danger to the productive process. And all of this is fuelled by a global arms trade, to say nothing of the military firms that are often involved from the now defunct Executive Outcomes to the more recent Executive Solutions, Global Solutions, Blackwater, etc.

Political and economic fragmentation can be linked to vaster representations of the world, historical schismatic schemes that can be expressed in the opposition Orientalism/Occidentalism. If Orientalism is the classificatory scheme of the imperial order, Occidentalism is its inversion, one that becomes available in periods of declining hegemony. Thus current Islamist alternatives to the world capitalist order take the form of a return to a world organised as a Califate, a renaissance of Sharia as a public order. But this unified image is a projection of a proliferation of networks rather than a state project. The unification of a Califate is an oppositional imaginary, an Occidentalism with a positive project for the replacement of the decadent Western world system.

Finally, the simultaneous presence of the above tendencies toward fragmentation, and their representation, might appear disordered; but the fragments are neither divergent nor autonomous entities. On the contrary they are related in logics that might even be said to be predictable. This collection aims to understand these logics, a sorely needed exercise in these times.

How does this increasing disorder relate to the distribution of different forms and conditions of strategic raw material extraction? In areas with strong states, still primarily in the Western states, while there is a great deal of decentralisation, production of valuable minerals such as oil still occurs under stable conditions. In such conditions, revenues of this process are intricately coupled to other industrial processes in which they do not, by and large, dominate. Norway is an extreme example due to the relative dominance of oil in total national production. It is potentially a victim to the Dutch Disease that might force other forms of production off the market due to the price levels in the country. In Russia there are several patterns depending on the degree of maintenance of state-backed order, as documented in this volume, with a strong contrast between Siberia and the Central Asian border zone where violent disorder has been on the rise. On the other hand the oligarchic structure of the economy that emerged in the 'transition' process led to massive transfers of wealth to the new dominant classes at the same time as poverty has been abundant. The Middle Eastern oil states represent yet another pattern of single-resource dependence with the revenues going to a lesser degree to citizens, while imported labour forms the lower classes. South America displays interesting recent variations that range from typically peripheral oligarchic orders to tendencies to state redistribution of revenues. Finally in those areas of the world where former Western peripheral states have declined, or collapsed, we find the extremes of violence documented for Africa in which fragments including state classes of the former order are reorganised into 'gangs', private militias very often linked to regional and/or ethnic leaders in lethal competition over the lucrative resources.

Technology?

Does technology play any role here? Oil extraction requires a massive technological input compared to gold, uranium, coltan and other precious minerals;[5] one that cannot be dealt with by gangs. On the contrary, and despite the possibilities of siphoning oil from continental pipelines, oil extraction remains an issue that involves large transnational firms and states or at least regional representatives who can act independently of formal state regimes. Thus gangs cannot easily vie for direct control over the extraction of oil as opposed to other precious minerals. Now the relation between states, territorial populations and the companies is structured by the nature of the state regimes as well as by the organization of extraction. Where states have become privatised in disintegrating situations, they function like so many gangs. Where, on the contrary, there is a strong pressure to transparency and the use of revenues for the territorial population we find a very different arrangement. This is of course a continuum somewhat like that drawn by Reyna and Behrends in the introduction to the book. In any case the technologies of extraction influence the large structures in which they are implemented primarily by way of the constraints that they impose on the social and political activities that surround them. In this respect there is an important difference between offshore oil and land-based production. The latter can enter into direct conflict with the social projects and even existence of native populations and can easily be confronted by local demands, whereas the former is largely beyond the control of the local society and even to a large extent of the territorial state. Utilisation of deep-sea drilling technology places oil producers entirely beyond the jurisdiction of states. The variations in the extraction process, thus, affect the conditions of interrelation between states, local populations and the producers. They do not, however, impose particular ways of dealing with that process.

The mad scramble for coltan, diamonds and even gold is founded on conditions of appropriation that are quite unlike those of oil so it is important to detail the articulation of technological process and social process in the study of such phenomena. On the other hand, as documented in this volume, the difference in political orders is clearly of greater significance in diagnosing the contemporary world and its vicissitudes.

The Strange Yet Obvious Linkage between Sixteenth-century Silver Mining and Oil Production

We started this text with a discussion of the effect of the accumulation of silver on the economy of Spain in the sixteenth and seventeenth centuries. The logic of accumulation of primary resources depends on the state structures involved. In the quote by Cortes, above, the latter complains of the way the wealth of Spain ends up in the hands of its 'enemies'. This is exactly the kind of expression that one finds in many places in the declining states of the West today. In newspapers and other media it is said that the consumer wealth of the country is only benefitting our enemies and competitors, from Venezuela and the oil states of the Middle East for oil and China for a large portion of Western consumer goods. What can be discerned here is the more general economic relation in which declining centres become the consumers of commodities including energy that they once produced at home and which now are produced in formerly controlled peripheries. The specificity of silver or of oil lies in its money like properties. Silver is like the oil of the entire imperial financial order. It undermines, tendentially at least, other forms of production by raising general costs relative to other areas of the system. This lowers the competitiveness of the centre via its own increasing consumption power, making it a target for developing production elsewhere. This is the problem that is expressed in the well-known Dutch Disease (discussed in this book's introduction) and which leads to the emergence of the rentier state. In our discussion, however, this issue is not directly related to oil, although oil might imply such a development itself. It is a general tendency in the decline of hegemony that industrial economies become financial/rentier economies. The debate about England before the First World War is very much about the decadence of what had become a rentier economy (Hobson 1902 Lenin 1968). It is the transition from world workshop to world banker. And this is a transition that is encompassed within the global process of hegemonic decline sketched above.

The export of capital, its decentralisation, the financial decline of the state, political fragmentation and ethnicisation occur to varying degrees in different parts of the system. And when discussing the Spanish 'silver disease' we note, of course, that in the mining areas we find the same large-scale violence and dislocation, including small-scale marauding operations that were common in the empire. The classic recent example is Leopold's Congo Free State. The latter was a privatised state, but also an enterprise for the rapid and violent extraction of rubber for the world market (Ekholm Friedman 1992). It created the kind of local genocidal chaos that one finds today in certain peripheries. It is important to recognise that contemporary petro-states do not face the same situation as hegemonic industrial states since their industrial development is quite secondary even if there are similar start-up operations, involving investment in complex technology. The normal tendency is the emergence of an immensely wealthy upper middle and upper class directly linked to, and reproduced by, the oil sector employing a much larger population of imported labour in low-end services and construction. The petro-states of the Middle East and Southeast Asia are not like the African post-colonial state order. The latter are states that began to fragment in the 1980s as a product of forced 'democratisation' schemes linked to structural adjustment programmes and the withdrawal of massive amounts of financial support (Gaddis 1992; Huband 2001; Rye Olsen 1997). The result was a reorganisation around strong 'ethnic' and/or regional leaders in a struggle for control of the state itself as the principle recipient of foreign rents and aid. And with the world in full-scale fragmentation there was a proliferation of networks of arms dealers, military firms, drug smugglers and even states or branches of states (as in the case of the French presidency versus the prime ministry), all involved in reaping profits by investing in armed violence. This fragmentation of the African state was so extensive as to make the chaotic situation a virtual institution. That such fragmentation did not occur in the Middle East was due to the different historical and contemporary circumstances in the development of that region's states. These states were stabilised because they used their accumulated oil wealth to support, to a larger extent, their own populations, i.e. their Arab populations. The typical state order in the Middle Eastern (and Southeast

Asian) oil states is one in which the national population lives off the proceeds or rents, directly or indirectly, while there is a large migrant, poorly dependent population that works in the various service sectors. This is not the case in the African cleptocratic regimes in which the money stays in the hands of the ruling families and is exported immediately to Swiss bank accounts, a special sort of flight capital (Hoogvelt 2001). I would not suggest any absolute differences here, not least since there is an important historical component that must not be forgotten. The variability over time of state structures is a fundamental principle of a global systemic analysis.

Neither Neo-liberalism Nor Assemblages

New approaches to understanding the global have blossomed in the past few years, many advertised by keywords – most importantly globalisation, neo-liberalism and now assemblages (Klein 2007). The notion of globalisation has served as an instant label for all kinds of contemporary phenomena, including witchcraft, magic, runaway mining and export processing zones, and not least, decentralised chaotic violence (Friedman 2002; Gurr 2000). But most of this 'analysis' is correlative rather than truly analytic. We have already suggested that much of what is referred to as globalisation refers to the breakup of hegemonic vertical structures in the world order, not as the result of new ideas of neo-liberal politics, but as a product of declining hegemony and weakening of hegemonic structures. That is, the transformation is internally orchestrated and not introduced from the outside. Thus neo-liberalism is not a new economic invention. It is simply market capitalism in its pure form, a model in which the market is said to resolve all problems. The role of the state is critical here insofar as it is government that maintains free-market conditions. Now if there is anything neo-liberal in this it is the economic policies of the state, not the economy itself, since the latter is always an expression of the self-same capitalist logic. The transition from vertical Fordist organisation to post-Fordism is not an evolutionary process, but the structural adaptation-reorganisation in declining hegemonic centres in which the vertical model no longer worked because it was too expensive and risky. Industrial dominance was replaced by financial capitalist dominance in which production that was not exported to newly industrialising areas was decentralised, outsourced and flexibilised so as to preserve the core financial capital in the larger system. While on the surface this may appear as disorganised capitalism, as a proliferation of subcontracting firms and savage speculation on anything that moves, the process that creates this situation is quite regular.

There is the decline in profitability of industrial capital and the consequent shift into financial operations at the same time as industrial capital is exported to more profitable regions of the world. When this occurs finance capital appears dominant with all its speculative accoutrements and remaining production and services are flexibilised. Thus post-Fordism is not an evolution but more of a devolution, and its structure is closer to an earlier putting-out system than to the large scale industrialism that characterises the industrialisation process.

The above reorganisation did not occur in China, for example, where Fordism has flourished in the same period (Appelbaum 2009; Henderson 2008), a period of double-digit growth. While neo-liberalism as both ideology and strategy can be linked to economists such as Hayek who represented the anti-Keynesian front, the implementation of neo-liberalism was not a struggle for a new economic policy but an adaptation to changing conditions of accumulation in the declining centre. The proliferation of military firms, arms dealers and transnational prostitution and their linking to fragmenting states in Africa is not a product of neo-liberal policy either. It is the result of a real fragmentation process within a disintegrating hegemonic order whose effects are different in differing local conditions, as we suggested above. Decentralised capitalism is not more capitalist than centralised capitalism even if it does represent a higher degree of commercialisation. It is merely a change in mode of accumulation. These changing conditions are outlined above: the geographical decentralisation of capital accumulation, declining profitability of Fordism and a fragmentation of production processes even as financial processes are increasingly centralised (this is a way of getting rid of costs via outsourcing). While centralisation may be occurring in East and South Asia, decentralisation is the tendency in the West.

So what can the term *neo-liberalism* tell us? It is certainly no system but refers to a summary of certain practices and doctrines concerning the world economy (Harvey 2005). And the latter relate to the state and to other governmental organs of regulation rather than to the economy as such. Harvey, following Duménil and Lévy (2004), sees in this a process of both re-establishing the profitability of capital and recouping the Gini coefficients of the past, i.e. a strategy for re-establishing the relative wealth of the capitalist class following decades of equalisation of class incomes. Whether or not this can be reduced to a strategy, neo-liberalism as such is a situation of deregulation and not a stage of development. And its once strongest proponents have been seriously re-considering its deleterious effects, not so much on the grounds of lost social welfare, but on the stability of capitalist accumulation as a whole (Soros 2000, 2006). To account for the ravaging of Central Africa by a combination of multinationals, privatised states, military firms and arms dealers by ascribing it to neo-liberalisation is simply incorrect, as incorrect as ascribing the sorcery epidemics in South Africa to globalisation (Comaroff and Comaroff 2001).

The recent fascination with the term *assemblage* is similarly inadequate to the issues mapped out in this volume. While it is clearly a contribution to the study of global processes to be able to circumscribe the sets of elements that are relevant, the concept seems to harbour an inherent avoidance of the systemic analysis required of a project of explaining global complexity. Consider that the term is defined as:

> how global forms interact with other elements, occupying a common field in contingent, uneasy, unstable interrelationships. The product of these interactions might be called the *actual* global, or the global in the space of assemblage. In relationship to 'the global', the assemblage is not a 'locality' to which broader forces are counterposed. Nor is it the structural effect of such forces. An assemblage is the product of multiple terminations that are not reducible to a single logic. The temporality of an assemblage is emergent. It does not always involve new forms, but forms that are shifting, in formation, or at stake. As a composite concept, the term *'global* assemblage' suggests inherent tensions: global implies broadly encompassing, seamless, and mobile; assemblage implies heterogeneous, contingent, unstable, partial and situated. (Ong and Collier 2005: 12)

The 'contingent, unstable, partial and situated' interrelationships would seem to be the ultimate reality, a total set of relations. But is this an adequate characterisation? The same issue was raised by Lévi-Strauss in elaborating on the difference between statistical and mechanical models (Lévi-Strauss 1965). Reality is usually unstable and full of contingencies, so our understanding of it necessitates constructing models that account for instability and contingency, by discovering or hypothesising the hidden logics that account for these. Otherwise we can never get beyond the messiness of the world. This is the rule of thumb in most sciences and to jettison it is tantamount to intellectual suicide. Now, it might be argued that social life is like the weather, but then even the weather has its chaos theory and the latter is not chaotic in itself. The understanding of systemic processes is founded on the existence of multiple logics, but these form in their turn a contradictory larger system that is susceptible to our comprehension, no matter how complex it might appear. The chaos of the chaos theorist is a systemic chaos and not merely randomness (Gleick 1997). The chaos of assemblage theorists is a systematic avoidance of the systematic.

The Logic of Increasing Disorder

With the recent collapse of credit institutions and the debt crisis that has hit the financial sectors of the world followed by the drying up of credit more generally, we have the conditions that one might want to pin onto notions like assemblages since they take the pressure off a more serious attempt at accounting for the situation. The fact that many economists for the most part did not predict the crisis is somewhat surprising given the rather well known logics of accumulation that we discussed above. The chapters in this book focus on peripheral areas of extraction in the world system in a situation of fragmenting economic and political organisation. The scale of variations lies along an axis of more to less state integration. The different situations described in this book are not the products of disorderly processes. They are the disorderly situations generated by orderly processes, processes that can be understood and even, hopefully, explained. And if, as would seem to be the case, we are in for a period of prolonged recession and even more chaos in our economic worlds, violence in our social worlds, even in the 'rich' world that has been producing its own internal 'third world' for the past twenty-five years, then we need the kind of attempts at linking the specificity of local conditions to the larger articulations of global process that are engaged with in this work.

Notes

1. This is not really a question of technological determinism, but a focus on a particular resource as the basis of a significant social phenomenon, such as warfare or paradoxical underdevelopment, as in petro-states etc.
2. Thus the way oil is appropriated depends on the configuration of social relations in which it occurs, including the relation to state actors and local populations, all of which have specific organisations and harbour specific strategies. This is summarised as the 'who does what to whom' scenario.
3. 'Fictitious capital' is Marx's term for capital that is entirely created within the sphere of monetary accumulation, 'M-M'. It signals perhaps *the* major contradiction in capitalist accumulation – the tendency toward monetary accumulation at the expense of real accumulation, which is its ultimate foundation.
4. The local control project began in New York City in the 1960s, aimed at black communities and focused on the school system. The Ford Foundation played a crucial financial role in this development of local ethnically based politics (Gitel 1971; Edgell 1998; Gordon 2001; Traub 2002).
5. This massive technological input does not contradict the fact that the actual intervention in the territory is minimal since the latter refers to the fact that the extraction process can occur without any broader participation from the larger society. This is all the more so for offshore exploitation.

References

Appelbaum, Richard. 2009. Giant Factories, Militant Labor: The Rise of Fordism in China? *Paper presented at the annual meeting of the American Studies Association*, 22 January. http://www.allacademic.com/meta/p105673_index.html (last accessed 26 March 2011).

Cipolla, Carlo M. 1993. *Before the Industrial Revolution: European Society and Economy, 1000–1700*. London and New York: Routledge.

Comaroff, Jean. and John. L. Comaroff. 2001. *Millennial Capitalism and the Culture of Neoliberalism*. Durham, NC: Duke University Press.

Duménil, Gérard and Dominique. Lévy. 2004. *Capital Resurgent: Roots of the Neoliberal Revolution*. Cambridge: Harvard University Press.

Edgell, Derek. 1998. *The Movement for Community Control of New York City's Schools, 1966–1970: Class Wars*. New York: Edwin Mellen Press.

Ekholm Friedman, Kasja. 1992. *Catastrophe and Creation: The Transformation of an African Culture*. London: Harwood Academic Press.

Friedman, Jonathan, ed. 2002. *Globalization, the State and Violence*. Walnut Creek: Altamira Press.

Gaddis, John L. 1992. *The United States and the End of the Cold War*. Oxford: Oxford University Press.

Gitel, Marylin et al. 1971. An Experiment in Local Control: Demonstration for Social Change. Institute for Community Studies, Queens College of CUNY Flushing, NY: Frederick Praeger, Inc.

Gleick, James. 1997. *Chaos: Making a New Science*. New York: Vintage.

Gordon, John. A. 2001. *Why They Couldn't Wait: A Critique of the Black-Jewish Conflict over Community Control in Ocean Hill-Brownsville, 1967–1971*. New York: Routledge Falmer.

Gurr, Ted. R. 2000. *Peoples Versus States: Minorities at Risk in the New Century*. Washington, DC: United States Institute of Peace Press.

Harvey, David. 2005. *A Brief History of Neoliberalism*. Oxford: Oxford University Press.

Henderson, Jeffrey. 2008. China and the Future of the Developing World: The Coming Global-Asian Era and Its Consequences. Research paper: 2008/58. Helsinki: United Nations University, UNU-WIDER.

Hilferding, Rudolf. 1910. *Das Finanzkapital; eine Studie über die jüngste Entwicklung des Kapitalismus, Marx-Studien, Blätter zur Theorie und Politik des wissenschaftlichen Sozialismus*. Vienna: I. Brand.

Hobson, John. A. 1902. *Imperialism; A Study*. London: A. Constable & Co.

Hoogvelt, Ankie. 2001 [1997]. *Globalization and the Postcolonial World. The New Political Economy of Development*. Baltimore, MD: The Johns Hopkins University Press.

Huband, Mark 2001. *The Skull beneath the Skin: Africa after the Cold War*. Boulder, CO.: Westview Press.

Karl, Terry Lynn. 1997. *The Paradox of Plenty: Oil Booms and Petro-states*. Berkeley: University of California Press.

Klein, Naomi. 2007. *The Shock Doctrine: The Rise of Disaster Capitalism*. New York: Metropolitan Books/Henry Holt.

Lenin, Vladimir Ilyich i. 1968. *Imperialism, the Highest Stage of Capitalism: A Popular Outline*. Moscow: Progress.

Levi-Strauss, Claude. 1965. The Future of Kinship Studies. *Proceedings of the Royal Anthropological Institute for 1965*. London: Royal Anthropological Institute.

Luxemburg, Rosa. 1964 [1915]. The Accumulation of Capital: An Anti-critique. In *The Accumulation of Capital: An Anti-critique/Imperialism and the Accumulation of Capital*, ed. Kenneth J. Tarbuck, . New York: Monthly Review.

New York Times. 2008. 15 December.

Ong, Aihwa. and Steven J. Collier. 2005. *Global Assemblages: Technology, Politics, and Ethics as Anthropological Problems.* Malden, MA: Blackwell Publishing.

Polgreen, Lydia 2008a. Congo Warlord Linked to Abuses Seeks Bigger Stage. *New York Times*, 19 December.

———. 2008b. Battle in a Poor Land for Riches Beneath the Soil. *New York Times*, 14 December.

Ross, Michael. 1999. The Political Economy of the Resource Curse. *World Politics* 51: 297–322.

Rye-Olsen, Gorm. 1997. Western Europe's Relations with Africa since the End of the Cold War. *The Journal of Modern African Studies* 35: 299-319.

Sassen, Saska. 2000. *Cities in a World Economy.* Thousand Oaks, CA: Pine Forge Press.

———. 2006. *Territory, Authority, Rights: From Medieval to Global Assemblages.* Princeton, NJ: Princeton University Press.

Soros, George. 2000. *Open Society: Reforming Global Capitalism.* New York: Public Affairs.

———. 2006. *The Age of Fallibility: The Consequences of the War on Terror.* New York: Public Affairs.

Spiegel, Claire. 2008. Uranium Under the Sand. Anger Above. *Washington Post*, 27 April, p. B03.

Traub, James. 2002. A Lesson in Unintended Consequences. *New York Times Magazine* 6 October 6, pp. 1–6.

Tuareg Culture and News. 2008. 6 March. http://tuaregcultureandnews.blogspot.com/2008/03/tuareg-concerns-about-uranium-mining-in.html (last accessed 26 March 2011).

PART II

AFRICA

Chapter 3

BLOOD OIL

The Anatomy of a Petro-insurgency in the Niger Delta, Nigeria

Michael Watts

The secret of great wealth with no obvious source is some forgotten crime, forgotten because it was done neatly.
– Honoré de Balzac, *Father Goriot* (1834)

The courtroom was sterile and cold, in its own way threatening and intimidating. Sitting on her elevated platform and bracketed on each side by US and Californian flags, Judge Susan Ilston presided over the proceedings with a firm hand, staring intently at the legal teams over a mountain of documents of Himalayan proportion. The federal courtroom reminded me of nothing more than the drab socialist office spaces I had seen in the 1980s populated by Russian or Polish *nomenklatura*. The jury appeared utterly bored, a posse of locals whose sartorial standards were not about to launch any of them onto the runways of Milan or New York: sneakers, stained sweatshirts, blue jeans. At least two jurors were rarely awake. From my vantage on the witness stand, looking out over a sea of faces, it was not the lawyers barking questions or the studied indifference of the jury that struck me so powerfully. Rather it was the stark contrast between a rainbow coalition of youngish Chevron lawyers posing in their Armani and Prada suits, and the legal counsel for the plaintiffs, to a person badly dressed, dishevelled, and suffering from a very bad hair day – all of whom, in fact, looked (and indeed were) rather like me: 1960s Lefties, in their case flown in from Venice, California and Manhattan, New York.

On the stand at the invitation of the plaintiffs' legal team, I was ostensibly to educate the jury on the operations of the oil industry in Nigeria.

Providing 'expert' testimony in a federal court, moreover, did not resemble a graduate seminar. Quite the reverse, what was requested was not complexity, nuance and subtle distinction ('well, it's complex you see...') but rather a Manichean vision of the world full of confidently drawn sharp contrasts delivered with a haiku-like brevity as an unassailable expert. The experience of having smart young Harvard lawyers pore over every word I had written twenty-five years earlier for a Marxist journal now long gone was, to say the least, a salutary experience.

The case in question – Chevron v. Bowoto et al. – was heard in late 2008 in the San Francisco northern California Federal District Court, finally coming to trial after nine years of baroque legal wrangling (Center for Constitutional Rights). The case pitted the unimaginably poor and disenfranchised against the unthinkably rich and powerful; the wretched of the earth against the Olympian powers of the corporate behemoths, the biggest of Big Oil. Fourteen villagers from some of the most isolated and desperate communities on the Nigerian oil fields brought a class action charging Chevron/Texaco Corporation (as it then was) with gross violations of human rights including extrajudicial killings, crimes against humanity, and cruel, inhuman and degrading treatment. In May 1998, roughly 150 Ilaje villagers occupied Chevron's Parabe Platform eight miles offshore, demanding to meet with senior executives of the corporation to discuss resources for community development and compensation for environmental destruction associated with oil and gas exploration and production along the Atlantic coastal littoral and especially across the deltaic creeks from which most Ilaje eke a miserable existence. The occupation of a barge and platform – populated by a rainbow coalition of one hundred or so expatriate and Nigerian oil-workers – came on the heels of what the Ilaje saw as a history of serial neglect and abuse. A deep well of local resentment and frustration seeded, inevitably, an unstoppable surge of political energy.

Direct action against oil installations was a way of drawing the attention of senior oil executives holed up in their corporate compounds in Port Harcourt and Lagos, for whom the only Nigerian constituency to appear on their Blackberries was a venal and corrupt political class presided over by a military psychopath, then President Sani Abacha. Even though negotiations between the protesters' leaders and representatives of Chevron Nigeria Ltd (the local subsidiary of Chevron Corporation) appeared to be making headway and a tentative agreement reached, on the morning of 28 May 1998, a group of the protesters were shot (some in the back) and killed by Nigerian government security forces and Chevron security personnel transported to the platform on Chevron-leased helicopters and paid for by the company.

The plaintiffs sought injunctive compensation and other relief under the federal Alien Tort Claims Act (ATCA, 28 U.S.C. 1350) – a statute two centuries old, framed as part of the original Judiciary Act – which provides a sort of testing ground within the federal court system on which victims of individuals or corporations that commit human rights violations outside of US territorial jurisdiction can be have their day in court. Chevron won, fully exonerated on all claims in a unanimous jury verdict rendered on 1 December 2008 after barely one day of deliberation. The Chevron strategy of having few live witnesses – virtually all of the testimony consisted of white workers on tape describing being held hostage by hundreds of juju inspired, drunken and armed black men – and of representing the Niger Delta as a zone of Conradian primal violence, paid off handsomely.

Chevron v. Bowoto et al. revealed, among other things, the extent to which oil occupies a distinct place in the popular US consciousness, one that is a product of actual violent history and real political economy (the fall of the Shah, military bases in Dhahran) but also of a particular mix of the *material* (the technics and the infrastructure of the oil business), the *natural* (reservoirs and sulphur content) and the *cultural* (expertise, nation, addiction). Oil is, in this sense, *synthetic*. Resources as constitutive of a particular way of life as is oil – the very foundation of hydrocarbon capitalism – are exemplary illustrations of the Janus-faced character of all world or mass commodities: they are at once things that enter into the realms of use and exchange as commodities (they arrive in the marketplace with their price tag, as Walter Benjamin put it), yet are simultaneously, in their variety of forms, fetishes and fetishised, bewildering and metaphysical things surrounded by magic, mystery and necromancy, as Marx once said. It was Marx after all who traced the transformation of gold from the natural (a naturally occurring metal in particular geological formations) to the social (its use as money, as universal element of exchange) to the symbolic (an obligation, promissory note, a token). Oil is natural, material, symbolic, political and spectacular. A sensitivity to the synthetic and multi-faceted quality of oil is central to any understanding of the relations between oil, violence and lawlessness – relations that have come to define, as the Chevron case revealed, the regime of living and dying in Nigeria's Niger Delta, home to some of the world's sweetest crude.

Ruins and the Prophetic Landscape of Oil

Oil is fluid and fugitive.
    – A petro-geologist, cited in *Variant* (2007)

The first barrels of Nigerian crude oil destined for the world market departed from Port Harcourt harbour almost exactly fifty years ago, on 17 February 1958. To navigate its way through the shallows of the Bonny River, the eighteen thousand ton tanker *Hemifusus* left from the Port Harcourt dockside half-full. A shuttle tanker accompanied the *Hemifusus* to Bonny Bar, eight miles from the coast, where another nine thousand tons was pumped into the hold. The oil on board had been discovered in the central Niger Delta in 1956 at Oloibiri, a small, remote creek community near Yenagoa – now the capital of Bayelsa State – located ninety kilometres to the west of Port Harcourt. Wildcatters had begun drilling in 1951 in the northern and eastern reaches of what was then called Eastern Nigeria, and finally on 3 August 1956 discovered oil in commercial quantities in tertiary deposits at twelve thousand feet. In its first year of operations Oloibiri produced five thousand barrels of heavy ('sour') crude oil each day. A year later, the first crude oil pipeline connecting Oloibiri to Kugbo Bay, seven miles distant, came on line. Two hundred ton barges shuttled the oil to two storage tanks in Port Harcourt; from there it was then shipped to the Shellhaven refinery at the mouth of the River Thames. Within a few weeks of its arrival, Nigerian gasoline was fuelling cars in and around London, the new symbols of post-war British prosperity. The Nigerian oil industry had been born.

When the first helicopters landed in Oloibiri in 1956 near St Michael's Church to the astonishment of local residents, few could have predicted what was to follow. A camp was quickly built for workers; prefabricated houses, electricity, water and a new road followed. Shell-BP (as it then was) sunk seventeen more wells in Oloibiri and the field came to yield, during its lifetime, over twenty million barrels of crude oil before oil operations came to a close twenty years after the first discovery. Misery, scorched earth and capped wellheads are all that remain now.

In the decade that followed, the Nigerian oil industry grew quickly in scale and complexity. A giant field was quickly discovered at Bomu in Ogoniland, west of Port Harcourt in 1958, and Shell-BP, which had acquired forty-six oil mining leases covering fifteen thousand square miles, rapidly expanded its operations across the oil basin. Ten years of feverish activity saw the opening of the Bonny tanker terminal in April 1961, the extension of the pipeline system including the completion of the Trans

Niger Pipeline in 1965 connecting the oil fields in the western Delta near Ughelli to the Bonny export terminal, and the coming on stream of twelve 'giant' oil fields including the first offshore discovery at Okan near Escravos in 1964. Oil tankers lined the Cawthorne Channel like participants in a local regatta, plying the same waterways that, in the distant past, housed slave-ships and palm oil hulks. By 1967, 300 miles of pipelines had been constructed, and 1.5 million feet of wells sunk; output had ballooned to 275,000 barrels per day (b/d). By the first oil boom in 1973, Nigerian oil crude production was comparable to the present day (2.4 million b/d), accounting for more than 3.5 per cent of world output. Nigeria the oil nation had arrived. Despite the slide into a bloody civil war – the Biafra War 1967–1970 – fought on and around its oil fields, the Niger Delta had come of age. Nigeria emerged as a theatre of major significance in the global search for low cost, high quality oil. By some industry estimations, the Nigerian exchequer now takes in over US$1.5 billion in oil revenues each and every week, supplying a larger share of US crude imports than Saudi Arabia.

A rusting sign sits next to the 'Christmas tree' – the capped wellhead – at Oloibiri. Well No. 1. It reads:

Drilled June 1956. Depth: 12,139 feet (3,700 meters).

It is a monument to an exploit-and-abandon culture, just as Oloibiri itself is a poster child for all of the ills and failed promises of what Ryszard Kapuscinski (1980) calls the fairy tale of oil. In the 1960s the town had a population of ten thousand; it is now a wretched backwater, a sort of rural slum home to barely one thousand souls who might as well live in another century. No running water, no electricity, no roads, and no functioning primary school; the creeks have been so heavily dredged, canalised and polluted that traditional rural livelihoods have been eviscerated. 'I have explored for oil in Venezuela and … Kuwait', said a British engineer, 'but I have never seen an oil-rich town as impoverished as Oloibiri'. In the last few years the town has been rocked by youth violence; the Aso Rock armed 'cult group' dethroned the traditional ruler amidst allegations of corruption and half-finished community development projects.

It is a bleak picture, a dark tale of neglect and unremitting misery. Oloibiri, said one local, is now a 'useless cast-away snail shell after its meat has been extracted and eaten by the government and SPDC [Shell Petroleum Development Company]'. When I visited in 2001, the chief, drunk on local gin, thrust into my hand a tattered copy of the original lease agreement with Shell, hoping that I might be able explain why the terms of the agreement had been abrogated. As if to mock the sad fact that Oloibiri is a now a sort of fossil, a piece of detritus cast off by the oil industry, a gaudy plaque dating from a Presidential visit in 2001 sits next to Well No. 1. It is a foundation stone for the Oloibiri Oil and Gas Research Institute, and for a museum and library, an homage to Oloibiri and the early history of oil. Noble ideas. But the ground has not been broken, and never will. Regularly defaced, the plaque is policed by touts looking for a commission from erstwhile visitors who want to record where it all began, the ground zero of Nigeria's oil age.

Oloibiri's intimate association with oil contains another crucial lesson, this time a sort of prophecy. It was here that Isaac Adaka Boro, an Ijaw nationalist and leader of the Niger Delta Volunteer Service ('remember ... your petroleum ... pumped out daily from your veins and then fight for your freedom'), was born at midnight on 10 September 1938. Declaring an independent Niger Delta Republic on 24 February 1966, Boro's famous 'Twelve Day Revolution' was a foretaste of what was to come twenty years later as the abandonment and despoliation felt so harshly by Oloibiri was replicated, with terrifying fidelity, across the Niger Delta oil fields. As if to convert tragedy into farce, in August 2010 the governor of Bayelsa State announced his intention to build, with Chinese finance, a greenfield oil refinery at Oloibiri (*ThisDay* 2010).

These industrial landscapes – let's call them petrolic surfaces – become, over time, relics and ruins, residual and abandoned landscapes. The transformative powers of oil, that is to say the human ecology of hydrocarbon capitalism, dwarfs virtually every other sector (with perhaps the exception of the spectre of nuclear winter). The collateral damage associated with producing and moving vast quantities of oil – the nightmare of Exxon Valdes, and the Gulf Of Mexico spill, the massive scarification of the Canadian tar sands – is hard to calculate. In any inventory of the most polluted spots on the face of the earth, the oil field figures prominently. Virtually none of these costs show up in the price we pay at the gas pump. When deployed as a target of war or insurgency, oil infrastructure becomes a weapon all of its own. The stunning aerial images of Kuwait's incendiary oil fields, detonated by Saddam's retreating forces, have become part of the iconography of war. The underwater rupture in the Gulf of Mexico confirms the popular suspicion of an industry sustained by a culture of irresponsible risk-taking, cutthroat cost-cutting, and the unregulated lawlessness of the oil frontier.

Lawlessness and Disorder on the Nigerian Oil Frontier

Some years ago the *Economist* (2001) published a witty piece recommending to its tourism-inclined readership a menu of 'unusual excursions'.

Pyongyang topped the list of prime destinations, but close behind was Port Harcourt, a sprawling conurbation of almost three million located in the heart of Nigeria's oil-rich Niger Delta region. 'Hot, humid, malarial, polluted and prone to sporadic bursts of violence', Port Harcourt's local colour also allegedly included 'potholes up to half a mile long' and cars driven 'at incredible speeds on the wrong side of the road to avoid the potholes'.

In pre-oil days, Port Harcourt – set among a maze of forest-lined creeks and rivers where the Niger Delta empties into the Atlantic – was referred to locally, and with good reason, as 'the Garden City'. Nowadays Port Harcourt provides a perfect vantage point from which to predict the end of civilisation and the failure of state-led development. A rough-and-tumble oil town, the city is a ramshackle nightmare of waterside slums, unplanned residential development and dilapidated urban infrastructure. And yet Port Harcourt is the undisputed capital of a multi-billion-dollar Nigerian oil and gas industry. During the summer of 2007 the city descended into another of its sporadic periods of bloodletting, but this time the crisis was deeper and more kinetic than anything, outside of the Biafran civil war that erupted in 1967 in which perhaps one million perished, previously witnessed. Beginning on 2 August, on the back of a rash of hostage taking – including the seizure of young children and aged mothers of senior-ranking politicians and businessmen along the Port Harcourt–Yenagoa axis (see Figure 3.1) – the city descended into an orgy of gang violence. Amnesty International noted that beginning on 6 August, there was an eleven-day period of total mayhem in which gangs fought one another openly in the streets and randomly shot ordinary civilians. The Institute of Human Rights and Humanitarian Law located in Port Harcourt estimated that four to five hundred people died in a one-month period. *Médecins sans frontières,* in its small clinic, treated more than one hundred gunshot wounds, as well as wounds from stabbings and beatings, in the first two weeks of August. Economic and social life in the city was effectively paralysed. Estimates by the Port Harcourt Chamber of Commerce concluded that almost US$1 billion in revenues were lost in the violence that followed in the wake of the April 2007 Nigerian elections.

The grim reality is that in the wake of the elections, Port Harcourt became to all intents and purposes ungovernable: it was disorderly, violent and lawless, and this lawlessness now extends from the waterside slums to the middle-class neighbourhoods in the Government Residential Area (GRA). Organised robbery by well-ordered gangs of alienated and angry youth has increased dramatically during the post-election months. I myself was a minor casualty of this explosion in July 2007 when a group of close to a dozen heavily armed thugs followed me from a commercial bank to the offices of the *National Point* newspaper, edited by the brilliant

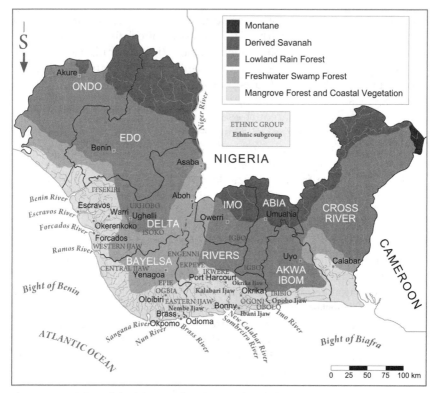

Figure 3.1. Map of the Niger Delta. *Source*: drawn by Daren Jensen.

young journalists Ibiba Don Pedro (see Don Pedro 2005, 2006) and Asume Isaac Osuoka. Shooting their way into the walled compound, the thugs made off with money and laptops after threatening the staff and ransacking many of the offices. Brazen criminality of this sort might not seem surprising in an oil city with a reputation for political violence, but it cannot be fully understood unless it is placed on the larger canvas of the wider collapse of security within the city of Port Harcourt (that is to say, the militancy and violence associated with the rural oil fields and creeks which dramatically entered the urban arena and pulled apart the region's oil capital). The crisis of the summer and autumn of 2007 is not solely or even largely about crime narrowly construed but about politics, or more properly, about the legitimacy of government, the rule of law, and the unravelling of a political order however corrupt it may be and however beholden to the powerful regional political godfathers.

Endemic robbery across the city reflected the fact that criminals knew full well they could operate with impunity because so much of the government is a fraud and a racket: state functions and public office are both widely understood to be nothing more than organised crime. How else would any sensible person interpret the images in the mainstream press of high-ranking politicians cavorting with political thugs, warlords and gang leaders? The proliferation of armed robbery in the summer of 2007 pointed to quite specifically a wider struggle for power within the fraudulent and violent world of Rivers State politics in the wake of the massively corrupt elections (by most estimations one of the most corrupt in Nigeria's postcolonial history). At stake was a legal tussle between Chief Rotimi Amaechi (former Speaker of the Rivers State House of Assembly) and incumbent governor Celestine Omehia (former special advisor to Governor Odili) over the governorship, a contest that ultimately was fought out on the streets of Port Harcourt by young men armed with Berettas and AK-47s.

Amaechi was elected in the People's Democratic Party (PDP) primaries by an overwhelming majority to run for the Rivers governorship, but following accusations of corruption by the Economic and Financial Crimes Commission (EFCC), and considerable internecine struggle within the party, he was deemed ineligible to run for office and was in fact arrested in December 2006. The PDP then substituted Omehia as its candidate in the April voting. Amaechi sued, claiming that he was in fact the party's candidate when the April voting took place, but the Federal Court of Appeals ruled against him on 20 July 2007. On 25 October 2007, the Supreme Court appointed Amaechi as the legitimate governor of Rivers State. Amaechi and Omehia are part and parcel of the PDP political machine that emerged under the previous governor, Peter Odili, an almost archetypical example of the new breed of 'godfathers' who wield enormous power within a decentralised federal system. Vast quantities of oil money (the Rivers State local governments alone collectively receive more than US$200 million per year) now course through the godfather network because of elevated oil prices and the expansion of the so-called derivation principle by which states of origin within the Nigerian federation receive 13 per cent of the revenues of oil located within their territorial jurisdiction.

While the Omehia government was right to say that the July 2007 violence 'is not an isolated scenario but part of the Niger Delta crisis', it is mildly astonishing to read that Governor Omehia also believes that the 'sporadic gunfire … was the handiwork of people who plan to discredit the Government for their own selfish gains' (Fyneface 2007). A part of the violence was related to what an insurgent group called MEND (the Movement for the Emancipation of the Niger Delta) – who exploded onto the political stage in December 2005 – cleverly called 'government workers'. MEND, a militant group engaged in a ferocious struggle with state security forces over who owns oil and how the proceeds are to be distributed, were making the point that street warfare was a result of gangs demanding that they be paid for political operations they undertook during the April elections. Odili allegedly approved some 400 million naira (US$3 million) for gangs to prevent the disruption of Omehia's inauguration. The rumours were that 'boys' from the area of Tombia – a centre of militia activity in 2003–2004 during vicious struggles between two rival Ijaw militias, Ateke Tom's Niger Delta Vigilante (NDV) and Asari Dokubo's Niger Delta People's Volunteer Force (NDPVF)[1] – were primed to cause a commotion (Sampson 2007). Gang warfare in the oil city of Port Harcourt was in this sense an excrescence of the desperate attempts by machine politicians, in an environment of great political instability and indeterminacy, to gain the upper hand by making use of political thuggery (a phenomenon that has mushroomed across the oil region, indeed the federation, over the last decade (Human Rights Watch 2008)). The gangs were attempting to reassert their power after being marginalised and in some cases hounded by the security forces as they fell out of favour during the last years of the Odili administration, and reacted by turning on their erstwhile employers. In this maelstrom of urban violence, Port Harcourt was exposed to a level of brutality and conflict that it has probably not witnessed since the Nigerian Civil War of 1967–70.

Through the autumn of 2007 Port Harcourt was in lockdown. A curfew, declared on 11 August by President Musa Yar'Adua in conjunction with the chief of defence staff and acting inspector general of police, lasted for several months. There was a call by Chief Edwin Clark, a prominent Ijaw leader and high-ranking government civil servant, for the imposition of a state of emergency, but for obvious reasons the ruling political classes at the local level did not want to cede control to the federal centre. In fact, the city was in an effective state of emergency for the latter half of 2007 and into 2008 (nineteen people were killed in a massive attack on a major hotel in Port Harcourt in January 2008) as federal troops occupied key points in the metropolis and security forces patrolled the streets and the peri-urban communities.

Oil Insurgents or Petro-criminals?

Blood may be thicker than water, but oil is thicker than both.
– Perry Anderson, *Scurrying toward Bethlehem* (2001).

The problems of political disorder and insecurity in the Niger Delta extend far beyond the fraudulent elections of 2007 in Port Harcourt and the local resentments in Oloibiri. The fact is that since the late 1990s, the oil fields of the Niger Delta generally have been more or less ungovernable (International Crisis Group 2006a, 2006b). The Nigerian oil fields have, in effect, become home to a full-blown insurgency. According to a United Nations Development Programme (UNDP 2006) report, there are 120 to 150 'active and high-risk violent conflicts' across Bayelsa, Delta and Rivers states (the three core oil-producing states). Remotely detonated car bombs and highly sophisticated arms and equipment are the tools of the trade. More than 250 foreign hostages have been abducted in the last eighteen months, and close to one thousand Nigerian workers have been detained or held hostage. Spectacular, and disruptive, attacks on both offshore and onshore facilities are endemic and can be perpetrated at will. In an astonishing raid on 19 June 2008, MEND took over and damaged the Floating Production, Storage and Offloading vessel (FPSO) associated with the massive Bonga field (Nigeria's largest field and developed at a cost of US$3.6 billion), seventy-five miles off shore, resulting in Shell declaring *force majeure* for deliveries of 200,000 barrels a day for June and July. Militants are now willing and able to directly confront federal and state security forces, which was not the case in the 1980s and early 1990s. A vast cache of sophisticated arms is skilfully deployed in an environment – the mangrove creeks running for hundreds of miles along the Bight of Benin, and increasingly the open sea – in which it was clear that the Nigerian security forces could not cope with the situation. Pipeline breaks due to vandalism and sabotage have almost doubled, from 497 to 895, between 1999 and 2004 (with costs estimated currently at US$6.8 billion). Product loss due to pipeline ruptures has grown steadily from 179,000 to 396,000 metric tons over the same period – a figure roughly equal to four supertankers.

The costs of the oil insurgency over the last decade have been nothing short of astonishing. A report prepared for the Nigerian National Petroleum Company (NNPC) published in 2003 and entitled *Back from the Brink* paints a very gloomy 'risk audit' picture for the Delta. The NNPC estimated that between 1998 and 2003, there were four hundred 'vandalisations' on company facilities each year (and 581 between January and September 2004); oil losses amounted to more than US$1 billion annually. In early 2006 MEND claimed a goal of cutting Nigerian output by 30 per cent and has apparently succeeded. Within the first six months of 2006, there were nineteen attacks on foreign oil operations and nearly US$2.2 billion lost in oil revenues; the Department of Petroleum Resources claims this figure represents 32 per cent of the revenue the country generated that year. The Nigerian government claims that between 1999 and 2005, oil losses amounted to US$6.8 billion, but in November 2006 the managing director of Shell Nigeria reported that the loss of revenues due to 'unrest and violence' was US$61 million per day (a shut-in of about 400,000 barrels per day), amounting to a staggering US$9 billion since January 2006. Against a backdrop of escalating attacks on oil facilities and a proliferation of kidnappings, the Joint Revolutionary Council (apparently an umbrella group for insurgents) in early November 2006 threatened 'black November' as an all out (*sic*) attack on oil operating companies. In the last three years, costs of the insurgency have increased dramatically to US$60 million per day, or roughly US$4.4 billion per annum. In May 2007, Nigeria drew upon US$2.7 billion from its 'domestic excess crude' (a windfall profits account) to plug revenue shortfalls from oil deferment. In mid-2006 President Obasanjo ordered the military to adopt a 'force for force' policy in the Delta in a vain effort to gain control of the creeks. In early 2007 the Nigerian navy embarked upon its biggest sea manoeuvre in two decades, deploying thirteen warships, four helicopters and four boats to the Bight of Bonny to test operational capability. Yet the month of May 2007, according to a Norwegian consulting company, Bergen Risk Solutions, witnessed the largest monthly tally of attacks since the appearance of MEND in late 2005. On 22 September 2007 MEND issued a new pronouncement, in the wake of the arrest of one of its operatives, Henry Okah, in Angola, inviting its supporters to resume attacks.

The massive escalation of violence across the Delta oil fields is in fact complex and multi-faceted, encompassing attacks on oil installations and infrastructure. But also civil violence among and between oil-producing communities and between and among militias and the state security forces is endemic (it is estimated that more than one thousand people die each year from oil-related violence). The tactics and repertoires deployed against the companies and the state have been various: demonstrations and blockades against oil facilities; occupations of flow stations and platforms; sabotage of pipelines; oil 'bunkering' or oil theft (from direct hot tapping of fuel lines to large-scale appropriation of crude from flow stations);[2] litigation against the companies; hostage taking; and a raft of organised and sometimes improvised strikes. A widely reported occupation of a Chevron refinery and tank farm near Warri by hundreds of Ijaw women in 2002, demanding company investments and jobs for indigenes (*New York Times* 2002), reflected the tip of a vast political iceberg, and a gradual escalation of militancy since the return to civilian rule in 1999. Ten years after the hanging of Ken Saro-Wiwa and the militarisation of the Ogoni oil fields, little had changed, and where it had it was for the worse. An Amnesty International report (2005) entitled *Nigeria: Ten Years On: Injustice and Violence Haunt the Oil Delta* noted that security forces still operated with impunity, government failed to protect communities in oil-producing areas while providing security to the oil industry, and the oil companies were partly responsible for the appalling misery and political instability across the region (see ICG 2006c, 2006b).

Since late 2005, the situation in the Delta has only worsened. Following attacks on oil installations and the taking of hostages in late December 2005 and early 2006, MEND, a hitherto unknown group of insurgents from the Warri region, began calling for the international community to evacuate from the Niger Delta by 12 February or 'face violent attacks'. Two weeks later, the group claimed responsibility for attacking a federal naval vessel and for the kidnapping of nine workers employed by the oil servicing company Willbros, allegedly in retaliation for an attack by the Nigerian military on a community in the western Delta. Claiming to be, according to an email communiqué from their erstwhile PR man Gbomo Jomo, a 'union of all relevant militant groups', MEND's public face is a shifting and sometimes contentious cadre of aliases: Major-General Godswill Tamuno, Tom Pollo, Oyinye Alaibe, Cynthia White and an articulate spokesperson, Gbomo Jomo. Beginning with a massive attack on the Opobo pipeline in Delta State in December 2005, MEND subsequently destroyed the offshore Forcados loading platform, the Ekeremore-Yeye manifold, and the state oil company Escravos-Lagos gas pipeline in Chanomi Creek. In a single day something like 20 per cent of output was compromised. The MEND insurgents, claimed Jomo in 2006, were 'not communists ... or revolutionaries. [They] are just very bitter men' (Bergen Risk Solutions 2007: 14). Between January 2006 and March 2007, more than two hundred expatriate oil-worker hostages were taken and forty-two attacks on oil installations took place. Within a year of their appearance MEND had, as they themselves predicted, shut in more than one-third of Nigeria's oil output. An article in the *New York Times* (2007) captures vividly the brave new world ushered in by MEND:

> Companies now confine employees to heavily fortified compounds, allowing them to travel only by armoured car or helicopter. ... One company has outfitted bathrooms with steel bolts to turn them into 'panic' rooms, if needed. Another has coated the pylons of a giant oil-production platform 130 kilometres, or 80 miles, offshore with waterproof grease to prevent attackers from climbing the rig. ... Some foreign operators have abandoned oil fields or left the country altogether. 'I can't think of anything worse right now,' said Larry Johnson, a former U.S. Army officer who was recently hired to toughen security at a Nigerian site operated by Eni, an Italian oil producer. 'Even Angola during the civil war wasn't as bad.'

By November 2007 oil revenues were down by 40 per cent, and 900,000 barrels a day shut in; Shell, the largest operator, accounting for almost half of all oil output, had alone lost US$10.6 billion since late 2005. In the

Port Harcourt and Warri regions – the two hubs of the oil industry – there were over five thousand pipelines breaks and ruptures in 2006 and 2007. By the summer of 2009, Shell's western operations were in effect closed down. Ken Saro-Wiwa's desolate prediction in 1990 of a 'coming war' had seemingly come to pass.

The armed robbery, gangland turf wars, and political thuggery that congealed in the crisis of urban disorder and violence in Port Harcourt in 2007 are part and parcel, in other words, of a long-festering political struggle about oil in the Niger Delta: who 'owns' it, who gets access to the federal allocation of oil revenues and how, and who amongst the competing political forces – political godfathers, the military, angry and alienated youth, ethnic movements, corrupt government and company officials, customary chiefly powers – will take home the vast proceeds of the black gold. The Niger Delta's crisis – multi-faceted and violent, in which the driving forces are a lethal mix of organised crime and insurgent politics – is nourished by a gigantic reservoir of anger and dissent (UNDP 2006; WAC 2003). More than fifty operating military camps are dotted around the creeks. A large survey of Niger Delta oil communities discovered that an astonishing 36 per cent revealed a 'willingness or propensity to take up arms against the state' (Oyefusi 2007: 16). The incontestable fact, as Ledum Mittee, the Ogoni human rights campaigner, has noted, is that there is overwhelming popular sympathy for what the militants are doing. Some sources estimate the number of trained militants now operating in the creeks at more than twenty-five thousand, commanding monthly salaries of more than 50,000 naira – well above the wage that might be secured by an educated youth employed in the formal sector. For their part the oil companies have lost their so-called 'license to operate'. Ken Saro-Wiwa, the pipe-smoking writer equipped with the power of the pen, has now been replaced by the figure of the masked militant armed with the ubiquitous Kalashnikov, the 'typewriter of the illiterate', to deploy the colourful language of Hungarian artist Janos Sugar (2003). But even Saro-Wiwa's gravest fears could not have anticipated the calamitous descent into violence over the last decade. How did it all come to this? How did a story that began with wildcatters and company officials preaching the virtues of oil to chiefs and traditional diviners in Oloibiri, where the first oil well was sunk in 1956, ultimately culminate in car bombs, a kidnapping industry, massive oil theft, rocket-propelled grenades, and full-blooded insurgency?

The Nigerian Oil Complex and the Failure of Secular National Development

The state is not even corruption. It is organised crime.

– Nuhu Ribadu, Nigerian Economic and Financial Crimes Commission, cited in The Economist November 12th 2009, (http://www.economist.com/node/14843563?story_id=14843563&source=hptextfeature) [EFCC],

One of every five Africans is a Nigerian – the country's population is currently estimated to be 150 million – and Nigeria is the world's seventh largest exporter of petroleum, providing the US market with roughly 12 per cent of its imports. A long-time member of OPEC, Nigeria is an archetypical 'oil nation'. With reserves estimated at close to forty billion barrels, oil accounted in 2004 for 80 per cent of government revenues, 90 per cent of foreign exchange earnings, 96 per cent of export revenues, and almost half of GDP (IMF 2007). Crude oil production in 2008 ran at more than 2.3 million barrels per day, bringing roughly US$5 billion a week to Nigerian state coffers at prevailing prices. Mostly lifted on shore from about 250 fields dotted across the Niger Delta, Nigeria's oil sector now represents a vast domestic industrial infrastructure: more than 300 oil fields, 5,284 wells, over 10,000 kilometres of pipelines, 10 export terminals, 275 flow stations, 10 gas plants, 4 refineries (Warri, Port Harcourt I and II, and Kaduna), and a massive liquefied natural gas plants (at Bonny Island and Brass).

The rise of Nigeria as a strategic player in the world of oil geopolitics, largely in the wake of the civil war that ended in 1970, has been explosive. In the late 1950s petroleum products were insignificant, amounting to less than 2 per cent of total exports (see Figure 3.2). Between 1960 and 1973 oil output exploded from just over 5 million to over 600 million barrels per year. Government oil revenues, in turn, grew by more than one hundred times between 1970 and 1980. And yet the multi-billion-dollar oil industry has proved to be little more than a nightmare. An El Dorado Nigeria is not. Flying into Port Harcourt or Warri at night – viewing the panorama of harsh gas flares burning bright – conveys a sense of the Dantean universe one is about to enter, the unforgiving, ruthless and austere world of oil. To compile an inventory of the achievements of Nigerian petro-development is a salutary, if dismal, exercise: 85 per cent of oil revenues accrue to 1 per cent of the population. According to former World Bank president Paul Wolfowitz, at least US$300 billion of the US$600 billion in oil revenues accrued since 1960 have simply 'gone missing'.

Nigerian anti-corruption czar Nuhu Ribadu claimed that in 2003, 70 per cent of the country's oil wealth was stolen or wasted; by 2005 it was 'only'

40 per cent (BBC 2006). By most conservative estimates, almost US$130 billion was lost in capital flight between 1970 and 1996. Over the period 1965–2004, the per capita income fell from US$250 to US$212 while income distribution deteriorated markedly. Between 1970 and 2000, the number of people subsisting on less than one US dollar a day in Nigeria grew from 36 per cent to more than 70 per cent, from nineteen million to a staggering ninety million. Over the last decade, both GDP per capita and life expectancy have fallen, according to World Bank estimates. The Bank put it this way in 2007: 'Per capita GDP in PPP [purchasing power parity] terms fell 40 per cent from US$1,215 in 1980 to US$706 in 2000. Income poverty rose from 28.1 per cent to 65.5 per cent and other indicators of welfare – notably access to education and health – also declined' (World Bank 2007: 1). According to the United Nations Development Programme (UNDP 2006), Nigeria ranks in terms of the human development index (HDI) – a composite measure of life expectancy, income and educational attainment – number 158, below Haiti and Congo; over the last thirty years the trend line of the HDI index has been upward, but barely. In a terrible indictment of so-called oil development, the IMF has concluded that oil 'did not seem to add to the standard of living' and 'could have contributed to a decline in the standard of living' (Sala-i-Martin and Subramanian 2003: 4).

It is not simply that Nigeria is a sort of Potemkin economy – it is, of course – but the cruel fact is that the country has become a perfect storm of waste, corruption, venality and missed opportunity. To say that Nigeria

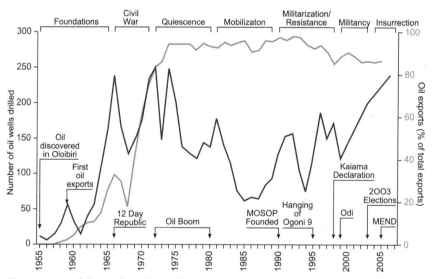

Figure 3.2. Oil graph and timeline. *Source:* drawn by Daren Jensen from IMF and World Bank statistics.

suffers from corruption – organised brigandage is how Ken Saro-Wiwa once put it – does not really capture the nature of the beast: money laundering and fraud on gargantuan scales; missing billions and inflated contracts in virtually every aspect of public life; areas boys, touts, and mobile police all taking their cuts and commissions on the most basic of everyday operations. Perhaps there is no better metaphor for this oil-fuelled venality than the stunning fact that huge quantities of oil are simply stolen every day. Over the last five years between 100,000 and 300,000 barrels of oil have been stolen daily (perhaps 10 to 15 per cent of national output), organised by a syndicate of 'bunkerers' linking low-level youth operatives and thugs in the creeks to the highest levels of the Nigerian military and political classes and to the oil companies themselves. The managing director of Chevron Nigeria, Jay Prior, once observed that he had 'run companies that have had less production than is being bunkered in Nigeria' (Peel 2005: 11).

What is on offer in the name of petro-development is the terrifying and catastrophic failure of secular nationalist development. The paradoxes and contradictions of oil are nowhere greater than on the oil fields of the Niger Delta (see Don-Pedro 2005, 2006; Okonta and Douglas 2002). In political terms, the Niger Delta consists of nine of the thirty-six states within the Nigerian Federation and 185 Local Government Councils (LGCs) occupying a surface area of about 112,110 km^2 – 12 per cent of Nigeria's territory. In 2007 the population of this region was estimated to be twenty-eight million, the overwhelming proportion of which is rural and poor (there are 13,329 settlements in the Niger Delta region, 95 per cent of which have fewer than five thousand inhabitants). The core states of the Niger Delta – Bayelsa, Rivers, Delta and Akwa Ibom – cover 45,000 km^2 and account for half of the regional population and more than three-quarters of onshore oil production. Across the Niger Delta almost 90 per cent of the rural inhabitants fall below the conventional poverty line (US$1 per day) and depend largely upon aquatic resources and petty trading for their livelihoods. Overall, the population is young and dirt poor: 60 per cent of the population is less than thirty years old, and almost 40 per cent are between the ages of fifteen and twenty-nine. According to the Niger Delta Development Commission (NDDC), the population continues to grow very rapidly – 3.1 per cent per year – and is projected to be over forty-five million by 2020. Sustained population growth is partly responsible for driving one of the highest rates of rural–urban migration in the world, a huge and relentless movement of humanity to the vast slum worlds of Port Harcourt and Warri – modern oil cities whose infrastructure resembles that of eighteenth-century Naples. In the oil-rich states of Bayelsa and Delta, there is one doctor for every 150,000 inhabitants. Oil has wrought only poverty, state violence and a dying ecosystem, says Ike

Okonta. The government's presence, Okonta notes, 'is only felt in the form of the machine gun and jackboots' (2005: 206). It is no great surprise that a half-century of neglect in the shadow of black gold has made for a combustible politics. All the while the democratic project initiated in 1999 appears ever more hollow.

The nightmarish legacy of oil politics must be traced back to the heady boom days of the 1970s. The boom detonated a huge influx of petro-dollars and launched an ambitious (and largely autocratic) state-led modernisation program under military rule. Central to the operations of the new oil economy was the emergence of an 'oil complex' that overlaps with, but is not identical to, the 'petro-state' (Watts 2005). The latter is composed of several key institutional elements: first, a statutory monopoly over mineral exploitation; second, a nationalised (state) oil company that operates through joint ventures with oil majors who are granted territorial concessions (blocs); third, the security apparatuses of the state (often working in a complementary fashion with the private security forces of the companies), who ensure that costly investments are secured; fourth, the oil-producing communities themselves, within whose customary jurisdiction the wells are located; and finally, a political mechanism by which oil revenues are distributed.

The oil revenue distribution question – whether in a federal system such as Nigeria or in an autocratic monarchy such as Saudi Arabia – is an indispensable part of understanding the combustible politics of imperial oil. In Nigeria there are four formal distribution mechanisms: the federal account (rents appropriated directly by the federal state); a state derivation principle (the right of each state to a proportion of the taxes that its inhabitants are assumed to have contributed to the federal exchequer); the Federation Account (or States Joint Account), which allocates revenue to the states on the basis of need, population and other criteria; and a Special Grants Account (which includes monies designated directly for the Niger Delta, for example, through the notoriously corrupt NDDC). Over time the derivation revenues have fallen precipitously (and thereby revenues directly controlled by the oil-rich Niger Delta states have shrivelled) and the States Joint Account has grown vastly. In short, there has been a process of radical fiscal centralism in which the oil-producing states (composed of ethnic minorities) have lost and the non-oil producing ethnic majorities have gained – by fair means or foul.

Overlain upon the Nigerian petro-state is, in turn, a volatile mix of forces that give shape to the oil complex. First, the geo-strategic interest in oil means that military and other forces are part of the local oil complex. Second, local and global civil society enters into the oil complex either through transnational advocacy groups concerned with human rights and the transparency of the entire oil sector, or through local social movements and NGOs fighting over the consequences of the oil industry and the accountability of the petro-state. Third, the transnational oil business – the majors, the independents and the vast service industry – are actively involved in the process of local development through community development, corporate social responsibility and stakeholder inclusion. Fourth, the inevitable struggle over oil wealth – who controls and owns it, who has rights over it and how the wealth is to be deployed and used – inserts a panoply of local political forces (ethnic militias, paramilitaries, separatist movements etc.) into the operations of the oil complex. In some circumstances oil operations are the object of civil wars. Fifth, multilateral development agencies (the IMF and the International Bank for Reconstruction and Development) and financial corporations such as the export credit agencies appear as key brokers in the construction and expansion of the energy sectors in oil-producing states (and latterly the multilaterals are pressured to become the enforcers of transparency among governments and oil companies). And not least, there is the relationship between oil and the shady world of drugs, illicit wealth (oil theft, for example), mercenaries and the black economy.

The operations of the oil complex under the conditions of US military neo-liberalism creates the violent and unstable spaces that David Harvey (2003, 2005) identifies as undergoing accumulation by dispossession. The oil complex is a vast forcing house – a sort of incubation chamber – of primitive accumulation, repeating the original sin of robbery. It operates as if through a chain of enclosures, violent economies that dispossess at a variety of levels and through a raft of modalities. The rise of the resource control movement over the last fifteen years, the rise of the so-called oil minorities – the small ethnic groups claiming control over oil and gas resources located on what they take to be their territories – and the attendant mix of ethno-nationalisms and insurgent politics across the Delta are reactions to, or, drawing from Polanyi (1947), one might say a 'double movement' against, imperial oil. What this insurgent politics has produced, of course, is a fragmented polity in which we have a form of parcellised sovereignty (Mbembe 2001) – that is to say, a sort of political fragmentation of the national space called Nigeria – characterised by the emergence of highly contentious and insurgent political (and criminal) spaces, rather than a robust sense of nationalism and a modern petro-state.

Anatomy of an Oil Insurgency

How then can one understand the genesis of an oil insurgency in the Niger Delta since the mid- to late 1990s? I cannot offer a full accounting here (but see Watts 2007 for a fuller treatment) but rather wish to highlight a number of structural forces all of which cast a rather different light on the so-called 'resource curse' (see Collier et al. 2003). The first is what one might call local petro-nationalisms – the process by which the ethnic minorities of the delta became 'oil minorities' with a political project for resource control. Over the last decade this has been most visible in the deepening of Ijaw nationalism and a popular mobilisation of youth especially in the wake of the state-repression of the Ogoni during the 1990s. The Ijaw are the largest ethnic or so-called oil minorities in the Delta and are distributed across the heart of the oil fields, especially in Rivers and Bayelsa States. Their exclusion from the oil wealth (and the federal revenue allocation process), to say nothing of their bearing the costs of oil operations across the oil fields, became central to the emergence of a new sort of youth politics (in effect, a disenfranchised generation). Nwajiaku (2005) has traced the origins of Ijaw nationalism to the 1920s and 1930s but it was a group of politically connected Ijaw elders that emerged from the 1950s onwards who mobilised around state-formation – an Ijaw state for Ijaw indigenes – and established organisations like the Rivers State Forum and the Ijaw National Congress to promote their ambitions. But this establishment and elder-dominated movement was overtaken during the 1990s by youth politics and the establishment of the Ijaw Youth Council in 1998 and its radical founding document, the Kaiama Declaration (see Okonta and Douglas 2000), which marked a watershed in the growth of popular mobilisation from below and in the gradual turn toward direct actions against both the federal state and the international oil companies. Control of oil in relation what they saw as a deep history of theft, appropriation and unjust exploitation provided a powerful idiom to mobilise Ijaw claims and a discourse of rights (including legal, constitutional and fiscal reforms). Ijaw nationalism proved to be a complicated category because of the internal heterogeneity of so-called Ijaw peoples (differing clan and community structures, differing language and cultural histories). Oil, as Nwajaiku points out, provided a way of drawing Ijaw together but also generated other local forms of identity at the clan, village or local territorial levels.

A second process was the inability and unwillingness of the Nigerian state in its military and civilian guises to address this political mobilisation in the Delta without resorting to state-imposed violence by an undisciplined military and police and security forces. In this sense the history of the Ogoni struggle was a watershed, too, insofar as it bequeathed a generation of militants for whom Ken Saro-Wiwa's MOSOP (Movement for the Survival of the Ogoni People) represented a failure of non-violent politics.

Third, the militant groups themselves were often the *products*, if not the creation, of state-supported electoral thuggery; a welter of so-called militias, cults, organised criminals and political militants were bankrolled by the state, ambitious corrupt politicians and local political godfathers. The NDV and NDPVF were both fuelled by machine politicians and the local state, especially during the notoriously corrupt 1999 and 2003 elections. Fourth, the proliferation of a massive oil theft business in which insurgent groups were able to insert themselves (though typically as underlings beneath high-ranking military and politicians) enabled them to acquire arms and embolden their military offensive (and their popular appeal to a generation of enraged youth). And finally, the operations of the companies – in their funding of youth groups as local security forces, in their willingness to use military and security forces against protesters and militants alike, and in their corrupt practices of distributing rents (so-called cash payments) to local elites in the name of community development – contributed to an environment in which violence and conflict was in effect encouraged and facilitated. Youths fought corrupt elders, youth groups fought each other to get access to standby payments, and communities fell into conflicts over land claims and the boundaries of oil-bearing lands – a process often seen as a divide and rule policy by the companies.

These structural forces operated within the circumference of what I have called the oil complex. One of the consequences of emphasising this relation is that it points to the deep problem of seeing the Nigerian oil insurgency as a simple function of the resource curse (Collier et al. 2003; Ross 1999). It is not the case that oil deterministically produces, as some predict, secessional tendencies (Le Billon 2005), nor that oil revenues were simply 'predated' (see Ross 1999) by the insurgents (oil rents were certainly extorted but also stolen through a highly organised bunkering trade in which the insurgents controlled the lower levels of these so-called oil syndicates). But more profoundly, oil did not play a determinative role – a sort of commodity determinism. Rather, the insurgency emerged from the political struggles over centralised oil rents, struggles in which party politics, the electoral cycle, intergenerational politics, organised oil theft and the history of ethnic exclusion played constitutive roles.

The appearance of MEND symbolises a new phase, both in terms of strategic capacity and in the franchise character of the insurgency, linking to and speaking for a number of militias and rebels. Whether it is, as Okonta (2006) suggests, not an organisation but 'an idea' is difficult to assess. Certainly the MEND militias operate with ease in and around Warri; the leadership appears, as Okonta says, articulate and politically very savvy. But MEND emerged and is inseparable from a number of local and regional issues, the most important of which are the long-standing antagonisms between the oil companies (especially Chevron) and local communities in the Gbaramantu and Egbema clan territories, and the crisis and struggles among ethnic groups and clans over the creation of local government councils in Warri – a region of long-festering interethnic struggle – that broke out in 1997. MEND has been framed by a wider and panethnic struggle for resource control but was at the same time detonated by what Ijaw see as a deepening assault under President Obasanjo on their nationalist aspirations, what Bello Oboko calls 'being cut off from being a nation' (cited in Human Rights Watch 2003). The extraordinarily violent gunship and helicopter attacks by the Nigerian security forces on Okerenkoko in February 2006 and the attacks by the Joint Military Task Force (the special forces of the Nigerian government deployed as counterinsurgency forces in the Niger Delta) on MEND in the wake of a truce brokered between MEND and the government in August of the same year were consistent with a much longer history of state violence across the Warri axis. In this sense, Okonta is surely right to say that MEND is 'the violent child of the deliberate and long-running constriction of the public space in the Niger delta. ... Behind the mask of MEND is a political subject forced to pick up an AK47 to restore his rights' (2006: 20).

Whether it is an umbrella organisation, a franchise or an 'un-united hydra', in the words of MEND spokesperson Jomo Gbomo (ICG 2006c: 7), MEND emerges on the back of a long process of grassroots mobilising and the widening of the social base of recruitment among youth, men in particular, across a wide array of ethnic groups and local communities. It also reflects the institutional incorporation of various youth groups in MEND in complex and unstable networks – MEND, for example, has allegedly made an alliance with the Outlaws, a renegade group previously linked to the Icelanders, a local militia involved in, among other things, drugs and protection rackets. The emergence of MEND, moreover, is part of the shift from non-violent protest and demonstrations to occupations, sabotage, vandalism and outright organised armed assault, including, since 1998, the tactical use of kidnapping and ransom. Running across this story is the deepening involvement of organised militias, since the late 1980s, in various economic 'enterprises' including oil bunkering (and refining), ransoms, extortion, protection services and drug trading. To see oil theft or hostage taking as either new or evidence of a simple linear shift from grievance to greed is not helpful, in part because one person's greed is another's grievance and because inevitably this mix of forces – always open to different definitions and meanings – always operates as part of a complex whole. In this sense the oil insurgency in the Niger Delta is not terribly different from any insurgency in the history of militant political struggles everywhere.

After a decade of deepening militancy, the reality on the ground is one of a dizzying and bewildering array of militant groups, militias and so-called cults[10] – the Niger Delta Militant Force Squad (NDMFS), Niger Delta Coastal Guerillas (NDCG), South-South Liberation Movement (SSLM), Movement for the Sovereign State of the Niger Delta (MSSND), the Meinbutus, the November 1895 Movement, the Arogbo Freedom Fighters, Iduwini Volunteer Force (IVF), the Niger Delta People's Salvation Front (NDPSF), COMA (Coalition for Military Action) , the Greenlanders, Deebam, Bush Boys, KKK, Black Braziers, Icelanders and a raft of others. By 2007, according to some sources, there were more than fifty military camps operating in the creeks. With good reason, MEND's spokesperson, Jomo, could boast in March 2007 that he had 'the oil industry by the balls' (*Economist* 2007; see Figure 3.3). On a wider canvas of frustration, especially after the 2007 elections and the heightened expectations among the militants with the emergence as Vice-President of a politician from the Niger Delta, the oil industry sank slowly into dysfunction and chaos. In the first nine months of 2008, $20 billion in oil revenues were lost to disruption (Technical Report 2008). By the summer of 2009 oil output had fallen to barely 1 million barrels per day (bpd) from roughly 2.5 million bpd in 2005.

Figure 3.3. Members of the Movement for the Emancipation of the Niger Delta (MEND) in the creeks of the Niger Delta near to Warri, Delta State. *Source*: Photo by Ed Kashi. See also Kashi and Watts (2008).

From Insurgency to Amnesty

The April 2007 elections were recognised as being perhaps the most corrupt in Nigerian history. Nowhere was electoral fraud and intimidation more pronounced than in the Niger Delta. Nonetheless, deeply flawed elections and a victory by the ruling PDP did produce an Ijaw Vice-President, Goodluck Jonathan, an ecologist from Bayelsa State with strong connections to a younger generation of activists and civic groups. Musa Yar'Adua, the new Nigerian President – a machine politician from an influential Katsina political family in northern Nigeria – clearly put some stock in his Niger Delta running mate's capacity to address the insurgency and indeed there were some positive signs early on: the 14 June 2007 release from detention of Ijaw leader Asari Dokubo and the 27 July freeing of Chief Alamieyeseigha met key demands of many of the Ijaw militants. Alamieyeseigha, the former Governor of Bayelsa State, was apprehended in London for money laundering but escaped, dressed in drag, to triumphantly return to the Delta, wherein some quarters of the Ijaw community hailed him as a freedom fighter. Whatever their respective track records, both are seen as Ijaw heroes to many across the Delta.

None of this is made easier by the constant drumbeat of US geopolitics and regional militarisation. In February 2006 Nigeria's vice-president, Atiku Abubakar, unsuccessfully requested two hundred patrol boats and a military package from the United States. In turn, Nigeria appealed directly to China for military aid, claiming that the United States was slow to support them in this area. It is in the intersection of a more aggressive scramble for African oil by China and the US, twin concerns of secure oil supply (national energy security) and the global War on Terror that a perfect storm of political volatility is created.

United States energy security has always been military in tone since at least the 1930s, but after 9/11 it was merged into the portfolio of the Global War on Terrorism (GWOT). What distinguishes this military incorporation is a trio of forces: first, a proactive counterterrorism effort rather than training for peacekeeping and human rights; second, the growing role of China in African oil zones; and third, bureaucratic competition among the regional commands of the US military. The former Defence Secretary Donald Rumsfeld offered a new strategic doctrine, force transformation, which emphasised flexible mobility operating through a network of 'lilly-pads' in conflicted zones such as the Gulf and thereby reinforced the strategic shift to counterterrorism in Africa. In short, the GWOT offered the US European Command (USEUCOM) strategists an opportunity to compensate for lost opportunities by looking southward and repositioning and redeploying their forces to the Sahel and the Gulf of Guinea. All of this was facilitated by an unholy alliance of energy lobbyists, politicians and right-wing activists who promoted the new energy security–military fix. Against a backdrop of spiralling militancy across the Delta, US interests have met up with European strategic concerns in the Gulf in the establishment of the Gulf of Guinea Energy Security Strategy (GGESS). By December 2005 the US ambassador and the managing director of the NNPC agreed to establish four special committees to co-ordinate action against trafficking in small arms in the Niger Delta, bolster maritime and coastal security in the region, promote community development and poverty reduction, and combat money laundering and other financial crimes. Not surprisingly, the oil companies – facing losses of five hundred thousand barrels per day and more – also put their shoulder to the wheel. A senior maritime analyst at the US Office of Naval Research revealed to participants at a conference in March 2006 at Fort Lauderdale that 'Shell led a group of oil companies in an approach to the U.S. military for protection of their facilities in the Delta' and warned that 'Nigeria may have now lost all ability to control the situation' (Carbon Web 2006: 5). The establishment in 2007 of the African Command (AFRICOM) and the desperate search by the United States for countries in which to locate forward bases is seemingly the capstone for the new African energy security policy.

The establishment of AFRICOM in 2007, while draped in the double-speak of humanitarian assistance, development, military professionalisation and so on, is rooted in the need to police what the US military calls the 'ungoverned spaces' in which political Islam and oil insurgents can flourish (Lipschitz, Lubeck and Watts 2007).

In practice it was internal, rather than foreign, forces which drove the complex dynamics of the contemporary oil-field conflicts. On 2 July 2007, the federal government inaugurated a twenty-member Peace and Conflict Resolution Committee for the Niger Delta with Senator David Brigidi and the Hon. Kingsley Kuku as chairman and secretary respectively. The committee, inaugurated by Vice-President Goodluck Jonathan, facilitated the cessation of hostilities by militants, and release of hostages. But the activities of the Brigidi committee were hampered by mistrust between government and the militants as well as composition of the committee and as a result the situation continued to deteriorate. In response the federal government announced the setting up of a forty-member Technical Committee on the Niger Delta on 8 September 2008. The important report emphasised the question of good governance and laid out a clear plan of action. But once more the report went unheeded. An escalation of militancy continued to the extent that by May 2009 the oil fields were in effect barely functional. At this point the government launched a counter-insurgency attack by the Joint Military Task Force especially focused on the western

Delta along the so-called Warri axis with considerable displacement of people and loss of life. Within a month the government, on 25 June 2009, announced a sixty-day (from 6 August to 4 October 2009) amnesty package for ex-militants in which the militants were expected to disarm and forswear violence. Arms collection centres and withholding camps were established and some twenty six thousand militants including most 'commanders' accepted the amnesty. A large budget of $430 million was allocated to a Presidential Monitoring Committee on Amnesty with promises of monthly stipends of N65,000 and conflict mediation and not least the expectation of some type of employment training thrown in too.

But history intervened once again lending, this time, a strange surreality to the Niger delta question. President Yar'Adua was taken gravely ill in November 2009 and was shipped to Saudi Arabia for treatment. Nobody other than a handful of close advisors knew anything of his actual condition. He mysteriously returned to the country in on 24 February 2010 but died suddenly on 5 May. Delta native Vice-President Goodluck Jonathan assumed the presidency but over this entire period the amnesty process – indeed the whole country – had in effect stalled for almost six months. Indeed the country drifted, there were rumors of a military coup. For the amnesty process these events turned out to be disastrous. There was after all good reason to believe that some militants had not taken the amnesty, that the disarmament process was woefully incomplete, and that many of the militants who had been waiting in holding camps for months were about to return to the creeks.

Against the backdrop of the political crisis, frustrations and resentments bubbled up almost immediately. In Yenagoa, the capital of Bayelsa State ex-combatant protests turned ugly:

> In the first such violent demonstration, the militants defied a heavy down pour, barricaded the major highway in the city and crippled commercial activities while shooting sporadically into the air...A couple of days later, hundreds of the militants trooped out of their temporary guest house and stormed the secretariat and Government House demanding to meet their leaders who are sheltered there. The militants have since issued dire threats of abandoning the amnesty programme and returning to the war path (*The Guardian*, editorial, September 17, 2009:14).

The militants' firepower suggested that de-militarization was far from complete.

The Government had constituted a Presidential Committee on Disarmament and Amnesty for militants in the Niger Delta chaired by then Minister of Defense, Major General Godwin Abbe (rtd) (Abbe was also chairman of the Amnesty Implementation Committees). The Committee was immediately unpopular largely due to the top-down and arrogant disposition of its leadership and in any case was at odds with other arms of government charged with managing the program. Amidst deepening criticism and contention, the federal government sacked the Presidential Committee on Disarmament and Amnesty and in its place appointed five new committees inaugurated on December 16, 2009 (the new committees were Presidential Monitoring Committee on Amnesty headed by the Presidential Adviser on Niger Delta, Mr. Timi Alaibe; Infrastructural Development Committee Chaired by the Minister of Niger Delta Affiars, Chief Ufot Ekaette; and Disarmament and Rehabilitation Committee headed by the Minister of Defense, Major General Godwin Abbe(rtd). The two others are Oil and Gas Assets Protection Committee headed by the Minister of Petroleum Resources, Dr. Rilwanu Lukman; and Environmental Remediation Committee chaired by the Minister of Environment, Mr. John Ode).

Inevitably the funding mechanisms of the new dispensation were thrown into question. Although the office of the President announced an initial take off grant of N50 billion for the Amnesty project on July 30, 2009, the Senate approved only a budget of N10billion for the Presidential Committee on the Amnesty Program chaired by Abbe. The initial release of N450 million for the commencement of the activities of the Amnesty by the former National Security Adviser, Major General Saki Mukar was shrouded in secrecy and claims of fraud. Payments delays to the militants occurred because the budgeted funds were diverted and accusations that the militants leaders were absconding with large quantities of money.

By their protests, the former militants have raised serious issues about transparency, accountability and, above all, competence in the management of the amnesty program

The new Amnesty Committee structure operated a multi-camp training system in Alua, Rivers State, Agbarho in Bayelsa State, as well as Egbokodo-Itsekiri in Delta State. But in practice there were no structures on ground at the various camps for effective rehabilitation purposes: there were no camp commandants, no camp rules, in adequate and dilapidated facilities, no camp clinic or sick bay as well as security. Not surprisingly, the Federal government in April 2010 abandoned the multi-camp arrangement for the demobilization process, settling instead for a uniform camping system for the ex-militants at Obubra in Cross River State.

Such was the situation in August 2010 with the final if rather shambolic training camps finally beginning in Cross River State. Yet once more the first camps were disorganised and intense conflicts developed around the training sessions and the imported US "mediators". In early August 2010 there were protests in Warri, Yenagoa and the federal capital itself by disgruntled militants: payments, stipends, eligibility, the nature of the training were all thrown into doubt. It was a rickety and very delicate situation and whether the 'Big Four' militant leaders – Asari, Ateke, Farah and Boyloaf – would be prepared or indeed able to keep their boys from a renewal of militancy remains a very big question. The signs were ominous. And indeed the worse seemed to come to pass when massive bomb explosions killing 12 people and injuring many others were detonated during the Independence Golden Jubilee celebrations in Abuja the capital city on 1 October 2010. While President Jonathan immediately claimed the events were not related to the Niger delta (to defend himself against the accusation that he could not control "his people") , shortly afterwards a number of militants were arrested and Henry Okah, a purported mastermind of MEND, was seized by police in South Africa accused of terrorists acts (he is currently waiting trial as of March 2011). Within a month there were renewed attacks on pipelines in Bayelsa and Akwa Ibom states, a dramatic hostage taking incident 8 miles offshore and the apparent appearance of a "new MEND" as recalcitrant commanders – notably Commander Obese and John Togo – claimed responsibility for a rash of new attacks. On 17 December the Niger Delta Liberation Front (Togo's group) attacked Alero and Abiteye flow stations in Delta State; three of the four major refineries were shut because of earlier attacks. MEND informed news outlets that they intended to shut in 500,000 barrels as the new year opened.

With the elections looming in April, the situation looks anything but rosy. Between the first peace initiatives in 2007 up to the amnesty and post-amnesty programs of 2010–2011, the insurgency had cost Nigeria over N3 trillion and was responsible for over 3000 oil spills (*Worldstage*, 13 February 2011: http://www.worldstagegroup.com/worldstage/index.php?active=news&id=2027). The amnesty now seems in tatters. Recent electoral history of Nigeria has been marred by extraordinary political violence and thuggery; as unscrupulous politicians look for ways to intimidate both voters and their political competitors, they will not have to look far for a large community of disgruntled ex-militants who can be hired as thugs. This after all is how many of the militants got their start in 1999 and 2003. It is a bleak prospect.

Notes

1. The Ijaw represent the largest ethnic group (perhaps fourteen million) within the multiethnic Niger Delta, a nine-state region within the Nigerian federation with an estimated population of twenty-eight million and almost fifty different ethno-linguistic groups.
2. The oil theft business in Nigeria runs to several billion US dollars each year, organised by criminal gangs, the military, and high-ranking politicians and businessmen. Some of the oil is popularly appropriated by tapping pipelines directly (the cause of devastating oil pipeline explosions) but also the direct diversion of oil from the flow stations by well-organised criminals (often former oil workers with knowledge of the oil infrastructure). See Kemedi (2006).
3. Coup attempts were launched against Equatorial Guinea, Sao Tome and Chad in 2004–2005; Gabon, Congo and Angola all face internal political instabilities and civil conflict.
4. The Petroleum Finance Company (PFC) acknowledged the enhanced significance of Nigerian oil in a March 2000 presentation to the US Congressional International Relations Committee Sub-Committee on Africa. By early 2002, the Jerusalem-based neo-conservative think tank the Institute for Advanced Strategic and Political Studies was actively promoting Africa as 'a priority for U.S. national security'. (see IASPS, *African Oil: A Priority for US National Security*, 2002: http://www.israeleconomy.org/strategic/africawhitepaper.pdf)
5. African gas production – a by-product of oil drilling – was close to 4 trillion cubic feet by 2000; Algeria produces almost 70 per cent. Algeria and Nigeria account for the largest reserves of gas. African gas consumption is expected to grow substantially as domestic and transnational gas-to-power plants are developed and as major oil producers such as Nigeria and Angola develop their liquefied natural gas capacities (the majority of gas is currently flared).
6. For example, the 1984 Ogharefe and Ekpan uprisings, and those by Ogoni and other ethnic 'minority' groups in 1994 and 1995.
7. The Chicoco Movement and the Kaiama Declaration were the two founding Ijaw movements, both of which marked the escalation of demands for resource control by a panoply of youth movements across the Niger Delta.
8. It is commonplace to see the Kaiama Declaration in 1998, the ferocious state violence that followed, and the so-called Egbesu Wars of 1998–1999 as the founding moment of Niger Delta militancy (Ikelegbe 2006). In fact, Isaac Boro (of the NDPVF) and his sixty or so comrades were their forerunners three decades earlier in 1966. In any case, the use of various tactics currently employed, such as the seizure of flow stations, was already in evidence in the 1980s and early 1990s, especially in the so-called Warri axis.
9. A major study on the relations between gangs, cults and militias has been published by CASS (the Centre for Advanced Social Science) in Port Harcourt (see Peterside 2007).
10. The Rivers State Secret Cult and Similar Activities Bill passed in 2004 identified 103 different cults in the state and more than fifty thousand small arms in circulation.
11. This section draws directly from a paper prepared for the Center for International Policy in Washington, DC (Lipschitz, Lubeck and Watts 2007).

References

Amnesty International. 2005. *Nigeria: Ten Years On: Injustice and Violence Haunt the Oil Delta.* http://www.amnesty.org/en/library/info/AFR44/022/2005.

Anderson, Perry. 2001. Scurrying toward Bethlehem. *New Left Review* 10: 5–30.

Bannon, Ian and Paul Collier, eds. 2003. *Natural Resources and Violent Conflict.* Washington, DC: World Bank.

Barnes, Sandra. 2005. Global Flows: Terror, Oil, and Strategic Philanthropy. *African Studies Review* 48(1): 1–23.

BBC. 2006. Nigerian Leaders Stole $380 Billion. 20 October. http://news.bbc.co.uk/2/hi/africa/6069230.stm.

Belida, Alex. 2004. US Navy to Deploy Aircraft Carrier Strike Group in Gulf of Guinea. *Energy Bulletin,* 30 May. http://www.energybulletin.net/498.html.

Bergen Risk Solutions. 2007. *Security in the Niger Delta.* Bergen: Bergen Risk Solutions.

Carbon Web. 2006. Government Fiddles while Delta Burns. *Carbon Web Newsletter,* 7 April, p. 5. www.platformlondon.org/carbonweb/documents/utcw_newsletter04.pdf.

Center for Constitutional Rights. [2010]. Bowoto v. Chevron. *http://ccrjustice.org/ourcases/current-cases/bowoto-v.-chevron* (accessed 15 July 2010).

Center for Strategic and International Studies (CSIS). 2004. *Promoting Transparency in the African Oil Sector.* Washington, DC: Center for Strategic and International Studies.

Christian Aid. 2003. *Behind the Mask: The Real Face of Corporate Responsibility.* London: Christian Aid.

Clearwater. 2003. *Back from the Brink: Niger Delta Risk Audit 1999–2003.* London: CWC Publishing.

Collier, Paul, Victor. L. Elliott, Håvard Hegre, Anke Hoeffler, Marta Reynal-Querol and Nicholas Sambanis. 2003. *Breaking the Conflict Trap.* New York: Oxford University Press.

Don-Pedro, Ibiba. 2005. *Out of a Bleak Landscape.* Lagos: Foreword Communication.

———. 2006. *Oil in the Water.* Lagos: Foreword Communication.

Economist. 2001. Sunhat, Bikini, Flak Jacket. 22 December. http://www.economist.com/node/883977.

Economist. 2007. Blood and Oil. 15 March. http://www.economist.com/node/8861488.

Frynas, George. 2004. The Oil Boom in Equatorial Guinea. *African Affairs* 103: 527–46.

Fyneface, Senior. 2007. Between State of Emergency and Omehia's Who Wants to Be a Millionaire. *Sahara Reporters,* 11 August. http://www.saharareporters.com/www/interview/detail/?id=56.

Gary, Ian and Terry Lynn Karl. 2003. *Bottom of the Barrel: Africa's Oil States and the Poor.* London: Catholic Relief Services.

Harvey, David. 2003. *The New Imperialism.* London: Clarendon.

———. 2005. *A Brief History of Neoliberalism.* Oxford: Oxford University Press.

Hodges, Tony. 2001. *Angola: From Afro-Stalinism to Petro-diamond Capitalism.* Bloomington: Indiana University Press.

Human Rights Watch. 2003. *The Warri Crisis: Fuelling Violence.* Washington, DC: Human Rights Watch.

Ikelegbe, Augustine. 2006. The Economics of Conflict in the Oil Rich Niger Delta Region of Nigeria. *African and Asian Studies* 5(1): 23–55.

International Crisis Group (ICG). 2006a. *Nigeria: Want in the Midst of Plenty.* Report No. 113. Dakar: International Crisis Group.

———. 2006b. *Swamps of Insurgency.* Report No. 115. Dakar: International Crisis Group.

———. 2006c. *Fuelling the Delta Crisis.* Report No. 118. Dakar: International Crisis Group.

International Monetary Fund (IMF). 2007. Nigeria: Poverty Reduction Strategy Paper. Report 07/0270. Washington, DC: International Monetary Fund.

Kapuscinski, Ryzard. 1980. *Shah of Shahs.* New York: Bantam Books.

Kashi, Ed and Michael Watts. 2008. *Curse of the Black Gold: Fifty Years of Oil in the Niger Delta.* New York: Powerhouse Books. http://www.powerhousebooks.com/blackgold.pdf.

Keenan, Jeremy. 2006. The Making of Terrorists: Anthropology and the Alternative Truth of America's 'War on Terror' in the Sahara. *Focaal – European Journal of Anthropology* 48: 144–51.

Kemedi, Dimieari Von. 2006. *Fuelling the Violence.* Working Paper no. 10, Economies of Violence Project. Berkeley: University of California. Http://geography.berkeley.edu/ProjectsResources/ND%20Website/NigerDelta/pubs.html.

Klare, Michael. 2004. *Blood and Oil.* New York: Metropolitan Books.

———. 2008. *Rising Powers, Shrinking Planet.* New York: Metropolitan Books.

Le Billon, Philippe. 2005. *Fuelling War.* London: Routledge.

Lipschitz, Ronnie, Paul Lubeck and Michael Watts. 2007. *Convergent Interests.* Washington, DC: Center for International Policy.

Lyman, Princeton. 2006. *More than Humanitarianism: A Strategic US Approach toward Africa.* Task Force Report No. 56. New York: Council on Foreign Relations.

Mbembe, Achille. 2001. At the Edge of the World. *Public Culture* 12(1): 259–84.

National Energy Policy Development Group (NEPDG). 2001. *Reliable, Affordable, and Environmentally Sound Energy for America's Future: Report of the National Energy Policy Development Group.* Washington, DC: US Government Printing Office.

New York Times. 2002. 'Women Block Chevron and Shell Offices'. 10 August. http://www.nytimes.com/2002/08/10/world/women-block-chevron-and-shell-offices-in-nigeria.html?src=pm.

New York Times. 2007. Oil Companies in Niger Delta Face Growing List of Dangers. 22 April. http://www.nytimes.com/2007/04/22/business/worldbusiness/22iht-oil.1.5388689.html.

Nwajiaku, Kathryn. 2005. *Oil Politics and Identity Transformation in Nigeria.* PhD Dissertation, Oxford University.

Okonta, Ike. 2005. Nigeria: Chronicle of a Dying State. *Current History* (May): 203–208.

———. 2006. *Behind the Mask.* Working Paper 11, Niger Delta Economies of Violence Project. Berkeley: University of California. http://globetrotter.berkeley.edu/NigerDelta/.

Okonta, Ike and Oronto Douglas. 2002. *Where Vultures Feast.* London: Verso.

Omeje, Kenneth. 2006a. *High Stakes and Stakeholders: Oil Conflict in Nigeria.* Aldershot: Ashgate.

———. 2006b. Petro Business and Security Threats in the Niger Delta. *Current Sociology* 54(3): 477–99.

Oyefusi, Aderoju. 2007. *Oil and the Propensity for Armed Struggle in the Niger Delta Region of Nigeria.* Post Conflict Transitions Papers No. 8 (WPS4194). Washington, DC: World Bank.

Peel, Michael. 2005. *Crisis in the Niger Delta.* Chatham House, London. Africa Programme. Briefing Paper # AFP BP 05/02.

Peterside, Sofiri. 2007. *Rivers State: Explaining the Phenomena of Ethnic Militias.* Port Harcourt: Center for Advanced Social Science.

Polanyi, Karl. 1947. *The Great Transformation.* Boston: Beacon Press.

RETORT. 2005. *Afflicted Powers: Capital and Spectacle in a New Age of War.* London: Verso.

Ross, Michael. 1999. Does Oil Hinder Democracy? *World Politics* 53: 325–61.

Sala-i-Martin, Xavier and Arvind Subramanian. 2003. *Addressing the Resource Curse: An Illustration from Nigeria.* IMF Working Paper. Washington, DC: International Monetary Fund.

Sampson, Akanimo. 2007. Nigeria: Rebels Spoil for Fresh Oil War, Target US Giants. 27 August. http://www.scoop.co.nz/stories/HL0708/S00379.htm.

Shelley, Toby. 2005. *Oil: Politics, Poverty and the Planet.* London: Zed Books.

Sugar, Janos. 2003. Interview, 23 May. http://www.nettime.org/Lists-Archives/nettime-l-0305/msg00076.html.

Taiwo, Juliana. 2007. Country Moves to Halt U.S. Military. *Legal Oil*, 14 September. http://www.legaloil.com/NewsItem.asp?DocumentIDX=1190457384&Category=news.

Technical Report. 2008 *Report of the Technical Committee on the Niger Delta.* Volume 1, Abuja: Nigerian Federal Government.

ThisDay. 2010. At Last Oloibiri Gets its Due. 2 August, p.19. http://allafrica.com/stories/201008020464.html.

United Nations Conference on Trade and Development (UNCTAD). 2005. *World Investment Report: Transnational Corporations and the Internationalization of R&D.* New York: United Nations.

United Nations Development Programme (UNDP). 2006. *Niger Delta Human Development Report.* Abuja: United Nations Development Programme.

United States European Command (USEUCOM). 2005. Statement of General James L. Jones, USMC, Commander, United States European Command before the Senate Armed Services Committee. 1 March. http://www.eucom.mil/english/Command/Posture/SASC_Posture_Statement_010305.asp.

WAC Global Services. 2003. *Peace and Security in the Niger Delta.* Port Harcourt: WAC Global Services.

Watts, Michael. 2005. Righteous Oil? Human Rights, the Oil Complex and Corporate Social Responsibility. *Annual Review of Environment and Resources* 30: 373–407.

———. 2007. Petro-insurgency or Criminal Syndicate? *Review of African Political Economy* 144: 637–60.

Whelan, Theresa. 2005. Africa's Ungoverned Space: A New Threat Paradigm. Rethinking the Future Nature of Competition and Conflict Seminar Series, 19 December. http://www.jhuapl.edu/POW/rethinking06/video.cfm#whelan.

World Bank. 2007. *Nigeria: Competitiveness and Growth*, Volume II. Washington DC: The World Bank, Report no. 36483-NG.

Yates, Douglas. 1996. *The Rentier State in Africa: Oil Rent Dependency and Neocolonialism in the Republic of Gabon.* Trenton, NJ: Africa World Press.

Zalik, Anna. 2004. The Peace of the Graveyard: The Voluntary Principles on Security and Human Rights in the Niger Delta. In *Global Regulation: Managing Crisis after the Imperial Turn,* ed. Kees van der Pijl, Libby Assassi and Duncan Wigan, pp. 110–27. London: Palgrave.

— *Chapter 4* —

FIGHTING FOR OIL WHEN THERE IS NO OIL YET

The Darfur–Chad Border

Andrea Behrends

The Sudan Liberation Movement (SLM) wishes to make clear to foreign investors and the Sudanese government that so long as the people
of Darfur are denied their basic rights, the exploitation of natural resources in Darfur for the benefit of the National Congress Party regime
or any foreign firm will not be tolerated.
    – Rebel leader Abdelwahid al-Nur, *Sudan Tribune* 2007.

Oil is shit!
    – Oil worker in southern Chad, 3 June 2007.

Tout l'argent du pétrole va à l'est du pays – pour la guerre (all of the oil
money goes into the war in the east).
    – Head of a Christian NGO working in southern Chad, 5 June 2007.

This article analyses how the possibility of oil and conflict mobilises local,
national and global actors on the Chad/Sudan border, where there is in
fact no oil yet. It poses two questions: how has oil, both as local possibility
and as national reality in Chad and Sudan, influenced the fighting on the
border of Darfur (Sudan) and Wadai (Chad)? And, from another angle,
how do the actors involved in this fighting relate to the factor of oil? The
first question suggests a reflection on the resource of oil as an element in
promoting conflict. Here, I follow Marchal and Messiant (2002) and Watts
(2004) in stating that war, as in Darfur, cannot be explained by possible

resource gains for the different sides of the conflict alone. Increasing social disintegration results rather from problems relating to the historical socioeconomic conditions in the area and to the arrangements concerning the distribution of power and wealth among local, regional and national regimes: there is often a noticeable refusal of central regimes to let the rest of the population share in the profits gained from a country's natural resources. Oil, of course, is a vital part of these arrangements.

Concerning the second question, not just facts but also rumours and widespread speculation will go into the discussion of oil as a factor in processes of identity formation among those directly or more indirectly involved in the fighting. In the first part of this chapter, we encounter national and international actors: governments and multinational companies. It is not, however, their intentions, policies, decisions and moves themselves so much as what is known about them, or what people think they know, that will be of interest to this analysis. More visible actors appear in the second part of this chapter. The quotations that began this chapter offer different perceptions of oil. The first speaker leads a seemingly unified Darfurian rebel group, the Sudan Liberation Movement/ Army (SLM/A). He expresses his apprehension about oil gains being taken away by the Sudanese government or international forces.[1] The speculation that there might be oil under the soil of his people's land on the one hand provides him with the aim of fighting any interested party looking for oil profits without intending to share the revenues. On the other hand, he knows that the possibility of oil makes his region attractive to powerful potential allies.

The other two quotations represent views on the consequences of oil and oil wealth from persons not directly involved in the fighting. The Chadian oil worker, who does not speak English, knew enough to grumble: 'Oil is shit!' Although he makes money working as a security guard for the US oil base, his family has not received any share in the profits from the long-awaited oil. The NGO employee had meticulously planned how Chadian oil gains were to flow into the socioeconomic infrastructure. However, what he observes so far is that the government spends all the money on combatting rebels in eastern Chad.

Self-defined entities such as rebel groups and militias, but also institutionalised groups such as the Sudanese and the Chadian army participating in the wars on both sides of the Chad/Sudan border, cannot be assumed to be clear-cut communities with a unified interest. They neither have the permanence of a fixed and clearly definable group nor do they actually speak with one voice. According to what I saw and heard during several stays in the oil region of southern Chad and the Chadian border area with Sudan,[2] as well as what is to be read in the many publications on the Darfur War, these interest groups rather form transient constellations that can easily regroup. Even to suggest that all group members have a common aim – as the rebel leader al-Nur does in the above quotation – appears redundant. While al-Nur expresses national political aims, some of his rebel fighters may well have joined the group for personal feelings of revenge or simply to make a living. Thus, when I speak of actors or groups of actors, I will keep the differing expectations and interpretations of individuals in focus. I believe this is what an anthropological approach can contribute to the study of a global phenomenon such as oil: linking the perspective of individuals to larger entities and even global processes without levelling them.

This chapter begins with a discussion of the literature on oil and the oft-proclaimed African 'resource curse'. Rejecting strictly resource-oriented explanations for the outbreak of civil wars in Chad and Sudan, one objective of this chapter is to analyse oil through the impact it makes on local, regional and national processes that make war possible. After a general introduction to the situation in Chad and Sudan in the late 1950s when oil was discovered there, the analysis will concentrate on the Chad/Sudan border area, where two separate wars are currently occurring: one involving anti-Khartoum rebels fighting for inclusion in national power-sharing arrangements in Sudan, the other directed against Déby, the President of Chad, and having its roots in the breakup of the patronage system through which Déby has governed the country since his takeover in 1990. I show that both wars are linked to oil. This chapter will conclude by arguing that the events, expectations and explanations leading to war in the Chad/Sudan border region cannot be analysed without realising the extent to which they are interrelated with the extraction of oil and its unintended side effects.

Theories on Civil War

Three interrelated bodies of literature in the social sciences connect natural resources to politically motivated, violent conflicts. The first classifies violent civil wars as the typical consequence of a neo-liberal, post–Cold War world order. This discussion maintains that though international observers were hoping that the long-standing proxy wars fought in economically and institutionally 'weak states' would come to an end after 1989, many wars in fact continued because ruling elites, who previously received financial backing from the rival Cold War superpowers, now lacked the means to maintain their patronage networks, thus leading to state collapse. Conceptualised as 'new wars' (Kaldor 1999), another form of international involvement took the place of former Cold War strategies. Governmental and non-governmental actors now started operating directly on the basis of economic, political, military or humanitarian interests and thereby circumvented the level of the central state administration (Bayart, Ellis and Hibou 1999; Callaghy, Latham and Kassimir 2001; de Waal 2002; B. Ferguson 2003; J. Ferguson 2005; Reno 1998). Mark Duffield believes these 'network wars' supersede the territorial level, not in their actual venue of fighting but with respect to those who have stakes in it:

> The new wars can be understood as a form of non-territorial network war that works through and around states. Instead of conventional armies, the new wars typically oppose and ally the transborder resource networks of state incumbents, social groups, diasporas, and so on. These are refracted through legitimate and illegitimate forms of state–non-state, national–international and local–global flows and commodity chains. Far from being a peripheral aberration, network war reflects the contested integration of stratified markets and populations into the global economy. (Duffield 2001: 14)

Some of the elements depicted by Duffield can be found in the Chad/Sudan border crisis: local rebel groups and state-supported militias are all sponsored from abroad, be it because of business interests or the political motivations of outside national regimes. Humanitarian aid in refugee camps is redirected by rebels and militias to create the conditions for forced recruitment and to loot the cars, food or other commodities available. In this chapter, I adopt the new wars approach to discuss in which way oil or the prospect of oil revenues influences those who have come to power on the Chad/Sudan border.

The second field of literature on the role of oil in civil wars directly links natural resources to increased violence and civil war. In this tradition, economic greed determines the onset of wars, their duration, and the amount of violence – including the type and number of weapons used (Collier 2000; Collier and Hoeffler 2001; Ross 2004). Paul Collier, analysing statistical data of civil wars between 1965 and 1999, concluded that rebellion and violence did not occur as a result of social grievances but that civil wars were the 'ultimate manifestation of organised crime' (Collier 2001: 144). He argued that 'the motivation of conflict is unimportant; what matters is whether the [rebel] organisation can sustain itself financially' (ibid.: 145). According to this hypothesis, rebellion occurs where natural resources make it financially feasible for actors to organise it. This approach has been criticised on several grounds: first, for completely denying the importance of historical, political and social reasons for rebellion; second, because of Collier's inappropriate use of statistical data; third, for limiting itself to a correlational logic without showing the ways in which

conflicts actually escalate; and finally, because of his emphasis on the national level rather than that of the insurgents, which necessarily elimi-
nates essential information on the origins of violent conflict (see Ballentine 2003; Marchal and Messiant 2002; Tarrow and Tilly 2007; Watts 2004).

Michael Ross refines Collier's argument by suggesting that resources
determining civil wars are predominantly those promising very high revenues, such as diamonds, gold, drugs, gas or oil and sometimes copper
and timber, whereas natural resources gained from conventional agricultural production have no correlation to civil war and rebellion (Ross
2003a). Ross differentiates between various kinds of resource conflicts on
the basis of a resource's 'lootability' (Ross 2003b). A resource that is easy
to loot, such as riverbed diamonds, more often provokes non-separatist
conflicts. Non-lootable resources, oil and gas being the main examples,
are more likely to generate separatist rebellions and wars, particularly if
the resource is situated in the area where the rebels are based (ibid.).

Oil not only generates huge capital for those involved in its extraction
but also severely affects the people living on the land of oil concessions.
As a resource it is prone to attract the economic and political interests
and expectations of international companies, state governments, and local people living in the areas of extraction. The latter are most often the
ones who suffer most and gain least from the resources, as the case of
Nigeria amply shows (Watts 2004). Many examples show that national regimes – particularly in otherwise poor countries – tend to monopolise
the revenues derived from these resources, thus provoking local interest
groups to use force in claiming a share. Whether oil actually triggered
insurgency in Chad and Sudan will be examined in this chapter in light
of the implications of Collier's and Ross's positions.

A third approach to the interlocking dynamics of oil riches and conflict in otherwise poor countries is that of the resource curse. Resource
curse theory points out that oil production in developing countries leads
to a host of economic and political problems that inhibit development.
The political scientist Terry Karl (1997) locates the main reason for the destructive impact of oil on poor countries in the combination of economic
and political power that it engenders. Because the oil business is so capital intensive, only the biggest players – multinational oil companies or
states – can deal with it. Once oil revenues start to flow, all other previous
sources of state income tend to become marginalised, together with the
need for new investments into other economic fields.[3] Non-oil taxation,
normally the link between the population and its government or the 'es-
sence of popular control', decreases in such a situation and thus 'frees governments from the types of citizen demands for fiscal transparency and
accountability' (Gary and Karl 2003: 23). Monopolisation of oil rents in

the hands of a few further concentrates the affected governments' already strongly condensed economic and political power. In such a situation political leaders spend more on security to consolidate their power. Furthermore, human rights abuses in dictatorial political structures are often disregarded by international business partners and governments alike. This situation provokes an overall increase of popular unrest, armament and militarisation. Studies about the resource curse conclude that oil rents hinder democratic processes and maintain authoritarian rule.[4] Civil wars, as a result, become more violent and protracted (ibid.: 18ff).

In the case of Chad and Sudan, the resource curse took hold in very different forms. While war in Sudan indeed intensified with oil extraction since the early 1980s, Chad, as Africa's most recent oil exporter, was meant to follow a different path with the help of a new approach to oil revenue distribution induced and partly controlled by the World Bank. The next section will take a closer look at the impact of oil on Chad and Sudan and the larger African context.

The International Significance of African Oil

African oil production, as Gary and Karl (2003: 9ff) predicted, would 'jump from 3.8 million bpd [barrels per day] to 6.8 million bpd in 2008, with increases concentrated in Nigeria, Angola, Chad and Equatorial Guinea.' Further estimates have it that reserves in the area amount up to 24 billion barrels by 2008. These reserves have become ever more important in a world market facing waning oil reserves. As a result of turbulence in the Middle Eastern oil-exporting countries, particularly Chinese and other Asian oil companies have shifted their interests increasingly to African countries, although major US and European players, such as the US-based Chevron and ExxonMobil and the French companies Total/ Fina/Elf and Royal Dutch/Shell, plus some independent US corporations, remain prominent among the companies operating in the region (Maidment 2003).

On a world scale, primary energy consumption rose 23 per cent between 1994 and 2004. During these years, China increased its consumption by about 71 per cent. Today it ranks as the second largest consumer of oil worldwide, closely followed by Indonesia, South Korea and India. China's thirst for oil has increased, and because Euro-US oil companies dominate elsewhere, China has oriented prospecting and production to crisis-prone countries in Africa and Central Asia (see Jiang 2003; Zhang 2006). Sudan – barred from trade with the United States since 1996, following Khartoum's alleged involvement in the attempt to assassinate Hosni

Mubarak, the former president of Egypt (Duffield 2001: 198) – is an example of this orientation. Before 1992, China's supply of Africa's hydrocarbons came solely from Angola. In 1993 China started to look for other African suppliers, searching particularly for direct investment opportunities. In 1997 its major oil company, China National Petroleum Corporation (CNPC), entered a partnership with Malaysia (Petronas) and Canada (Talisman) to conclude an agreement with the Sudanese state oil company (Sudapet) in order to jointly develop the oil sector. The Muglad Project, the area of the first oil fields under Chinese concession in south-central Sudan, 'is the first and largest program of this type headed by a Chinese state company on the African continent' (Jiang 2003: 67).

Chad and Sudan offer an interesting point of comparison, particularly when looking at Chinese and US policies of oil extraction and at the international perception of these policies. While the US-based multinational oil companies Chevron and ExxonMobile had first been the main investors and oil producers in Chad, China holds the major part of oil concessions in Sudan. It has been widely discussed in the Western international press that China's influence on Sudan through its policy of non-interference in the internal politics of its Sudanese contract partner acted as a spoiler to attempts by the United States, the European Union, the United Nations and others to influence Sudanese politics during the war in Darfur.

On the other hand, the heavy involvement of the United States and other Western states in Darfur has raised speculation about these countries' true motives. Although more moderate voices assure us that the United States does not interfere in Darfur out of an interest in Sudanese oil, many assume that a new governmental regime in the Sudan would reallocate Sudanese oil concessions in favour of Western companies. Although regime change has never been officially acknowledged by Western states as their aim, rumours that this is indeed their true aim persistently re-emerge in the Darfur literature (see Hennig in *Afrol News*, 10 September 2007). Similarly, oil interests in Darfur have been mentioned as one of the main reasons for the Sudanese government's aggressive retaliation against the Darfur rebellion starting in 2003 (Köndgen 2004).

In Chad, US politics and its relation to oil extraction has been less openly discussed and is therefore less visible, but it is nevertheless noticed by the people in Chad. As the main investor in the Chadian oil sector and the main importer of Chadian oil, the United States tries to create the image of abiding by the World Bank's demand for good governance. Beneath the surface, however, it seems the US government is mostly interested in maintaining good relations with a stable Chadian government, with lesser concern over the kind of governance it follows. This interest goes so far as to train Chadian army soldiers at US military bases in Chad. The Chadian oil extraction contract signed with the US-based oil companies first restricted Chinese oil interests in Chad and thus serves the economic interests of the United States above any considerations about socioeconomic development in Chad. China, however, has a growing influence on the Chadian oil competition and began prospecting in 2006. In 2011, China is preparing to produce oil in the Bongor Basin south of N'Djamena and is constructing a refinery for the country's own consumption. But US-based multinational companies are also further exploring in Chad, and so the struggle for African oil comes to resemble the Scramble for Africa during the period of new imperialism before the First World War (see also Frynas and Paolo 2007).

Oil and War in the History of Chad and Sudan

This part of the chapter investigates the historical impact of oil on war in Chad and Sudan. At the same time that colonial rule in Africa was ending, former colonial rulers started to become increasingly interested in Africa's natural resources and particularly in its oil, which they hoped might provide an alternative to Middle Eastern oil. During the late 1950s, oil explorations were under way in many African countries, north and south of the Sahara desert, with French, British and US companies taking the lead. French colonial government in Chad and British colonial rule in Sudan left the two countries at about the same time in the late 1950s and had a particular impact on these countries' sociopolitical setting. In both countries today, the most important oil fields are situated in the south, while the government is controlled by northerners. Also, both countries are religiously divided: an increasing number of settled, agropastoral peoples in the south started converting to Christianity, while the predominantly cattle- and camel-herding peoples of the north remained Muslim. In Sudan a northern Muslim elite captured all ruling positions from the British regime, while in Chad the first postcolonial government had come from the Christianised south. Southern Sudanese rebels revolted against political exclusion and long-standing neglect of the south. The resulting civil war lasted from 1955 to 1972 and flared up again from 1983 to 2005. Chad likewise experienced fierce internal conflict starting in 1963 (Buijtenhuijs 1978, 1987), during the course of which a northern regime took power in the country, supported by France and Libya. While rebellion in the south of Chad ceased after it was brutally suppressed by government forces in the 1990s, northern regional rebel movements continue to challenge the regime in power even today.

United States and European oil companies started exploring for oil in Chad and Sudan in the late 1950s. By this time, oil production had already started in Libya. In 1969 Muammar al-Gaddafi, still the leader of Libya today, came to power through a military coup. Two of his first acts were to expel US and British military bases from the country and to nationalise oil production. With the money he gained by selling the oil, Gaddafi purchased arms in great quantity, not only to equip his own army but also to bolster those forces in neighbouring Sudan and Chad that most suited the Libyan leader and his ideas about an Arab corridor reaching far beyond the Sahara desert (Harir 1994).

Oil in Sudan

Agip, an Italian oil company, began Sudan's oil explorations in the Red Sea area in 1959, followed by different French and US companies. No oil was found during the next fifteen years (Verney 1999: 15). Meanwhile, a 1972 peace agreement ended the seventeen years of civil war, granting the south autonomous government and authority to administer its territory through an executive council. The president of the executive council, Abel Alier, was part of the group that invited Chevron to start oil exploration in the south, originally against the will of the northern government (Alier 1990: 236ff). The issue was sensitive because the prospect of larger oil finds in that area promoted northern fears of southern separatist trends. Chevron by then knew that the oil fields with the greatest production potential in Sudan lay in the south. It was granted concessions in 1974, after cumbersome deliberations between the two parts of the country. When in 1978 Chevron found oil near Bentiu, the Sudanese government immediately changed the name of the place, and the oil field was called Unity.[5] The oil discovery boosted anxieties within the central government about maintaining control over the new oil wells, which were assuaged by rearranging the regional setup so that Bentiu became part of the north. Southerners interpreted this as a plan to deprive them of their wealth (ibid.: 238). When Chevron announced that the company had agreed with the northern government to extract southern oil and that a pipeline would be built to connect these fields with Port Sudan on the northern Red Sea coast, people of the south demonstrated on the streets for an alternative suggestion. They suggested that the pipeline could also go to Mombasa, Kenya, and thereby service the 'most deserving markets' for Sudanese oil, which many Southern Sudanese believed lay in East and Central Africa (Kok 1992: 108).

These protests notwithstanding, the political elites in Khartoum under President Jafaar Al Nimeiri risked a breach of the 1972 peace agreement by placing Chevron's operational base in southern Kordofan, an area ascribed officially to the north. The boundaries of the former Sudanese regions were redrawn to make the oil fields become part of the north. Khartoum then moved its southern army to the north, while northern soldiers were stationed in large numbers in the south to protect the oil fields. Khartoum's policies of denying the south their share in the oil gains, plus imposition of Sharia law throughout the whole country in 1983, undermined the legal and political basis for southern autonomy and contributed to renewed north–south civil war in 1983 (Kok 1992: 105). The oil fields were heavily contested from the beginning of this war.

Sudanese oil production finally started in 1999, with the country holding proven oil reserves of 563 million barrels (Energy Information Administration, 2009). Still considered to be vastly underexplored, the country's potential oil reserves are estimated at between 600 million and 1.2 billion barrels with recoverable reserves estimated at greater than 800 million barrels. A more recent estimate has it that Sudan holds 5 billion barrels of proved reserves (Energy Information Administration, 2011). Oil business is booming. There are plans to expand production to generate US$30 billion in revenues during the next twenty years. Assuming an uninterrupted development of the so far most profitable Blocks 1 and 2, production sources estimate a production of an overall 400,000 bpd of crude oil, with an increase up to 600,000 bpd by the end of 2006 (*Afrol News* 2010; Gary and Karl 2003: 35; *Oil and Gas Journal Online* 2003). Since in January 2011 a referendum was held over the separation of the country, northern Sudan started to explore its possibilities for production apart from southern oil reserves. While overall oil production in Sudan decreased to 500,000 bpd, of which the north is producing 100,000 bpd, northern oil production alone is expected to rise to 195,000 bpd by 2012 (*Sudan Tribune*, 2011).

In 2003 the Canadian company Talisman and the Swedish company Lundin ended their operations in Sudan, after years of massive protests by human rights organisations, which accused them of condoning the gross human rights violations caused by the Sudanese civil war (Duffield 2001; Gagnon and Ryle 2001; Human Rights Watch 2003). China, however, continued investing in Sudan. Today, Sudanese oil is exploited mainly by China, Malaysia and India, with changing constellations among several smaller shareholders.[6] The largest and yet unexploited concession in the south is Block B (formerly Block 5), which used to be operated by the French Total Exploration with Marathon Petroleum from Houston, Texas, the Kuwait Foreign Petroleum Exploration Company, and the Gulf Petroleum Corporation from Qatar as shareholders. Here, operations were stopped in 1981 due to the civil war in the south. Total Oil intends to resume operations, though, and is engaged in negotiations with the Sudanese government (Total.com 2010), while Marathon had to pull out its 32.5 percent interest due to US sanctions on Sudan (Energy Administration Information, 2011).

Oil in Chad

In 1960 three potential oil basins were identified in Chad. At that time the former colonial power, France, was not interested and declined to promote further explorations (see Reyna, this book). Therefore, Chad's first president, Ngarta Tombalbaye, turned to the US company Conoco, which started to explore for oil throughout Chad. But when, in 1974, oil was found in Sedigui around Lake Chad, Tombalbaye was overthrown and killed.[7] After that, the oil consortium continually changed in composition, bringing in the Dutch Shell and US Chevron and Exxon oil companies. The outbreak of the most violent phase of civil war in 1979 between Hissène Habré, supported by France and the United States, and the then President of Chad, Goukouni Weddeye, supported by Libya, caused Conoco to leave Chad (Petry 2003). Oil operations in Chad continued at a slower pace in the 1980s and picked up in the early 1990s during a period of relative stability after Idriss Déby, a former army general of Habré, staged a successful coup against Hissène Habré with the help of Gaddafi and Omar al-Bashir, the new Sudanese President who had just come to power (see Behrends 2007; Burr and Collins 1999; Marchal 2004). But although the civil war had decreased in intensity at the onset of Déby's presidency, rebellion and insecurity were still prevalent, causing Total and Shell to announce their withdrawal in November 1999 (Petry 2003: 128).

A new oil consortium emerged in April 2000, including ChevronTexaco, ExxonMobil, represented by Esso Chad, and the Malaysian Petronas, which together formed the Esso Exploration and Production Chad, Inc. (EEPCI). This group entered into partnership with the Chadian government to form the Tchad Oil Transport Company (TOTCO) to build a pipeline from the Chadian oil fields to the Cameroonian coast at Kribi.[8] Smaller companies were allocated further oil exploration rights, for example, in Block H, which borders the Central African Republic. Recently, China has become a major prospector, particularly in the Bongor Basin, south of N'Djamena.

The consortium's US$3.7 billion decision to drill the wells and construct the pipeline made it the largest private-sector investment in sub-Saharan Africa (Gary and Karl 2003: 60). The main shares of the Chad oil project were financed by the consortium, various credit agencies and the World Bank. Chad started exporting oil in 2003 from three basins near Doba in the south of the country (Bolobo, Kome and Miandoum) through a 1,080 km pipeline to Port Kribi on the Atlantic Ocean in Cameroon. Close to one billion barrels of oil were planned to be carried from three hundred wells in the Doba fields over a planned twenty-five-year period. In 2004 production reached 225,000 bpd, which was predicted to continue for the following five years. By 2013 this quantity is likely to have declined

100,000 bpd, according to oil consortium documents. It is estimated that Chad will receive more than US$5 billion over the span of the project. But real revenues already are much larger than originally predicted, taking into consideration new negotiations over tax income from oil and the new explorations in the country. ExxonMobil is setting up five 'satellite' fields in the present area of extraction. At the same time, China will start to produce oil by 2011 in four fields of the Bongor Basin, meant for local Chadian consumption (Gary and Karl 2003: 60ff; Gary and Reisch 2005; Geointelligence Network, 2010).

The consortium's project was designed to avoid previous failures associated with the above-mentioned resource curse. In consultation with Chadian and international NGOs, a model was formulated by the World Bank to guarantee a transparent use of oil revenues through enactment of a law specifying oil revenue allocation for the country's development. This model was made the condition for foreign oil companies' investments in the 1,080 km pipeline that connects the oil fields in southern Chad to Port Kribi. The law was enacted as the 1998 Revenue Management Law, which specifies oil revenue distribution, the main actors in this process, and a committee to oversee the oil revenue. Out of 100 per cent of oil revenues, 10 per cent was to be placed in a London-based escrow account reserved for future generations. The remaining 90 per cent was to be allocated as follows: 80 per cent of the money to education and development, 5 per cent to administration, and 5 per cent to developing the area of extraction. The law provided for the creation of a Chadian Oil Revenues Control and Monitoring Board (Collège de contrôle et de surveillance des ressources pétrolières, or CCSRP), responsible for authorising and monitoring disbursements from the escrow account. The board would include members from Chad's judiciary, churches, civil society and trade unions (Krasner 2004: 112).

This model was acclaimed worldwide for its innovation in oil investment transparency and poverty alleviation. But it has its weaknesses: NGOs and the International Advisory Board set up to supervise the flow of revenues and to consult the Chadian government and the World Bank criticise the fact that the oil project proceeds much faster than reforms in governance. If institution building proceeds too slowly, the supervision of the sharing of oil revenues cannot be guaranteed.[9] So far, none of the preparations for oil production has rendered the situation in Chad more stable. Dathol Antione Berilengar, a Chadian bishop and a former member of the CCSRP, does not think that anybody supervising revenue shares from oil extraction will have a chance to influence the Chadian government. Regarding recent changes in the oil revenues allocation to the Chadian government after long negotiations with the oil companies and the World Bank, Berilengar in 2007 maintained that 'until 2005 the government had only 15 percent of the oil revenues. Since 2006 they have 30 percent and all revenues from taxes – and tax revenues are by now higher than the direct oil revenues. They are by now at about 1,000 billion CFA francs[10] – the money of the government can thus originate from the 30 percent or the taxes, no one can control it' (interview with author in N'Djamena, 18 June 2007).

Who Is Fighting (for Oil) in Darfur and Wadai?

For more than six years (eight in the case of Darfur), two wars have been fought simultaneously along the Chad/Sudan border. One is the war in Darfur, widely covered by the world media from mid-2004 into 2005, which began with a rebel attack on Sudanese army bases in February 2003. The rebels had gathered in various local groups from different parts of Darfur and from among the diaspora. Their first public demand was the inclusion of all marginalised regions of Sudan in the peace negotiations on the sharing of power and wealth, then only still occurring between the northern and southern parts of the country.[11] As is by now well known, the reaction by the Sudanese government was prompt and extremely violent and involved the unleashing of militia groups, called the Janjawid (generally translated as 'devils' or 'gunmen on horseback') in the area. These groups of very diverse origin attacked villagers all over Darfur and, since 2006, also across the border in Chad (IRIN Humanitarian News and Analysis 2006). The war in Darfur so far has not ended, although in May 2006, the largely ineffective Darfur Peace Agreement (DPA) and, in 2009, a peace treaty between the governments of Chad and Sudan were signed and mixed forces from both countries are now patrolling the border from both sides (*Jeune Afrique*, 2009). But since this peace is still extremely volatile, refugees and displaced people have not yet returned to their villages and towns.[12]

Less well known – and closely connected to the Darfur crisis – has been the war in eastern Chad, where, since August 2005, Chadian rebels have openly fought to oust President Déby. Back in December 2005, a united front of Chadian rebel groups attacked Adré, a garrison town on the Sudanese border. This attack was followed by defections of senior Chadian army officers over the next six months, who formed an ever changing number of different rebel groups, most of whom operated from Darfurian bases – at least in the beginning with the support of the Sudanese government (Human Rights Watch 1999; ICG 2006).

Currently, some of these movements are defunct, and new ones have emerged. Thus, the Chadian rebels not only operated within the same area as the Darfur insurgents and the Sudanese militias, but many of them also came from the same, cross-border ethnic groups to which most Sudanese rebels belong. In contrast to which most Darfurian rebels belong, however, the justification given by the Chadian rebels for taking up arms did not rest upon a deep-rooted and enduring feeling of exclusion and neglect by the state. Rather, their oft-proclaimed aim to oust President Déby lay in their former closeness to the president and in the breakdown of what might be called Déby's patrimonial system. It therefore makes sense to speak of two separate wars – although they have been intricately interconnected, which makes it difficult to distinguish different underlying motives or power structures. I will nevertheless try to do so by discussing the role of oil in both wars.

Oil and the Rebellion in Chad

When oil money started to flow during July 2003, the Darfur crisis was already well under way. In Darfur many of Déby's Zaghawa kin had been under Sudanese attack as they had joined the rebels fighting against the Sudanese government. His kin also occupied all higher ranks in both the Chadian government and the army. They were disappointed that Déby would not help them against the Sudanese aggressors. The reasons for Déby's reluctance concerned the failed coup against him in May 2004 by his nephews, the twin brothers Tom and Timan Erdimi. Tom Erdimi was formerly in charge of oil operations in Chad and had been the speaker of Déby's presidential cabinet, while Timan Erdimi was the former director of Cotonchad, Chad's cotton parastatal (Human Rights Watch 2007: 72). After the failed coup, Déby stopped his attempts to mediate the conflict between the Sudanese rebels and the Sudanese government, though he tried not to oppose the Sudanese government openly. His own interests also went in two directions. On the one hand, he sought a solution for the dangerous situation in the country's east – from where he himself had prepared his successful coup against Hissène Habré, with the help of Sudan. On the other hand, he did not want to jeopardise his chances of receiving the newly flowing oil revenues – which overwhelmingly go to the head of state.

Thus, to secure the oil money first, Déby in 2006 changed the election law that originally denied him a third presidential term. This further heightened opposition to his regime. Defections from the army and rebellion escalated, triggering further coup attempts in 2005, 2006 and early

2007 and, most severely, in February 2008, when the capital, N'Djamena, came under direct rebel attack. Backed by the French army and by 'friendly' African governments (the Central African Republic, Burkina Faso and Libya), Déby beat the rebel attacks back and managed to stay in power. While the east of the country was struck by mounting violence, he renegotiated taxes with the oil consortium. In a power struggle with the World Bank, he also managed to secure access to the oil revenues intended for 'future generations' – a sum of about US$425 million. This provided him with additional funds to fight the rebels.

In a second move, Déby started to support the Sudanese Zaghawa faction of the Darfurian rebels who revolted against the Sudanese regime. Déby had repeatedly accused the Sudanese regime of supporting rebellion against him (ICG 2006: 12). After that Darfurian rebel groups could roam freely in Chad, partly in army attire, to fight Chadian rebels and the Sudanese army.[13] By the end of 2006, Déby had also started a 'Darfurisation' of the conflict by arming local militias along the border with Sudan to fight against the Chadian rebels (and their direct neighbours) in a move to weaken armed opposition against him and restrict the fighting to the border region.[14]

How precisely did the war in Chad pertain to the resource of oil – and what were the narratives by which the main actors involved made sense of the war, also in relation to oil? For the case of Chad, we may follow Brian Ferguson's argument (2003: 10) that many of the internal conflicts in Africa are about access to the government as the only place to secure a share of revenues from primary commodity exports. The disillusionment of Déby's followers within the army and the civil service with his failed internal politics – combined with anger over unpaid wages – was probably aggravated by the prospect of participating in profits coming from Chadian oil revenues as part of a 'new government of Chad' after the elections. Along the same line, it makes perfect sense that Déby, in order to maintain his power, used the future generations fund to strengthen his military to fight the insurgents. The argumentation resembles in reverse Collier's approach, which asserts that rebellion occurs if the outcome is economically profitable for the rebels. In this case, however, it makes more sense to speak of the governing regime's failure to preserve its supporters' allegiance (or its disinterest in doing so) by maintaining the patrimonial system on which it was built.

Thus, concerning the previously discussed resource-oriented approaches to oil, the resource curse position seems to fit this case best. The Chadian dictatorial regime – in democratic disguise – has been so far able to stay in power with rising international and shrinking internal support; and violence goes hand in hand with sociopolitical and developmental decline.

Partly supported by the evidence is Ross's hypothesis that nonlootable re-sources are likely to cause separatist rebellions, as there were separatist rebel movements in the south in both Habré and Déby's regimes (Reyna, this book). Nevertheless, the most recent rebellion has been in the east.

Here, even though discontent with Déby's alleged embezzlement of oil revenues might have been a motivation to start a rebellion for some of the president's inner circle, this explanation does not account for the many other personal reasons to join the fighting. During my first stay in the Chad/Sudan border area in 2000 and 2001 – two years before oil revenues started to flow – I noticed that dissatisfaction with the Zaghawa, Déby's ethnic group who enjoyed impunity all over Chad, was generally very high. Particularly the Tama of northeastern Chad had suffered un-der continuous harassments and injustice by their Zaghawa neighbours. When a group of Tama under Mahamat Nour went into rebellion, young men from all over Chad saw their chance to help end a regime that they had hated for a long time. A German friend working for a development agency, for example, told me that her Chadian colleague in N'Djamena suddenly disappeared. Worried about his whereabouts, she contacted his family, who said that their son had been ill. Later they said he was trav-elling. When the organisation suggested announcing his disappearance over a radio station, the family reluctantly announced that he had joined Nour's rebels in the east. After Nour had signed a peace contract with Déby in December 2006 and became minister of defence, his rebels were free to move around and so the absent son came to Abéché in full army attire. In his case – as in very many similar cases – oil probably played no major role in his joining the rebel movement. It is more likely that he was motivated by anger at a hated regime. Still, the movement's leader might have used oil corruption as one reason to fight Déby, just as oil money helped both, fighting the rebels and later arming them when they had joined the government side.[15]

In another case, a rebel group used oil as a factor to denounce an in-ternational presence in the Chadian border region. As the United Nations funded Integrated Regional Information Networks (IRIN) reported,

'I personally question the EU's intentions,' said Albissaty Saleh Allazam, who is based in Dakar, Senegal, as a speaker of the rebel group *Rassemblement des Forces du Changement* headed by Timan Erdimi. Albissaty suggested that the EU was more interested in exploiting the country's oil resources than bringing lasting peace to the country. (IRIN Humanitarian News and Analysis 2007)

In this way, the supposed oil interests of international interveners in the Chad/Sudan border area figure as a 'killer argument' in the power struggle between rebels and the state rather than a realistic fear of foreign exploitation.

Oil and the Darfur Crisis

Some review of history is needed to connect the Darfur crisis and oil in Sudan. Darfur had been a marginalised region since the fall of the Fur sultanate in 1916 (see Behrends 2007; Kapteijns 1985; Prunier 2005). Tensions between different parts of the population rose during the famine years in the early 1980s, when the long-established system of transhumance and temporary migration ceased to function. At the same time, the Chad/Libya war spilled over into Darfur, where the two countries fought a proxy war, inundating the area with weapons and soldiers while the Sudanese government turned a blind eye (de Waal 1989, 2002; Prunier 2005; Suliman 1992). After the renewed outbreak of the southern rebellion of the SPLA[16] in 1983, Sadiq al-Mahdi, during his presidency starting in 1986, armed the southern Darfurian Rizeigat Arabs as militias to prevent the SPLA from going farther north. But many of the Rizeigat, as a result of the existing tensions inside Darfur, also turned against their northern neighbours. After 1985, the arming of local militias as proxy fighters became the standard method of all subsequent Sudanese regimes (Johnson 2003; Marchal 2007).

Besides spreading mutual distrust and hatred in the region, by the early 1990s the regime started effecting political changes in Darfur's government. President Omar al-Bashir divided the large province of Darfur into smaller units, each of which was to be administered by Arab civil servants closely allied to the regime. Those ethnic groups in the existing government, such as the Fur, the Masalit and the Zaghawa, thus feared replacement by central government puppets. In 1995 this measure triggered the so-called Masalit War in the westernmost region of Darfur, around the regional capital of El-Geneina (Flint and de Waal 2005: 57ff). During this time, Hassan el-Turabi, the charismatic leader of the Muslim Brotherhood and confidant to President al-Bashir, encouraged the hope of – mainly northern – Darfurians that they could be of influence in the national regime through him. When al-Bashir placed Turabi under arrest in 1999, the last hope of many Darfurians died, prompting a spike in the rebellion (de Waal 2004; El-Tom 2005; Flint and de Waal 2005; Marchal 2004; Prunier 2005; Ryle 2004).

In contrast to the case of Chad, where a link between oil revenues and the motives of rebellion has been more evident, the insurgency in Darfur has not displayed a direct connection to oil. As is obvious from the opening statement to this article by the Darfurian rebel leader Abdelwahid al-Nur – that 'the exploitation of natural resources in Darfur for the benefit of the National Congress Party regime or any foreign firm will not be tolerated' (*Sudan Tribune* 2007) – the rebels were certainly always aware of national and international interests in (potential) primary resource exploitation in Darfur. But, as in Chad, this information could also be used as a propaganda campaign vis-à-vis the state. The possibility of oil has neither triggered separatist desires, as was Ross's hypothesis, nor functioned as a means to economically support and thus cause rebellion, thus also negating Collier's position.[17] The resource curse theory, which partly fits the Chadian case, is also not fully able to explain the fighting in Darfur: although the state government had failed to develop its marginal areas with the oil gains, it already severely and purposefully neglected those areas long before oil revenues started to flow (see Duffield 2001; Johnson 2003). And although this has also been the case in Chad, the beginning of revenue flows from oil did heighten tensions within the Chadian government in such a way as to lead to the typical crises predicted by resource curse theorists (such as Terry Karl, also mentioned above).

In the case of Darfur, Duffield's approach explains some aspects of the situation best. Here, no direct resources could be looted by the rebels, but resources did influence the fighting indirectly through the networks of the actors involved. I will therefore briefly readdress the specific role of international actors and network wars as defined by Duffield (2001). Liberal markets and globalisation trends have made it possible for actors such as companies, rebel leaders or heads of governmental operations to have access to a largely diversified and open world economy. Therefore, in the 1980s, Libyan oil revenues first financed and thus caused the overall abundance of trained fighter groups and the flow of weapons into Darfur – to support Gaddafi's Chadian and Darfurian (in both cases mainly Arab) allies against the regime of Hissène Habré in Chad. Or, when the United States and the UN put an embargo on Sudan, the Canadian Talisman company, for example, found loopholes to circumvent these resolutions and establish economic ties with key actors in the Sudan, although the Canadian government supported the political line of the United States. China, as the main exploiter of Sudanese oil and, simultaneously, one of the suppliers of weapons in the cross-border warfare activities, is against the UN sanctions on Sudan and thus plays an important role in limiting them to a diplomatic embargo.

In different ways, therefore, oil has influenced and continues to influence the war in Darfur, expressed by way of rumours or recognisable in hard facts. It is a fact, also during the 1980s, that oil was part of the reason for the Sudanese regime to instrumentalise militias to fight against their direct neighbours in the newly escalating conflicts in the south – to clear the land where oil was found from its inhabitants (Gagnon and Ryle 2001; Human Rights Watch 2003); weapons were bought with oil money, and today rumours again spread the notion that the Janjawid's repeated cry of hate to 'kill all blacks' in Darfur (as repeatedly mentioned in the media representations of the conflict) might reflect the regime's strategy to manifest its claim to Darfurian – supposedly oil-rich – land.[18]

The individual narratives by which those fighting in Darfur make sense of the war might – as was argued for the Chadian case – touch the factor of oil only marginally. They might, however, allude to issues such as the international interest in the region, the possibility of inclusion of Darfur in global economics, or, simply, an upgrade of the very land on which and over which the fighting takes place. In response to my question of whether oil was a factor for the Justice and Equality Movement (JEM) – a rebel group that originally mainly recruited among the Sudanese Zaghawa temporarily allied to the Chadian president – Abdullahi El-Tom, who was then the JEM's spokesperson in Great Britain, told me that the rebels were promoting oil exploration in Darfur. When the government of Sudan wanted to stop foreign companies from further explorations in Darfur, the rebels tried to convince them to continue.

Fighting for Oil?

Has the fighting on both sides of the Chad/Sudan border occurred because of oil? Both answers could be given: yes and no. Yes, because it was through the direct or indirect influence of oil that tensions in both countries rose to the point of exploding into violence – more recently in Chad and since the 1980s in Sudan. No, because there is no oil actually exploited on the border, and thus, one could argue, oil cannot be a reason for the fighting, because it is not there to fight for. But none of the two answers is complete. As the above deliberations tried to make explicit, the fighting on both sides of the border is – for different reasons – strongly connected to the implications of oil but was not as such triggered by the desire to have direct access to oil revenues gained on the ground. So I argue that in the course of the two Chad/Sudan border wars, oil became one of the reasons to continue fighting: for the rebels in Darfur it was a reason not to accept agreements for not being far-reaching enough, while for the rebels in Chad it remains a reason not to cease trying to get the desired access to state power. For the governments in both countries oil became a reason not to let the insurgents win. This means that the fighting certainly gained momentum through the knowledge of the possibility of the resource's existence on the ground.

It did so through different dynamics in Chad and Sudan. While in Sudan oil gave rise to tensions in Darfur over the past twenty-five to thirty years, it was not one of the triggers for the insurgency in 2003. But, in the course of the fighting, it gained importance again as a narrative to make sense of and justify the fighting, as the initial rebel statement shows, and as the international entanglements of, mainly, China with Sudanese politics demonstrate. In Chad oil has not played a significant role in giving rise to regional tensions along the border. It was, however, a likely trigger for the rebellion against Déby, which originated in his closest political and kin circles. In contrast to the situation in Sudan, oil seems to be of lesser importance to the most recent spread of the fighting in Chad as it spilled over to local groups turning against each other. The intention of President Déby to divert the aggression against him into a regional issue might, one can assume, still be directly linked to his own wish to stay in power and continue benefiting from oil.

Conclusion

In spite of the oil revenues, the Chadian and Sudanese governments have failed to bring peace, stability, general education or economic growth to the larger parts of their countries. Both countries remain in a state of (latent) civil war. Although Chad has acquired millions of petro-dollars, it still ranks fifth on the UN Human Development Index of the world's poorest countries. Since 2003, when oil money began coming in, the government has internally been weakened by several failed attempts to overthrow the president. Since December 2005, army soldiers and generals have deserted and formed rebel movements against Déby, apparently supported by the government of Sudan. In Sudan, in spite of the 2005 power- and wealth-sharing CPA, neither the war in Darfur nor violent confrontations in the south immediately ceased. But, in both cases, the two governments are backed internationally: in the case of Chad, the African Union, the United States and France support the present regime, fearing that a military overthrow would render the country even less stable than under the current president's rule. Sudan receives Chinese support, and international intervention was slow to begin; and when the European Union Force (EUFOR), from 2008–2009, and, from 2007–2010, the United Nations Mission in the Central African Republic and Chad (MINURCAT) were stationed on the other side of the border in Chad, they did not have the appeasing impact some might have hoped for.

Economic explanations of this situation, argued by Collier and Hoeffler (2001), Ross (2003a), or Le Billon (2001) tend to lack, as Ballentine (2003: 280) and Watts (2004: 76) maintain, a contextualisation into the 'pre-resource' history of countries where military dictatorial rule, weak institutionalisation, mismanagement of finances and regional tensions prevailed before oil or other natural resources came into play. In most cases of civil war that actually can be traced back to, or have been at least partly caused by, the quest for resource revenues, a situation of exclusion already existed. Here, resource gains intensified existing grievances instead of initiating them. Ballentine (2003), among others, therefore suggests applying a more holistic approach to research or policy development for incidents of resource-related war: one that integrates economic, political, military and diplomatic measures.

In my analysis of the Chad/Sudan border wars, I have followed Ballentine's suggestions and tried to trace not only the history of the local tensions but also the entanglements of national and international actors and their connection to oil in relation to the ongoing conflicts. I conclude that the fighting might not have been started by oil but that on both sides, fighting for oil eventually became part of the continuation and intensification of aggression.

Notes

1. See also IRIN Humanitarian News and Analysis (2007), for the same apprehensions of the Chadian rebels.
2. Anthropological research in Chad was carried out first in 2000 and 2001 on the Chad/ Sudan border about the integration of refugees among Arab and Masalit villages and again in 2007, 2008, 2009 and 2010, partly together with Stephen P. Reyna, on the consequences of oil wealth. All research activities have been funded by the Max Planck Institute for Social Anthropology, Halle/Saale (Germany) and the Volkswagen Foundation.
3. Economic aspects of this process are termed the Dutch Disease. Here revenues from natural resources raise the exchange rate of the nation's currency so that most other exports become noncompetitive. Services, transportation, and construction servicing oil grow while the agricultural sector and other industries go down (see Gary and Karl 2003; Gylfason 1999; Karl 1997).
4. Exceptions are the oil exporters Canada and Norway, whose oil gains did not lead to a decline in other economic sectors. Botswana is the only African country that seems to have succeeded in turning incomes from the export of natural resources, in this case diamonds, into an improvement of the overall health and social situation (Sarraf and Jiwanji 2001).
5. The naming of the first oil field in Sudan has been subject to much debate. While some hoped that the name Unity, *Al Wihda* in Arabic, would signify the wish to finally unite the two parts of the country, it rather revealed the growing concern and suspicion against the south on the part of the northern government concerning the continued unity of the country 'in the face of the dynamics of oil in a potentially oil rich Southern Sudan' (Alier 1990: 237).
6. See, for instance, *Oil and Gas Journal Online* (2003).
7. Although not officially asserted, rumours about a connection between Tombalbaye's intended refusal to sign oil contracts with France and turn to the United States instead and his death have been ever present in Chad (personal communication with Khalil Alio, 7 May 2007).
8. Long discussions over the course of the pipeline had preceded the decision to build along the Cameroon route that was suggested by the United States, with the acknowledgement to France, which had lost in the deliberations, to let it end in the francophone

part of Cameroon. Nigeria and Algeria were interested in a trans-Saharan pipeline, a project that is still on the table. China had suggested building the pipeline via Sudan with the help of the Sudanese government. I thank Bertram Turner for making me aware of this discussion in *Le Monde Diplomatique* in early 2001.

9. For criticism of the Chad/Cameroon oil project see Basedau (2006, 2007), Gary and Karl (2003), Guyer (2002), Krasner (2004), Pegg (2005), Petry (2003) and Reyna (2007).

10. The CFA (Communauté Financière Africaine) franc is the Chadian currency; one euro is worth 656 CFA francs.

11. There are numerous reports on the origins of the Darfur crisis; especially prominent is the coverage by Human Rights Watch and by the International Crisis Group. See also Flint and de Waal (2005), Prunier (2005), and Mamdani (2009).

12. See de Montesquiou (2007). Social scientists who have extensively published on the war in Darfur, such as Alex de Waal or Roland Marchal, question the effectiveness of any military solution (de Waal 2006; Marchal 2006). Without political agreements between the actors involved, Marchal strongly doubts that any military intervention would be able to bring peace to the region (personal communication, April 2007).

13. It is these groups, locally called 'Toroboro' after the Al-Qaida mountain hideout in Afghanistan, that have been most attractive to many young men in the border area. The rebels and their families often stay in Chadian refugee camps, and one could argue that they are thus directly supported by international aid organisations.

14. See the report of Human Rights Watch (2007: 9ff), which shows how local groups were provided with weapons by Déby's army to weaken the rebellion and turn attention from the original desire of the rebels to oust Déby. See also Marchal (2007) on Chad 'turning into a militia state'.

15. Soon after, Nour left N'Djamena again to oppose Déby once more, now with new equipment, thanks to oil revenues.

16. The Sudan People's Liberation Army was formerly the main rebel group in the south under the leadership of John Garang. Garang, who became first vice-president of Sudan after the signing of the CPA, died three weeks after his official inauguration to office in a plane crash in July 2005.

17. Financial and other aid does, however, reach the rebel movements from other sources than oil. I discuss the Chadian government's open support to the insurgents in Darfur and the Sudanese government's help to the Chadian rebels elsewhere (Behrends 2007; see also Marchal 2006). I still maintain, however, that these forms of support were not the major causes for the outbreak of rebellion, since they only developed in the course of the events.

18. There are certainly more links to the southern rebellion in 2005 and the outbreak of the Darfur War in 2003 than mentioned here. The desire of other neglected areas in Sudan to 'get the same' in forms of participation in government as the south is one factor; another might be the availability of newly 'unemployed' fighters from the south who started to look for new lines of action.

References

Afrol News. 2010. Sudan Now Africa's Third Largest Oil Producer. http://www.afrol.com/articles/21889 (accessed 12 August 2010).

Alier, Abel. 1990. *Southern Sudan: Too Many Agreements Dishonoured*. Exeter: Ithaca Press.

Ballentine, Karen. 2003. Beyond Greed and Grievance: Reconsidering the Economic Dynamics of Armed Conflict. In *The Political Economy of Armed Conflict: Beyond Greed and Grievance*, ed. Karen Ballentine and Jake Sherman, 259–83. Boulder, CO: Lynne Rienner.

Basedau, Matthias. 2006. Politische Krise und Erdöl im Tschad – Ein Modell am Ende? *GIGA Focus*, vol. 3. Hamburg: Institut für Afrikakunde.

———. 2007. Erdölkriege – Kriege der Zukunft? *GIGA Focus*, vol. 6. Hamburg: Institut für Afrikakunde.

Bayart, Jean-François, Stephen Ellis and Béatrice Hibou, eds. 1999. *The Criminalization of the State in Africa*. Oxford: International African Institute in association with James Currey.

Behrends, Andrea. 2007. The Darfur Conflict and the Chad/Sudan Border – Regional Context and Local Re-configurations. *Sociologus* 57(1): 99–131.

Buijtenhuijs, Robert. 1978. *Le Frolinat et les révoltes populaires du Tchad, 1965–1976*. The Hague: Mouton Publishers.

———. 1987. *Le Frolinat et les guerres civiles du Tchad (1977–1984). La révolution introuvable*. Paris: Karthala.

Burr, Millard and Robert Collins. 1999. *Africa's Thirty Years War: Libya, Chad and the Sudan, 1963–1993*. Boulder, CO: Westview Press.

Callaghy, Thomas, Robert Latham and Ronald Kassimir, eds. 2001. *Intervention and Transnationalism in Africa: Global-local Networks of Power*. Cambridge: Cambridge University Press.

Collier, Paul. 2000. *The Economic Causes for Civil Conflict and Their Implications for Policy*. Washington, DC: World Bank.

———. 2001. Economic Causes of Civil Conflict and Their Implications for Policy. In *Turbulent Peace: The Challenges of Managing International Conflict*, ed. Chester Arthur Crocker, Fen Osler Hampson and Pamela Aall, 143–62. Washington, DC: United States Institute of Peace Press.

Collier, Paul and Anke Hoeffler. 2001. Greed and Grievance in Civil War. Policy Research Working Paper, No. 2355. Washington, DC: World Bank.

de Montesquiou, Alfred. 2007. Questions Remain Whether Sudan Will Honor Its Darfur Pledge. *Sudan Tribune*, 17 April. http://www.sudantribune.com/Questions-remain-whether-Sudan,21430 (accessed 30 May 2007).

de Waal, Alex. 1989. *Famine That Kills: Darfur, Sudan, 1984–1985*. Oxford: Clarendon Press.

———. 2002. *Famine Crimes: Politics and the Disaster Relief Industry in Africa*. Oxford: James Currey.

———. 2004. Counter Insurgency on the Cheap. *London Review of Books* 26(15): 1–8.

———. 2006. Chad in the Firing Line. *Index on Censorship* 35(1): 58–65.

Duffield, Mark. 2001. *Global Governance and the New Wars: The Merging of Development and Security*. London: Zed Books.

El-Tom, Abdullahi Osman. 2005. Darfur People: Too Black for the Arab-Islamic Project of Sudan. Paper presented at the DGV Conference on 'Konflikte, Menschenrechte, Interventionen', 4–7 October 2005, in Halle/Saale, Germany.

Energy Information Administration. (2009). Sudan. http://www.eia.doe.gov/emeu/cabs/Sudan/Background.html (accessed 10 August 2010).

Energy Information Administration. (2011). Sudan. http://www.eia.doe.gov/cabs/Sudan/Oil.html. (accessed 3 March 2011).

Ferguson, Brian R. 2003. Introduction: Violent Conflict and Control of the State. In *The State, Identity and Violence: Political Disintegration in the Post-Cold War World*, ed. Brian Ferguson, 1–58. London: Routledge.

Ferguson, James. 2005. Seeing like an Oil Company: Space, Security, and Global Capital in Neoliberal Africa. *American Anthropologist* 107(3): 377–82.

Flint, Julie and Alex de Waal. 2005. *Darfur: A Short History of a Long War*. London: Zed Books.

Frynas, Jedrzei George and Manuel Paulo. 2007. A New Scramble for African Oil? Historical, Political, and Business Perspectives. *African Affairs* 106(423): 229–51.

Gagnon, Georgette and John Ryle. 2001. *Report of an Investigation into Oil Development, Conflict and Displacement in Western Upper Nile, Sudan*. Canadian Auto Workers Union, Steelworkers Humanity Fund, World Vision, Symons Foundation, Sudan Inter-Agency Reference Group. www.ideationconferences.com/sudanreport2001/resourcepage.htm. (accessed 26 March 2003).

Gary, Ian and Terry Lynn Karl. 2003. *Bottom of the Barrel: Africa's Oil States and the Poor*. Baltimore, MD: Catholic Relief Services.

Gary, Ian and Nikki Reisch. 2005. *Chad's Oil: Miracle or Mirage? Following the Money in Africa's Newest Petro-state*. Baltimore, MD: Catholic Relief Services.

Geointelligence Network. 2010. The New Chinese Partnership. http://www.geosint.com/index.php?option=com_content&view=article&id=90&Itemid=90. (accessed 3 March 2011).

Guyer, Jane. 2002. Briefing: The Chad-Cameroon Petroleum and Pipeline Development Project. *African Affairs* 101(402): 109–15.

Gylfason, Thorvaldur. 1999. *Natural Resources and Economic Growth: A Nordic Perspective on the Dutch Disease*. Helsinki: UNU World Institute for Development Economics Research.

Harir, Sharif. 1994. 'Arab Belt' versus 'African Belt': Ethno-political Conflict in Darfur and the Regional cultural factors. In *Short-cut to Decay: The Case of the Sudan*, ed. Sharif Harir and T. Tvedt, 144–85. Uppsala: Nordiska Afrikainstitutet.

Human Rights Watch. 1999. *The Price of Oil: Corporate Responsibility and Human Rights Violations in Nigeria's Oil Producing Communities*. New York: Human Rights Watch.

———. 2003. *Sudan, Oil, and Human Rights*. New York: Human Rights Watch.

———. 2007. *'They came here to kill us': Militia Attacks and Ethnic Targeting of Civilians in Eastern Chad*. New York: Human Rights Watch.

IRIN Humanitarian News and Analysis. 2006. Sudan-Chad: Chadians Look for Refuge in Volatile Darfur. http://www.irinnews.org/Report.aspx?ReportID=59508, 29 June 2006. (last accessed 2 March 2011).

IRIN Humanitarian News and Analysis. 2007. Chad: Rebels Warn of 'total war' if EU Force Is Not Neutral. http://www.irinnews.org/Report.aspx?ReportID=74310, 14 September 2007. (last accessed 2 March 2011).

International Crisis Group (ICG). 2006. *To Save Darfur*. Africa Report No. 105, 17 March. Nairobi: International Crisis Group.

Jeune Afrique. 2009. Accord de Reconciliation entre le Soudan et le Tchad. 4 May. http://www.jeuneafrique.com/Article/DEPAFP20090504T074527Z/soudan-tchad-libye-paix-accord-de-reconciliation-entre-le-soudan-et-le-tchad.html. (accessed 3 March 2011).

Jiang, Chung-lian. 2003. Oil: A New Dimension in Sino-African Relations. *African Geopolitics* 14: 65–77.

Johnson, Douglas. 2003. *The Root Causes of Sudan's Civil Wars*. Oxford: James Currey.

Kaldor, Mary. 1999. *New and Old Wars: Organized Violence in a Global Era*. London: Polity Press.

Kapteijns, Lidwien. 1985. *Mahdist Faith and Sudanic Traditions: The History of the Masalit Sultanate, 1870–1930*. London: KPI.

Karl, Terry Lynn. 1997. *The Paradox of Plenty: Oil Booms and Petro-states*. Berkeley: University of California Press.

Kok, Peter Nyot. 1992. Adding Fuel to the Conflict: Oil, War and Peace in the Sudan. In *Beyond Conflict in the Horn: The Prospects for Peace, Recovery and Development in Ethiopia, Somalia, Eritrea, and Sudan*, ed. Martin Doornbos, Lionel Cliffe, Abdel Ghaffar M. Ahmed and John Markakis, 104–13. London: James Currey.

Köndgen, Olaf. 2004. Tragödie in Darfur. *Inamo* 10(39): 31–34.

Krasner, Stephen D. 2004. Sharing Sovereignty: New Institutions for Collapsed and Failing States. *International Security* 29(2): 85–120.

Le Billon, Philippe. 2001. The Political Ecology of War: Natural Resources and Armed Conflicts. *Political Geography* 20: 561–84.

Maidment, Paul. 2003. The Other Gulf. *Forbes.com*, 31 March. http://www.forbes.com/global/2003/0331/018.html. (last accessed 2 March 2011).

Mamdani, Mahmood. 2009. *Saviors and Survivors: Darfur, Politics, and the War on Terror.* New York: Pantheon Books.

Marchal, Roland. 2004. *Le Soudan d'un conflit à l'autre.* Paris: Centre d'études et de recherches internationales (CERI).

———. 2006. Chad/Darfur: How Two Crises Merge. *Review of African Political Economy* 33(109): 467–82.

———. 2007. Chad: Towards a Militia State? Unpublished Manuscript at *Centre d'études etde recherches internationales (CERI)/ Centre nationalde la recherché scientifique (CNRS).*

Marchal, Roland and Christine Messiant. 2002. De l'avidité des rebelles. L'analyse économique de la guerre civile selon Paul Collier. *Critique Internationale* 16 (July): 58–69.

Oil and Gas Journal Online. 2003. Sudan Could Support Growth as Non-OPEC Oil Exporter. 27 October. http://www.ogj.com/index.html. (accessed 2 January 2004).

Pegg, Scott. 2005. Can Policy Intervention Beat the Resource Curse? Evidence from the Chad-Cameroon Pipeline Project. *African Affairs* 105(418): 1–25.

Petry, Martin. 2003. *Wem gehört das schwarze Gold? Engagement für Frieden und Gerechtigkeit in der Auseinandersetzung mit dem Erdölprojekt Tschad-Kamerun. Erfahrungen eines internationalen Netzwerks.* Frankfurt am Main: Brandes & Apsel.

Prunier, Gerard. 2005. *Darfur: The Ambiguous Genocide.* London: Hurst & Company.

Reno, William. 1998. *Warlord Politics and African States.* Boulder, CO: Lynne Rienner.

Reyna, Stephen P. 2007. The Traveling Model that Would Not Travel: Oil, Empire, and Patrimonialism in Contemporary Chad. *Social Analysis* 51(3): 78–102.

Ross, Michael. 2003a. Natural Resources and Civil War: An Overview. Unpublished Manuscript submitted to the *World Bank Research Observer.*

———. 2003b. Oil, Drugs, and Diamonds: The Varying Roles of Natural Resources in Civil War. In *The Political Economy of Armed Conflict: Beyond Greed and Grievance,* ed. Karen Ballentine and Jake Sherman, 47–70. Boulder, CO: Lynne Rienner.

———. 2004. How Do Natural Resources Influence Civil War? Evidence from 13 Cases. *International Organization* 58: 35–67.

Ryle, John. 2004. Disaster in Darfur. *New York Review of Books* 51(13): 3–37.

Sarraf, Maria and Moortaza Jiwanji. 2001. Beating the Resource Curse: The Case of Botswana. *Environmental Economics Series,* Paper No. 83. Washington, DC: World Bank.

Sudan Tribune. 2007. Rebel Leader Warns Foreign Firms of Exploiting Darfur Oil. 17 April. http://www.sudantribune.com/Rebel-leader-warns-foreign-firms,21423. (last accessed 2 March 2011).

Sudan Tribune. 2007. Questions Remain Whether Sudan Will Honor Its Pledge. 17 April. http://www.sudantribune.com/Questions-remain-whether-Sudan,21430. (last accessed 2 March 2011).

Sudan Tribune. 2011. Sudan's Oil Output to Reach 195 bpd by the End of 2012. http://www.sudantribune.com/Sudan-s-oil-output-to-reach-195,37897. (last accessed 3 March 2011).

Suliman, Mohamed. 1992. Civil War in Sudan: The Impact of Ecological Degradation. Occasional Paper No. 4. Zurich/Bern: Environment and Conflict Project.

Tarrow, Sidney and Charles Tilly. 2007. Contentious Politics and Social Movements. In *The Oxford Handbook of Comparative Politics,* ed. Charles Boix and Robert E. Goodin, 435–60. Oxford: Oxford University Press.

Total.com. (2010). Ethical Business Conduct. http://www.total.com/en/corporate-social-responsibility/Ethical-Business-Principles/Human-rights/Questions-Answers_9151.htm (accessed 10 August 2010).

Verney, Peter. 1999. *Raising the Stakes: Oil and Conflict in Sudan.* Hebden Bridge: Sudan Update.

Watts, Michael. 2004. Resource Curse? *Geopolitics* 9(1): 50–80.

Zhang, Zhong Xiang. 2006. China's Hunt for Oil in Africa in Perspective. *Energy & Environment* 18: 87–92.

— *Chapter 5* —

ELVES AND WITCHES

Oil Kleptocrats and the Destruction of Social Order
in Congo-Brazzaville

Kajsa Ekholm Friedman

According to World Bank figures on economic performance, oil-producing African countries, such as Congo-Brazzaville, which this chapter deals with, are doing fairly well.[1] Congo-Brazzaville is today Africa's fourth largest oil producer. Nigeria is number one, Angola number two and Gabon number three. To anthropologists and certainly to most political scientists the picture of sub-Saharan Africa in general, with a few exceptions, is by contrast grim and alarming. As Jean-Francois Bayart pointed out as early as 1990, the process of change does not bring forth development and improvements but entails, instead, a return to 'the heart of darkness', now as well as then in the form of 'a noxious cocktail of commerce and violence' (Bayart et al. 1999: xiv).

I have done fieldwork in Congo-Brazzaville from the mid-1980s onwards. From the mid-1980s until 2005, I witnessed accelerating pauperisation, increasing insecurity and violence; sectarian conflicts and a grim civil war in 1997; horrific onslaughts on civilians by soldiers and milititas, a growing number of children living on the street; in short, the breakdown of ordered social life. Ironically, the conditions massively worsened with the so-called 'democratisation process', initiated at the beginning of the 1990s. Child witches emerged out of this noxious cocktail. It is this witchcraft that I seek to understand and explain in the following pages. First allow me to introduce child witchcraft and, then, the new holism I will employ in its investigation.

Child Witchcraft and Its Explanation:
Towards a New Holism

At the end of the 1990s there was a sudden outbreak of witchcraft accusations against children. The first accounts on the BBC came from Kinshasa, and from there the phenomenon seems to have spread like an epidemic to both Congo-Brazzaville and Angola.[2] Witchcraft has been, and remains, a central aspect of Congolese culture and society (Ekholm Friedman 1991). Certain individuals are supposed to be witches and in this capacity able to cause all kinds of misfortune to their social surroundings. They fly out, especially in the night, on their own or in groups as members of an association of witches, and in this dimension of reality attack other people. In the most severe cases witchcraft accusations have throughout the twentieth century led to the killing of the alleged witch. It has been more common, however, to find other methods for combating the problem.

A difference between Africa and modern Europe is the persistence of magical thinking about witches in the former part of the world. The difference is clearly distinguishable in our notions of reality vs fantasy, or of 'day' vs 'night'. In Western thought the distinction is accentuated. We only recognise the day world as real. Fantasies and dreams are of a less 'real' nature, even if they, as noted by Freud, may teach us something about ourselves. In many parts of Africa, the night world (or 'the second world') is conceived as equally real, perhaps even more real than the day world. Here the two worlds are parallel dimensions of social reality. When the person falls asleep, he leaves 'day' for 'night', and in the latter world, or dimension, he can go to places and also influence others by 'mysterious' means. Other persons, especially witches, may approach him in his dreams, harming him, sometimes by having illicit sex with him. A dream of a sexual encounter might lead the dreamer to accuse his partner of witchcraft the next morning (see Ekholm Friedman 1994; Yengo 1999).

During the colonial era witchcraft was viewed as typically African (Evans-Pritchard 1937). It was depicted popularly as 'superstition' and was in this sense negatively contrasted with modern rational thinking in Europe. This literature fell into disrepute in post-colonial Africa and new approaches were suggested. For example, *Witchcraft Dialogues: Anthropological and Philosophical Exchanges* (ed. Bond and Ciekswy 2001) argues that both witchcraft and African philosophy must be seen within the framework of colonialism, as a result of the encounter of the African world with European hegemony and modernity (see also Eze 1997). Other recent anthropological contributions emphasise the modernity of witchcraft (Comaroff and Comaroff 1993; Fisiy and Geschiere 1995; Geschiere 1997, 2000). Here it is claimed that witchcraft is not a 'traditional' phenomenon, related to the backwardness of village life, but instead a way of understanding and practising modernity.

It is easy to sympathise with this approach. Certainly, social phenomena taking place in the present must be analysed within the framework of the present. But even if today's African witchcraft is modern in this sense, it still bears the stamp of African culture and society, some aspects of which were there before colonialism and continue during globalisation. What has to be taken into account is the specific form of magical thinking and why it has remained so strong. I shall in the following argue that child witchcraft in the Congo area constitutes a multifaceted complex of which some aspects can be understood as a consequence of economic and political conditions as mediated by an existing culture of witchcraft. What sort of approach is needed to make this argument?

Although anthropological fieldwork is essential for providing data of what happens locally, it has its shortcomings, especially when it comes to explanation. In his famous article *Thick Description: Toward an Interpretative Theory of Culture* (1993: 5), Clifford Geertz declared that anthropology in his opinion was 'not an experimental science in search of law but an interpretative one in search of meaning'. Because meaning is local, Geertz claimed that anthropologists do not need to go beyond the local/cultural setting when interpreting their material. Interpretation was to be found in the same unit where fieldwork was conducted. This approach was thus bound to the fieldwork situation. My fieldwork experience in Congo-Brazzaville suggests a different opinion. Not everything that happens in local areas is explained by events in those areas. What happens in small Congolese villages is influenced by events in the capital, Brazzaville, Paris and elsewhere. So a major conclusion of my research, and a main argument in this chapter, is that we have to take higher levels of the global system into account when trying to explain the local. Fieldwork in some locality is not enough. Other types of observation utilising different methodological approaches are needed.

Oil and witchcraft represent, one might say, the opposite poles of the global–local continuum. Although witchcraft is a local phenomenon it is, as I shall argue, influenced, even determined, by forces active at higher levels of the global system. In the old holistic approach, analysis was limited to 'local society' where fieldwork was conducted, and the various parts that were shown be a coherent whole were conceived in terms of local economy, social structure, religion etc. I suggest that analysis of child witchcraft takes into account transnational corporations (TNCs) and other international actors, national and local actors, and their interrelatedness. This that means parts of the whole would then be of a different character compared to the previous holism. In this new holism what are to be combined analytically are phenomena at different (territorial) levels of the system. At higher, global levels we explore, in the particular instance of child witchcraft, the role of Elf, the French oil company now called Total; the French government; the functioning (or malfunctioning) of the Congolese state as these produced the gradual impoverishment of the Congolese people and a violence that accompanied the transition from a one-party political system to parliamentary 'democracy'. At the local levels, we discuss how these higher level transformations affect families, the clan system and individuals and, finally, how changes to these influence child witchcraft. The following section of the article addresses the higher level transformations, showing how the Congolese state, plagued by struggles over oil wealth and control of the government, prompted destruction of social order, marked by increasing pauperisation and violence for ordinary people.

Higher Level Transformations: Destruction of the Social Order

I shall in this section take up the play of higher level forces within the arena of the Congolese state. First, I analyse the nature of this state and then document the various events occurring there that produced the pauperisation and violence which characterise Congolese social disorder. First, an overview of the post-colonial history of this state: Congo-Brazzaville became independent in 1960. It was relatively wealthy and quite developed economically at independence. Its wealth emanated partly from its position as a transit country for trade with Chad, the Central African Republic and Gabon, and partly from its position as headquarters of AEF (*Afrique Équatoriale Francaise*). Wealth also came from production for export in agriculture, forestry and industry. The country exported industrial products, such as soap, cigarettes, shoes and textiles to neighbouring countries, and sugar even to Europe and the Middle East. So Congo-Brazzaville was actually characterised by a relatively high level of industrialisation in the late colonial period (Amin and Coquery-Vidrovitch 1969).

Foulbert Youlo became the first president and governed until 1963 when the military intervened and installed Alphonse Massamba-Débat, who was himself overthrown in a coup (1968); after which Captain Marien Ngouabi took power, declared Congo-Brazzaville a Marxist-Leninist socialist republic, and ruled until his assassination (1977). Denis Sassou Nguesso succeeded to the presidency after a few troubled years in 1979 and governed until electoral defeat (1991). Pascal Lissouba triumphed in this election, which ended over two decades of socialist rule. His regime controlled the country until 1997; at which time Sassou returned; there was severe violence, whose outcome was Lissouba's defeat. Sassou has ruled the land since that time.

From 1968 until the abrupt changes at the beginning of the 1990s, political power was in the hands of political clans from the north, and during the Sassou I regime (1979-1991), more narrowly within the Mbochi ethnic group. Since there was only one political party it has often been assumed that this particular political system was an exclusive arrangement, which was not entirely the case. What characterised the one-party system was rather its inclusive character. Instead of two blocks, one in power and one in opposition, leading politicians from various provinces and ethnic groups were invited to share power and economic resources, even if one ethnic network was more central than the others. But Sassou conceived of the state and of the public wealth as 'his thing' (Verschave 2001: 20), regardless of how many were invited to share in the 'thing'. It is likely that other rulers of Congo-Brazzaville had identical conceptions of the state. Let us further explore 'his thing' from structural and cultural perspectives.

A Structural Perspective

The Congolese state appears to me as more or less equivalent to the group of power-holders. It consists of a central hierarchical network of politicians plus a peripheral sector of low-paid clients with the task of supervision and control. The political class is world-class rich because it controls all foreign funds; above all in the form of oil revenues but also in the form of foreign loans and development assistance. Oil has since the 1970s been the number one income source. In the 1980s there were a couple of transnational oil companies of which Elf was, and still is, by far the most powerful (Bissila 1999). The collaboration with TNCs made, I argue, the state independent of its people.

The state's alliance with foreign TNCs and entrepreneurial groups constitutes a threat to the Congolese people because it makes them unnecessary in the production process and as taxpayers. The oil business is run by foreigners. Very few Congolese, if any, work on the platforms. There are on the whole few jobs for Congolese and where they exist they are not always combined with a salary. The poor are of course also in a weak and precarious position because they do not constitute an electorate. This is a problem that cannot simply be resolved by the introduction of elections.

In the second half of the 1980s, Congo-Brazzaville was a one-party system, with parallel hierarchies of state and party and, as in the communist world, with a *Bureau Politique* and a *Comité Central*. The Congolese people were controlled through various 'mass organisations'. The party was called 'The Congolese Labour Party' (*Parti Congolais du Travail*, PCT), which I found a bit strange since there was no real working class and the conditions of the existing workers seemed of no political interest. Those appearing on television, shouting in unison '*Tout pour le Peuple!*', with their right fists up in the air, and then adding '*Rien que pour le Peuple!*', were politicians and high ranking military. At the beginning of the 1990s when the political class was exposed suddenly to severe criticism, the latter part of the slogan was changed to '*Rien pour le Peuple*'. And the poster of a smiling Sassou holding a bunch of tomatoes in his hands was furnished with a new text, 'this is for you', i.e. after 'I have taken my part'.

This state structuring is by no means unique to Congo-Brazzaville (Bayart 1993). It can be found in other parts of Africa as well where the economy is dominated by TNCs engaged in the extraction of raw materials (cf. Hodges 2001, for Angola). Difficulties of the African state have been chronicled from the 1980s onwards (Ake 1985, 1996; Bayart 1993; Ekholm Friedman 1990a, 1991, 1994; Frimpong-ansah 1991; Hyden 1983; Jackson 1990; Médard 1982, 1991; Migdal 1988). Médard documented its 'neo-patrimonialism'. Bayart, Ellis and Hibou (1999) spoke of its 'criminalisation'. Reno (1998) has emphasised its recent disintegration into warlords fighting over the loot of raw material extraction. .-.

The economist Frédéric Clairmont (2001) discusses the threat to the world's poor in general in this sort of state, where there is an alliance between the TNCs and the political class. The danger emanates, he says, from the built-in conflict between the economic forces represented by TNCs and the world's poor populations. We are, he argues, involved in a global process that is neither about the well-being of people, nor about optimal resource allocation, as is usually claimed by economists. Instead, 'il a pour vocation l'enrichissement d'une minorité d'actionnaires des sociétés transnationales' (ibid. 3) (the goal is the enrichment of a minority of stockholders in the transnational companies). Here the TNCs are depicted as the dominant actors which is certainly correct, but the politicians are also responsible for the situation. They might after all behave differently, offer resistance, say no to the money, and so on. Let me explore the political culture that enables the political classes' practices.

Political Cultural Strategies

What I argue below is that the structure of the Congolese political system is the outcome of a political cultural strategy, which is characterised by an anti-production attitude and the dominance of politics over economy. Remember Congo-Brazzaville was relatively wealthy and developed economically at independence. In the 1960s there also existed a vibrant Congolese entrepreneurial sector, predominantly from the south and more specifically from the Lari. During the reign of Massamba-Débat (1963-1968) repeated political demands for nationalisation were rejected. However, with the military coup d'état in 1968, a new anti-production cultural strategy was adopted as state ideology. A key characteristic of this strategy was the tabooing of commodity production for export. Consequently foreign capital left the country.

As for the anti-production attitude and the dominance of politics over economy it is worth noting that such ideas, in the 1960s and 1970s, were popular even in Western Europe. An African export oriented economy was abhorred, or at least mistrusted. In Congo-Brazzaville a number of articles appeared as late as the 1980s by 'social scientists' close to the Marxist-Leninist regime, arguing that the economy unfortunately was still dominated by imperialist actors and dependent on external markets but that the revolutionary regime was constantly working on this problem and would in the immediate future bring about a complete rupture with imperialism. The new and truly progressive economy would then be *'au-to-centré'* and *'auto-dynamique'*, i.e. no longer dependent upon export and external markets but instead focused on, and driven by, internal needs (see Mouamba 1985). This idea came of course to a certain extent from the communist ideology. But it also strongly resonated with Congolese political culture with its over-emphasis of politics over economy (see Ekholm 1972; Ekholm Friedman 1991); where access to, and benefits from, economic resources result from political rather than economic practice.

The Congolese one-party system can be comprehended as a specific (cultural) strategy. It has often been suggested that its roots are to be found in colonialism. A foreign state was implanted from the outside, as an organisation separate from the indigenous society, and therefore, the argument goes, it has continuously been looked upon as something to be invaded and conquered. It might also be conceived as a borrowing from the Soviet system. A number of Soviet elements were copied – the red flag, the International as national hymn, the parallel hierarchies of state and party, the Marxist-Leninist jargon.

However, the one-party system was also anchored in central African political culture. Marxism-Leninism suited the political class at a deeper level. It masked the fact that Congo-Brazzaville to a large extent was still constructed as a traditional central African kingdom (see Ekholm Friedman 1994; Ekholm Friedman and Sundberg 1995). The idea of parliamentary democracy, with its implied dualism, has always been viewed as foreign. When discussed among political leaders before independence it was usually rejected with the argument that it did not fit local realities. A multi-party system would, it was argued, easily open the doors to ethnic conflicts and thereby endanger political unity. A one-party system would therefore be a better solution. Everybody could fit convivially in the same organisation. In fact, around 1960, when indigenous power structures were shattered and a first phase of democracy was introduced in the newly independent state, competition among ethnic factions increased. Both Brazzaville and Kinshasa experienced outbreaks of ethnic violence, which certainly confirmed the negative view of what the 'Whites' called 'democracy'. Congo-Brazzaville was not officially proclaimed a one-party system until 1963 when Massambat-Débat carried through his so-called 'socialist revolution'. But 'democracy' was actually practised from the very beginning. Although the French had insisted on parliamentary democracy, the newly elected president in 1960, Youlou from the south (a Lari), immediately invited his main opponent, a politician representing the north, to share political power.

What was the impact of such a state upon ordinary folk? One point should be clear. The wealth that flowed into Congo-Brazzaville from oil and other revenue sources was treated as the 'thing' of the governing elite, as their private property, when it legally belonged in the public sector (Bazenguissa-Ganga 2001). In this sense it was stolen from the Congolese people, making the state was a sort of kleptocracy. The lack of investment from these sources, in conjunction with a disinvestment in productive activities, put in motion a pauperisation which characterises the current situation. I now turn to explain why this state became so violent in the 1990s (Ekholm-Friedman 1990).

Ethnic Conflicts and the Disintegration of the State in 1993-1994

Democratisation was a stipulation of advanced capitalist states' neo-liberal structural adjustment policies (SAPs) imposed on developing states starting in the 1980s. Conformity to this stipulation was coerced by making development assistance contingent upon it. The so-called 'democratisation process' meant dismantling of the former one-party system. Congo-Brazzaville, due to grave problems in its oil sector (documented below), needed development aid, and so was obliged to re-install a multi-party system. 'Free and fair elections' in 1992 brought Pascal Lissouba to power, an old man who had occupied a position as one of the Prime Ministers during the regime of Massambat-Débat (1963-1968) and thereafter spent most of his time abroad. Yet he had the capacity of mobilising a major ethno-political network in his support, a factor that is of central importance for political leaders in Congo-Brazzaville.

Quite soon the introduction of 'democracy' precipitated an upsurge of ethnic conflict. Since the population in 1992 mainly voted along ethnic lines and the south was so much more populous, the northerners lost their hegemonic position in the power structure. Losing an election means of course much more in countries such as Congo-Brazzaville than in the West, since access to economic resources is obtained via control over the state. Therefore the 'free and fair' elections, with their implications for uncertainty and a shattered political hierarchy, were deeply threatening to both politicians and common people. They evidently experienced fear and thought they had to struggle for their very survival. The introduction of parliamentary democracy plunged political leaders, both old and new, into intense competition and conflict with one another. And in this situation they experienced a need for the young men who in the previous period were hopelessly unemployed and not needed (see Ekholm Friedman and Sundberg 1995). A new type of political unit appeared in which political actors recruited young men, or boys, from their own ethnic groups, who were used as bodyguards and militias.

Thus a disintegration of the state into three ethno-regional factions began, each one with its own political leadership and its own militia. There was Nibolek, an association of three provinces in the south under Pascal Lissouba; Pool, the central province under Bernard Kolelas; and the North under ex-president Sassou. As President Lissouba did not trust the army, which was dominated by Sassou's supporters, he set up his own militia, at the beginning called the Aubevillois. The other two militias were Kolelas's Ninjas and Sassou's Cobras. Ethnic conflict in 1993 escalated, mainly between the two competing factions in the south, the Nibolek and the Pool. There was extensive violence associated with ethnic cleansing. When fighting eventually stopped, in early 1994, civilians on both sides seemed genuinely regretful, sometimes even shocked, about their own behaviour during that time. 'It will never happen again', was a common statement. In May 1994 the state had still no effective control over the country. Both the army and the police were fragmented along ethnic lines, and soldiers as well as policemen participated in looting activities.

This was a clear case of ethnic conflict, very different from the civil war of 1997 which took place above the heads of common people. It was 'ethnic' because it involved ordinary people. It is probably true that political leaders wherever such violence appears bear the ultimate responsibility as they are the dominant actors in the conflict, who recruit militias and who turn their own armed men against ethnic enemies. But this is an attempt to reduce the phenomenon, with which we are increasingly acquainted and therefore need to understand, to something else. In this particular case, *les responsables* certainly opened the doors to the turmoil but when it broke out they seemed surprised and uncertain about what to do. They were even criticised in 1994 for remaining silent, for not appearing on radio, on television or in the streets in order to 'talk' to the people. In Congo-Brazzaville a chief must 'talk'. His interpretation of the situation as well as his admonition/criticism of his subjects' behaviour have always been important aspects of his obligations.

The city was divided into different zones, controlled by ethnic militias and successively cleansed of their 'foreign' elements. This kind of agency produced a great number of internally displaced persons on both sides. The militias killed one another and also attacked unarmed and helpless civilians. Among the victims were men, women and children who were brutally killed, decapitated, slashed with machetes, buried alive, or thrown into the rivers. Gang rapes of enemy girls and women became for the first time in the postcolonial period a common phenomenon. Grimmer warfare was to follow.

The Civil War of 1997

The introduction of parliamentary democracy in African countries was applauded by many, in both Africa and the West, as it was assumed that this would improve the conditions for economic development at the same time as freeing the poor and oppressed from dictatorship. But nothing became of this democracy. On the contrary, the economic problems augmented. Employees in the civil service and retired people were still not paid on a regular basis. This problem appeared for the first time at the end of the Sassou regime. Many of my Lari informants accused Lissouba and his entourage of 'eating' even more than the previous regime. Sectarian conflicts and violence continued although of a less intense character, and various militia groups and bandits continued to terrorise civilians.

After Sassou was defeated 'at the urns' by Lissouba in 1992, he temporarily withdrew from the political scene. In January 1997 he returned to Brazzaville from Paris, and there was something ominous and foreboding in the air when his plane descended towards Maya-Maya. 'No', my Congolese friend laughed, 'Sassou no longer constitutes a threat, he could never win an election because his Northerners are simply too few'. But elections were apparently not on his agenda. It is time to bring oil into the narrative, because it is crucial in what happened next.

Given the fact that both Elf and the Congolese state have constantly concealed information regarding various crucial aspects of the oil business, it is difficult to take existing figures completely seriously. Nevertheless, the first part of Sassou's presidency was, it seems, an economically bright era due to increasing oil revenues:

'La première moitié des douze années de règne de Sassou I (1979-1991) a coincidé avec les vaches grasses de la rente pétrolière' (The first half of the 12 year reign of Sassou (1979-1991 coincided with the fat years of oil rents) (Verschave 2002: 19f).

In the second part of his reign (1986-1991) the era of the 'fat cows' was, however, gone, with mounting economic problems, generally resulting from decreasing oil revenues to the state budget. This was the explanation I obtained during my fieldwork in the second half of the 1980s and it is repeated by Verschave (2000). Congo-Brazzaville received 17 per cent of the oil companies' profit (however this was determined) at this time. At the National Conference in 1991 it was claimed that only 2 per cent went to the state budget while 5 per cent was appropriated by the oil minister and the rest, 10 per cent, by the president himself. If this is true, the figures for the state budget are quite relative.

According to Verschave, while official oil production doubled between 1979 and 1991, the state budget only increased until 1985, from 1.37 billion francs in 1979 to 10.35 billion in 1985. Thereafter a remarkable economic deterioration occurred. At the end of the 1980s it was down to 5 to 6 billion, explained as a consequence of 'la chute conjointe des cours du baril et du dollar'(the combined fall of the price of the barrel and the US$) (Verschave 2002: 19). The abrupt fall is thus explained by external factors; the falling oil prices and the falling value of the US dollar.

At their establishment in Congo-Brazzaville, both Elf and Agip, the Italian oil company, had obtained very favourable conditions, if not exorbitant, by being guaranteed a margin of US$5 per barrel. This meant, says Verschave, that Congo-Brazzaville at the end of the 1980s, when both the oil price and the US dollar fell, received very little from its oil production. After Elf and Agip had taken their part, there was almost nothing left for the Congolese state.

During the years of the 'fat cows' the Congolese state had taken huge foreign loans. In 1985 its foreign debt amounted to 10 billion francs, in 1986 the debt had, in spite of certain renegotiations, gone up to 15 billion francs (US$2.5 billion) and in 1987 to US$4.6 billion. Congo-Brazzaville was in 1987 the most indebted country in the world in relation to its GDP. The economic situation was already precarious by 1985 when the budget amounted to 4 billion francs and the debt service to 4.4 billion francs. After 1987 it was not able to pay any debt service (Verschave 2002: 20, 25).

What then did the Congolese political class do with all this money? First, a state such as Congo-Brazzaville is an extremely costly operation. The members of the political hierarchy, with their family and kin, live luxurious lives. When 5 per cent of the oil revenues goes to the oil minister and 10 per cent to the president it means that large sums of money are distributed through the hierarchical, patrimonial channels of clan membership and alliances. Second, the army with all its sophisticated military equipment is costly. Third, there is the problem of 'capital flight'. Money enters the state but is immediately taken out to foreign bank accounts and landed property abroad. Fourth, money invested in the country is wasted because of the political anti-productionist strategy. At the end of the Sassou regime, the IMF demanded cuts in the budget and the liquidation, or privatisation, of state enterprises. At the same time, foreign capitalist actors maintained a strong interest in the country.

At the *Conference Nationale Souveraine* in 1991 a tremendous amount of repressed rage came to the surface among the citizens of Congo-Brazzaville. One of the topics was, 'what happened to all the money?' A document was distributed where the sum of the country's foreign debt was compared and found approximately equal to the private fortunes (source unknown) of about twenty high-ranking politicians, Sassou at the top of course.

In the last period of his reign, Sassou tried to attract additional money. Besides turning to the IMF and the World Bank for help, he invited a number of foreign entrepreneurial groups, based in Lebanon and North Africa, mainly into the forestry sector (Verschave 2001: 21f). He also went to the US in 1990 (Verschave 2001: 27, 29), evidently in order to counterbalance the power of Elf by an alliance with US oil companies. He was received by both Republicans and Democrats. A dinner was given in his honour by the Kennedy clan. Ethel, the widow of Robert, and her son Michael, owner of a non-profit energy company, had the year before (1989) visited Brazzaville and on this occasion donated US$2 million to Congo-Assistance, an organisation run by Mme Sassou with the reputation of being her private source of income.

Sassou and his entourage evidently experienced a constant and insatiable need of money. A possible explanation would be that the financial need, or appetite, of the political class increased over time because of its continuous expansion. So it had to turn to all kinds of sources; oil revenues, foreign loans, the IMF, foreign aid, and the taxation of foreign entrepreneurial groups. An imbalance between demand and supply appeared, it seems, early and rapidly led to virtual bankruptcy in spite of the increasing amounts of appropriated wealth.

The transition to parliamentary democracy thus occurred in the worst kind of situation. When Lissouba entered the scene in 1992 the state was in a precarious state in more than one way. Apart from the fact that he could not rely on the loyalty of the army, he had no money. Congo-Brazzaville was bankrupt. 'Le pays est en faillité. Sa dette extérieure est le triple de son produit intérieur brut' (The country is bankrupt. Its external debt is three times its gross domestic product) (Verschave 1998: 310). The oil revenues had not only shrunk but, as just shown, entirely disappeared. Gone were employee salaries and pensions.

New elections were scheduled for 1997. Instead, Sassou returned in January, and civil war exploded (Yengo 2006). Lissouba had done two things that angered Elf. First, he renegotiated the deal with the oil companies and managed to raise the Congolese state's share from 17 per cent to 33 per cent. Second, he invited the US oil company Oxy to invest in newly discovered oil fields, which apart from counterbalancing Elf's power secured him an advance of US$150 million (Verschave 2002: 39). In both cases it amounted to defying Elf's hegemonic position in Congo-Brazzaville.

Even if oil has been a source of constant wealth for the Congolese political class since the 1970s, the relationship between oil companies and presidents has not always been entirely harmonious. In the mid-1970s, Marien Ngouabi made an attempt to increase his control over the oil business, a manoeuvre that certainly did not please Elf. Ngouabi was murdered in 1977 and replaced, in 1979, by the much more collaborative Sassou, called *le chouchou* (teacher's pet) of Elf. Both Elf and Sassou might have been implicated in the removal of Ngouabi (2000: 47), and even if Elf was not, it clearly benefitted from it. From 1979 to 1991 oil flowed without any attempts from the state's side to oppose Elf.

When the civil war broke out on the 4th of June 1997 it was evident that both warlords had access to considerable financial and military resources. Sassou had, to many people's surprise, a well-equipped and well-trained militia. A war of this scale could not be carried out without huge economic resources on both sides. Both parties had been able to buy weapons on the international market. In order to do so both warlords used 'stolen money'; 'ils ont assez volé pour faire la joie des marchands d'armes'(they stole enough to bring joy to the arms dealers) (Verschave 1998: 310). Whence, then, did these resources emanate? This is less clear in Lissouba's case. He obtained, as mentioned above, an advance of US$150 million from Oxy, and, in addition, a loan from the IMF of US$150 million for the rebuilding of the secondary school sector in 1996, money that was evidently used for other purposes. After being defeated and obliged to leave the country, Lissouba brought charges against Elf at the *Tribunal de grande instance* in Paris. He accused Elf of complicity in the destruction and killing of between five thousand and fifteen thousand persons, of acts of terrorism, and of having financed Sassou's war activities with, he estimated, more than US$100 million (Verschave 1998: 315).

In Verschave's understanding both Elf and the French state were major actors in this war. President Chirac declared at the very beginning of the war that France would keep out of it, but this was but 'une neutralité de façade' (a superficially false neutrality) (Verschave 1998: 312). It has been pointed out by John Clark (2002) that resources from France initially flowed to both sides of the conflict, but that at its end they were concentrated upon their old and more reliable ally Sassou.

There are a number of details indicating the involvement of both Elf and the French state in this civil war. On 3 June, the day before the war broke out, 25 tons of material, in the form of weapons, were sent by air from le Bourget to the Presidency of Gabon for further transport to Sassou, the son-in-law of Gabon's president Omar Bongo. Troops were also sent from Chad to Sassou in French planes. The states of Gabon and Chad were thus involved in the war on Sassou's side and in both cases there was a connection to the French state. In addition, Sassou obtained mercenaries from various sources, such as Hutu Power, Mobutu's old presidential guard, and the military firm Executive Outcomes. The decisive military support came from Angola, even here with connections to Elf/the French state. The Angolan troops sent to the Sassou side were transported from Cabinda to Pointe-Noire by boats usually used by Elf for providing its oil platforms with food and other necessities.

The war was short but highly destructive. Its main arena was Brazzaville, which was completely destroyed by aircraft, grenade throwers and 'Stalin organs'. This conflict was radically different from that of 1993-1994. It was a large-scale war over oil and oil rents which entailed large sums of money, converted into weapons and military manpower. Unlike in the previous conflict, ordinary people did not take any active part. Instead they were unambiguously victims of a combat waged between major economic and political actors. They were killed, mutilated and traumatised, their homes and small businesses destroyed and, in sum, their entire existence imperilled. The fighting, apart from the two indigenous warlords and their militias, involved a number of foreign actors; the oil company Elf, the French state, neighbouring states, and mercenaries of various origins from Hutu Power, Executive Outcomes and Mobuto's old presidential guard. The intervention by Angolan troops on Sassou's side proved decisive for its military outcome. The war of 1997 was a war over oil, and in retrospect it seems quite predictable that Elf's *chouchou* would win. Even if Lissouba was an old politician from the 1960s, he did not have the same kind of powerful network with Elf and the French state as Sassou.

In October 1997 Sassou was back in power, and so he has remained ever since. A quasi-election has been held, in overwhelming favour of the president. The only dark clouds in his sky are the Lari rebels or bandits, the Ninjas, who still roam the Pool countryside. They constitute, according to the official ideology, the main threat to peace and the future development of the country and must, therefore, be eliminated. After his victory Sassou directed, unprovoked it seems, a deadly attack on the Lari. During 1998 his militia, the Cobras, committed repeated assaults on individuals of both Nibolek and Lari origins. The more systematic attacks targeted, however, the latter group. Boys and young men were killed and women, as well as young girls, were victims of brutal gang rapes. It has been claimed (among the Lari) that these type of acts were ordered from above: rape them, infect them with AIDS, kill them, eliminate them! But downtown Brazzaville is rebuilt, traces of the war have been removed, and Sassou II has become chairman of the African Union. Today he is presented, by himself and others, as a true democrat. It is time to summarise the themes of this section.

At the higher level of global/state actors, the post-colonial economic and political record of Congo-Brazzaville has been one where the political class, the French state and the Elf, along with surrogates of these actors, have submitted the Congolese people to impoverishment and a bloody charnel house of violence. Certainly, such pauperisation and hostility meant that things fell apart for ordinary Congolese. The time has come to consider how this social disorder is related to child witchcraft.

Local Level Transformations: The Making of Child Witches

This section investigates the consequences of social disorder for child witchcraft in lower local levels of the family, clan and individual subjectivity. I begin with the family.

The Family and Child Witchcraft

In the 1980s the most common pattern of witchcraft accusation was young people indicting their elders. At this time, I repeatedly came across cases where old men or women were accused of witchcraft and sometimes also killed. However, at the end of the 1990s, witchcraft accusations took a new turn. Parents began to accuse their children and this on an alarming scale. Sadly, there was little attention from international media as long as only elderly people were targeted. When children started to be accused there was considerably more interest. There were reports from Kinshasa as early as the autumn of 1999 (BBC report, 10 December 1999) claiming that thousands of children had recently been thrown out of their homes amidst accusations of witchcraft. The accused children were taken to healers and religious sects where miscellaneous forms of treatment were practised, sometimes with devastating consequences for the children.[3]

Human society has generally been based on the social bond between generations. The relationship between parents and their young has always been of major importance for social reproduction. The young are incorporated into the society of the older generation in the sense that they adapt and conform. Parents' ability to care for their children seems to be intimately linked to parental authority and control. When the latter, for one reason or another, is weakened (and there are no other structures to replace it), parents seem to lose their capacity to care for their young.

This is recognised today as a problem in many impoverished parts of the world. Children come to be experienced as an insupportable burden and even worse, as a threatening, destructive force in their families, suspected of vicious and life-threatening attacks against their surroundings. When parents are seriously weakened in their roles as parents, the child often becomes an autonomous actor in a manner that seems contradictory to ordered social reproduction. The child appears as out of control, an element of disturbance – and parents and other members of the older generation may respond by turning away, by abandoning the child or by aggression.

In this respect I want to stress the common nature of the problem. Children are abandoned and abused by their weakened parents all over the world, in developed as well as in developing countries. Child witches may seem a marginal phenomenon while the increasing number of street children is seen as more general. However, child witches are often also street children. They are either abandoned by their parents or leave home by their own will due to violence and miserable material conditions. But all street children are not accused of witchcraft.

Why, then, did parents believe their children were witches? What was special about these children? First, alleged child witches come from extreme poverty. Both sexes up to the age of fifteen were targeted as witches. However, the alleged witch was predominantly a boy of twelve, described as depressed, with nightmares and concentration problems, fearful, nervous, aggressive, impolite, insecure, delinquent, disobedient and anxious. He or she steals, isolates himself, is indifferent, mistrusts his surroundings, has sleeping problems, and has a tendency to run away.

There was a third kind of actor in this witchcraft, the self-proclaimed 'pastors' who diagnosed and treated the affected children. We found out that parents who believed their children were witches and who also wanted to get rid of them were very seldom biological parents. This was because these parents, directed by the principles of clan social solidarity, had, even though they were in already desperate economic situation, taken in close relatives' children who came from even more disadvantaged parents. Here the business-minded 'pastors' with their ideas about child witches entered the scene and immediately carved out a lucrative niche for themselves. In northern Angola these 'pastors' all came from the Kinshasa area. It was they who declared uncontrolled children to be child witches. Their existence and role in the drama explain to a large extent the epidemic nature of witchcraft accusations against children at the end of the 1990s. The very idea of 'child witches' was, in all probability, their invention.

Allow me to summarise my position: pauperisation has both reduced the resources a family has to care for its members and led some families to take in more distant kin. Under both such conditions parents are less able to parent. They have less to give their children in terms of food and the things money can buy such as education and health. They are challenged by the business of emotional nurturing. Such parents, being ineffective, lose their authority and control over their children, and so are still less able to parent. Offspring in this situation, especially those who are more distant kin, become wild and out of control. This raises in their parents' minds the question: what could make children act this way? To which there is a common answer. They have become witches, and 'luckily' there are pastors to diagnose and deal with this situation.

The Clan System and Child Witchcraft

The witchcraft pattern that I encountered in the 1980s was an aspect of the clan system and its disintegration tendencies due to mounting economic problems. In this period the most probable 'witch', responsible for sickness, death and other kinds of misfortune, was an elderly person, male or female, who was accused by the younger generation, acting as a group. In some cases the accusation led to the killing of the alleged witch, often by fire. The person was tied up and thrown into a hole dug into the ground, then gasoline was poured over the body and lit. These were, however, relatively rare cases. More commonly, 'the problem' was resolved at a clan reunion which entailed speeches, confession, the transfer of money, and reconciliation.

The witchcraft accusations of the 1980s against elders were quite comprehensible when seen within the logic of the clan system. The specific form of clan system which I encountered during fieldwork in the 1980s and early 1990s and which today is rapidly disintegrating is to a large extent a construct of the colonial era. Political entities as well as local societies were crushed by Europe's penetration and colonisation of the area. Following this destruction, the indigenous society was recreated from its remnants in a new form. The clan system of the twentieth century was part of a colonial re-creation because it incorporated clans into the colonial administration. It was based on the elders' power and dominance over the young, who as a rule, were remarkably obedient and well-behaved. The fact that the clan had priority over the individual had to do with the substantial security the former offered. The principle of mutual rights and obligations meant that people had to give to others and that they were, at the same time, guaranteed the support of others. In the beginning of my fieldwork I met with many middle-aged persons who nostalgically talked about how good it was when they were little. Then they had a number of older relatives who cared for them and to whom they could turn for help. In the 1980s I saw clan members constantly transferring money in kin relations as well as participating in costly clan reunions and often thought they wasted their money on 'unnecessary' objects, such as coffins and stones for the graves.

So in the 'traditional' clan system, the relationship between generations is characterised by reciprocity. The parents initially give to the child, first of all his life, then their care and material support, and finally, and highly important, they transmit 'Life Force' to the young person without which he/she would not survive in social life. In the matrilineal south both father and maternal uncle had magical power to offer. Young folk needed Life Force in order to be bright students, earn money, get a job, have a wife or a husband, and of course have children. The junior, who received all these blessings from his parents, had to reciprocate with money, services and respect. I often heard about fathers and uncles using their magical power as an argument when they felt disappointed in the young person. The father could curse the child, usually by malediction. He did not have to do more than walk around in his yard complaining about his worthless offspring. An uncle was supposed to protect the child by 'putting up his leg' and thereby preventing witches and evil spirits from entering the matri-family.

However, the elders' magical power proved to be a double-edged sword when the economic situation deteriorated in the 1980s making them vulnerable when the young did not obtain a reasonable amount of success. This happened, for example, if young women did not get pregnant, or had one child after the other with no stable husband in sight; or the young men remained unemployed, had no money, and therefore were unattractive to the opposite sex. I met with many young men in this period who had to stay in their father's house and who complained about not even having their own bed. This category of men talked about their lack of self-confidence, and their feelings of exclusion and worthlessness. Who was to blame for this state of affairs? Who was the cause of all their unjust suffering? Clearly, it was the elders, those who should have transmitted Life Force and protected them from Evil but who obviously had not done so. Given the preceding, it is understandable why it was easy for the politicians to recruit such young men to their militias in the beginning of the 1990s. It is equally understandable that juniors would see elders as witches.

The clan system has shown disintegrative tendencies as early as the 1980s, but this process has accelerated in the last two decades with increasing pauperisation. Poor clan elders have nothing to offer their young. More affluent clan relatives wish to liberate themselves from poor relatives and their exorbitant demands. Gangs as well as militias offer alternative support to poor youth. With the pauperisation comes a relaxing of law and order and cultural norms, and in this situation young frustrated men, armed and often drugged, feel free to commit horrible assaults on the more vulnerable categories, i.e. women, children and older people. In interviews with street children in Brazzaville (2004 and 2005) the gang, of eight to twelve boys, appears to be the only social unit where these children experience feelings of solidarity and security. One of them says: 'There is no love at home, love only exists in the street.' They love one another and treat all others as prey in their struggle for survival.

Clan ties of mutual reciprocity and nurture no longer exist. They cannot provide for security, as they did in the past. So, in this situation, who needs clans? A younger clansperson who is violent, drugged and brutal is not so much your clan relative as a vicious gang or militia member. How could he or she be so evil? To which the answer is: only witches are like that, which explains the rise of child witchcraft accusations. Finally, let us consider what the social disintegration does at the level of a person's subjectivity.

Individual Subjectivity, Dreams and Resistance

It is easy to emphasise the clearly negative aspects of witchcraft; i.e. that innocent people are accused of imaginary activities and, consequently, in some cases killed. This is a recurrent theme in literature from the colonial period, and it has also played a role in my own fieldwork. Witchcraft is, however, a complex phenomenon including positive characteristics. People are, for example, full of enthusiasm and admiration when they tell about the mysterious powers of witches. Alleged witches do not always claim they are innocent. On the contrary, they may admit that they are witches and be quite obstinate about it. The message is, 'yes, I am a witch and you better watch out' (Ekholm Friedman 1994: 106f; see also Laman's early nineteenth century material, 1962: 224). At the end of the 1980s I was repeatedly told a story about some old men from a village, Makanna II, who flew to Paris in a magical bamboo plane in order to 'eat' a sister's son. 'Eating' is often what witches do in southern Congo-Brazzaville. The plane arrived unannounced at a Paris airport, impossible to identify. The airport personnel read 'Makanna II' on the plane and shook their heads in consternation at the powers of poor Congolese. I shall argue below that such beliefs, including those involving child witches, express a resistance to those with greater political or economic power.

Witchcraft certainly has a base in pre-colonial religion, where it was believed the king and all the chiefs under him, down to the father, were supposed to uphold society by their own creative power and by their intimate link to God and the ancestors (Ekholm Friedman 1991). The king, as well as any father, was like God, the Creator. In matrilineal society it is still the father who creates life, i.e. the child, while the role of the mother is reduced to that of a container. The idea of Life Force flowing from God and via the ancestors down the political hierarchy had serious consequences for power-holders when the political system collapsed at the end of the nineteenth century. Since the universe's order was supposed to be maintained by kings and chiefs, these were held responsible for the catastrophe. Instead of focusing on the real reason, i.e. foreign intrusion and colonisation, people often directed their aggression towards their own chiefs (Ekholm Friedman 1991).

Current Congolese witchcraft beliefs are based upon two closely intertwined ideas. One is the notion that certain people, above all older poor men with a will to power, are able to influence reality by magical means. In northern Angola I was told about an old man in rags who informed a young, energetic man, working his field, ' your field is really impressive, but you must acknowledge the fact that it is I who has caused these plants to grow and that I therefore am entitled to part of what you earn'. The other is the belief that events in dreams taking place in the night world are as real as what takes place in the day world. When the individual falls asleep he enters into the parallel world of the night. He flies out at night, in his dreams, and engages in various kinds of activities. If he is a witch, he may do harmful things to others. If he is not a witch he may be attacked by witches and evil spirits. A belief in two parallel dimensions of reality has a number of problematic consequences for both the dreamer and his/her surroundings. Nightmares are, logically, much more frightening for those who conceive of nocturnal attacks as real than for those who think they are merely dreams. Consequently, if someone dreams of being approached sexually in an illicit relationship, he or she may accuse this person next day, as is reported to have occurred in my fieldwork (Ekholm Friedman 1994).

Dreams are of central importance in relation to alleged child witches. When meeting with them at various types of centres for abandoned children in Angola, I was initially astonished by the fact that they so willingly accepted their identity as witches. 'In which sense then are you a witch?' I asked; 'What do you do when practising witchcraft?' The standard reply was that they fly out at night in their dreams, to visit other places where they eat, drink, dance and meet with the opposite sex, and where they also engage in harmful activities, such as strangling other people. What these informants were telling me was that witchcraft is a magical power confirmed by dreams and that they, child witches, had that power, and relished it. And what a power it is, allowing flight back and forth to New York in a couple of seconds.

During my stay in northern Angola in 2000, I participated in a radio programme addressing the issue of children being accused of witchcraft. In the middle of the program the reporter turned to me and posed the question, 'Dona Kajsa, you who call yourself an international expert in this matter, do you believe in witchcraft?' I answered, 'No, I do not believe in witchcraft', although I realised that my disbelief would cause indignation. Afterwards my Angolan colleague was furious. He concluded his lengthy criticism of my behaviour by saying, 'You cannot come here declaring in public that you do not believe in witchcraft. This is a scandal.'

My disbelief was thus conceived as 'a scandal', or an insult. But why? When I said, 'I do not believe in witchcraft', it meant I do not believe in the night world but only in my own culture's view of reality where a clear demarcation exists between reality and phenomena such as dreams, fantasies and delusions. What they found provoking was certainly not my disbelief in the children's stories about flying out in their dreams but, instead, my rejection of the very idea of magical power. When I say, 'I don't believe in witchcraft', they find it arrogant since it seems as if I depreciate their own unique power on this point.

The West has had its technological marvels, which the ruling class in both Angola and Congo-Brazzaville have taken over; but ordinary people, deprived of wealth and political power, have their magical power. By magical means they are as powerful, or even more powerful than others. When my Congolese assistant visited Lund at the beginning of the 1990s she was asked by a student group to speak. The students immediately raised the issue of witchcraft and, to their consternation, she said, 'your witchcraft is better than ours because it does not lead to such tensions and conflicts'. When trying to clarify what she meant she identified 'your witchcraft' with technology and Congolese witchcraft as magic and thereby dangerous to social relations.

The belief in magical power and the night world is not only rooted in pre-colonial religion but is also a form of cultural resistance. Witchcraft beliefs allow the poor to still be in control, and to oppose the power of Western civilisation as well as their own political class. Western technology and the very concrete political power of their ruling elites constitute a threat, not only to their own cultural self-confidence but to their very survival, a threat that has been counteracted culturally by the persistence of the belief in the magical power of the night world. This view is not confined to the Congo area but is found in other parts of Africa. In Naipaul's book *Finding the Centre* (1986) there is a description of a woman in the Ivory Coast who excitedly keeps talking about 'the night'. Naipaul also refers to archival material from the eighteenth century in the West Indies in which he has found an account of a slave who in the day world was weak and of no importance but who in the night world was a powerful chief. How do child witches fit into this understanding?

While the power of magic is cherished, child witches are unanimously considered a serious problem. They are in no way admired. Instead their kind of power, which the parents evidently experience, is dangerous, unacceptable and must be combated. The following interpretation was suggested to me by one of my assistants. Originally, when social order prevailed, the magical power was concentrated into the hands, or minds, of responsible elders and traditional leaders. What has now happened is a diffusion of this power down the hierarchy to children, which of course creates chaos. A solution to the problem of child witches, according to this person, would be the return of their magical power to the elders, in the form of a rehabilitation of the Congo Kingdom.

Allow me to summarise the position I have just developed. The belief in witches is exceptionally widespread. It is a belief that even poor people have a magical power. This power can further devolve into that of child witchcraft. One solution of the child witch problem would be to restore the Congo Kingdom and the magical power's proper possessors, all of whom are some sort of elders. Lurking in the subjective consciousness of the poor, who have borne the brunt of the impoverishment and violence of social disorder, is the knowledge that they too have their magical powers. Even child witches have these powers. These powers are there in spite of the powers of Westerners and their own Congolese political class, and so they offer a resistance to them. Who else can fly to New York and back in seconds?

Conclusion

The evidence is as follows: Congo-Brazzaville, from independence (1960) to the 1990s, at the higher level of state and global actors, experienced increasing social disorder due to pauperisation and violence. Then at the end of the 1990s child witches were reported in Congo-Brazzaville, Congo-Kinshasa and Angola. This child witchcraft is explained in terms of events occurring at the local level of family, clan and individual subjectivity, which are products of the social disorder at the upper level. Impoverished, violence-devastated parents and elders in family and clan are no longer able to be functional parents or clan elders. Under these conditions, some children and juniors accordingly become disoriented and rebel against their seniors. This rebellion is diagnosed as child witchcraft by the 'pastors'. Finally witchcraft is a form of magical power, subjectively imagined by ordinary Congolese to be stronger than that of the political class and their Western allies, and so helps them to resist the social disorder provoked by these elites. Child witchcraft is evidence that that magical power is everywhere, and real, if malign.

Notes

1. This chapter has been produced within a project financed by the Guggenheim Foundation. A word on the names of states: Congo-Brazzaville is the Republic of the Congo, a former French colony, with its capital at Brazzaville. Congo-Kinshasa is the Democratic Republic of the Congo, a former Belgium colony, with its capital at Kinshasa.
2. A shorter study on the sudden outbreak of witchcraft accusation against children has been conducted in northern Angola where the population is also Bakongo (Ekholm Friedman and N'senga 2002).
3. Child witches have been recognised in three countries in the lower Congo River Basin: Congo-Brazzaville, Congo-Kinshasa and Angola. At the end of 1999, a case occurred in Stockholm, Sweden, in an immigrant family from Kinshasa. Two children had been accused of witchcraft and subjected to exorcism, including elements of torture, in order to drive out evil. I was the expert court witness in 2000. In 2001, I served as a consultant in Angola to a project investigating child witchcraft accusations among the Bakongo (unpublished report, Ekholm Friedman and Biluka Nsakala N'senga 2003).

References

Ake, Claude. 1985. *The Social Sciences in Africa*. mimeo
Ake, Claude. 1996. *Democracy and Development in Africa*. Washington, D. C.: The Brookings Institution.
Amin, Samir and Catherine Coquery-Vidrovitch. 1969. *Histoire économique du Congo 1880–1968*. Paris: Éditions Antropos.
Comaroff, Jean, and John Comaroff, eds. 1993. *Modernity and Its Malcontents: Ritual and Power in Postcolonial Africa*. Chicago: University of Chicago Press.
Bayart, Jean-Francois.1990. L'Afro-pessimism par le bas. *Politique africaine* 40: 103–108.
———. 1993. *The State in Africa: The Politics of the Belly*. London: Longman.
Bayart, Jean-Francois, Stephen Ellis and Béatrice Hibou. 1999. *The Criminalization of the State in Africa*. Bloomington: Indiana University Press.
Bazenguissa-Ganga, Rémy. 2001. *Une guerre contre les civiles*. Paris: Éditions Karthala.
Bissila, Paul. 1999. La Compagnie pétrolière Elf, facteur s'insécurité. In *Congo-Brazzaville: dérives politique, catastrophe humanitaire, désirs de paix*, ed. Patrice Yengo, 144–151. Paris: Éditions Karthala.
Bond, George and Diane Ciekawy. 2001. *Witchcraft Dialogues: Anthropological and Philosophical Exchanges*. Athens: Ohio University Press.

Clairmont, Frédéric. 2001. Menace sur l'économie mondiale. *Le Monde Diplomatique*, May, page 3.

Clark, John F. 2002. The Neo-colonial Context of the Democratic Experience of Congo-Brazzaville. *African Affairs* 101: 171–192.

Ekholm, Kajsa. 1972. *Power and Prestige. The Rise and Fall of the Kongo Kingdom*. Uppsala: Skrivservice.

Ekholm Friedman, Kajsa. 1990. Obstacles to Rural Development in Africa: The Congolese Case. *Social Movements and Strategies in Third World Development* 18: 52. Department of Sociology, Lund University.

———. 1990a "Den politiska eliten struntar i folket" in *Sida rapport* 3: 28–29.

———. 1991. *Catastrophe and Creation: The Formation of an African Culture*. London: Harwood Academic.

———. 1994. *Den Magiska Världsbilden: om statens frigörelse från folket*. Stockholm: Carlssons Förlag.

Ekholm Friedman, Kajsa and Biluka Nsakala N'senga. 2002. A Study of Children at risk in Zaire, Uíge and Luanda Provinces. Report for Save the Children, Luanda.

Ekholm Friedman, Kajsa and Anne Sundberg. 1995. *Ethnic War and Ethnic Cleansing*. Occasional Paper, IDS. Roskilde, Denmark: Roskilde University Press.

Jackson, Robert. 1990. Quasi-states: Sovereignty, International Relations, and the Third World. Cambridge: Cambridge University Press

Evans-Pritchard, E.E. 1937. *Witchcraft, Oracles and Magic among the Azande*. Oxford: Clarendon Press

Eze, Emmanuel Chukwudi 1997. *Postcolonial African Philosophy: A Critical Reader*. Cambridge, Mass.: Blackwell.

Frimpong-Ansahm Jonathan. 1991. *The Vampire State in Africa: The Political Economy of Decline in Ghana*. London: Currey.

Geertz, Clifford. 1993 [1973]. Thick Description: Toward an Interpretative Theory of Culture. In *The Interpretation of Cultures*, 3–32. London: Fontana Press.

Geschiere, Peter and Cyprian Fonyuy Fisiy. 1995. Sorcellerie et politique en Afrique: la viande des autres. Paris: Karthala.

Geschiere, Peter. 1997. *The Modernity of Witchcraft: Politics and the Occult in Postcolonial Africa*. Charlottesville. University Press of Virginia.

Geschiere, Peter 2000 Sorcellerie et modernité :retour sur une étrange complicité. *Politique Africaine* 79 : 17–32.

Hodges, Tony. 2001. *Angola from Afro-Stalinism to Petro-Diamond Capitalism*. Oxford: James Currey.

Hyden, Göran. 1983. *No Shortcuts to Progress*. Berkeley: University of California Press

Jackson, Robert. 1990. *Quasi-states: Sovereignty, International Relations, and the Third World*. Cambridge: Cambridge University Press.

Laman, Karl. 1962. *The Kongo III*. Uppsala: Studia Ethnographica Upsaliensia.

Lindell, Henrik. 1999. Vu de l'Occident: la guerre au Congo-Brazzaville n'est pas assez affligeante. In *Congo-Brazzaville: dérives politique, catastrophe humanitaire, désirs de paix*, ed. Patrice Yengo, 40–60. Paris: Éditions Karthala.

Médard Jean François. 1982. *L' Etat Sous-Développé en Afrique Noire: Clientélisme Politique ou Néo-Patrimonialisme?* Bordeaux: Centre d'Etude d'Afrique Noire.

———. 1991. L'État néo-patrimonial en Afrique noire. In *États d'Afrique Noire: Formations, mécanismes et crises*, ed. Jean François Médard, 323. Paris, Karthala.

Migdal, Joel S. 1988. *Third World*. Princeton: Princeton University Press.

Mouamba, Clément. 1985. La Stratégie de développement auto-centré et auto-dynamique et la transition au socialisme. *La Revue des Sciences Sociales* 1.

Naipaul, Vidiadhar Surajprasad. 1984. *Finding the Center.* London: André Deutch.

Reno, William. 1998. *Warlord Politics and African States.* Boulder, CO: Lynne Rienner Publishers.

Verschave, Francois-Xavier. 1998. *La Francafrique. Le Plus long scandale de la République.* Paris: Éditions Stock.

———. 2000. *Noir Silence. Qui arrêtera la Francafrique.* Paris: Les Arènes.

———. 2002. *L'envers de la dette. Criminalité politique et économique au Congo-Brazza et en Angola.* Marseille: Agone.

Yengo, Patrice. 1999. Anthropo-logiques de la violence politique. In *Congo-Brazzaville: dérives politique, catastrophe humanitaire, désirs de paix,* ed. Patrice Yengo, 121–143. Paris: Éditions Karthala.

———. 2006. *La Guerre civile du Congo-Brazzaville, 1993–2002, 'Chacun aura sa part'.* Paris: Éditions Karthala.

— *Chapter 6* —

CONSTITUTING DOMINATION/
CONSTRUCTING MONSTERS

Imperialism, Cultural Desire and Anti-Beowulfs in the Chadian
Petro-state

Stephen P. Reyna

Let us begin with one of those verbal texts found in anthropologists' note-
books. This one contains an exchange between myself and a chauffeur in 2003,
during which I became a participant in the diffusion of gossip prevalent in the
Doba Basin (the southern Chad region roughly between Doba to the east and
Moundou to the west). We were at a petrol station in a crowded, dusty and
hot market town. The chauffeur was filling the tank. I leaned against the 4X4.
The conversation was serendipitous. We had been talking about animals in
the bush. I knew that there were not many left, all hunted out. So I was flab-
bergasted when I caught something about big game eating people:

Anthropologist: What did you say is out there?
Chauffeur: There are lions eating them.
Anthropologist: But there are no lions left.
Chauffeur: There are *these* lions.
Anthropologist: What do you mean – *these* lions?
Chauffeur: You know…
Anthropologist: No, I don't.
Chauffeur: You know, *them*…
Anthropologist (thinking, maybe I'm getting it): I don't…
Chauffeur: Lionmen.
Anthropologist: You mean lion *men*?
Chauffeur: Yes.
Anthropologist (thinking, 'got it!'): So lionmen eat consortium flagmen?
Chauffeur: Yes.
Anthropologist: Why?
Chauffeur: Those flagmen are sorcerers.

This brings us to *Beowulf* (Anon 1999), the oldest surviving Old English epic. It was written circa AD 1000 somewhere in England and evokes the good-old days in the Danish homeland around AD 450 to 600. England at the end of the first millennium was a violent place. Kingdoms incessantly fought each other, vying to be petty empires; and, indeed, Anglo-Saxon realms would fall to a Norman Empire in AD 1066. *Beowulf* tells the story of earlier times but, in doing so, it informs its audience of the way things are and what to do about them for all time (at least to the tenth century Anglo-Saxon mind). The way things were is that there were *cynings* and *thanes* – kings and aristocratic warrior retinues; and in this in-*thane* world there was reciprocity between *cyning*, who gave to his warriors the means to be aristocrats, and *thanes*, who gave to their king the violent wherewithal to be king. One king, Hrothgar, began to experience bad things in his feasting hall. Grendel, a troll-like monster, broke into it and feasted on the *thanes*. Beowulf, a great warrior, sought to help Hrothgar. He fought Grendel, and killed him; then went out to kill Grendel's mother, and killed her; and, finally, tried to kill their terrifying associate, a fire-breathing dragon, and got killed. The epic's eleventh century audience was likely to be the rulers' aristocratic retinue. The bards who narrated and renarrated the epic broadcast its moral to them. There are terrifying monsters out there who threaten the empire. A great aristocrat, like Beowulf, kills them, winning everlasting glory.[1]

So here are two texts: one concerning rumour in the southern Chadian bush, and the other Beowulf. What could they possibly have in common? For starters both texts are about fear and monsters in imperial systems of domination. But the modes of this domination vary. In *Beowulf* the domination was that of pre-modern empires, and the function of the text might be seen as motivating its aristocratic audience to overcome fear of monsters to become agents fighting for their king; thereby helping to reproduce pre-modern imperial domination. The lionmen/sorcerer rumours take place within a developing petro-state undergoing integration into a modern system of imperial domination. This integration involved constitution of an oil complex in Chad by structural actors – ranging from a consortium of petroleum transnationals led by Exxon (hereafter referred to as 'the consortium'), the World Bank, and the Chadian state – that allowed the majority of the capital from Chadian oil revenues to be accumulated by the consortium. Specifically, this chapter proposes that the gossip, resulting from Doba Basin peoples' experiences of the constitution of the oil complex, constructed fear among those sharing the rumours of a particular monster (consortium sorcerers), creating a desire to oppose them (as do lionmen); and thereby helping Doba Basin peoples to distrust modern imperial domination. It is as if the rumour produces anti-Beowulfs in the Chadian bush; agents disposed to resist, not reproduce, imperial domination. The argument advancing this position develops over two stages. First, a theory of the rumour is proposed in critical structural realist terms. Second, this explanation's plausibility is tested by observing whether the events which occur in Chad from 1995 until 2007 are those predicted by the theory. A conclusion speculates about the role of fear and monsters in other petro-states in current systems of imperial domination.

Theory

Since the 9–11 attacks on the World Trade Center there has been an outburst of talk of imperialism (see Harvey 2003 for a discussion of this). This conversation agrees on two matters: first, imperialism *is* prevalent in the current global political economy; second, the preeminent imperialism *is* US American, so we had better 'Get Used to It' (Cover, *New York Times Magazine*, 5 Jan, 2003).[2] 'Imperialism' is a logic of domination involving states whose agents create, maintain or expand domination within two sorts of spaces: one where there are dominators accumulating valuable resources; and the other where there are the dominated, from whom are extracted valuables to be accumulated by the dominators. In capitalist empires the key resources accumulated are economic ones which can be transformed into capital. Different institutional complexes in capitalist empires can be named after the commodity which the dominated control and from which they are accumulating capital. For example, US oil investments result in oil complexes –organisations of institutions through which oil and oil revenues flow – favourable to US capital accumulation. Gallagher and Robinson emphasise the importance of distinguishing between formal and informal empires, because empires expand both 'by acquiring dominion' over territory 'in the strict constitutional sense', and by eschewing such formalities (1953: 1). For our purposes, empires are 'formal' when a centre and periphery are institutionalised in the same state, with the centre providing an administration to govern the periphery. The periphery in formal empires is a 'colony'. Empires are 'informal' when the centre and periphery are different polities, and where there is no hierarchical administrative apparatus whereby the centre governs the periphery. However, informal empires *are* empires because the centre still has institutional complexes that allow it to extract resources from the periphery. The periphery in informal empires is a 'client' state. The US ruling class is generally seen as managing an informal imperialism (Mann 2003: 13).

Analysis of current, informal imperialism emphasises its economic aspects (Arrighi 2005; Harvey 2003; Hudson 2003). Elsewhere (Reyna 2005) I analysed US imperialism, seeking to bring violent conflict into the theoretical limelight; suggesting violence, like peaceful buying and selling, is a normal part of the constitution, maintenance and enlargement of empires. Some of those who have experienced violent domination construct cultural desires to resist it. There has been considerable violence in Chad as it has become a petro-state. So theorising about what is happening in the Chadian bush as the country begins oil production should include generalisations about the constitution of imperialism and the construction of cultural desires resisting it. What type of theory might perform such a job? Below I argue for a structural realist theory that has two sets of generalities: those that account for constitution of imperial domination; and those that construct its resistance. It is the latter generalisations that will involve monsters.

Four Generalisations

This chapter's goal is to argue the plausibility of a theory. Consequently, first, the theory is presented in the form of generalisations, which are as abstract and as general as possible to increase their explanatory reach. Then, as much as possible, the theory is validated. There is a problem. Abstract generalisations explain a lot. The difficulty is that they are not experience-near, in the sense of being closely tied to observations. The ethnographer's art in such situations is to grasp how to tie observation to abstraction. This is done by surveying observations of reality, to discover if what is observed to occur in reality is consistent with what the generalisations state should be observed in the reality. Such explorations of experience are what is meant by validating theory.

The four generalisations are derived from a structural realist approach (Reyna 2002). The perspective is 'realist' in the sense that is posits that there is independent reality; and that it is the job of investigators to discern the truest knowledge of it possible.[3] It is 'structural' because its credo is that once one has explained the organisation and dynamics of structure, one has completed one's work because reality is, to all intents and purposes, the creation, occurrence or destruction of different structures. The structural realism I propose considers the human condition to occur within a social monism (Reyna 2002) consisting of two connected realms of objective and subjective structures. 'Objective' realms are those external to, but inclusive of, individuals. They are of individuals doing things in groups, which groups exhibit structures of force and power (Reyna 2001,

2003a). Creation of such structures is said to be their constitution. 'Subjective' realms are those internal to individuals, and pertain to their biological structures; especially those involved in experiencing objective realms, what I term their cultural neurohermeneutic system (2002, 2006). Creation of such structures is said to be their construction; by which I mean not the developmental biology building neuronal structures, but the adjusting of those structures to the objective realm in which individuals live.

The first two generalisations concern creation of a novel objective situation in the Doba Basin, constitution of imperial domination. The final two generalisations are about the effects of that novel structure of power upon the indigenous peoples' subjective structures. The third and fourth generalisations explain how Doba Basin peoples' subjectivities reacted to the novel objective and subjective realities. They responded by the construction of cultural desire, using performitivity logic, a concept derived from the work of Judith Butler (1993). This desire functions as a force resource arranging resistance to the consortium.

The generalisations, and elucidation of the concepts which compose them, are presented below.

1. *Competition between France and the US for constitution of imperial domination in Chad involved strings of a constitutional logic that added a new oil complex to the US informal empire.*

The concepts of strings and power need to be explained in order to understand the first generalisation. At the heart of structural realism is the recognition that what groups do is to perform 'strings', observable causal sequences of events. Recurring strings will be said to be 'iterative'. Football matches and factory assembly lines perform iterative strings. Strings exhibit 'logics', which are abstract, generalised categories of strings with characteristic spatio-temporal forces and powers. Football matches exhibit logics of non-violent conflict; assembly lines exhibit those of capitalism. Force and power make possible strings.

A structural realist notion of force derives from distinctions made between power and what causes it (Reyna 2001, 2003a). 'Power' is effects of exercises of force. Force, as cause, is institutional means at some antecedent time to produce outcomes at some subsequent time, thereby adding to some string; raising the question, what makes antecedent 'institutional means' into forces? This is due to utilisation of force resources by groups. 'Force resources' are what necessarily get consumed during the exercise of social force. There are four such resources. The first of these involves 'instruments' – tools, monies etc. – inanimate things that individuals use to make things happen. A second force resource is actors performing practical or discursive 'action'. 'Discursive' action is use of the body to write or speak. 'Practical' action is use of the body, usually with tools, to get something done. Labour, of course, has been a particularly important sort of practical action in economic groups.

'Culture', a third force resource, involves signs of the times learned and shared by those in populations. It is helpful to distinguish between 'neuronal' and 'discursive' culture: the former is in the subjective realm, learned and stored in cortical memory networks, and the latter in the objective realm, expressed in speech or writing (Reyna 2002). Further, we can distinguish 'perceptual' and 'procedural' forms of neuronal and discursive culture, with the former being information about *what is* and the latter information about *what to do about it*. Associated with perceptual and procedural knowledge are feelings. Some perceptual and procedural knowledge feels good; other perceptual and procedural knowledge feels bad. Perceptual and procedural knowledge plus the associated emotion may be said to be 'cultural desire'. Choreographers arrange human body movements over space and time in a dance. Cultural desire is like a choreographer, arranging other force resources over space and time, and it is in this sense that it is a force resource. When explaining the third generalisation, we shall treat cultural construction as the placing of cultural desires within the subjectivity to serve as the force resource that organises other force resources.

The fourth variety of force resources is 'authoritative' and is really a particular type of cultural resource; it is *formally sanctioned* cultural desire specifying actors' rights and responsibilities to instruments, actions and cultural information. The notion of a sanctioned resource is one that will have other resources added to it to augment the force of which it is a component. The concept of a formally sanctioned authoritative resource concerns rules applying to populations (laws or regulations) that have been specified by some procedure (a vote in the case of laws, an administrative decision in the case of regulations). Authority is cultural desire with a club, the formal sanctions, to help it out. 'Exercises of force' in this structural realist perspective are utilisations of cultural and/or authoritative force resources which choreograph other force resources to cause some effect; which effect is some event occurring after another; and it is the placing of events in temporal sequences which is the making of strings. Now it is time to apply what has just been learned to understanding the first generalisation

Some strings may exhibit the logic of structural constitution; that is, they may exercise force in ways that has the power of constituting other novel groups. Indeed, the first generalisation is about the constitution of a structure of imperial domination in Chad. The generalisation proposes this constitution will involve a competition between weaker and stronger imperial states to perform strings that involve utilisation of resources to create an 'oil complex'; sets of institutions whose strings operate: (1) to pump crude from the ground and to deliver it to markets; as well as (2) distributing oil revenues to various beneficiaries, especially the capitalist enterprises of imperial states. Constitution of such complexes is necessary for imperial domination because it allows one state's dominators to accumulate capital from another state's dominated people. Let us explicate the second generalisation.

> 2. Some strings associated with the constitution of this oil complex exhibited a threat logic that produced fear among some indigenous peoples in the Doba Basin.

Some of the strings constituting the oil complex involved violence. Violence threatens the subjectivities of those experiencing it. So the same strings that exhibited a constitutive logic also exhibited a threat logic. 'Threat logics' are ones in which the events in a string have the power of evoking fear in some actors. Fear is an emotion. Emotion involves operations of certain parts of the body, especially the brain. The brain's amygdalae are critical in the case of fear (Rolls 2005). Fear is normally directed against something, and is a feeling that the something is dangerous, bad or horrifying, i.e., a threat. The second generalisation is simple: strings constituting the oil complex exhibited a threat logic to the subjectivities of those living in the Doba Basin. Consider now the third generalisation, which is about what happened in the objective realm of the threatened to construct altered cultural desires in their subjective realm. This generalisation employs a concept derived from the work of Judith Butler.

> 3. *Consequent upon the operation of the threat logic, a performativity logic – involving gossip about the consortium sorcerers and village lionmen – constructed a new cultural desire.*

Butler states that,

> Performativity cannot be understood outside of a process of iterability, a regularised and constrained repetition of norms. And this repetition is not performed *by* a subject; this repetition is what enables a subject .... This iterability implies that 'performance' is not a singular 'act' or event, but a ritualised production. (Butler 1993: 95)

Perfomativity can be conceptualised in structural realist terms. At its heart it is iterable (repeatable) 'ritualised production'; as such, it is repeated events in some sequence. This is what I understand strings to be. However, what sort of string are we considering? Here Butler tells us that they involve 'repetition of norms'. Norms are cultural phenomena. They are understandings that something (the perceptual culture) should result in doing, or not doing, something else (the procedural culture). For example, the norm, 'Should not eat the poodle' has a bit of perceptual culture (the poodle) and some procedural cultural direction (don't eat it), and if revulsion is associated with the idea of eating the poodle, then emotion is associated with the procedural culture, which means that norm is another term for cultural desire. 'Cultural construction' is the placing of cultural desires within the subjectivity to serve as a force resource that organises other force resources. 'Performativity' logics can include strings that construct cultural desires in peoples' subjectivity. This occurs when the iterative strings people perform teach them what their cultural desires should be. So understood, the third generalisation posits that gossiping about sorcerers and lionmen is a performativity logic that constructs new cultural desires in Doba Basin people. The fourth generalisation concerns the substance of this desire.

4. *The new cultural desire specified monster culture, identifying who were monsters (consortium sorcerers) and what to do about them (oppose them, as do lionmen) and, as such, functions as a novel cultural force resource in certain Doba Basin Chadian subjectivities impugning the consortium and motivating resistance.*

A concept of monsters needs to be specified. A 'monster' is a perceptual cultural category of threat that stimulates the amygdalae, provoking fear. Something must be done about monsters because they are so threatening. Late at night, when all were sleeping, Beowulf heard noise in Hrothgar's feasting hall, interpreted it as Grendel (the perceptual culture) and knew he had to kill it (the procedural culture) because it was so monstrous. 'Monster culture' consists of a perceptual cultural category that something is horribly threatening; a strong fear attached to that perceptual culture; and a procedural cultural category, of some disposition to resist the fearful threat. When threat logics are so new that people may not appreciate them, then ways are needed to impress on people that threats are a danger. What better way to do this than with a monster. The argument here is not that the monster culture bearing upon the consortium is a form of resistance (Scott 1990). Rather, it is that such culture is a pre-condition of resistance. The following section reports observations bearing on the above generalisations.

Analysis

Analysis proceeds in the following manner. First, evidence reveals strings of imperial competition that eventually constituted a consortium-built oil complex. Second, information is offered indicating that a threat logic has operated in the Doba Basin in association with the consortium since the early 1980s. Third, more evidence is presented revealing how performativity logic constructed a new cultural desire; and how this novel desire can be a cultural force resource disposing some Doba Basin Chadians to resist the consortium.[4]

Imperial Competition in the Chadian Periphery

A word is in order about the Doba Basin. This has been one of the most isolated places in the world – cut off to the north by the Sahara and the south by the Congo River basin jungles. It is largely populated by Sara-speakers. Those living around the oil fields are for the most part Sara Ngambay. There is no strong ethnography of the Ngambay. However, the patrilineage, called *gel ka* among Ngambay, was the 'fundamental element of Sara societies' (Magnant 1986: 27). One of its senior members, widely termed the *chef de terre* (or *ngar nàng* in Ngambay), established, and maintained through ritual, ties between Earth Spirits and the patrilineage. These ties gave the patrilineage rights to the land allowing them to cultivate cereals, especially sorghum. Sara raised relatively few cattle in the past, though they supplemented their cereal diet with fish from the Logone River and its tributaries. For the most part, they were a highly acephalous people living in dispersed hamlets. Leaders were largely ritual specialists, like the aforementioned *chefs de terre*.

In the nineteenth century, Sara were subjected to slave raiding from Muslim empires and, as a result, began centralisation (Brown 1975; Reyna 1990). The Sara region was the part of Chad most touched by French colonisation. Especially important was education that allowed southerners to be more educated in a Western manner, which facilitated their control of the central government following Independence. Further, such 'modern' economic development as occurred took place in the south, with cotton production being introduced in the 1930s. Manioc has been gradually added to cereal production in part because its lower labour requirements release labour to produce cotton (Gaide 1956). Commercial and administrative centres grew to gin and distribute the cotton especially in the new Doba Basin cities of Doba and Moundou. This introduced new ethnic groups in the area. A key point to grasp is: the Sara and other peoples' incorporation into modern imperialisms puts at risk their relationship to the land; because land access becomes not a matter of Earth Spirit alliances, but of imperial interests, and imperial welfare is prioritised over the welfare of the Doba Basin peoples. It is time to consider how Chad and the Sara became entangled in imperial strings.

Chad was one of the last places – due to its remoteness – to be integrated into a formal, Western empire. It became part of French Equatorial Africa in 1910. France gained little from its new colony due to high military costs; absence of exploitable natural resources; and presence of an impoverished and tiny population, unable to buy much (Bouquet 1982: 56–119). African independence (1960) started a second round of informal imperialism throughout the former French colonies and involved organisation of 'an integrated system of dependence' based upon 'client states' (Survie 2000: 1–2), involving strings of collaboration between the French government and African political elites to aid French capital accumulation. Some term this organisation 'Françafrique' (Verschave 1998). Jacques Foccart, who was De Gaulle's Chief of Staff for African and Malagasy Affairs, was a person central to constituting it. However, France was not to be allowed to monopolise Chad as its imperial plaything. United States capital equally developed an interest in Chad, which provoked an imperial competition for a prize worth acquiring, oil. The USA, the winner of this rivalry, then constructed an oil complex. How this happened is explicable following a brief discussion of Chad's political history.

The first president of Chad, François Tombalbaye (1960–1975), was a Sara from southern Chad. Starting in 1963 opposition to his government turned violent in the north. The Front de Libération Nationale du Tchad (FROLINAT) organised this rebellion. The French military had intervened in support of Tombalbaye's regime by the 1970s when it became clear that his Forces Armées Tchadiennes (FAT) could not defeat FROLINAT, which had developed into two major military factions that were increasingly hostile to each other: the Forces Armées du Nord (FAN) under Hissen Habré and the Forces Armées Populaires (FAP) under Oueddei Goukouni. Actors in the FAT, fearful that the government was doomed under Tombalbaye, staged a coup against him in 1975. Colonel Wadel Abdelkader Kamougue played a central role in this coup. However, a more senior officer, Félix Malloum, a FAT general who had earlier fallen out with Tombalbaye, became the new president. There followed more FAT losses to FROLINAT. Malloum bowed to the inevitable and in 1978 signed a *Charte Fondamentale* which allowed FROLINAT equal power in the central government. Habré was appointed Prime Minister. Immediately, Habré sought to dominate the government, provoking years of extreme, violent conflict (1979–1982).

By 1979, southern influence in the central government ended and a fight began between Goukouni, supported by Libya and the Soviet bloc, and Habré, supported by the US. The US's client won, and Habré ruled (1982–1990) in what became an increasingly brutal dictatorship that was in turn overthrown, with French assistance, by Idris Déby, who had once been the commander of Habré's army. Déby's rule has been 'legitimated' by three elections widely believed to be fraudulent (May and Massey 1999: 29; Verschave 2002: 225–29). His violence against his own people is only slightly less brutal than that of his predecessor. However, Chad under Déby has become a petro-state, pumping its first oil in June of 2003. It is the oil that is at the heart of Franco-American imperial competition. Let us now explore this contention.

Informal imperialism also alternates between strings of 'gifts' and those of violence. Elite actors in the imperial power give something desired by elite actors in the government or economic sector of the client state. The client elites, in return, furnish something desired by the imperial elites, and that something is normally directly or indirectly helpful to core capital accumulation. If imperial sweeteners fail their intended effects, then imperial violence may be applied. France worked hard at gift-giving in the early days of independence, providing financial assistance for the military, budgetary support and development aid, and technical workers (*corpérants*). French officials wanted certain things from Chad in return for these sweeteners, one of which had to do with natural resources. These expectations were made explicit at Independence when Chad signed an accord with France stipulating that 'sensitive materials … such as oil, minerals … could not be developed without the agreement of French authorities' (in Djimrabaye 2005: 4). Chad might be independent, but its natural resources were a gift to France.

French oil exploration in Chad was half-hearted, probably because there were better regions in which to develop oil deposits in the former French Equatorial Africa. Some exploration did occur in the 1950s and was promising. The reports of these explorations were probably the source of some Tombalbaye's *fonctionnaires'* belief that, 'the French knew of the existence of oil in Chad prior to Independence' (in Magrin 2001: 370). So Tombalbaye urged the French to exercise their privilege of natural resource development and to begin serious oil prospecting. Some studies were performed by the Bureau de Recherches Pétrolières (BRP), a branch of Elf oil (the French parastatal petroleum firm purchased by Total in 1999) between 1962 and 1966. No oil was found and in 1966 BRP informed Tombalbaye 'that there was only sand and pebbles in Chad, not a drop of oil' (Djimrabaye 2005: 5).

The French game at this time was unclear. There is a hint that they actually knew that there was, or was likely to be, oil but preferred to not develop it because 1960s oil prices were low and the costs of bringing isolated Chadian oil to the market high (see AgirIci-Survie 1999: 9). Kamougué, then head of the Chadian Parliament, announced in 1976, after oil had been found and 700 million barrels of reserves were known of, that it would take a billion barrels to make production profitable (in Ravignon 2000: 5). Further, Elf was already committed to bringing the easier-to-produce oil in other African client states on line (Yates 1996). Finally, the French knew their petroleum industry to be smaller, less capitalised and less experienced than that of US competitors. So, perhaps, Paris in the 1960s wanted to play possum; keeping the oil in the ground; avoiding competition, until it could be profitably developed.

Tombalbaye's reported response to the French claim of an oil-free Chad was: 'Furious and skeptical' (Djimrabaye 2005: 5). Consequently, he turned to the US firm Continental Oil Company (CONOCO), giving them in 1969 prospecting rights throughout the country. CONOCO was known for efficient project management and cutting edge technology. Perhaps most importantly from Chad's perspective, it had found the huge Libyan Dahra oil field; and if it could find oil in neighbouring Libya, why not in Chad? CONOCO was successful. Oil was found in 1971 in southern Chad near Doba. In 1974, CONOCO declared Chad to be 'an African El Dorado' (ibid.: 5).

This was a blow to Françafrique. Foccart reported in his journal that American prospecting was considered by Michel Débre (De Gaulle's foreign minister at the time) to be 'a veritable insult to the French army' (in Verschave 2000: 155). The Chadian press reported, 'Many [Chadians] are convinced' that Tombalbaye 'signed his own death warrant the day he offered exploration permits to an American firm' (*N'Djamena Hebdo* in Buijtenhuijs 1998: 31). This is probably because Tombalbaye had appealed on *Radio Tchad* for peoples' watchfulness in early April 1975 because, he explained, a coup was being organised against him as punishment for allowing Americans to discover the oil fields. He died in a coup a few days after this broadcast (13 April 1975).

Tombalbaye's demise intensified belligerency over who would rule Chad, especially between leaders in FROLINAT, Oueddei Goukouni and Hissen Habré (1979–1982). Fighting became exceptionally heavy in the capital at the beginning of 1979 between southerners and Habré's soldiers. This especially brutal time is referred to by many Chadians laconically as *les événements*. There were terrible massacres of southerners, who, consequently, fled the city and returned home. A provisional government was set up under Kamougué in Moundou. A *Comité Permanant*, composed of senior southern officials from the Tombalbaye and Malloum regimes, was organised to administer the southern provinces (see Lanne 1981, 1983). Secessionist fever swept through the south (Dadi 1987). People spoke at this time of there being a *République du Logone;* partly as a wish to be fulfilled, partly out of pride over how well the south governed itself.

However, throughout *les événements* the central conflict was between Goukouni and Habré for control over the central government. At first Goukouni was successful and, with Libyan assistance, drove Habré from N'Djamena. However, Habré received considerable military assistance, in part from the French, and in greater part from the Americans in his exile in the Sudan (Reyna 2003b). On 7 June 1982, Habré recaptured N'Djamena and began extending the central government's authority throughout the country. To a considerable extent, Habré was Washington's man during this time. President Reagan's administration is said to have provided him with '100s of millions of dollars' (Nolutshungu 1996: 238–39.) Especially malign was US support for the *Direction de la Documentation et de la Sécurité* (DDS), Habré's personal security service, responsible for forty thousand to fifty thousand tortures and murders (Brody 2001). Development of a Chadian oil sector proceeded apace during these years.

As Kamougué had indicated, there appeared to be 700 million barrels of reserves by 1976. The events of 1979 'interrupted' oil prospecting (Magrin 2001: 376). CONOCO withdrew from the oil business in 1979 at least partially due to the difficulties of working in a war zone. Where possible, Habré supported US oil prospecting and 'the apparent stabilisation' he provided at the end of the 1980s allowed Exxon, the new lead transnational in the consortium that now included Shell and Chevron, to intensify prospecting in the Doba Basin. For example, five US oil company employees were kidnapped by rebels in 1985; Habré freed them (Terrorism Knowledge Base 1985). Three areas of exploitable oil-fields were located at Komé, Miandoum and Bolobo, which held the billion barrels of reserves that Kamougué had said were necessary to bring the oil on line. In 1988, the Chadian government and the consortium signed an agreement specifying that the consortium would build the oil wells and a pipeline to move the crude from Chad to the port of Kribi in Cameroon, whence it could be shipped to refineries. So by 1988, prospects for actually building an oil complex were rosy, and it looked as if the US had won the imperial competition with France.

France's response was to find its own client. This was Idris Déby, a gifted FAN military leader, whom the French championed as 'the cowboy of the desert', and who went on to command the new Chadian army, then called the Forces Armées Nationales Tchadiennes (FANT). Not unsurprisingly, Habré grew distrustful of the 'cowboy' and his cousin Hassan

Djamous, also a brilliant commander. Consequently, Déby (1985) was sent to the École de Guerre in France for military training, and it is possibly here that his close association with the French began. Déby returned to Chad in 1986. Habré became convinced in 1988 that Déby and Djamous planned a coup against him, so he struck against them in a counter-coup. Déby and Djamous fled in a running gunfight like something in an old cowboy movie. Djamous was killed. Déby took refuge in Darfur in Sudan. The French government, then, appears to have organised what has been termed by some a *'coup d'État militaro-pétrolier ELF'* (Ley-Ngardigal 1999: 8; and discussed in Verschave 2000: 156; Verschave and Beccaria 2001:184; and Petry and Bambé 2005: 23). Paul Fontbonne, an officer of the French secret service (DGSE) in Khartoum, supervised a flow of military and financial resources to Déby, who used these to raise and train an army that invaded Chad in 1990. This force was spectacularly successful. On 1 December 1990 Habré fled N'Djamena. France had considered 'Chadian oil as a priority economic interest' (Ravignan 2000: 50). The Americans in their imperial competitive zeal had stymied this interest. Now, French prospects were looking up thanks to the 'coup d'État militaro-pétrolier ELF'. In 1992, with pressure from Déby, Elf entered the consortium with a 20 per cent share to Exxon's 40 per cent and Shell's 40 per cent shares.

Imperial competition relaxed with partial French victory. The French had a client who was *their* client, as well as a share in the oil profits. The Americans found out that Déby was just as strong a supporter of their petroleum interests as Habré. Then in 1999 something unexpected occurred. Elf along with Shell withdrew from the consortium. A new consortium was reconstituted by adding Chevron and Petronas. Elf's withdrawal was puzzling. Two explanations have been offered. The first, that of Elf itself, was that there were other regions in Africa where it could more profitably do business. The second explanation, offered by some familiar with Elf, is that at the time it withdrew from Chad it was under investigation in France for corrupt practices. Chad was just the sort of place that promised even more scandal, something Elf desperately needed to avoid. However, France would still benefit from the implementation phase. This was because building the petroleum infrastructure cost billions of dollars, and much of this construction money went to French business (Agir Ici-Survie 1999: 31). Thus, the end of the prospecting phase of the Chad oil complex witnessed imperial cooperation, with the Americans scheduled to receive profits from the oil, and the French in return receiving profits from supplying the materials for, and building, much of the oil infrastructure. Let us move on to the complex's implementation phase.

In November of 1996, the consortium signed an agreement with the Chadian government to develop the Doba oil fields and to build a 1,070 km pipeline from southern Chad through Cameroon to Kribi. Here off-shore storage and transferral facilities would be constructed to get the oil onto boats for refinery elsewhere. Start-up production costs for this oil complex were calculated in 1997 US dollars in the order of $3.72 billions, an investment that would deliver 225,000 barrels per day for about twenty-five to thirty years.

Non-governmental organisations, sensitive to the nature of Chadian politics and of the wretched record of oil in assisting development, especially for the poor, vigorously campaigned against the consortiums plans for the oil complex (Petry and Bambé 2005). Consequently, the World Bank in 1997 initially declined participation in the project. However, it did specify conditions which, if met, would result in its support. The consortium was required to develop elaborate environmental safeguards, which it did. Chad's government was required to legislate distribution of Chad's portion of the oil revenues in ways the Bank considered would fight poverty. Without the Bank other investors were reluctant to provide financial support. Chad's parliament passed a law in 1999 (# 001/PR/99) which specified that 10 per cent of all revenues were to be held in trust for future generations and 80 per cent of the remaining funds were to be devoted to poverty reduction. Crucially, there is a phrase in the 1999 law which rendered moot how rents will actually flow because the law specifies that 'for sovereignty reasons the Government of Chad alone decides how to use the funds' (Environmental Defense Fund 1997: 1). Further, the Bank was allocated a 'role ... in managing royalties generated by oil production' (Ellis 2003: 136). This was a 'precedent ... that some Washington sources are keen to extend' (ibid.: 136). 'Keen', indeed, for the Bank's 'role' in the Chadian oil sector was classic informal imperialism; because, to the extent that the Bank marches to a US Treasury Department drummer, it meant that the US government was involved in 'managing' Chad's oil revenues. The consortium and Chad's efforts satisfied the World Bank. On 6 June 2000 it approved the project. The years 2002–2003 witnessed the actual construction of the oil complex.

According to the Bank's projections, total receipts from oil production should reach $12 billion in 1997 US dollars. These petro-dollars will be the basic capital flow in the Chadian oil complex. Chad would earn about $2.5 billion in 1997 US dollars over the project's life, with annual revenues up to $200 million 1997 US dollars per year.[5] This would come from a 12.5 per cent royalty on oil sales and a 40 to 50 per cent tax on the consortium's taxable profits. However, there were to be deductions from gross profits including all the costs of oil exploration since 1969 as well as the costs of operating the business (Ravignon 2000: 17–18). Roughly five times the petro-dollars were projected to be accumulated by the consortium as by Chad. This is not a huge amount by Exxon's standards, but every little bit helps.[6]

Let us summarise this section's findings. Strings of Franco-American competition began in the 1960s over who would develop Chad's oil. The Exxon consortium eventually won this competition, and in 2000–2003 performed strings that constructed the complex; allowing it to accumulate most of the capital generated by the complex. This is evidence consistent with the first generalisations because the strings of imperial competition are those of a logic that constituted US imperial domination. Now it is time to explore whether there was fear among people in the oil producing region during this time.

Fear in the Doba Basin (1995–2000)

Bluntly put: there was an enormous amount of fear that came from physical and structural violence. This section documents strings of both sorts of violence suggesting that the fear produced by it can be analysed as a threat logic. Much of the physical violence was outsourced. A company 'outsources' when it allows another agency to perform some of its necessary operations. Consortiums constructing oil complexes need stability for their efforts to be successful. One way they achieve this is by hiring security services. Another way to do it is by having the state security services maintain stability. This latter is preferable because it lowers security costs. Chad's governing elite was aware that without protection for the consortium there would be grave problems in prospecting for, and building the oil complex. So they were willing to use government troops to protect the project. This constituted an outsourcing of security, which began in Habré's regime. The following two sections scrutinise this outsourcing.

Fear in the Time of Habré

Fighting in the south began at the very onset of Habré's regime in 1982 when he attacked Moundou. The immediate objective of this offensive was to defeat Kamougué and the *Comité Permanant*. In this it was successful. However, a bit later, the FANT (Habré's old militia, the FAN, enlarged to become the new national army) began operations in the south in support of the replacement of southern officials with those loyal to the central government. Violent clashes erupted starting in May 1983, as these new officials attempted to perform their duties, especially taxation. This led to the formation of a rebel movement called the Codos, short for commandos. At their height there were five Codo groups: Codos rouges, in the Moyen Chari; Codos cocotieres in Mayo Kebbi; Codos vert in Logone Oriental; Codos espoir in Tandjile; and Codos panthères in Logone

Occidental. Habré at first tried to negotiate with the Codos, but by August 1983 negotiations had broken down, and fighting spread through four of the five southern provinces. Habré responded in the autumn of 1984 with a 'pacification' campaign that came to known as *Septembre noir*, during which cruel suppression was visited on Codos and civilians alike. Repression was widespread throughout the south in late 1984, slackened by 1985, and largely terminated in 1986. The Codos were defeated, or withdrew across the border into the Central African Republic. Thereafter there was little open rebellion in the south during Habré's regime. The south, and with it the oil producing region, became occupied territory, garrisoned by the FANT and administered by northern officials.

It is important to grasp the brutality of this situation. A report marked 'Highly Confidential' obtained by Human Rights Watch detailed the *Septembre noir* repression as follows:

> Since the events of 15.09.84, the military situation is in the FANT's hands. One thing to note, the security of the population has been disrupted since elements of FANT launched into acts of vandalism sowing *terror* among the peasant population as well as the civil servants.

> The population lives in *fear*..., young men and women have fled the zone in the direction of Bongor.... The peasant masses are truly terrorised, they have seen their possessions fall in FANT's hands like a ripe piece of fruit, and they do not dare say a single word in the presence of the soldiers because they are so stricken with *fear* (2006: 5; emphasis added).

Mark the words: Doba Basin peoples lived in 'fear' and 'terror' during Habré's occupation.

Was the fighting in southern Chad during this time over oil? A case can be made that the Habré regime had more pressing concerns than oil. The state itself was at risk. Civil war following the *événements* of 1979 had broken Chad asunder. Goukouni to the north, supported by Libya, was in open rebellion by 1982. The south at this time seemed to be fast becoming a *République de Logone*. So, certainly, Habre's attack on Moundou was intended to maintain Chad's territorial integrity. Elites on both Kamougué's and Habré's side made clear that they knew that oil was in the south. They also knew that oil promised a vast source of state wealth. Further, Codo tactics appeared aimed at controlling areas where there was oil. Hence, even if Habré's southern 'pacification' was intended to preserve the state's integrity, this meant securing the richest part of the state, that with oil. It is time to consider violence in the time of Déby.

Fear in the Time of Déby

Déby overthrew Habré and came to power in 1990. There followed two southern rebellions. The first was that of the Comité de Sursaut National pour la Paix et le Démocracie (CSNPD), active between 1991 and 1994. The second was that of the Forces Armées pour la République Fédérale (FARF) from 1994 to 1998. The CSNPD was formed by Moïse Ketté, who had served in Habré's security forces and who recruited certain of Habré's henchmen and elements of the Codos into the CSNPD. Ketté operated in the extreme southeastern Chad, using bases across the border in the Central African Republic and Cameroon. His major goal was to drive Déby's army out of the south and to acquire reparations for the damages done by it. He explicitly made oil part of his military strategy warning: 'oil would not flow from Doba' unless his conditions were met (Buijtenhuijs 1998: 39).

The CSNPD joined a failed coup attempt against Déby in 1992. The FANT was now renamed the Armée Nationale Tchadienne (ANT). One part of which was the Guarde Républicaine, specially trained by the French to be vicious. They 'roamed the land in Toyota pick-ups holding six or seven, seeking victims' (Verschave 2000: 165). The botched coup led to 'an uninterrupted series of massacres, rapes, and village burnings' (ibid.: 152). Initially centred in Doba (August 1992), these soon became widespread throughout the south. In response to these repressions, the CSNPD signed a peace agreement with the government. However, peace was not achieved. There were reports in January 1993 of 246 people killed in twenty-two villages in Logone Oriental. Two months later there were further reports of 203 persons '*égorgées*' around Goré (MAR 2004: 9). The Chadian Association of the Rights of Man accused the army of 'genocide' (Amnesty International 1996). CSNPD in response to this campaign threatened to 'sabotage government-supported oil exploration' (MAR 2004: 10). However, early the next year (February 1994) Ketté signed a second peace accord with the central government. A month latter the CSNPD attacked, and apparently bested, a government installation at Bekerou. The Republican Guard in reprisal assaulted Ketté's home village of Beboungai. These attacks and counter-attacks effectively destabilised southern Chad, and Déby urgently needed tranquillity because the 'oil giants' were 'all investigating oil resources' (MAR 2004: 11). So in August 1994, the government and the CSNPD signed yet another peace agreement. Ketté agreed to end his resistance; the government agreed to remove its troops from the south; Ketté and a number of his troops were incorporated into the Chadian army.

Some of those in the CSNPD regarded Ketté's final peace accord with Déby as a sell-out. These rebels formed FARF, under the leadership of Laokin Bardé in 1994. FARF made it clear that its was fighting for oil, for as one leader put it, 'I'm ready to die for oil' (Petry and Bambé 2005: 101). Remember that FARF stood for Forces Armées pour la Republique Fédérale with the word 'federal' meaning that the south would control its own affairs, especially those of oil. Government troops and the FARF engaged in sporadic fighting from the end of 1994 into 1995. The intensity of the fighting increased in the spring of 1996 into what one observer labelled a 'regime of terror' (Verschave 2000: 166). On 10 October 1996 Amnesty International published a report accusing both sides, but most especially the government, of fighting a war of atrocities involving the 'banalisation' of torture (Amnesty International 1996).

During this time Déby's diplomats negotiated with Central African Republic and Cameroonian counterparts to deny FARF use of Central African or Cameroonian territory as rear-bases. This diplomacy succeeded and Bardé, realising the loss of his safe havens, signed a peace treaty with his opponent. The conditions of this agreement resembled those of earlier ones with the CSNPD and were equally ineffective in stopping combat. In fact Bardé soon recognised that they were simply a way for Déby to buy time (May and Massey 2000: 14). Time ran out on 30 October 1997, when his headquarters were attacked in Moundou in yet another round of fighting there. Many FARF leaders were killed. One account of this fighting reported, 'They killed local personalities passing by, they molested a bishop, kidnapped children, killed their parents. Forbid burial, throwing bodies to the pigs' (in Verschave 2000: 166). Then security forces, numbering an estimated five thousand, 'spread the terror' in an offensive throughout southwestern Chad (ibid.: 167): police and soldiers, 'trained by French instructors[, c]ontinued the assassinations: local officials, high school students, peasants …. The techniques of liquidation had not changed [from those in Habré's time]: torture was made banal, especially that of the *arbatachar* …, drowning, ingestion of acid …, or simply the Kalashnikov' (ibid.: 167). This round of fighting lasted until 1997 (Petry and Bambé 2005: 64–65). February 1998 witnessed yet another outburst in Moundou which lasted into May (ibid.: 90–93) New peace accords were signed in May. Bardé chose exile, was betrayed by his own kin and was killed, after which FARF effectively ceased to exist.

This pattern of fighting reveals a type of iterative string between 1982 and 1998 in southern Chad. At some place or time, government security forces provoked southern rebels, who retaliated, provoking government forces to retaliate more strongly with terror tactics. These events repeated themselves until the rebels were unable to respond. Then in another space and time, this string reiterated itself. To recapitulate: the consortium outsourced its security needs to the Chadian government which prevented any of the rebel movements from disrupting oil prospecting. Stability reigned in the Doba Basin from the perspective of the government and the consortium based upon iterative strings of attack and counter-attack that provoked 'terror' among those in the oil producing zone. 'Terror' because the violence fixed in people's memory the sights, sounds and smells of horrific death – jagged gaping wounds in sons and daughters, rotting bodies of mothers and brothers, genitalia without torsos, torsos without genitalia. It is time to consider another form of physical violence operating in southern Chad at this time.

Fear from Herder-farmer Violence

Chad is one of the poorest countries in the world. It was expensive for the Déby regime to garrison the south and provide for the consortium's security. One way of reducing these costs was to settle northerners in the south who were less prone to rebellion. Hence, the central government encouraged north–south migrations. This might be said to be the government's outsourcing of the consortium's outsourcing of its security needs. Fulani, Arabs and others arrived in 'massive' numbers (Magrin 2000: 539) and soon clashed with indigenous farmers. The conflicts intensified because of the appearance of a new type of livestock owner in the south; northern *fonctionnaires* who had used the wealth they derived from their offices to acquire large numbers of cattle, sheep and goats. These herds were entrusted to herdsmen, who were often armed and protected by the herd's owner. Such herders, confident of protection in high places, treated farmers with an aggressive arrogance (Buijtenhuijs 1995: 23). This provoked fighting often over farmers' manioc fields because these stay green late in the dry season and tempt hungry animals. Such fighting is reported as early as 1990 (Arditi 1999).

There is an iterative string at work in this herder/farmer violence. Somewhere, sometime, herders' animals destroy farmers' crops in a field; verbal fighting occurs; fighting escalates to violence; somebody kills someone else; retaliation occurs. Some other place, some other time, the animals do it again, and the string repeats itself, and so it goes throughout the south. A person killed here; another wounded there. There is a niggling trepidation, in both farmers' and herders' perceptions, that maybe sometime, somewhere, somebody will kill you. Remember the nagging drip-drip of a tap when you are trying, but not succeeding, to sleep. In the oil producing zone there is a nagging, drip-drip into peoples' unsleeping hours of the interminability of physical violence.

Fear from Structural Violence

Elsewhere I have written about the fear in the Doba Basin resulting from structural violence (Reyna 2007). Before proceeding, let me address the question of the reality of structural violence. Violence is about making bodies dysfunctional. Structural violence produces stress. Links between stress and illness are documented (Kendall-Reed and Reed 2004). Illness makes bodies dysfunctional. Physical violence uses grenades. Structural violence uses stress. Both wreak havoc on bodies. Stress was increased among people in the oil producing region by the strings involved in the construction of the oil complex, which had the power of elevating peoples' uncertainties concerning their, and their loved ones', welfare.

Sara interviewed were anxious about losing farmland, having their water polluted, receiving inadequate compensation for lost property, visits by security forces, unfair competition from new migrants, inflation and reduced access to medical and educational services. This uncertainty was existential in the sense that it was about events that at best made existence more difficult or at worst threatened it. Villagers spoke of their fears over uncertainty as *tab* (Chadian Arabic for 'suffering'). Further, they were conscious that theirs was not an ordinary suffering. The described it in Sara as *kon*, a deep suffering, like that experienced when something horrible happens, such as from witchcraft (Fieldnotes, 16 Jan 2003).[7] Otherwise put, 'deep suffering' existed for some at the beginning of the US Empire in the Chadian periphery; a lurking terror, which if Exxon was not solely responsible for, it was certainly complicit in.

Conclusion

In sum, certain strings of events that provided the security the consortium required to build the oil complex involved strings of physical or structural violence experienced by villagers in the Doba Basin as *kon*. Fear was everywhere: the grotesque torture of the *guarde républicaine*, a sly fight with pastoralists, just not knowing what might become of your land, water and the prices of things. Clearly, this fear was subjective experience of events that profoundly threatened lives. So, it was in this sense that some of the strings that strung Chad into US imperialism involved a threat logic, which is evidence consistent with the second generalisation. The following section considers observations bearing upon whether or not a performativity logic operated to construct a new cultural desire involving monsters subsequent to operation of the threat logic in the Doba Basin.

A Monstrous Performativity Logic

Some imagine the current 'US Empire' as a 'misshapen monster' (Mann 2003: 13). However, neither the US government in Chad, Exxon, nor their Chadian clients announced they would threaten peoples' welfare in the Doba Basin. Far from it, the consortium publicised a study it commissioned, which it claimed demonstrated it had brought 'improvement in the local population's living conditions' (*Report 14* 2004: 41). Further, the consortium dispatched its employees for 'consultations'. These, in principle, were to demonstrate that the consortium was a good citizen of the globalising world engaged in bottom-up development. However, most 'consultations' simply propagandised 'the dream of petroleum boom and its benefits … in the hearts of the young' (Petry and Bambé 2005: 171). The Chadian government, for its part, erected signs in the Doba Basin trumpeting: 'Oil. The hope for a better future' (Petry and Bambé 2005: in photographic section). The sequence of events that produced the consortium's self-congratulatory study, its consultations and the Chadian government haudings were strings. Because the strings sought to hide the threats consequent upon building the oil complex, these strings may be said to have exhibited a cloaking logic. But the cloaking failed.

I have twice interviewed (2002–2003, 2007) in the Doba Basin concerning peoples' attitudes and actions towards the consortium. These interviews did not involve formal sampling. Nevertheless, they included the full variety of the region's people in smaller hamlets and larger cities; males and females, old and young, educated and uneducated, farmers, merchants, local government officials, NGO workers, even the odd lower-level consortium employee. A striking attribute of these interviews was their near unanimity of one view: The consortium *dá* (Ngambay for 'does bad'). Almost everyone was sceptical of the consortium, resistant to its claims, and in many instances angry at it. However, I hasten to add that not all those interviewed criticised the consortium. A minority of higher officials in the regional government supported it. Further, the consortium was not the only object of peoples' scorn. Frequently, there were fierce critiques of the government in the same sentences that blasted the consortium.

These interviews should be seen as strings of discursive action. A first event in the string was the interviewer's question; a second event was the respondent's answer; and everywhere the response was the same: the consortium*n does not do good things, watch out*. These strings, because they recurred, were iterative. They are evidence of the failure of the Consortium/Chadian government cloaking logic. Those in the Doba Basin were *tab* ('suffering') from the 'misshapen monster'. Further, they knew theirs was not an ordinary suffering. It was *kon*, deep suffering. Such suffering can only be made by the most horrible of events, such as bereavement or sorcery. It is to the latter that attention now turns, and to the emergence of a performativity logic that breached the cloaking of the 'misshapen monster'. However, in order to understand this logic, we need to first understand certain aspects of Doba Basin peoples' cultural desire.

Cultural Desire in a World of Sorcerers and Lionmen

Actors monitor strings of events in which they participate in terms of perceptual and procedural culture already stored in their neural networks. This is an abstract way of saying that Sara, and others in the Doba Basin, worried about the suffering in their lives provoked by the consortium. In order to understand how this monitoring led to a performativity logic that produced the resistance just reported, there needs to be discussion of the cultural desire already stored in their neuronal memories. We can begin to grasp this desire by considering Chadian ontology. By 'ontology' I understand views about the nature of being. Many Chadians tend to apprehend being as 'visible' and 'invisible' worlds where forces operate. The invisible and visible worlds are, to use a phrase from the Chadian Arabic, *kulu wahid*, 'all one', i.e., a monad. The visible world is a place where a person can observe what brings about what. The invisible world may be the same place, but now it is a place where a person cannot tell what brings what about. Things are occult.

For example, once I was with a man who purchased a chicken. He tied it up so it would not run away. You could see the cord that tightly bound the poor animal's legs. We went away to do more marketing. We came back. We looked. No chicken! This occasioned astonishment, which stimulated discussion whose consensus was that some invisible force must have loosened the chicken's bondage. The chicken was some sort of shape shifter: a force popped into the visible world from the invisible one, flitting from one shape of being to another. Witches and sorcerers are shape shifters metamorphosing from their human self to animals to other, more bizarre monsters. For example, during the time of President Habré a hippopotamus waddled out of a river in the Salamat region prophesying war. People speculated, 'Maybe the hippo was a sorcerer?' In the case of the missing chicken, the interpretation was that it must have been a witch, and the man was lucky not to have introduced it into his household.

Shape shifters do their shifting because of invisible forces. Among Barma, a Sara-speaking people, *mal* is perhaps the most widespread of these forces. People warned that *mal* is a complex and difficult term. At its base, it might be imagined as an invisible causality that makes things occur. Individuals may control *mal* and use it for good or bad. Evans-Pritchard

(1937) provided the classic ethnographic distinction between witchcraft and sorcery: the former being the doing of evil without any use of implements, and the latter being doing evil with implements. A person using *mal* to achieve evil could be a sorcerer or witch, depending upon the use or the non-use of implements. For example, among the Barma, a *malamal* is a sorcerer. Some persons may use *mal* to do good things, as do the earth-chiefs of the Sara.

Many accounts have it that sorcerers 'eat' their victims (Chapelle 1986: 137; Hagenbucher-Sacripanti 1977: 261; Pairault 1995: 331; Vincent 1975: 84). Certain Sara believe that it is not the body that the sorcerer eats, but its *ndil* (a concept resembling the 'soul'). It is consumption of the *ndil* that kills, and 'Sorcerers, because they kill people, symbolise the negation of the life of the group' (Jaulin 1971: 229). They cause, in perceptual cultural terms, *kon*. How should people deal with sorcerers? Because they are terribly frightening and multiply *tab* and *kon*, they should be resisted. Sorcerers are to Sara what Grendel was to Anglo-Saxon aristocrats, monsters stored in neuronal cultural memory. So we have identified a cultural desire that is widespread in Doba Basin peoples' subjectivities. The perceptual culture of this desire is that certain creatures are sorcerers, who are monsters. Its emotional component is that such monsters eat you and so provoke great fear. Consequently, its procedural culture is resistance to them.

Where do lionmen fit into this ontology? Certain villagers among Sara peoples are believed to be able to turn themselves into a lion (*tubo*; Sara *mbai*), just as other men who are sorcerers can turn themselves into chickens, panthers or hippos. Some Sara believe that this ability is inherited, though it has to be confirmed by initiation (Brown 1975: 34–35). Sometimes lionmen are spoken of as if they were sorcerers (Fortier 1974: 135). Like sorcerers, they eat their victims; also, like sorcerers, they use invisible force. Further, lionmen have special implements that they use to exercise their force. Special lionmen lances and musical instruments have been found and were on display in Chad's National Museum (Chapelle 1986: 138). Lionmen moralities were and are ambiguous. Sometimes they do bad things, when they are sorcerers; at other times they can do good things, as we shall see below. It is time to link sorcerers and lionmen to gossip about monsters and, in so doing, to construct a new, monstrous cultural desire.

Monster Construction

Consortium cars and trucks roared by, bulldozers cleared bush, planes landed, buildings got built, dust spread everywhere. People in the oil-producing zone had seen that the consortium did a number of fearful things, and it was unclear how they did some of what they did. For example, Nodji told me that the company's flagmen had *'cet chose'* (this 'thing') that they pointed at a car driving along a road. Flagmen were consortium employees who stood by the side of consortium-built roads at spots – like sharp curves or narrow bridges – that required giving guidance to drivers. They looked hot, listless and uninterested, for the most part their flags drooping at half-mast. Then a vehicle would come and they would raise or lower their flag. But some flagmen also had the 'thing'; the radar gun is a device familiar to, and feared by, every American speeding along US motorways. It is used by police to measure your speed and, all too often, pull you over for a ticket. There is utterly no Chadian perceptual culture of 'radar guns'. Nodji told me, after flagmen pointed the 'thing', they stopped the car, and said it was going too fast. The driver would incredulously ask, 'how did you know?' Consortium people would say that the 'thing' knew. Now only sorcerers act this way, so the company's people must be sorcerers.[8] Once company employees appeared within the cultural category of sorcerer, they were placed within the realm of something monstrous – because those hot, bored looking men standing by the side of the road with their wilting flags actually ate you. Further, if flagmen did it (sorcery) then by a sort of contagious magic the consortium in general did it. Flagmen, then, might be interpreted as a monstrous metonym for the consortium.

This brings us back to lionmen prowling in the night. Nodji told me that lionmen had been attacking flagmen. Actually, he did not say 'lionmen'. Rather, he said 'lions'. At which point I told him, as I had the chauffeur, that there were no lions left in this part of Chad. He replied that yes there were, but that these were very special sorts of lions that came from shape shifting villagers. These lions were attacking, materialising out of a dark nowhere, and mauling their victims as they stood alone with their flags and 'things'.[9] In general, people appeared not to have been awfully upset about these attacks. There was a sense that the flagmen deserved it. Many flagmen had been village school teachers, paid out of villagers' scarce funds, who left teaching for higher consortium salaries. Such desertion deserved punishment.

How many lionmen attacks had there been? Nodji was uncertain, maybe three. 'How did you know they were lionmen?' I asked. The wounds on the flagmen were from lions was the response. I posed the same question to Étienne – university-educated in Paris, son of an *haute fonctionnaire*, member of the Moundou elite – if there had been lionmen attacks. He responded with a double take (as if thinking, 'how did you know?') and announced that he knew of no attacks by 'lions' in the recent past. However, implicit in his body language was that there were 'lions' prowling out in the bush in the darkness snacking on the odd flagman.

Implicit in Nodji and Étienne's accounts is a string. The first event in the string was the unexplainable action of the flagmen with the 'thing'. The second event was that someone interpreted this first event in terms of their perceptual culture of sorcery that led them to know that consortium flagmen were sorcerers to be combated. This short string had a punch. It was cultural desire-making because now a new perceptual category, consortium employees, had been added to the pre-existing perceptual culture of monstrous sorcerers, and everybody knew the procedural culture of monsters: resist them. Next I show how this new cultural desire became part of the performativity logic that diffused resistance to the consortium to others in the Doba Basin.

The novel cultural desire had become part of gossip in the oil-producing zone at the beginning of 2003. Those spreading the rumours were, as the Barma might put it, the *malawayage* (the masters-of-gossip). They were not people who had directly seen the consortium sorcerers or the lionmen, but they got the story from somebody who knew. There was a network of truck drivers, chauffeurs and itinerant traders, among others, who went from place to place spreading the tale, especially to the owners and patrons of bars, restaurants, shops and markets. These people then recounted it again to their customers who had come in on some errand from the countryside who, in turn, took the story back to their relatives, neighbours and friends in the bush. So, in a world saturated with *kon*, Doba Basin people learned: Consortium employee sorcerers ate villagers; villager lionmen ate consortium employees.

Of course, the strings that spread this gossip were exercises of force. The force resources utilised were the new culture desire about resisting consortium monsters and the discursive action that communicated this desire. The rumour takes the monstrous cultural desire from the gossiper's neuronal culture, makes it into a discursive cultural message (event 1), which is transmitted to the message's hearer, where it becomes part of the hearer's neuronal culture (event 2). Remember the strings of this gossip were repeated over and over again at the beginning of 2003. Remember, further, that these strings were those of cultural construction, the placing of the new cultural desire of consortium monsters into peoples' subjectivity. Remember, finally, that these strings of gossip occur just after the construction of the oil complex, and the operation of the threat logic. This gossip, then, is evidence consistent with the third generalisation, because it provides the observation that after operation of the threat logic, a performativity logic, gossip, constructed in the subjectivities of those Doba Basin people a new cultural desire, and a disposition to resist a new, scary monster, the consortium's sorcerer. Let us review the presentation of evidence.

The first part of this section provided observations consistent with the first generalisation; the second part offered such observations for the second generalisation; while the section immediately above did the same for observations bearing upon the third generalisation. Such evidence means that the new cultural desire specified who were monsters (consortium sorcerers) and what to do about them (resist them, as lionmen do) and, as such, function as a novel cultural force in some Doba Basin peoples' subjectivities, disposing them to resist the monstrous consortium; which, of course, is the fourth generalisation.

Conclusion

What are the implications of the preceding analysis for anthropological study of oil? Let us return to the *New York Times'* recognition that there *is* an 'American Empire', and that we had better 'Get Used to It'. Of course, this is over-simplification. Globally the predominant structuring is of competing informal imperialisms with, at the current conjuncture, US imperialism dominant, if probably in decline. Oil is of such importance to the success of these structures of imperial domination that imperialists need to control it. It has been controlled in the case of developing petro-states when oil complexes have been constituted that operate to ensure substantial capital accumulation of oil revenues from the developing states in the coffers of their imperial dominators. However, we have seen in the case of Chad how such constitution leads to construction in Chadian subjectivities of novel cultural desires. These were a veritable new monster culture that was a pre-condition of resistance to imperial domination.

There is a more general literature concerning what happens to people's subjectivities in developing states during the construction of capitalist complexes. The Comaroffs, for example, report that 'millennial capitalism', their term for the contemporary capitalist conjuncture, is coupled in southern Africa with increased witchcraft, sorcery and other preternatural malevolencies (Comaroff and Comaroff 1999). Others have noted that as capitalist complexes develop so too do cultural desires about witchcraft, sorcery, vampires and devils (Geschiere 1997; Nash 1993; Ogembo 2007; Stewart and Strathern 2004; Taussig 1994; White 2000; Whitehead 2002). Why? I believe formal and informal capitalist empires seeking to constitute imperial domination generally cause fear, due to either physical or structural violence. The strings of violent events – butcheries galore – making this fear are threat logics. Because the role of capitalist institutions in this fear is often 'occult' (Comaroff and Comaroff 1999) (outsourced in the case of Chad), threat logics are subject to interpretation on the basis of pre-existing monstrous invisible worlds. Such interpretations may construct old or new monster cultures, whose cultural desires motivate resistance to the monstrous. Sometimes resistance goes astray as, for example, in a case described by Ogembo (2007) where resistance is not directed against agents of capitalist imperialism, but against elderly, innocent women accused of witchcraft. A similar situation seems to exist for Ekholm-Friedman (in this volume) in Congo-Brazzaville where people have been impoverished by the development of an oil complex, and where witchcraft accusations are directed against children. What is striking about the Doba Basin situation is that the link between building the oil complex to augment the US capitalist empire and the people being dominated by these strings is less occult. After all, flagmen were caught red-handed with their 'things' going about the business of sorcery.

The preceding suggests that an anthropological analysis of oil might emphasise constituting and constructing. By this I mean it should describe, and explain, the constitution of the objective structures involved in the production, distribution and consumption of petroleum revenues; which I believe to be those of informal, capitalist imperialism. It should equally depict, and explain, the subjective structures such imperialisms provoke; which I believe to be for many the result of the threat logics these imperialisms operate. The subjective structures resultant from these threat logics should be analysed to reveal if there is construction of cultural desires to resist the monsters of imperial threats. Finally, I predict that such cultural constructions may well produce anti-Beowulfs: lionmen who are heroes, seeking to do unto imperial sorcerers what Beowulf did unto anti-imperial Grendels.

Notes

1. Chadwick (1959) emphasises the monsters' role in *Beowulf.*
2. Hunt (2006) reveals how widespread the acceptance of the US as an empire is among non-Marxist thinkers.
3. Devitt (1991), Leplin (1997) and Psillos (1999) provide rigorous rationales for realism.
4. Empirical data comes from four sources: recent fieldwork in Chad (2002–2003, 2007); earlier fieldwork (1968 to 1980); document study of institutions involved with building the oil complex; and previously published ethnographic sources. Some informants were involved in oil exploration.
5. Descriptions of Esso's proposed activities in Chad can be found in Esso (1999) and those of the World Bank are in IBRD (2000).
6. Discussions of the distribution between Chad and the members of the oil consortium of the money generated by oil production agree that Exxon and its partners will receive 'the maximum and spend the least' (Agir Ici-Survie 1999: 33 and 36–38); see also Ravignon 2000 and Djimrabaye 2005).

7. I am uncertain to what language *kon* belongs. I first heard it in a largely Ngambay village. However, some informants indicated it is a word in non-Sara languages.
8. Informants elsewhere in Chad have described sorcerers' instruments in terms of Western technology. For example, I gathered material on *masass*, a form of sorcery experienced by Chadian Arabs. One instrument used to cause the sorcery was described to me by one informant as like a 'television camera'.
9. There is another account of lionmen attacks just prior to the onset of oil production (Margonelli 2007). Interviews conducted in villages around Komé during the summer of 2007 suggested that the lionmen had gone into abeyance.

References

Agir Ici-Survie. 1999. *Projet pétrolier Tchad-Cameroun: des pipes sur le pipe-line*. Marseilles: Agone.

Amnesty International. 1996. Chad: A Country Under the Arbitrary Rule of the Security Forces with the Tacit Consent of Other Countries. Report #: AFR20/011/1996. http://amnesty.se/women.nsf/. (Accessed: 11 November 2008).

Anon. 1999. *Beowulf*. New York: Signet Classics.

Arditi, Claude. 1999. Paysans sara et éleveurs arabes dans le sud du tchad: du conflit à la cohabitation. In *L'homme et l'animal dans la basin du lac Tchad*, ed. Catherine Baroin and Jean Boutrais, 555–73. Paris: IRD.

Arrighi, Giovanni. 2005. Hegemony Unravelling, Part 1. *New Left Review* 32: 23–80.

Bouquet, Christian. 1982. *Tchad: genèse d'un conflit*. Paris: Harmattan.

Brody, Reed. 2001. The Prosecution of Hissène Habré-An African Pinochet. *New England Law Review*. 35: 23–31.

Brown, Ellen. 1975. *Family and Village Structure of the Sara Nar*. PhD dissertation. Cambridge: University of Cambridge.

Buijtenhuijs, Robert. 1995. *Democratisation en Afrique au Sud du Sahara, 1992–1995*. Leiden: Centre d'Études Africaines.

———. 1998. *Transitions et élections au Tchad 1993–1997: restauration autoritaire et recomposition politique*. Paris: Karthala.

Butler, Judith. 1993. *Bodies That Matter: On the Discursive Limits of 'Sex'*. London: Routledge.

Chadwick, Nora. 1959. The Monsters and Beowulf. In *The Anglo-Saxons*, ed. Peter Clemoes, 171–203. London: Bowes and Bowes.

Chapelle, Jean. 1986. *Le Peuple Tchadienne: ses racines et sa vie quotidienne*. Paris: Harmattan.

Comaroff, Jean and John. 1999. Occult Economies and the Violence of Abstraction. *American Ethnologist* 26(3): 279–301.

Dadi, Abderahman. 1987. *Tchad: l'état retrouvé*. Paris: Harmattan.

Devitt, Michael. 1991. *Realism and Truth*. Princeton: Princeton University Press.

Djimrabaye, Renodji. 2005. *Pétrole et dette: cas du Tchad. Reseau de suivi des activités liées au pétrole du moyen Chari*. http://www.oilwatch.org/2005/documentos/deuda_tchad_fra.pdf. (Accessed 17 December 2008).

Ellis, Stephen. 2003. Briefing: West Africa and Its Oil. *African Affairs* 102: 135–8.

Environmental Defense Fund. 1997. *Questions Concerning the World Bank and Chad/Cameroon Oil and Pipeline Project*. (Ed. Korinna Horta). New York: EDF.

Esso. 1999. *Chad Export Project: Project Description*. Vols 1–6. http://Essochad.com/Chad/Library/Documentation/Chad_DO_Support_V1.asp.(Accessed: 16/12/2008)

Evans-Pritchard, Edward Evan. 1937. *Witchcraft, Oracles and Magic among the Azande*. Oxford: Oxford University Press.

Fortier, Joseph. 1974. *Dragon et sorcières du pays mbai.* Paris: Colin.

Gaide, M. 1956. Au Tchad, les transformations subies par l'agriculture traditionnelle sous l'influence de la culture cotonnière. *L'Agronomie Tropicale* 11(5–6): 597–623, 707–31.

Gallagher, John and Ronald Robinson. 1953. The Imperialism of Free Trade. *Economic History Review* 9(1): 1–15.

Geschiere, Peter. 1997. *The Modernity of Witchcraft: Politics and the Occult in Postcolonial Africa.* Charlottesburg: University of Virginia Press.

Hagenbucher-Sacripanti, Frank. 1977. Éléments de magie et de sorcellerie chez les arabes d'Afrique centrale'. *Cahiers O.R.S.T.O.M., sér. Sci. Hum.* 14(3): 251–88.

Harvey, David. 2003. *The New Imperialism.* New York: Oxford University Press.

Hudson, Micheal. 2003. *Super Imperialism: The Origins and Fundamentals of U.S. World Dominance.* London: Pluto Press.

Human Rights Watch. 2006. *Hissène Habré – The Political Police Files.* New York: HRW Global Issues, International Justice. http;//www.hrw.org/justice/habre/habre-police.htm. (Accessed: 19 September 2008).

Hunt, Michael. 2006. Review of Charles S. Maier, *Among Empires.* H-Diplo-Roundtables. http://www.h-net.org/~diplo/roundtables/PDF/Hunt-MaierRoundtable.pdf (Accessed: 12 September 2008).

IBRD. 2000. Project Appraisal Document on Proposed International Bank for Reconstruction and Development Loans to Chad and Cameroon. Report # 19343 AFR. Washington, DC: World Bank.

Jaulin, Robert. 1971. *La Mort Sara.* Paris: Plon.

Kendall-Reed, Penny and Stephen Reed. 2004. *The Complete Doctor's Stress Solution: Understanding, Treating, and Preventing Stress-related Illness.* Toronto: Robert Rose.

Lanne, Bernard. 1981. Le Sud du Tchad sans la guerre civile (1979–1980). *Politique Africaine* 3: 75–89.

———. 1983. Le Sud, l'état et la révolution. *Politique Africaine* 16: 30–44.

Leplin, Jarett. 1997. *A Novel Defense of Scientific Realism.* Oxford: Oxford University Press.

Ley-Ngardigal, Djimadoum. 1999. *Dossier Françafrique.* http://www.communisme-bolchevisme.ner/dossier_france_afrique.htm (Accessed: 10 August 2008).

Magnant, Jean-Pierre. 1986. *La Terra Sara, terre tchadienne.* Paris: Harmattan.

Magrin, Géraud. 2000. Insécurité alimentaire et culture contonnière au Sud du Tchad. *Cahiers d'Études Africaines* 159: 525–49.

———. 2001. *Le Sud du Tchad en Mutation: des champs de coton aux sirènes de l'or noir.* St.-Maur: Sépia.

Mann, Michael. 2003. *Incoherent Empire.* London: Verso.

MAR. 2004. *Chronology for Southerners in Chad. Minorities at Risk.* University of Maryland. http://www.cidcm.umd.edu/inscr/mar/chronology.asp?groupID=48302. (Accessed: 8 September 2008).

Margonelli, Lisa. 2007. *Oil on the Brain: Adventures from the Pump to the Pipeline.* New York: Nan A. Talese.

May, Roy and Simon Massey. 1999. *Chad: Social, Political and Economic Situation Par. 1999.* Writenet Country Papers. http://unhcr.ch/refworld/country/writenet/writed.html. (Accessed: 14 September 2008).

Nash, June. 1993. *We Eat the Mines and the Mines Eat Us: Dependency and Exploitation in Bolvian Tin Mines.* New York: Columbia, University Press.

Nolutshunga, Sam. 1996. *Limits of Anarchy: Intervention and State Formation in Chad.* Charlottesville, VA: University Press of Virginia.

Ogembo, Justus. 2007. *Contemporary Witchcraft in Gusii, Southwestern Kenya.* Leiston, NY: Edwin Mellon Press.

Pairault, Claude. 1995. *Retour au pays d'Iro: chronique d'un village du Tchad.* Paris: Karthala.

Petry, Martin and Naygotimti Bambé. 2005. *Le Pétrole du Tchad: rêve ou cauchemar pour les populations?* Paris: Karthala.

Psillos, Stathis. 1999. *Scientific Realism: How Science Tracks Truth.* New York: Routledge.

Ravignan, Antoine de. 2000. Tchad-Cameroun: pour qui le petrole coulera-til? Paris: FIDH. http://www.fidh.org/afriq/rapport/2000pdf/fr/petchcam.pdf. (Accessed: 12 October 2008).

Report 14. 2004. Chad Export Project Report # 14. 1st Quarter 2004. N'Djamena, Chad: Esso Exploration and Production Chad Inc.

Reyna, Stephen. 1990. *Wars Without End: The Political Economy of a Precolonial African State.* Hanover, NH: University Press of New England.

———. 2001. Force, Power and *String Being?* Max Planck Institute for Social Anthropology Working Papers. Working Paper # 20.

———. 2002. *Connections: Brain, Mind and Culture in a Social Anthropology.* London: Routledge.

———. 2003a. Force, Power, and the Problem of Order. *Sociologus* 3(2): 199–223.

———. 2003b. Imagining Monsters: A Structural History of Warfare in Chad. In *Globalization and Violence*, ed. Jonathan Friedman..279–309. Walnut Park, CA: Altamira.

———. 2005. American Imperialism: 'The Current Runs Swiftly'. *Focaal: European Journal of Anthropology* 45(July–August): 129–151.

———. 2006. What is Interpretation? A Neurohermeneutic Account. *Focaal* 48: 131–43.

———. 2007. Waiting, the Sorcery of Modernity: Transnational Corporation, Oil, and Terrorism in Chad. *Sociologus* 57(1): 131–9.

Rolls, Edmund. 2005. *Emotion Explained.* Oxford: Oxford University Press.

Scott, James. 1990. *Domination and the Arts of Resistance.* New Haven: Yale University Press.

Stewart, Pamela and Andrew Strathern. 2004. *Witchcraft, Sorcery, Rumor and Gossip.* London: Cambridge University Press.

Survie. 2000. *La Françafrique. Survie.* http://www.survie-france.org/article.php?id_article=164. (Accessed: 8 August 2008).

Taussig, Michael. 1994. *The Devil and Commodity Fetishism in South America.* Chapel Hill: University of North Carolina Press.

Terrorism Knowledge Base. 1985. *Terrorism Knowledge Base.* MIPT. http://www.tkb.org. home.jsp. (2 February 2008).

Verschave, François-Xavier. 1998. *Françafrique: La Plus Longue Scandale de la République.* Paris: Stock.

———. 2000. *Noir silence: qui arrêtera la Françafrique.* Paris: Arènes.

———. 2002. *Noir Chirac.* Paris: Arènes.

Verschave, François-Xavier and Laurent Beccaria. 2001. *Noir procès: offense à chefs d'États.* Paris: Arènes.

Vincent, Jeanne-Francoise. 1975. *Le Pouvoir et le sacré chez les Hadjeray du Tchad.* Paris: Anthropos.

White, Luise. 2000. *Speaking with Vampires: Rumor and History in Colonial Africa.* Los Angeles: University of California Press.

Whitehead, Neil. 2002. *Dark Shamans and the Poetics of Violent People.* Durham: Duke University Press.

Yates, Douglas. 1996. *The Rentier State in Africa: Oil Rent Dependency and Neo-colonialism in the Republic of Gabon.* Trenton, NJ: Africa World Press.

PART III

LATIN AMERICA

Chapter 7

THE PEOPLE'S OIL

Nationalism, Globalisation and the Possibility of Another
Country in Brazil, Mexico and Venezuela

John Gledhill

As Karl (1997) has demonstrated, nations that possess an abundance of
'natural wealth' in petroleum have an abysmal track record on providing a decent standard of living for the majority of their citizens. Coronil's
(1997) book on Venezuela not only lends strong support to that argument
but also disentangles stories of 'development failure' from Occidentalist
explanations focused on Latin America's supposed social, cultural and
political deficits relative to the North Atlantic world. Scepticism about
such explanations is more vital than ever as northern powers and multilateral agencies insist that the region can only overcome its legacy of
deficits by abandoning all remaining barriers to foreign investment.

Any resistance to these prescriptions that envisages reassertion of national control over resources and the use of the revenues they generate to
reduce social inequalities is denounced as a return to an atavistic 'populist' tradition that can only thwart 'development'. This doctrine is maintained despite the fact that in Mexico, supposed exemplar of neo-liberal
virtue, the modest 2 per cent annual rate of growth of income per capita
produced by huge increases in exports and foreign investment since 2000
has been accompanied by continuing regression in the living standards
of the majority of citizens and an ever-growing informal sector filling the
gap left by the failure of benefits to trickle down.

In this chapter I broaden the discussion of oil and politics beyond petro-states in the strict sense, that is, countries in which oil exports are the
mainstay of the national economy, so that sheer abundance of revenues
underpins a rentier state. I examine the relationship between oil and politics through a focus on the relationships between governments and the

societies that they govern. One question is the relationship between political and social elites. An obvious contrast between Latin America and East Asia is the way that the groups governing the latter countries after the Second World War guided business elites toward a strategy for future success in the global economy (Wade 2003). In Latin America neither military regimes nor civilian political parties have ever had such a directive role. Even in Mexico, where, in contrast to Brazil, agrarian social property relations were transformed by comprehensive land reform, expropriated landlords were compensated by opportunities to invest in a politically featherbedded industrial sector. After 1940 state policies consistently favoured modernised capitalist farms and agro-industries. Leading figures in the 'revolutionary' political elite duly took their place in this reconfigured class structure, fostering a model of development in which politics protects elite incomes, which persists to this day. In the course of the crises provoked by the neo-liberal economic restructuring of the 1990s, this protection extended to schemes to compensate business groups for their losses, funded from general taxation (Gledhill 2002).

Intra- and inter-elite relations are not, however, the sole focus of my analysis. Latin America's largely undemocratic past is often explained by its supposedly weak 'civil society'. Yet that kind of Occidentalist perspective devalues the role of popular struggles to achieve greater social justice and better government in nineteenth- and twentieth-century Latin American history. What Hale (2002) describes as the historical 'volatility' of Latin American civil society is evident again today in the appearance of strong grassroots movements of opposition to neo-liberalism in many countries. The most powerful of these are responsible for the governments that North Atlantic critics dismiss as populist.

A word of caution is necessary at this point. The other side of this volatility is that precarious livelihood conditions, exacerbated by growing violence and insecurity, promote antagonisms amongst subaltern sectors of society: in striving to preserve a modicum of social dignity and dissociate themselves from yet poorer citizens subjected to racial stereotyping and criminalisation, some lower-middle-class, working-class and peasant Latin Americans remain susceptible to the politics of fear with which established political classes and media corporations seek to undermine radical alternatives at the ballot box. Nevertheless, the role of 'those below' in Latin American politics should not be discounted. The history of oil indicates that it has long been a central popular symbol of the possibility of creating a country whose wealth is shared. As such, oil is at the centre of a series of what I will term 'popular imaginaries'.

Let me say more about how I am deploying this term. Another example relevant to our case studies is that of racial democracy, the idea that, in contrast to the segregated United States, extensive miscegenation eroded discrimination based on phenotypic appearance, so that any residual social prejudice is based largely on class. The practice of Brazilians in regard to the situational interpretation of phenotypic differences does reveal that their multiple mode approach to locating individuals within a range of categories has a very different logic from the binary mode of racial classification of the United States: it may even produce a different reading of an individual's colour if the context suggests a class position (Fry 1995). Yet the everyday experience of poorer Brazilians tends to confirm the continuing assumption of an absolute superiority of 'whiteness' as a point of reference and the pervasiveness of discrimination against indigenous and black people. The way that race and class combine in the case of Brazil is neatly illustrated by an incident that took place in 2006 at a supermarket checkout in Salvador, Bahia. Frustrated by the length of the queue and refused priority, a middle-class white woman, who suffered from a nervous disorder that probably accounts for her willingness to articulate what is generally unspoken, told the cashier that she was 'uma negrinha que deve estar na cozinha' (a little black girl who should be in the kitchen).

As Sheriff (2001) has argued, as a description of reality that elites in Brazil (and Venezuela) have assiduously fostered, racial democracy is a myth whose fit to reality may be firmly rejected by poor citizens. Yet they can still appropriate it as myth in another sense, in their own imagination of what a better country could be like, and turn imagination into a desire that motivates actions. The political problem that such imaginaries pose for elites is that they are persistently rearticulated and may be fortified by unintended consequences of the neo-liberal project. In the case of racial hierarchy, an evident 'decline of deference' to some extent feeds off neo-liberal discourses about citizenship and the rights of the poor. The woman in the supermarket was not only instantly surrounded by an angry crowd but also failed to secure immediate release on being handed over to the police when she tried to establish her claims to impunity with the classic declaration, 'Do you know with whom you are talking?' In the case of the imaginary of 'the people's oil', loss of sovereignty over resources is symptomatic of the abandonment of any 'national project' by neo-liberal regimes seeking to deepen the 'opening' of national economies at whatever social cost. In this popular reassertion of the value of the national, opposition to privatisation of strategic resources (which include water as well as energy) becomes a moral economy argument in a double sense: the privatisers are seen as alienating what should be public goods in their personal interest as well as 'selling the patrimony of the nation' to foreign interests. The critique is insistent because privatisation has led to unsupportable increases in the everyday costs of household reproduction.

The idea that reformed national states might use oil and gas revenues to improve the lives of the poor and stimulate the development of other economic sectors might appear eccentric in Latin America because past political regimes so lamentably failed to fulfil their promises on these fronts, lending superficial credibility to the charge of a return to past populism. Yet an extraterrestrial visiting our planet might need help in understanding the claims of the Bush Administration that the governments of Evo Morales in Bolivia and Hugo Chávez in Venezuela were threats to democracy given that both gained unprecedented majorities of the popular vote in free elections and have exercised power in a scrupulously constitutional manner. It is therefore worth asking whether radically reformed national states, based on not only the electoral defeat of established political classes but also new kinds of popular participation in politics, might not do better than their predecessors in terms of delivering the benefits of national oil wealth to the mass of their citizens.

There are, however, still considerable grounds for scepticism about whether what might now seem a historical possibility can become an enduring reality. In this article I examine historical factors that have shaped political struggles over what is done with the wealth generated by oil in three Latin American countries. Venezuela, with 7.4 per cent of world reserves, and Mexico, with 1.2 per cent, are both oil exporters. Brazil, whose vast economy has been vulnerable to energy deficits, is not simply in the happy position of possessing newly discovered oil deposits that are now economical to exploit following the global oil price hike but is also at the forefront of development of biofuel alternatives to oil. Both the similarities and differences between these cases are illuminating, and examining the differences offers insights into the way the use of oil wealth is shaped by shifting balances of struggle and alliance between distinct social actors inside and beyond the industry itself, helping us grasp the structural conditions that promote or inhibit the benefits that ordinary citizens derive from such 'national' assets.

Differences, Similarities, Convergences

I begin by comparing Venezuela and Mexico. Oil accounts for the bulk of Venezuela's export earnings and almost half of all government revenues come from the state-owned Petróleos de Venezuela, S.A. (PDVSA) (Talbot 2002). From the time the nation's destiny was first coupled to petroleum in the 1930s, under the dictatorship of General Juan Vicente Gómez, oil exports have created a rentier state. As Coronil (1997: 391) shows, far from making state-projected fantasies of development more realistic, the oil boom triggered by the creation of the Organisation of the Petroleum Exporting Countries (OPEC) in 1973 consigned these dreams to ashes 'as foreign banks recycled petrodollars into loans', the national subsoil was mortgaged to acquire further loans that were dissipated in wasted investment, consumption and capital flight, and the ultimate 'harvest' of this 'sowing of the oil' was 'the highest debt per capita in Latin America and a decimated economy'. Pretty much the same epitaph might be recited over Mexico's contemporaneous 'oil boom', a project accompanied by spectacular growth of state-run enterprises throughout the economy and a vast increase in public-sector employment that ended with a catastrophic financial meltdown in 1982. In Mexico, oil production and distribution is monopolised by a state company, Pemex (Petróleos Mexicanos), created after the nationalisation of foreign oil companies' assets in 1938.

Yet, although Mexico failed as miserably as Venezuela in its efforts to 'sow' its oil wealth, it has never been a petro-state. Oil accounts for less than 2.5 per cent of Mexico's gross domestic product. Petroleum exports became a less significant source of foreign earnings than remittances from Mexicans working abroad for the first time in 2004. That the country needs to export its citizens to keep the national economy afloat underscores the weaknesses of Mexico's version of neo-liberal capitalism. While politically connected national business groups with transnational reach have prospered, especially in commercial and financial services, telecoms and electronic media, the destruction of domestic industry and agriculture has fuelled a growing informal economy alongside a growth of assembly plants and non-oil extractive industries. These extractive industries represent a worrying historical regression toward dependence on export of nonrenewable natural resources in states such as Chiapas (Villafuerte 2001).

Political civility was severely reduced between the 2000 and 2006 presidential elections. The 2006 victory of Felipe Calderón, candidate of the right-wing National Action Party (PAN) of the outgoing president, Vicente Fox, was challenged as fraudulent by the candidate of the Centre-left Party of the Democratic Revolution (PRD), Andrés Manuel López Obrador, the former mayor of Mexico City. In an unusually dirty campaign, López Obrador was presented by Calderón as the equivalent of Venezuela's Hugo Chávez and 'a danger to the country'. The less than transparent defeat of a platform that argued the case for redistributing wealth and reforming a capitalism based on the 'traffic of political influences' has increased polarisation not only between classes but also between those regions, particularly the northern border zone, to which increasing economic integration with the United States has brought some benefits, and the centre and south, where the impact has been generally negative. Yet the electoral parties of the Centre-left also faced a challenge in 2006 from more radical forces.

Calling for a construction of a new and 'pluralistic' Left outside the arena of electoral politics, 'The Other Campaign', led by the Zapatista Army of National Liberation's Subcomandante Marcos, condemned the PRD for being as neo-liberalised as the government of Luiz Inácio Lula da Silva in Brazil, while painting it as another expression of the wholesale corruption of Mexico's political class. Given that the PRD had incorporated an ever-growing number of defectors from the Party of the Institutional Revolution (PRI), which monopolised power for seventy years before Fox won in 2000 but came in a poor third in 2006, this charge seemed plausible to many. Yet one effect of the PRI's poor showing in the disputed 2006 elections was to drive the rump of the old ruling party into ever closer alliance with the PAN government, a process already incipient under Fox.

Despite the fact that the opposition (including the PRD itself) is divided and fragmented, this underscores the limitations of the regime change that followed Fox's election in 2000 in the eyes of many Mexicans. It also reawakened fears that the agenda of the new government and its PRI allies would include privatisation of Pemex. In April 2008 President Calderón submitted an energy reform plan to the legislature that would allow Pemex management greater autonomy and offer private capital new opportunities to invest in refineries and transportation infrastructure and to bid for service contracts. Calderón also proposed a 'citizens bond' scheme that would allow Mexicans to acquire a personal stake in Pemex, a proposal with interesting possibilities, since the bonds would be tradeable and could therefore become concentrated in a small number of private hands. Calderón's plans are considered a step toward privatisation by opponents of the government and too limited by spokespersons of some of the transnational oil companies. Yet Calderón's repeated insistence that Pemex would not be privatised replicated the posture of his predecessor, Vicente Fox. Fox, former boss of Coca-Cola Mexico and a self-avowed enthusiast for neo-liberalism, might well have had strong aspirations to move down the road of full privatisation on entering office, but by 2003 he felt obliged to declare publicly that 'Pemex is not for sale'. Despite repeated efforts to privatise parts of the national oil industry by stealth, oil nationalisation has remained a peculiarly potent symbol in Mexican political culture, for reasons explored in more detail below, and the political risks of seeming to embrace privatisation of Pemex remain substantial. Furthermore, in the past privatisation was not an attractive option for political elites for other reasons: milking the cash cow of the state-owned company provided governments with a means of reducing the short-term impacts of mismanagement of the rest of the economy and a covert source of finance for electoral campaigns.

While Mexico has not yet experienced a complete decomposition of its established political class, this is exactly what brought Chávez to power in Venezuela. For some this was a shock, but critics of the thesis of Venezuelan 'exceptionalism' within Latin America have rewritten the twentieth-century history of the country in a way that makes it look more like Mexico, deconstructing images of peaceful democracy and class compromise based on multiparty alternation and the inclusion of a plurality of social sectors, the communists excluded. Grassroots dissidence predated the 1989 Caracas riots that surprised Venezuela's elites when Carlos Andrés Pérez returned to power to invoke the magic of neo-liberalism as an unexpected alternative to the statism that had marked his disastrous first term in office from 1974 to 1978. Chávez's electoral success in 1998 and the sustainability of his Bolivarian Revolution since then are the product, under conditions of Gramscian 'organic crisis' in the old regime, of the convergence of distinct, multiclass social and political forces that are by no means all controlled by the figure of the president, whose own face, with its mixture of indigenous and African features, also embodies the possibility of making Venezuela's myth of racial democracy real (Cannon 2004; Valencia 2005).

Whilst Venezuela under Chávez uses oil exports as an instrument of foreign policy, Brazil only attained oil self-sufficiency in 2006. Nevertheless, Getúlio Vargas established a complete state monopoly over oil exploration and extraction in Brazil while presiding over a regime that had much in common with that which nationalised Mexico's oil. The differences between Mexico and Brazil have a lot to do with the historical role of the agro-export elite in the latter, since Vargas used rather than challenged the landlord class, and later moves toward land reform were halted by the military coup of 1964. The Brazilian state's monopoly was abandoned in the 1990s under the neo-liberal social democratic government of Fernando Henrique Cardoso, although the state company, Petrobras, has remained the dominant player in the industry, in its new guise as a public corporation that seeks to provide value for its shareholders but also has a legal duty of 'accountability to the Brazilian population' (*Petrobras Corporate Information*, 2004). In contrast to Mexico's Pemex, which has drifted into a crisis of undercapitalisation, Petrobras has successfully exploited its expertise in deep-water drilling and gas as a global energy corporation competing for contracts outside Brazil, including the types of contracts in which Mexico itself now allows foreign participation. Brazil is also world leader in the development of biofuels, developments with further social implications. Some of these renewable resource technologies entail giving more land over to transgenic crops that are not foodstuffs in a country where regional political magnates own farms the size of Wales. Pressures on migrant workers in a sugar cane industry striving to increase the production of alcohol have led to deaths from heart failure because they take amphetamines to keep pace with ever-rising productivity targets (Sartori 2007: 17).

To judge from the complaints of transnational oil companies about the terms that they are offered by the Brazilian state's National Petroleum Agency (ANP, Agência Nacional do Petróleo), the state-enforced economic nationalism once pursued by Getúlio Vargas and reproduced by technocrats under the military regime retains some purchase in the country. Many Brazilians who voted for Lula's Workers' Party (PT) government complain about the president's refusal to rock the boat with the international financial system, his prioritisation of the land and energy needs of agro-exporters over the interests of the environment, indigenous people and the landless movement, and the limitations of his measures to reduce poverty in Brazil's cities. Whilst most critics would concede that Lula's spending on this latter area is vastly greater than that of the previous administration, the long-term structural impact of his social programmes has been questioned (see, e.g., Hall 2006) and the PT's reforming image in the political field has been tarnished by serious corruption scandals. Nevertheless, despite conflicts of national interest (especially over the future of biofuels), Lula maintains cordial relations with Hugo Chávez. Both advocate adjusting the relations between national states and global power structures by building supranational coalitions of the south. Brazil therefore raises the question of whether national projects might be redefined in the region without departing from the broad premises of a neo-liberal market society. Public oil corporations are also potentially crucial test cases of the possibilities and limitations of stakeholder capitalism, not only because of the scale of the investments needed and the technological complexity of their operations but also because of the threat that oil exploitation has posed historically both to the environment and to the sustainability of livelihoods in regions where drilling and refining takes place.

I will begin further discussion with Mexico, the country whose industry seems most in crisis. Before analysing its causes, however, I will explore what the nationalisation of the industry in 1938 tells us about the relationship between the Mexican people and what was, by the standards of its day, the most radical reforming state in Latin America. This is also a story that brings out another side of Mexico's subsequently much-reviled oil workers' union.

Oil Nationalisation and Popular Nationalism

In 1938 the president of Mexico was Lázaro Cárdenas, who had already undertaken the largest land reform in Latin American history. The new challenge facing the Cárdenas government was a dispute over wages between the oil workers and the foreign companies dominating Mexico's fledgling oil industry. Throughout the negotiations the companies threatened to withdraw investments to Venezuela and argued that oil workers' wages in Mexico were already vastly higher than those earned by other sectors. The workers themselves were divided, since there were three different factions in their union's leadership, only one of which was willing to push the ongoing dispute over the collective contract to the point of demanding nationalisation of the companies (González 1981: 173). Cárdenas' own classically populist statecraft, orientated to demobilising the regional worker and peasant movements that had helped bring him to power by incorporating them into national organisations whose top leaders were appointed by the president, was partly responsible for this situation, since he had allowed two main trade unions to survive so that he could play one off against the other and ensure that the communists were kept out of the game altogether. Cárdenas was as strong as any postrevolutionary president. Yet he was not initially in favour of expropriation, not only because he feared international economic sanctions or even armed intervention but also because he doubted that Mexicans could run the industry themselves (González 1981: 174, 179ff). The country lacked tankers to ship its oil, and the companies had made it clear that they would withdraw their technical experts.

Nor was this an ideal moment to have another crisis. It was less than a decade since Mexico had emerged from its last major civil war, the *Cristero* rebellion provoked by President Calles' attempts to subordinate the Catholic Church to a secular state. The radical agrarian reform had caused new conflicts and economic disruption in what was still a predominantly rural country. Yet, after the companies remained intransigent in the face of a Supreme Court ruling that not only backed the Arbitration Tribunal's decision in favour of the workers but also added instructions to compensate them for lost earnings, mounting domestic political pressure, spearheaded by the Mexican Workers' Confederation (CTM, Confederación de Trabajadores Mexicanos) left Cárdenas with no alternative but to take a leap in the dark. He remained so uncertain about the outcome that he made plans to resign and leave the country if things went badly (González 1981: 183–84).

Yet Cárdenas was proved unduly pessimistic about foreign reactions: while the British protested, the US government under Franklin Roosevelt accepted the principle that sovereign nations have a right to control their own resources and acquiesced in the expropriation subject to reasonable compensation for the companies affected (González 1981: 187ff). The ambassador in Mexico whom Roosevelt instructed to carry forward this policy, Joseph Daniels, had not only been selected for this sensitive post because he was a loyal partisan of Roosevelt's Good Neighbour doctrine but also because he was personally wedded to the same ideas about moral improvement of the labouring classes as Cárdenas himself. Daniels publicly declared that oil expropriation would provide the Mexican state with resources to promote a general increase in living standards and purchasing power that would not only promote political stability but ultimately prove more beneficial to the economic interests of the United States than unreflective support for the transnational oil cartel (González 1981: 189).

In this crucial respect, the Mexican oil expropriation belongs to a different era than the one in which we now live, as evidenced by the difference between George W. Bush's reaction to the 2006 Bolivian gas expropriation and Lula's reaffirmation of Roosevelt's principle (despite the grumblings of Petrobras' top management). Yet ordinary Mexicans produced the biggest surprise of all.

The Cárdenas government had been obliged to 'engineer' public demonstrations in favour of its other policies, which divided public opinion. Yet, in the case of the oil nationalisation, thousands upon thousands of citizens took to the streets throughout the country in spontaneous demonstrations of enthusiasm that included people who were more generally found protesting about government actions. Even more impressively, these citizens responded generously to government calls for donations to pay compensation to the companies. Women queued to hand over their jewellery, and even the poorest of peasants turned up at the collection points clutching the few things of value they possessed, down to their last chicken (González 1981: 181). The queues brought together citizens who had been killing each other not very long before. Catholics who had fought with the *Cristero* rebels in the 1920s joined pro-government agrarian fighters to do their bit for the country and priests gave sermons praising the actions of a government that they normally detested for its anti-clericalism. This was not a country and 'people' conjured up by a nation-building elite seeking to hegemonise a society that lacked any sense of unity. Although Mexico remained fractured and conflictive on lines of class, region and ethnicity, nation builders could also draw on a *popular* nationalist imaginary. This was an imaginary forged by a century of territorial losses to the *gringos* and it embodied widespread yearning for the peace, education and 'material improvements' promised by a state born of social revolution, rather than from the kind of coup d'état that ushered in the *Estado Novo* (New State) of Getúlio Vargas in Brazil in 1937, or the ten-year dictatorship of Pérez Jiménez that followed the first short-lived government of Acción Democrática (AD) in Venezuela, itself installed by a military coup in 1945.

The other surprise delivered by the oil nationalisation was that Mexicans could run and develop the industry successfully without foreign technicians. By withdrawing their managers and encouraging all their lower-level expatriate technical staff to leave Mexico, the foreign companies left day-to-day management of the industry largely in the hands of unionised blue-collar workers (Philip 1999: 38). Contrary to expectations, the transfer of the industry into Mexican hands did not produce a technical meltdown. The unintended consequence of the transnationals' complete withdrawal was that the Pemex union, the STPRM (Sindicato de Trabajadores Petroleros de la República Mexicana), acquired extraordinary power, since it not only regulated access to jobs but also took control over much of the enterprise's subcontracting of goods and services.

The US administration's decision to opt for good neighbourliness did not, however, prevent Mexico from suffering serious economic reprisals and capital flight. This played an important role in Cárdenas' decision to back as his successor in 1940 not his closest cabinet ally in the petroleum expropriation, Francisco J. Múgica, but the conservative general Manuel Avila Camacho (Meyer and Morales 1990), who enjoyed close relations with North American capitalists in his home state, Puebla (Gómez 2003). Yet most domestic business groups kept a low political profile until the 1980s, prospering under an import-substituting industrialisation regime in which good relations with the political class provided handsome economic returns. Mexican capitalists agreed with that political class that national control of oil revenues was an asset and that preserving the nationalised industry fortified the regime's political legitimacy as it turned its back on the peasantry.

From 1964 to 1970, the Pemex director general was Jesús Reyes Heroles, a major figure in the ruling PRI who went on to become interior minister and secretary of education, as well as a distinguished academic and public intellectual. In contrast to his less active predecessors, Reyes Heroles attempted to confront the union and bring some of the more notorious practices of corruption in Pemex under control. In one of his public pronouncements, he declared that:

> It would be incongruous if the administrators [of this publicly owned enterprise] should begrudge the workers their legitimate rewards and social benefits, derived from the work that they carry out; but it would also be incongruous for the workers, in their demands for justice and a bettering of their social

status, to impede the growth of an industry that is the key to our economic development. This would be to sacrifice new jobs for other Mexicans and security in their jobs for the children of the oil workers themselves.' (Quoted in Sobarzo 1992: 11, my translation)

Don Jesús could be credited with the promotion of significant advances in the technical and scientific capacity of Pemex and a greater concern with issues of conservation. He also negotiated the termination of contacts that had been signed with private enterprises at the end of the 1940s and the beginning of the 1950s, in which Pemex paid contractors who were successful in finding oil with a 50 per cent share of the crude extracted from the new wells (Sobarzo 1992: 24). No one was a more effective advocate of state oil monopoly in the interests of development of the whole national economy, making Felipe Calderón's appointment of Don Jesús's son, Jesús Reyes Heroles González-Garza, as director general of Pemex an astute symbolic move in countering expected opposition to the government's 'energy reform' plans. What the reforming father did not, however, succeed in doing was transform the relationship between the union and the management of Pemex in the longer term, for reasons that were essentially political, given the STPRM's centrality to the patronage networks and vote-mobilising capacities of Mexico's ruling party. This contributed to failure of the industry to deliver what it promised to the national development model as a whole, as became only too apparent after the oil crisis made it profitable to exploit Mexico's less accessible reserves, a task for which Pemex was now technically equipped.

How to Turn an Asset into a Liability

Under the presidency of José López Portillo (1976–1982), Mexico became a major oil-exporting country. Between 1973 and 1982, Pemex's output increased from 191,000 barrels per day to 2,746,000 barrels per day, a staggering achievement (Philip 1999: 39). López Portillo's appointee as director general, Jorge Díaz Serrano, came from a background in the private sector but also harboured the highest political ambitions, despite the fact that he had not served his apprenticeship by working his way up through public office with the assistance of the clique structures that normally governed ascent through the ranks in the PRI (Gledhill 2002). He was also, inconveniently, seen as pro-American, having been an associate of the first President Bush in his private-sector career. Distrusted by the inner circles of the PRI, Díaz Serrano eventually went to jail rather than into the presidency, accused of corruption on a massive scale (Philip 1999:

39). Although he was later able to capitalise on fall-guy status for the catastrophic macroeconomic failure of the whole government strategy, which ended in the financial crash of 1982, the STPRM became equally implicated in the scandals that surrounded the management of the industry.

During the oil boom, Pemex's financial position actually deteriorated, thanks to price control and a tax burden that became even more of a barrier to investment after the country was plunged into generalised debt crisis (Philip 1999: 40). Between 1982 and 1988, undercapitalisation prevented the company from taking advantage of new opportunities to exploit natural gas reserves not associated with oil, but while the De la Madrid administration embarked on a course of privatisation in other sectors of the economy, it remained cautious in its handling of Pemex. Not only was economic nationalist sentiment still strong within sectors of the ruling party opposed to its hijacking by technocrats, but also there was a real and, as it turned out, well-founded fear that the PRI could not withstand the electoral consequences of abandoning what even many people whose loyalty to the regime was based on the land reform regarded as its greatest achievement of all.

A safer course was to attack the oil workers and STPRM. Already unhappy about falling real wages and investment cutbacks, their discontent was magnified when the new director of Pemex, Ramón Beteta, brought in three thousand nonunion managers and the government decreed that all contracts for goods and services should be awarded by public competitive tender, ending Pemex's traditional practice of awarding contracts to the STPRM, which would then subcontract the supply of the actual goods and services to the private sector for a percentage (Philip 1999: 41). Yet, although workers in the industry suffered the disadvantages of weakened union power, there was no compensating gain from reform of the way unions were run. This became only too apparent after 1988 brought Carlos Salinas de Gortari to the presidency in a contest against the son of Lázaro Cárdenas.

Cárdenas' lineage enhanced the credibility of his appeal to the popular imaginary of what post-revolutionary Mexico might have been, and, confirming the worst fears that the PRI's system of rule was unravelling, this election victory had to be achieved by fraud. Salinas' first act as president was to jail the boss of the STPRM on charges of corruption and murder of dissidents. This was largely an act of political vengeance, since Joaquín Hernández Galicia, 'La Quina', had supported Cárdenas in the election. The scale of La Quina's diversion of union funds was demonstrated by the fact that his home region suffered a severe recession after his incarceration, and his local popularity has proved enduring: one of his sons was subsequently elected as mayor. La Quina's removal did, however, also smooth the way for further attacks on the Pemex workforce.

Over the next four years the union lost more than one hundred thousand jobs nationally and was forced to swallow an unpalatable new collective contract (Philip 1999: 45). Nevertheless, despite the fact that Salinas did strike down the other sacred cow of the revolutionary legacy, land redistribution, he too left untouched the parts of Constitutional Article 27 that related to petroleum as national property irrespective of the ownership status of the land beneath which it was discovered, contenting himself with removing the remaining legal barriers to foreign ownership of secondary petrochemicals and restrictions on foreign companies' participation in Pemex procurement contracts (Philip 1999: 46). Economic meltdown and political crises during the last six years of PRI rule under Ernesto Zedillo allowed only a little further tinkering with foreign participation, and although Vicente Fox entered office with higher ambitions, he too was obliged to abandon any thought of denationalisation.

In 2002 a scandal promptly dubbed Pemexgate erupted around La Quina's successor as STPRM general secretary, Carlos Romero Deschamps, also a PRI congressman. Romero Deschamps was accused of conspiring with the directorate of Pemex to divert 1.1 billion pesos from the state company, of which half was supposedly used in the financing of the unsuccessful PRI campaign for the presidency in 2000. Although formal charges were laid against Romero, he managed not only to remain at liberty but also to keep his union post, despite the well-justified protests of dissident members (Cervantes 2004: 30). Another Pemex director general, Raúl Muños Leos, resigned in 2004 after the disclosure that he had signed an agreement with Romero Deschamps behind closed doors to transfer a further 8 billion pesos to the union as part of a 'salary review', suggesting that the STPRM was acting as banker for the PRI's election campaign in 2006. Since the PAN lacked a majority in Congress, it was now caught between the rock of having to let the PRI off the hook in order to continue ruling and the hard place of the possibility that the Mexican people might put the leftist PRD in power next time. As a party of capital, the first option was clearly preferable, while many *panistas* also felt more than comfortable reproducing established ways of doing political business.

Beyond the problem of the union, the management of the state oil company evoked controversy as the Fox government attempted to introduce further commercial flexibility into its operations. Luis Ramírez Corzo, previously head of Pemex Exploration and Production, became director general. While heading PEP, Ramírez Corzo was accused of violating the Constitution by use of a new formula, termed 'contracts for multiple services' (CSMs), to open the way for foreign companies to benefit illegally at the expense of the state company (Cervantes 2004: 28). The anti-constitutional element consisted in an apparent return to the risk contracts that

Jesús Reyes Heroles had eliminated, a charge subsequently to be repeated against Felipe Calderón's 2008 proposals for private-sector participation. While the PAN bloc in Congress defended the new director, members of other parties were disturbed to discover that one of the Canadian firms the new director had advised in the past, Nova Chemical, was leader of a consortium that won the contract to develop the Fénix petrochemical complex, a showcase project destined to receive a public investment of 49 per cent of its capital cost (Cervantes 2004: 29). That the PAN president of the Congressional Energy Commission, Francisco Salazar, tried to stop further discussion of Fénix reflected the embarrassing fact that the new director general had also been a member of Vicente Fox's transition team in 2000 (ibid.). Even so, the opposition continued to denounce the CSMs as backdoor privatisation. Detailed scrutiny of the contracts awarded indicated that the principal beneficiaries were foreign companies, including the US-based Lewis, Spain's Repsol, Argentina's Tecpetrol and Brazil's Petrobras.

These tactics on the part of the Fox government represented an effort to circumvent the ideological legacy of the days when women queued up to give their most precious possessions to the government to buy back the nation's oil. As the people of Mexico are only too aware, much of the wealth generated by Pemex historically has been squandered, stolen or diverted for political purposes, and citizens of diverse social backgrounds often utter phrases such as 'the nation's oil' in an ironic tone of voice. Pemex (and the STPRM) figured prominently in a popular imaginary of the post-revolutionary state that envisaged corruption at its heart, although most people tolerated the vices of the political class up to a point insofar as they were compensated by 'material improvements'. The regime's turn to neo-liberalism not only diminished the social functions of the state and provoked deepening impoverishment but also stripped the dignified masks from a PRI tarnished by murderous infighting and criminalisation (Gledhill 2002: 42ff). Pemex has been a major contributor to ecological catastrophes, not simply in rural zones where the victims are often indigenous people, who have on occasion joined forces with other social groups to oppose new oil-based megaprojects (Chevalier and Buckles 1995), but also in cities such as Guadalajara, where 230 people died and 1,224 houses were destroyed in 1992 due a concentration of petroleum vapour in a drain caused by leaks in Pemex ducts.

Yet popular imaginaries have become more rather than less sensitive about oil nationalisation. In 2002 Lázaro Cárdenas' grandson, Lázaro Cárdenas Batel, PRD Governor of Michoacán State, had to offer an abject public apology after making a speech to mark the 2002 annual celebration of the 1938 Expropriation in which he argued that times had changed and that greater private participation would not undermine national sovereignty over oil. Even if they are under no illusions, knowing that they are not the real masters of their oil wealth, the one thing to which a broad swath of actors from different social classes remain committed is that it should certainly not be handed over to the *gringos*. The entanglement of migration issues in the War on Terror and attacks on Afghanistan and Iraq only confirmed Mexicans' long-standing conviction that US imperialism remains a direct threat to their own country, since they believe it to be about controlling the oil and gas resources that remain a tangible symbol of Mexico's potential prosperity.

Venezuela and Brazil: Two Visions of the Public Interest

In contrast to Mexico, transnational companies remain central to the Venezuelan industry, with Phillips Petroleum, ExxonMobil, Chevron and Occidental the main US players. Chávez introduced a new hydrocarbons bill that increased production royalties for both private firms and PDVSA to 30 per cent. He also required PDVSA to own a majority stake in all joint ventures with foreign firms. Despite predictions to the contrary, Chávez has shown that these terms do not drive foreign investment away. Furthermore, his early record in government reveals a cautious approach in other matters.

During the 1998 election campaign, Chávez attacked not only the two main parties, AD (Acción Democrática) and COPEI (Comité de Organización Política Electoral Independiente), whose collusion had created a simulation of stable and democratic governance, but also the main trade union, the CTV (Confederación de Trabajadores de Venezuela), the equivalent of Mexico's CTM. He described the CTV as a 'mafia' tied to the parties and to the employers' federation, FEDECAMERAS (Federación Venezolana de Cámeras y Asociaciones de Comercio y Producción). The Venezuelan oil workers' union, FEDEPETROL (Federación de Trabajadores Petroleros), acquired much the same character as STPRM. Under the old regime, it enjoyed an equally cosy relationship with PDVSA management, whose top figures owed their position to patronage networks within the oligarchy, and its leaders were as adept as their Mexican counterparts in translating union power into other forms of power. In 1999, for example, riots broke out in the oil town of El Tejero, in the eastern state of Monagas, after an armed group led by the son of the local union boss, José Vicente Pereira, shot dead Rolando Marcado, an unemployed worker belonging to a movement that, with the support of local chavista parliamentarians, had challenged Pereira's control and demanded that he honour his union's promise to Chávez to desist from distributing jobs in return for payments

(Anonymous 1999). Like Mexico's La Quina, Pereira had turned his town into a personal fiefdom during his twenty-five years in union office, the proceeds from which had not simply financed wide-ranging business investments but also allowed him to fund his own political party. Allied to the traditional oligarchic groups in his state, this also conveniently provided him, like Romero Deschamps, with parliamentary immunity.

Yet the movement supporting Chávez split on how it should reform the labour movement. Those aligned with the pro-Chávez UNT (Unión Nacional de Trabajadores) argued for complete destruction of the CTV. Moderates within the chavista coalition argued that parallel unionism risked marginalisation of radical workers, advocating a strategy of working for reform within the CTV to break its links with the established parties (Ellner 2005: 52ff). Also at stake was the autonomy of the labour movement. Militants argued that replacing a union tied to AD and COPEI with another tied to Chávez's party, the MVR (Movimiento V [Quinta] República), might simply reproduce the political clientelism associated with the old regime. Some chavista labour leaders rejected a formal relationship with the MVR, forming the Fuerza Bolivariana de Trabajadores (FBT), an organisation that happily accepted members associated with other pro-Chávez parties, including the communists (Ellner 2005: 60). Yet there was another side to the coin.

In 2000 Chávez appointed Héctor Ciavaldini president of PDVSA. Chavista labour leaders who sought to undermine the power of the AD-dominated leadership of FEDEPETROL under Carlos Ortega argued for the need to end the corruption associated with allowing the union to control the hiring of workers and the extended paid leave granted to union officials (Ellner 2005: 56). Ciavaldini drew up a 'modern contract' designed to eliminate corruption without consulting FEDEPETROL (ibid.: 57). Yet even some chavistas rejected Ciavaldini's proposals to abolish company stores, while his arguments for abolishing bonuses and special payments echoed those already advanced by neo-liberal economists. This strategy enabled Ortega to argue that Ciavaldini and Chávez were closet neo-liberals and that the rights of organised labour had been trampled upon, and to call a strike that produced substantial gains for his members and forced Ciavaldini's removal (ibid.: 58).

Yet Ortega was unable to sustain this initial victory. His backing for unsuccessful attempts to oust Chávez alienated an increasing number of workers, and he turned increasingly to fraud in union elections (Ellner 2005: 62). Once installed as leader of the CTV as well as FEDEPETROL, Ortega forged an alliance with FEDECAMERAS that produced four general strikes between the end of 2001 and beginning of 2003. The second of these coincided with the failed coup of April 2002. FEDEPETROL's role in these politically motivated strikes was one of transparent collaboration with PDVSA managers opposed to Chávez's efforts to reform the industry, advancing again after he appointed the economist Gastón Parra as PDVSA president – promptly branded a '1960s big government leftist' by both domestic critics on the right and US commentators – along with three new board members and some new managers committed to his politics (Talbot 2002). The full privatisation of PDVSA was a prime objective of the leadership of the April 2002 coup. The coup leader, Pedro Carmona Estanga, had worked for the private oil company Venoco. One of its chief backers, Gustavo Cisneros, head of a transnational corporate empire that includes free-to-air and cable TV and the Coca-Cola franchise, hoped to benefit personally from privatisation of PDVSA's assets, which included a US subsidiary (Aharonian, 2002). Cisneros is a long-time associate of George H.W. Bush, and an oil company in which the Bush family has interests was also expected to share in the spoils of privatisation. One motivation for the coup leaders' immediate suspension of the rule of law was that privatisation of PDVSA is prohibited by the 1999 Constitution.

Although the coup failed, covert meddling by the United States continued. The congressionally funded National Endowment for Democracy (NED) channelled resources to FEDEPETROL through the AFL-CIO–associated American Centre for International Labour Solidarity (ACILS) (Talbot 2002). The ostensible purpose of ACILS grants in Venezuela has been to promote reforms that would increase rank-and-file participation in union life and transparency in internal elections. It seems odd that this project was not prioritised until after the election of Chávez, who had his own programme for achieving direct elections of union officials and transparency in voting, backed by independents not aligned with his Bolivarian movement or the MVR. Ortega and his associates responded by declaring themselves re-elected despite widespread accusations of fraud, refusing to submit the ballots to the government for further scrutiny. Yet the AFL–CIO and NED continued to praise the role of the CTV in supporting strikes organised by the employers against the Chávez government.

Ordinary oil workers are not the villains of this story. It is easy to forget, when painting them as a labour aristocracy relative to the rest of the working class, that there is considerable differentiation within the labour force, that, for many, working in the industry is extremely dangerous, and that a great many workers have lost their jobs as firms have rationalised in response to drops in the world oil price and other problems of a more localised kind. The risks of working in the industry have increased dramatically with the growth of subcontracting, as the unions in Mexico, Venezuela and Brazil have publicised. I have already mentioned the existence of unemployment in the Monagas region, which produces nearly 8 per cent of national output. As David Guss notes in his ethnographic work on this area, where peasants once queued up to abandon the land and seek work in the oil fields, there are now long queues of unemployed people who can no longer return to a rural way of life: 'the oil industry has been a factory for the production of urbanism, unemployment and destabilised social relations' (Guss 2000: 77). This produced a novel symbolic effort to try to piece back together the disintegrating elements of local society, a festival that parodies state models of 'progress' by celebrating incongruous symbols of 'indigenousness'. It is not difficult to discern the dangers perceived by external actors in any effort that might give these sectors of the population a new voice in determining the shape of regional development. There have now been examples of the Chávez government curtailing major extractive projects following local protests (Fernandes 2007: 19).

Although the final ten-week strike called by FEDEPETROL in 2002–2003 greatly strengthened the hand of the UNT hard-liners (Ellner 2005: 66f.) and a purge of eighteen thousand (mostly white-collar) PDVSA employees did follow, the pro-Chávez union movement continued to resist a return to a situation in which labour leadership is tied to the political forces controlling the state. Chávez's Venezuela thus remains a long way from replicating the model of the old regime or the populist corporatism built in Mexico and Brazil in the 1930s. Contrary to the stereotype that sees the regime as an idiosyncratic one backed by amorphous popular masses whose actions are spontaneous and uninformed, Valencia (2005) has argued that the state as elected government is acting as an ally of largely autonomous resistance movements, whose class composition is diverse and whose history in many cases predates 1998 and was initially unconnected with Chávez. Since the government maintained a commitment to participatory democracy and new forms of politics, Chávez fostered a process of 'negotiating hegemony with the state' (Valencia 2005: 95ff) that was reinforced by many activists' determination to preserve their independence.

Implementing effective social programmes did require a more bureaucratic and centralised approach, which alienated some of the activists who participated earlier in the voluntary Círculos Bolivarianos citizens' organisations (Hawkins and Hansen 2006: 124–25). Chávez might not have been so successful politically had he not been able to use the expanding revenues accruing to PDVSA as a result of a rising world oil price to increase government spending on social programmes targeted at poorer Venezuelans. Yet periods of high oil prices in Venezuela's past did not bring the poor free health care. Venezuela's economic growth contrasts strongly with Mexico's stagnation, despite the problems that an increase of government spending from 19 to 30 per cent of GDP since 1998 has caused for inflation and the relationship between supply and demand in consumer markets. The most serious problem that Chávez faced at the end of 2007, when he narrowly lost a referendum vote for constitutional changes, was a shortage of milk, eggs and chicken. Although price controls had produced perverse effects such as contraband exports of food to Colombia, it is also worth noting that per capita food consumption has risen since 1998 as a result of the government's pro-poor policies.

Advancing the redistributive and democratising potential of Chávez's Bolivarian Revolution may also depend on whether alliances can be built between like-minded states at the regional level. Yet the interest conflicts embedded in the energy sector are clearly a significant problem in this regard, as will become apparent as I turn in more detail to Brazil.

Brazil consumes more oil and gas annually than any other country in the Western Hemisphere, apart from the United States and Canada. In 2001, reflecting the country's dependence on hydroelectric power generation, widespread drought caused the country's lights to go out as it became necessary to ration power to the grid. Nevertheless, oil and gas production has been rising steadily since the beginning of the 1990s, and oil consumption as such has not increased significantly since the end of that decade, since the use of cane alcohol (ethanol) as a gasoline substitute is now being followed by development of other biofuels.

Getúlio Vargas created Petrobras in 1953 during his second period as president. For Vargas, oil sovereignty was a condition for autonomous development, and state monopoly a condition not simply for industrialising Brazil but also for achieving national independence. One section of the military, represented by the nationalist general Horta Barbosa, shared the view that oil was 'the basis of the economy and of the military defense of the country' (Ray 2004: 20). Barbosa became one of the leaders of the campaign *O Petróleo é Nosso* (The Oil Is Ours), which was organising large street demonstrations by the time Vargas returned to power in 1951. Yet the military was split on the issue, as were large sections of business. The agro-export bourgeoisie opposed Vargas's entire economic model since they were content with the notion that their country had an 'agricultural vocation' and feared the political consequences of a larger urban working class. Financiers and the commercial elites whose profits lay in the import of products and services were antagonistic to Vargas' emphasis on steel and other heavy industries as a basis for import-substituting industrialisation.

Oil was first discovered in Bahia, which still has unexploited reserves, a large refinery, and the Camaçari petrochemical complex, created in the 1970s. Although these developments have not, in the long term, resolved the problems of a region dominated by casualised work and unemployment, they did produce significant social mobility for some families. The most important oil production zone today is, however, the offshore Campos Basin, north of Rio de Janeiro. When it became apparent that the Brazilians were intent on developing their national resources, the US Department of State instructed its ambassador to apply every possible pressure to support US companies in obtaining exploitation concessions, apparently including bribery of deputies and senators (Ray 2004: 20). That Vargas succeeded in securing a majority for the passing of Law 2,004 granting Petrobras a monopoly similar to that of Pemex was one of his greatest political achievements. Despite the support of the communists, no friends of Vargas after their ruthless persecution in the 1930s under the *Estado Novo*, political conditions in Brazil were less favourable to such a move even at the start of the 1950s than they had been in Mexico in the 1930s. Yet by the 1990s, the balance of forces in Brazilian politics made it possible to move much further toward privatisation than in Mexico.

Under Cardoso, Petrobras was given more operational autonomy and allowed to function more like a private corporation. Under the new regime, the National Petroleum Agency would issue tenders, monitor the sector as a whole, and grant concessions to both domestic and foreign companies. Yet the differences between Brazil and Venezuela remain striking. Although the major oil transnationals retail gasoline in Brazil, only Shell and Chevron are actually producing oil and natural gas, and in partnership with Petrobras. Costs in Brazil are high, since much of the commercially viable oil is in deep water. All the recent commercially viable oil and gas fields have been found by Petrobras, although the transnationals frequently complain that the decks are stacked against them. Another cause of complaint has been taxes levied by state governments, notably Rio de Janeiro, in addition to those paid to the federal government. Nevertheless, in a national economy dominated by big capital with transnational ties, Cardoso's privatisation measures remain far from trivial. The conversion of Petrobras from a national oil and gas monopolist to an aggressive energy corporation with more global ambitions raises new issues of public accountability. The company is as interested as its foreign competitors in extracting the best deal it can from the different states since it is required to operate according to commercial criteria.

Domestic accountability is principally framed in terms of responsibility to other sectors of the national economy, although Petrobras also has extensive resource conservation and environmental protection programmes. In 2002 the federal government enacted a new law requiring Petrobras to purchase more locally sourced goods and services, which resulted in some production delays caused by the late construction of oil platforms, preventing the company from achieving the production targets in its strategic plan. Yet, as a Brazilian friend remarked to me, all that she really knew about Petrobras was its public face as a sponsor of educational and social development programmes, cultural events and the Brazilian film industry. The logo is everywhere as a sign that the public interest function of the company is being fulfilled. Petrobras does, however, impose very strict standards of confidentiality and nondisclosure of commercial information on its employees, who, I discovered, have a strong sense of being subject to surveillance by management.

If we compare Brazil to Mexico, it seems difficult to deny that the politics that have shaped the national oil industry have left Petrobras in better shape today than Pemex. Brazil has negotiated the opening up of its oil industry without complete sacrifice of national sovereignty, and Petrobras is a growing company that makes money. On the other hand, while Petrobras revenues do pay for public goods, how far poorer Brazilians benefit from what remains of economic nationalism in one of the world's most unjust societies depends on the delicate balances struck between wider social responsibility and the interests of the government in repaying international creditors, as well as those of shareholders and oil industry workers. If the share of revenues that accrue to the public purse through taxation and the sale of exploration rights are principally used to subsidise private corporate interests elsewhere in the country or repay debts, then having a healthy public energy corporation whose operations transcend national borders may not prove much of an advantage for those poorer citizens who notionally retain a share in 'the people's oil'. Even Venezuela still obliges us to ask whether spending on social programmes funded by oil revenues will eliminate poverty and produce a less polarised society, but this is a question that poses itself even more forcefully in Brazil.

Conclusion

An anthropology of oil focused on ethnographic studies of production zones offers important lessons about development. For locals and migrants alike seeking jobs, even in the early years of high hopes and boom times, the sudden influx of work and money can bring unexpected social problems (when men spend much of their new earnings on alcohol, prostitutes or second families, for example). Oil-related development can produce significant social mobility for some, and may even contribute to the advancement of families for groups previously located at the bottom of racialised class structures, especially when secondary petrochemicals development and other forms of industrialisation complement extraction, as in Bahia. Yet these positive effects remain limited in comparison with the overall needs of regional, let alone national populations.

As my examples show, even in the best of times the role of union bosses and other kinds of patronage relations skewed the distribution of benefits and diminished them absolutely by taxing access to jobs. The labour force was highly differentiated, and unskilled migrant workers hired to construct facilities were in a particularly vulnerable position: if they stayed, they often found themselves consigned to an informal second economy. Furthermore, we have seen that oil zones sooner or later experience harder times. What ethnography can add to depressing quantitative social, economic and environmental indicators is a deeper qualitative exploration of the meanings of these experiences of development. Ethnographies provide understanding of how people adjust their lives to changing conditions and rethink their identities and relationships with each other and wider powers in a variety of forms of symbolic and practical action.

A purely ethnographic perspective is, however, not sufficient to grasp all the dimensions in which oil relates to the political configuration of national societies. I have emphasised the broader significance of oil nationalisation to people who did not live in oil-producing regions, and indicated how the fate of national oil industries is the product of shifting political relationships within and between elites, specific interest groups, and subaltern classes. Although oil nationalisation proved a truly popular cause in all the countries that I have discussed, the subsequent history of each is different. Dependence of government revenues on oil exports is an important variable, but many of the vices of rentier petro-states seem to be duplicated in countries where oil is not the key sector, while the contemporary condition of the different national oil industries becomes more intelligible when it is related to the specific trajectories of political and social change that have provided the broader context for their development.

In arguing that national control over oil in these Latin American countries retains a popular symbolic importance that has, if anything, increased as neo-liberal capitalist globalisation has devastated the social fabric of these societies, I have also argued against those who contend that governments that espouse redistribution represent a return to an anachronistic Latin American populist tradition. Today's populists seem more a symptom than a cause of lower-class people asserting their own rights and dignity, a leadership that draws on popular imaginaries rather than fabricates them. In Brazil and Mexico it is difficult to deny that corporate capitalist interests have a dominant voice in the formulation of current state policies, and even in Venezuela, Chávez's government has worked hard to avoid confrontations with the private sector that might seriously damage economic performance. Yet the scope for popular leverage on government policy depends not only on which political forces can obtain power by democratic means but also on how economic elites articulate to political classes.

Although some of Mexico's business elite have successfully propagated transnational capitalist operations in Latin America and the United States, it is difficult to escape the conclusion that the historical fate of Pemex has been part and parcel of a configuration of intra-elite relations that has inexorably drawn the country into an international profile that makes it at most a junior partner in a US-centred web of transnational economic relationships. The same was broadly true of Venezuela before Chávez, but today both Brazil and Venezuela seem much more capable of forging alternative relationships (with China as well as their neighbours). The domestic configurations of political and social forces that have made this possible are clearly very different, as indeed are their oil industries. Petrobras reveals the benefits of developing a public corporation capable of capitalising on its technical capacity and expertise to extract commercial benefits abroad. PDVSA has enabled Chávez to make political alliances in the Caribbean by sacrificing short-term commercial objectives and even to twist the tail of the imperial dragon by offering poorer New Yorkers and Londoners subsidised heating oil. Different though the logics of these external deployments of national companies are, they nevertheless illustrate ways in which Latin American states can participate in the creation of a multi-polar world order by forging new relationships outside the framework of North Atlantic dominance. Although it can never be the whole of the story, the persistent imaginary of the people's oil is one of the subterranean processes that can push that historical possibility forward.

References

Aharonian, Aram Ruben. 2002. Venezuela. Un Golpe Con Olor a Hamburguesa, Jamón y Petróleo. *Proceso*, 27 April 2002. http://www.proceso.com.mx/rv/modHome/detalleExclusiva/732. (last accessed 3 March 2011).

Anonymous. 1999. Riots Against Venezuelan Oil Union Rock Monagas. *Drillbits & Tailings* 4(7).

Cannon, Barry. 2004. Venezuela, April 2002: Coup or Popular Rebellion? The Myth of a United Venezuela. *Bulletin of Latin American Research* 23(3): 285–302.

Cervantes, Jesusa. 2004. Misión: Privatizar Pemex. *Proceso,* 14 November: 28–31.

Chevalier, Jacques M. and David Buckles. 1995. *A Land Without Gods: Process Theory, Maldevelopment and the Mexican Nahuas.* London: Zed Books.

Coronil, Fernando. 1997. *The Magical State: Nature, Money, and Modernity in Venezuela.* Chicago: University of Chicago Press.

Ellner, Steve. 2005. The Emergence of a New Trade Unionism in Venezuela with Vestiges of the Past. *Latin American Perspectives* 32(2): 51–71.

Fernandes, Sujatha. 2007. A View from the Barrios: Hugo Chávez as an Expression of Urban Popular Movements. *LASA Forum* 38(1): 17–19.

Fry, Peter. 1995. O que a Cinderela negra tem a dizer sobre a 'política racial' no Brasil. *Revista USP São Paulo* 28: 122–35.

Gledhill, John. 2002. The Powers Behind the Masks: Mexico's Elite and Political Class at the End of the Twentieth Century. In *Elite Cultures: Anthropological Perspectives*, ed. Chris Shore and Stephen Nugent, 39–60. London: Routledge.

Gómez Carpintero, Francisco Javier. 2003. *Gente de azúcar y agua: modernidad y posrevolución en el suroeste de Puebla*. Zamora: El Colegio de Michoacán and Benmérita Universidad Autónoma de Puebla.

González y González, Luis. 1981. *Los Días del presidente Cárdenas. Historia de la Revolución Mexicana*, vol. 15. Mexico City: El Colegio de México.

Guss, David. 2000. *The Festive State: Race, Ethnicity and Nationalism as Cultural Performance*. Berkeley: University of California Press.

Hale, Charles. 2002. Does Multiculturalism Menace? Governance, Cultural Rights and the Politics of Identity in Guatemala. *Journal of Latin American Studies* 34(3): 485–524.

Hall, Anthony. 2006. From *Fome Zero* to *Bolsa Familia*: Social Policies and Poverty Alleviation under Lula. *Journal of Latin American Studies* 38(4): 689–709.

Hawkins, Kirk A. and David R. Hansen. 2006. Dependent Civil Society: The *Círculos Bolivarianos* in Venezuela. *Latin American Research Review* 41(1): 102–32.

Karl, Terry. 1997. *The Paradox of Plenty: Oil Booms and Petro-states*. Berkeley: University of California Press.

Meyer, Lorenzo and Isidro Morales. 1990. *Petróleo y nación (1900–1987): la política petrolera en México*. Mexico City: Fondo de la Cultura Económica.

Petrobas. 2004. www.petrobras.com.br. (accessed 12 November 2004).

Philip, George. 1999. The Political Constraints on Economic Policy in post-1982 Mexico: The Case of Pemex. *Bulletin of Latin American Research* 18(1): 35–50.

Ray, José Carlos. 2004. Petróleo nosso, apesar das forces poderosas. *Caros Amigos* 21(August): 20.

Sartori, Armando, ed. 2007. O Colossal Brasil. *Retrato do Brasil-Carta Capital* 1(August): 3–20.

Sheriff, Robin E. 2001. *Dreaming Equality: Color, Race and Racism in Urban Brazil*. New Brunswick, NJ: Rutgers University Press.

Sobarzo Loaiza, Alejandro. 1992. Jesús Reyes Heroles y su paso por Petróleos Mexicanos. In *Jesús Reyes Heroles y el petróleo*, ed. A. Sobarzo Loaiza, 9–27. Mexico City: Fondo de la Cultura Económica.

Talbot, Karen. 2002. Coup-making in Venezuela: The Bush and Oil Factors. Centre for Research on Globalization, 14 June. http://globalresearch.ca/articles/TAL206A.html. (last accessed on 3 March 2011).

Valencia Ramírez, Cristóbal. 2005. Venezuela's Bolivarian Revolution: Who Are the Chavistas? *Latin American Perspectives* 32(3): 79–97.

Villafuerte Solís, Daniel. 2001. *Integraciones comerciales en la Frontera Sur: Chiapas frente al Tratado de Libre Comercio México-Centroamérica*. San Cristóbal de Las Casas: Universidad Nacional Autónoma de México.

Wade, Robert. 2003. *Governing the Market: Economic Theory and the Role of Government in East Asian Industrialization*. Princeton, NJ: Princeton University Press.

— *Chapter 8* —

'Now That the Petroleum Is Ours'

Community Media, State Spectacle and Oil Nationalism in Venezuela

Naomi Schiller

Five days before the August 2004 presidential recall referendum in Venezuela, a young woman named Damales, together with eight neighbours from Lidice, a low-income neighbourhood in Caracas, arrived at Catia TVe. One of the founders of the community television station had invited Damales and her neighbours to appear on his talk show to discuss their efforts to mobilise voters in support of President Hugo Chávez. Looking nervous but excited, Damales sat on a faded brown couch in the television studio. A handmade Catia TVe sign hung on the wall behind her. Holding the microphone steadily with both hands, Damales spoke about the positive changes she saw taking place in her neighbourhood as a result of the government's new education and health initiatives, which were widely known to be a result of Chávez's effort to channel oil money to social programmes. What was less well known was that the faded brown couch where Damales sat, the camera recording her image, and the large antennae broadcasting the signal were all made possible by the alliance between Petróleos de Venezuela, Sociedad Anómina (PDVSA), the state-run oil company, and the flowering community media movement.

After discussing the upcoming referendum and the improvements in their everyday lives since Chávez came to power, Luis, the host of the Catia TVe programme, turned to the subject of PDVSA (pronounced pey-dey-VEY-sah). 'Does PDVSA belong to the people? Does it Damales?' he asked her. She responded emphatically, nodding her head. 'Of course it belongs to the people because it's doing things for us that it never did before. And, there were a lot of people before, myself included, who didn't know what PDVSA was. Imagine that!' Damales paused to reflect. 'I didn't know what PDVSA was. Now, I know that PDVSA is ours and is working for us.' Luis, the host, nodded in support. Damales concluded, 'I feel an immense love for the president. I hope he'll stay because this man has to be with us, so that we won't be the forgotten ones, the hidden ones, so that we can continue advancing ahead.'

Unmitigated celebration of Chávez over the airwaves of Catia TVe was not unusual in the weeks leading up to the presidential referendum. What caught my attention that day, as I sat in the back of the over air-conditioned studio observing the programme, was Luis' direct question about PDVSA and Damales' brief narrative of coming to consciousness about the existence of the state oil company. While nationalist appeals to Venezuela's vast oil resources have been a common refrain since the first oil legislation was drafted in the 1930s, Damales' comments concerning her change in understanding of what PDVSA is and what it does marked a departure from the past, when most inhabitants of Caracas' poor neighbourhoods had little knowledge of or feelings of connection to the state-run oil company.

Introduction: Reconfiguring State Spectacle

Venezuela is currently the fifth largest exporter of petroleum in the world, after Saudi Arabia, Russia, Iran and Norway. Venezuela boasts the largest reserves in the Western Hemisphere and has the sixth largest proven reserves of conventional crude oil on the planet (Lander 2007). In Venezuela, ideas about oil, the state and the nation are inseparable (Briceño-León 1990; Karl 1997; Lander 2003; Quintero 1972). Discussions of to whom oil-derived resources belong and by whom they should be administered provokes the question: what is the state? A study of the importance of oil in everyday life in Venezuela thus requires attention both to the 'state idea' (Abrams 1988) and the way that the state is linked to the 'nation' through the discourse of nationalism. Lomnitz argues that the power of the shared cultural construct of nationalism lies 'in the fact that it provides interactive frames in which the relationship between state institutions and various and diverse social relationships (family relationships, the organisation of work, the definition of forms of property, and the regulation of public space) can be negotiated' (2001: 14). During the period leading up to the 2004 presidential recall referendum, the 'interactive frame' of Venezuelan nationalism, through which state institutions and social groups relate, was slick with oil.

Venezuelan nationalism is strongly linked to the rights and responsibilities of the Venezuelan state to deliver the wealth derived from natural resources of its territory to the nation (Coronil 1997). Nationalist discourse about oil, which scholars often refer to as 'oil nationalism', has long been used to unite the population (Dávila 1993). The wealth found beneath the soil is invoked as the inhabitants' 'birth right' that connects the people with the state (Coronil and Skurski 1991). In *The Magical State* (1997), Fernando Coronil describes how at key periods in Venezuela's modern history governing elites have used oil wealth to stage spectacular magical displays that created the appearance of the state as an entity beyond the reach of human agency, thereby endowing it (and as a result, themselves) with god-like qualities (Coronil 1997: 4). He contends that the population's compliance in the state's monopoly over violence and the nation's natural wealth was achieved dramaturgically 'by manufacturing dazzling development projects that engender collective fantasies of progress' (ibid.: 5). Through awe-inspiring spectacle, he argues, the Venezuelan state 'casts its spell over *audience* and *performers* alike' (ibid.: emphasis mine). Given the sweeping changes that are taking place in Venezuela, the question emerges: are community media programmes funded by oil money simply a repetition of the vast and unrealistic mega-projects of Venezuela's past? Is Catia TVe co-producing the latest incarnation of the 'magical state'?

This chapter draws on ethnographic fieldwork conducted with Catia TVe over the course of thirteen months between 2003 and 2007. In what follows, I have two aims. First, I hope to illustrate how oil nationalist rhetoric like other forms of nationalism is polysemous and was deployed by the poor to legitimate struggles and demand access to resources. *Barrio*-based actors were involved in the process of creating their own media representations and participated in shaping the message of oil nationalism. Catia TVe's deliverance of an oil nationalist message – at times in tension with forces 'from above' – was a vital element of grassroots actors' bid for power. It was also, I argue, part of their effort to participate in creating new ideas about what the state is and should be. While attention has been paid to how politicians depend on oil nationalist rhetoric to advance their interests and the 'appearance of the Venezuelan state as a transcendent and unifying agent of the nation' (Coronil 1997: 4), there are few studies that attend to how 'the bases' deploy oil nationalism and take part in the production of state spectacle to serve their agendas. I argue that the legitimacy and coherency of the Venezuelan 'state-idea' (Abrams 1988) was co-produced by Catia TVe and formal government actors.

My second aim is to analyse the new participatory production of state spectacle in which the staging of empowerment and actual empowerment of the previously disenfranchised at times went hand in hand. My research with community television producers reveals that spectacle remained paramount for the production of everyday ideas about the state in Venezuela. However, while ideas generated about the state are no longer limited only to positing the state as magical and beyond the reach of human agency as Coronil suggests, a new fantasy about the state was nevertheless created through reconfigured practices of staging and the changing relationship between audiences and performers. Because Chávez's legitimacy during this period depended on the discourse that there is a 'new geometry of power' in Venezuela and that the Bolivarian Revolution was a social movement catalysed from below by the people, his authority could not be maintained without daily displays of popular or poor subjects assuming roles as protagonists in the Revolution.[1] State spectacle and discourse depended on the constant statement and exhibition of leadership and participation by the poor. At times these claims and displays were superficial and were not accompanied by the development of increased access to decision making, resources and self determination; at other times, producing statements and the appearance of popular protagonism worked to advance the agendas of activists. Barrio-based media producers were called upon by government actors to be present during acts of state spectacle (such as press conferences, celebrations and marches) not simply to produce media, but also and perhaps more importantly to display themselves as empowered central protagonists of the Bolivarian Revolution.

For grassroots leaders to build their power, they had to perform themselves as empowered subjects. This participation in state spectacle was part theatre and part constitution of a new kind of subject. While I take Coronil's attention to dramaturgy as a point of departure, I argue for a shift in analysis about the social production of state spectacle that draws attention to how the process of creating these spectacles was a generative experience for barrio producers. Particular kinds of political subjectivities were formed by the everyday normalisation of barrio participation in state media processes and their access to the 'behind the scenes' machinations of state spectacle. Attention to the experience of barrio producers during the social process of creating state spectacle reveals the complexity of the formation of subjectivity, which Sherry Ortner asserts is 'the basis of "agency", a necessary part of understanding how people (try to) act on the world even as they are acted upon' (2005: 34). While state spectacles are often dismissed as simply the production of traditional displays of state power, the further veneration of Chávez, and legitimisation of his centralised authority, I am interested in exploring the historical possibilities that the participation of barrio subjects in the productions of state spectacle created for barrio producers' lives and agendas.

This chapter is divided into three sections. First, I explore recent anthropological contributions to the study of 'the state' and the production of media. The second section outlines the history of oil nationalism in Venezuela and points to the way in which petroleum brings into stark relief the battle over the meaning of the state and its production in everyday life. In the third section I provide three ethnographic cases that allow insight into how barrio-based television producers were engaged as audience, producers and performers of messages of oil nationalism and state spectacle. I examine the cooperation between PDVSA Gas and Catia TVe to create informational segments about PDVSA Gas's work and explain how and why the antagonisms arose that ultimately led to the joint project being discontinued. I investigate the role of Catia TVe producers at a PDVSA press conference before the 2004 recall referendum. The final example examines Catia TVe's involvement in the hugely spectacularised celebration of the renegotiation of oil contracts concerning the Oil Belt of the Orinoco River in May 2007, which Chávez billed as the final historic assertion of Venezuela's independence and sovereignty.

Theorising the State and Media Worlds

In the past fifteen years scholars have begun to re-examine what 'the state' means in everyday life and to challenge received understandings of and approaches to state force and formation. One of the most salient contributions to emerge from this literature is ethnographic insight into how and why 'the state' is imagined, practised and represented as a *thing* that appears coherent, supreme, natural and agentive (Aretxaga 1997; Coronil 1997; Ferguson and Gupta 2002; Hansen and Stepputat 2001; Joseph and Nugent 1994; Scott 1998; Taussig 1993; Trouillot 2001). Anthropologists who study the state approach *ideas* about and *representations* of 'the state' not merely as reflections of the material world, but as actively shaping and producing the world. 'The state effect' is understood as a product of cultural processes and the abstraction of political practices (Mitchell 1999; Steinmetz 1999).

Anthropologists have examined the pitfalls and possibilities of cooperation between grassroots and state-run media initiatives (Ginsburg 1991; Wortham 2004). Scholarship that assesses state-funded media production maintains that even when television is government funded, it cannot be reduced to a hegemonic state apparatus; within state-run culture industries, producers negotiate and struggle to express their views (Abu-Lughod 2005; Mankekar 1999). This ethnographic scholarship on state-run media projects primarily focuses on the 'social life of television' in creating a sense of nationhood; this literature avoids exploration, however, of how state-run media is part and parcel of a project to create ideas about 'the state' as a coherent entity with unitary agency. In this chapter, I bring together the insights of scholarship on 'the state effect' with anthropological attention to media co-produced by formal government actors and grassroots producers to examine how sites of media production and spectacle are rich moments of production of ideas about the state. My close analysis of the process through which representations of 'the state' and the state oil company, PDVSA, are produced reveals the *ad hoc* everyday state formation taking place in Venezuela.

In Erica Wortham's work with indigenous media makers in Mexico she argues that the task of 'unraveling potentially "enlightened" government sponsorship from cooptation' presupposes certain notions about the state and local organisations. Wortham suggests that we recognise local community organisations as themselves 'institutions of power' and approach state power in Foucault's terms as 'a power bent on generating forces, making them grow and ordering them, rather than one dedicated to impeding them, making them submit or destroying them' (Foucault 1978, quoted in Wortham 2002: 15–16). Allowing for the possible positive outcomes of the government's role in local organising and power building, however, does not foreclose an analysis of the difficulties that arise when state hegemonic projects provide the very concepts or outlets that subordinated groups use to struggle for their autonomy.

Jeff Himpele's ethnography of media production in Bolivia advances the question of dialogical creation of agency. On a well-liked television programme called The Open Tribunal, impoverished Bolivians strategically engaged the host, an ascendant neo-populist politician, in order to secure help for their problems. Himpele (2007) explores how agency is always under construction through collusive discursive forms. He follows McDermott and Tylbor who explain that: 'Collusion refers to how members of a social order must constantly help each other to posit a particular state of affairs … . Participation in social scenes requires that members play into each other's hands, pushing and pulling each other toward a strong sense of what is probable or possible' (McDermott and Tylbor 1995, quoted in Himpele 2007: 161). At the heart of Himpele's exploration is whether the poor people who sought help by appearing on television can be defined as 'agentive historical subjects rather than as simulated effects of a ventriloquist's enunciation' (2007: 150). Himpele carefully traces how the new Bolivian popular classes were 'visualised as historical protagonists through the social alliances' formed with the television programme's host, and with other participants and viewers (ibid.).

Approaches to the everyday formation of the 'state effect' together with the above authors' contributions to the complexities of dialogical production of agency provide useful groundwork to understand Catia TVe's role in the production of state spectacle and message of oil nationalism. Just as indigenous producers in Mexico and the popular subjects who seek help on television in Bolivia, Catia TVe producers were involved in shaping the terms and outcomes of their engagement with the government within webs of constraint not always of their own choosing. I will show how the conceptual unity of the Bolivarian Revolutionary state idea was achieved on an everyday basis in the mid-2000s through performances that displayed newly empowered barrio-based media producers. First, I briefly narrate the history of oil nationalist claims in order to contextualise the latest incarnation of claims that 'now the petroleum is ours'.

The Formation of a Claim

The discovery and exploitation of petroleum resources in Venezuela in the early twentieth century precipitated vast social and economic changes that provided the basis for the emergence of notions of the Venezuelan state as a cohesive entity with unifying principles for individual and collective identification (Dávila 1993). Oil nationalism – a cultural and political artifact – served, first and foremost, the interest of the elite by channelling the outrage of the poor majority against foreign domination. Democracy in Venezuela was founded on limited concessions to contain Venezuela's poor and the concentration of power and resources in the hands of Venezuela's elite; the resources and symbolic content derived from petroleum helped to ease class conflict (Bustillos and Ferrigni 1981). The 1943 Law of Hydrocarbons, which placed all oil concessions under the same juridical framework for the first time, established the state as sole administrator of the territory's subsoil and made it possible for the Venezuelan government to declare national sovereignty on an international stage (Lander 2007).

During the 1930s the phrase *'sembrar el petroleo'* (to sow the oil) became a common refrain in political discourse and popularised the concept of oil as the national patrimony. The phrase was intended to convince the once agrarian nation that the government would redirect the capital accumulated from petroleum revenues into other productive sectors (Coronil 1997: 134; Karl 1997: 3). With the founding of the Organisation of the Petroleum Exporting Countries (OPEC) in 1960, oil was sharply politicised as an issue of sovereignty for Venezuela. Like the majority of other OPEC nations, Venezuela's effort to control the level of production and defend the price of oil was limited by the fact that the government had only partial control over the subsoil as a result of contracts with foreign companies.

The slogan that 'now the petroleum belongs to the people' was first used during the presidency of Carlos Andres Perez in the early 1970s in an attempt to win the support for nationalisation from both the poor and the professional elite with the promise that the country's wealth would no longer flow to the oil giants of the north. Oil was nationalised in Venezuela in 1976. Although nationalisation was invoked as an assertion of Venezuelan autonomy, in fact, oil nationalisation and the following decade of 'oil opening' (*apertura petrolera*) paradoxically accommodated foreign capital interests, strengthened the bureaucratic capitalist classes in Venezuela and their alliance with foreign capital, and weakened the state's control over PDVSA (Petras and Morely 1978: 232). Nationalisation and the 'oil opening' accompanied restricted wages, decreased social welfare benefits and loosened price controls. The oil boom, together with the ability of Venezuelan governments to easily secure international loans, made possible Perez's massive capital-intensive development projects. These projects – an effort to build a 'Great Venezuela' – led to the accumulation of a large foreign debt. Rather than seeing the national elites as their foes, Venezuelans were encouraged to believe that international oil companies were the cause of the economic inequality in Venezuela.

In 1979, the last year of Perez's first presidential term, the popular leftist Venezuelan folk singer, Ali Primera, wrote a song entitled 'Now that the Petroleum Is Ours'. His song is just one example of the prominent place of petroleum in the Venezuelan popular imagination and politics. Primera highlights the corruption of the Perez government and the false promise that the rising tide of petroleum wealth would raise all boats. In sharp lyrics, Primera observes:

> Now that the petroleum is ours,
> they raised the prices of sugar, beans, plantains, and rice.
> Now that the petroleum is ours,
> I don't talk about chopped meat, because that is how the people are left after demonstrations.
> Now that the petroleum is ours,
> the criminal at OPEC continues benefiting while the people are left with a square *arepa*.[2]
> Now that the petroleum is ours,
> long live sovereignty, what's new Mr President? Has the wealth been converted to food?

Primera reveals the hypocrisy of the mantra that 'now the petroleum is ours'. Primera criticised not only the poverty, oppression and corruption he saw around him but the rhetoric of oil nationalism itself. His lyrics expose how despite the nominal nationalisation of petroleum, Perez's policies led to increased prices, repression and hardship for Venezuela's majority. Primera's music was wildly popular with young people and those who supported progressive politics. Although Primera died at a young age in a mysterious car crash, his songs continue to be important anthems for the Left in Venezuela.

The myth of class harmony and inclusivity promoted by oil nationalism – which Primera's song so skillfully exposes as empty rhetoric – was violently ruptured in the 1980s. As concessions to the poor and working classes decreased in the face of massive debt payments and falling oil prices, tensions rose. For the next decade, Perez's successors turned increasingly to foreign loans and engaged in what Karl has called a politics of postponement (1997), attempting to avoid the reality of the financial crisis. In 1983, in an effort to refinance foreign debt, Venezuela devalued its currency. By the mid-1980s debt payments in Venezuela consumed more than half of the state's oil revenues (Karl 1997: 179).[3]

In 1989, massive urban uprisings took place in Caracas in response to the imposition of structural adjustment policies. Chávez's supporters consider the uprising – known as the *Caracazo* in Venezuela – as 'year zero' of the Bolivarian Revolution. The most immediate catalyst of the urban uprising was the doubling of the price of petrol. In defiance of the government's decree to limit the rise in bus fares by only 30 per cent, unofficial bus operators doubled their fares in twenty-four hours, arguing that fares had to reflect increased costs of fuel. The working poor found that they could not afford the increased cost of transport. This shock brought people together in the streets where looting and massive property damage took place. Many people viewed the increase in petrol prices as the ultimate affront to the national ideology that proclaimed that the nation's petroleum resources were jointly owned by the people and the state (Coronil and Skurski 1991: 314). 'To demand that people pay dearly for what was considered to be their national birthright,' Coronil and Skurski assert, 'was to rupture a moral bond established between the state and the *pueblo*' (1991: 315). In effect, the years of oil-nationalist rhetoric instilled in many the idea and expectation that Venezuela's wealth should guarantee not only affordable petrol, but an improved quality of life for all its citizens. Anger over empty promises of redistribution fueled the *Caracazo*, an uprising that made visible the racial and class divisions in Caracas (Hellinger 2003: 31).

The government responded to the uprising with unprecedented brutality in poor neighbourhoods. Politicians described the barrios as savage and irrational in an attempt to erase the questions of social class and the severe economic inequality that the *Caracazo* made so obvious. The memory of the *Caracazo* and the reality of class divisions it exposed so violently were potent elements in the background of changes I observed in the mid-2000s. The imposition of structural adjustment policies that catalysed the *Caracazo* formed part of the agenda of liberalisation and 'free market fundamentalism' initiated by the World Bank and the International Monetary

Fund (Harvey 2005). Following this market logic, PDVSA opened the company for foreign investment and weakened its ties to OPEC by breaking its commitments to production quotas. As a result, oil prices fell (Lander 2007). PDVSA executives, who shared an agenda and outlook with international oil companies with whom they had long ties, sought to limit its financial obligations to the state and asserted that international petroleum prices should be established by market laws, without interferences of the governments of consuming or producing countries (López-Maya 2005; Mommer 2003).

Chávez was first elected in 1998. His campaign advanced the critique that corrupt elites had stolen the peoples' birthright of oil wealth (McCoy 2004). His election was understood by many to be symptomatic of the disillusionment many felt with state institutions. Chávez's task as a leader of a new political movement was to reject wholeheartedly the politics, institutions and ideology of the past while restoring the nation's confidence and belief in the Venezuelan state. The Venezuelan state was perceived by many as otherworldly, in part because of the dazzling displays of magical spectacle that Coronil (2007) outlines. Participation in government was out of reach for the majority of the population. Chávez claimed that his political project would, in effect, do away with the alienation people felt from politics and the state. He promised that he would facilitate the remaking of state through the participation of Venezuela's poor.

Like previous Venezuelan politicians, Chávez depends on oil nationalism to build and unite his base. However, Chávez's rhetoric of liberation categorises the would-be usurpers of the nation's rich sub-soil as not only the international elite, but the Venezuelan elite as well. During his first few years in office, Chávez's reforms, according to Lander and López-Maya (2002), centred around four major shifts in policy: 1) the reestablishment of the power of the Executive over PDVSA through the Ministry of Energy and Mines to define and implement policy; 2) the privileging of the collection of petroleum royalties, an easier and more transparent process than the previous policy to collect revenues through taxes; 3) the defence of OPEC prices; and 4) the end to the privatisation of PDVSA, through laws such as the 2001 *Ley Orgánica de Hidrocarburos* that allowed the government to renegotiate contracts with oil companies signed under previous regimes.

The government's conflict with PDVSA culminated when PDVSA's leaders together with the country's largest trade union federation, the Confederation of Venezuelan Workers (CTV) and the business federation, Fedecámaras, led a one-day strike that culminated in a coup d'état. Elements of the Venezuelan military who turned against Chávez surrounded the Presidential Palace and Venezolano de Televisión, the only state television channel at the time, was taken off the air. The cooperate media's complicity in staging the coup has been widely recognised, leading some critics to call the 2002 fiasco the world's first 'media coup' (see Hernández 2004). The interim president, Pedro Carmona, reinstated Guacaipuro Lameda as President of PDVSA. Chávez had forced Lamenda out of PDVSA for his opposition to reforms. Lameda immediately sought to weaken Venezuela's relationship with OPEC and proclaimed 'not one more barrel of oil for Cuba' (Lander and López-Maya 2002). The coup suffered a surprising reversal when pro-Chávez supporters in the military who stayed loyal to Chávez worked to reverse the coup while large numbers of people from Caracas' poor barrios surrounded the palace and demanded that Chávez be reinstated. Thirty-six hours after being removed from office, Chávez reassumed the presidency.

Chávez's bid for political control and stability was challenged again less than a year later when an employers' trade-union strike paralysed the oil industry for over two months in an effort to oust Chávez from leadership. Seventeen thousand mostly white-collar skilled oil workers were urged by management to walk out to challenge Chávez's attempt to gain control of PDVSA. 'The hour has arrived to wage the great battle for oil,' Chávez said during the first week of the strike, which pro-government groups referred to as a management lockout. The strike, the longest and largest in Latin American history, brought the oil industry to a virtual standstill, while the informal sector of the economy which employs Venezuela's poor majority continued with business as usual.[4]

The two-month strike crippled Venezuela's oil industry and cost the country billions of dollars in lost profits. It resulted, however, in a golden opportunity for Chávez to gain control of the petroleum industry, converting it into a key instrument for the implementation of his political project (López-Maya 2005: 274). In the strike's aftermath, Chávez fired eighteen thousand of PDVSA's forty thousand employees. Ali Rodriguez, the newly appointed president of PDVSA, asserted that PDVSA was 'part of the state, even while being a corporation. That is, our effort is not just to add value to natural resources, not just to increase contributions to the state, not just to increase the income of the corporation, but to also valorise the human being' (Wilpert 2004). Chávez began emphasising his rejection of the logic of neo-liberal globalisation that seeks to 'turn resources like oil, previously defined as a national patrimony, into mere commodities subjected to the free play of market forces' (Coronil 2000: 364).[5] Venezuela's recent history demonstrates the centrality of the fight over how to administer oil. Unlike previous leaders, Chávez used the politics of oil not to smooth over class divides, but rather to expose, politicise and make use of socio-economic divides to build and unite his base and to argue for vast redistribution of oil profits.

Catia TVe had its origins shortly after the 1989 *Caracazo*. Residents of Manicomio, a small neighbourhood in west Caracas named after the near-by psychiatric hospital, organised a local *Casa de Cultura* (Culture House) in a building that had been looted and abandoned during the uprising. The *Casa de Cultura* functioned as a cultural and community centre, bringing together community members committed to organising to secure basic necessities for the neighbourhood while also providing arts and educational programs for Manicomio residents. A film club soon followed using a 16-mm projector purchased with a grant from the Federation of Centres of Cinematographic Culture (FEVEC), a state-funded initiative. The Manicomio Film Club aimed to bring people together as a community to watch films, rather than watching television alone in their own homes. A crucial moment in the station's history came later when the Film Club presented a proposal to the mayor of Caracas and received funding to buy a video camera. The film club's screenings expanded to include the documentaries made in the film club, and for the first time, members of Manicomio saw their own image projected on screen.

Ricardo Márquez, one of the founding members of the Film Club and Catia TVe's Director between 2004 and 2008, was born and raised in Manicomio. In a 2003 interview, Márquez explained,

> For fifty years we've been passive receptors of media. And the mass media have broadcast rubbish. When they come to a poor neighbourhood they denounce the murders, the criminals, the rapes. But they've never come to document the community organising itself, the community fighting for its children, the community doing cultural activities. Nothing. They come to make news that bleeds.... So community media has established itself to fill this gap that for so many years the commercial media has left open (Márquez 2003).

By 1996, Márquez had become a key cultural broker, mediating between the neighbourhood of Manicomio and the sympathetic politicians in local government. Reaching beyond the neighbourhood, Márquez and his middle-class ally Blanca Eekout, a young activist and university student living in the neighbourhood, also formed important alliances with several students and professors at the Central University in Caracas, who provided key technical support.

With new telecommunication laws passed in 2000 and 2002 Catia TVe became a licensed broadcaster. A grant from the government and donated equipment allowed Catia TVe to set up their operations in a hospital located in Manicomio. The station began broadcasting two hours daily and contributed to a weekly programming slot on VTV, the national government channel. From the beginning Catia TVe's programming included short educational and public service documentaries, which covered current neighbourhood issues and local history, and fiction films treating various issues such as health care, refuse management and domestic violence. In 2006, Catia TVe had thirty paid staff members and dozens of volunteers who were organised into small teams of independent producers, almost all of whom were from the station's surrounding poor neighbourhoods. After attending free filmmaking workshops organised by the station, volunteer producers contributed to the station's programming. The station provided an unprecedented opportunity for some of Caracas' poorest citizens to make their own media and document their diverse neighbourhoods.

Catia TVe's prominence in the changing landscape of power during this period was a result of its character as both a grassroots project and a media project. Media and politics became increasingly inseparable in Venezuela. With the collapse of traditional political parties in the 1990s, media outlets provided not simply a terrain for political debate; rather, media spokespeople became key political actors who shaped and determined politics in ways intended to resonate with local and global audiences. No longer 'a stage' for politics, media producers *staged* politics.[6] Becoming media producers, in other words, was crucial to becoming political prominent social actors. Hence, Catia TVe's participation in state spectacle had particular symbolic efficacy: evidence that popular subjects had become media producers suggest that the poor had assumed the status of politically influential actors.

Although the community television station had a high profile among barrio activists, government institutions and state television producers in Caracas, my research revealed that few people actually watched the station's broadcasts. The station's staff claims that their ultra high frequency signal reaches the homes of half of Caracas' almost five million people. However, in practice the signal's reach was unpredictable; moreover, the repetitive and unscheduled programming and the low production quality of sound and lighting limited audience numbers.

The station's producers recognised that their viewing audience was small but expressed ambivalent attitudes about the importance of audience numbers. The station's motto, 'Don't Watch Television, Make it!' articulated their primary interest in producing media producers, not viewers. When Catia TVe staff urged their community to become producers rather than remain passive audience members, they challenged the historical premises of the relationship between the popular masses and the state. In effect, their slogan was a rallying cry that placed front and centre the question of the relationship between structure and agency. They asserted their right to represent themselves and challenge relations of interpellation. In the three ethnographic examples that follow, I illustrate that Catia TVe producers by no means exercised complete control over relations of interpellation. Yet, they did take part in new forms of staging, co-producing messages about the state and oil in order to serve their own agenda, which at times simultaneously served the government agenda.

Given their small viewing audience, Catia TVe's prominence and political clout could not be attributed to the impact of their programming but was a result of the practices of Catia TVe's producers and leaders. These practices included the consistent presence of the station's leaders as spokespeople for the community media movement on state television and in face-to-face settings at meetings, press conferences and marches. Catia TVe's political and social capital was gained through the savvy engagement of social networks and participation in key political events between 2002 and 2006.

The three ethnographic examples that follow illustrate how Catia TVe producers took part in new forms of staging, co-producing messages about the state and oil in order to serve their own agenda, which at times simultaneously served the government agenda. I call attention to how the process of producing media is a rich site to examine the complex formation of subjectivity and how participation in spectacles, just as in other dramatised art forms, 'generate and regenerate the very subjectivity they pretend only to display' (Geertz 1973, quoted in Ortner 2005: 39).

Ethnographic Case One: Co-producing the State's Message

In 2003, the anti-Chávez Mayor of Caracas evicted Catia TVe from their original headquarters in a room of the local hospital in the poor neighbourhood where the station's founders lived. The Mayor, a former journalist, claimed that the television waves of the station's transmitter were a hazard to the hospital's patients. Fortunately for the station, just a few months earlier the Ministry of the Interior had granted Catia TVe a rent-free fifty-year lease to an abandoned building in a poor neighbourhood of Caracas. The move had been slow, however, because Catia TVe's founders had to raise the money to restore the dilapidated building. The media publicity generated by Catia TVe's eviction proved to be a boon in gaining recognition nationally and internationally. As a victim of Chávez's Opposition, Catia TVe gained notoriety and support among Chávez supporters and the government. Ricardo Márquez, Catia TVe's director, explained that when he went to PDVSA in search of funds, people at the state oil company had already heard of the station and were receptive. 'They gave us tables, chairs, lamps, things for them that weren't useful anymore but served us perfectly fine.' In addition to furniture, PDVSA provided Catia TVe large loans to purchase the materials to restore their new facilities, the technical equipment to broadcast their signal, and the computer and cameras to film and edit their productions.

In order to repay these loans, Catia TVe broadcast lengthy infomercials promoting PDVSA twice daily. After the loans were paid off, Catia TVe continued to broadcast PDVSA infomercials to finance the station. In the wake of the 2003 petroleum strike, which crippled the industry and ultimately granted Chávez complete control of PDVSA, the company launched an aggressive publicity campaign to market itself as the 'new' PDVSA. The campaign focused on sovereignty and self-determination of PDVSA, emphasising the message that the excluded and left behind *pueblo* benefits from the state's control of the oil company. Lengthy informational commercials about the 'new' PDVSA played not only on Catia TVe, but also on the state-run channels, as well as on Telesur, a pan-Latin American news channel started by the Chávez government and modelled on CNN.

Every few weeks in 2005–2007, Catia TVe received a new infomercial entitled 'PDVSA Advances' produced by PDVSA's publicity department. The infomercials, which lasted up to five minutes, contained information about the latest off-shore exploration, development projects and deals with international companies. Lengthy clips from PDVSA press conferences were included, that provide detailed information about PDVSA's earnings and the amount of money invested in social programnes. If before the population knew little about PDVSA and its day-to-day business, anyone who tuned into state or community television during this period could not possibly avoid this information.

PDVSA advertisements seemed effective in delivering their message to many of the producers I spoke with at Catia TVe, who in their daily lives were also witnessing the investment of oil money in social programmes. One afternoon, I found Andres, a 48-year-old volunteer at the television station, sitting in Catia TVe's small cafeteria area watching a PDVSA infomercial on a small television almost always tuned to Catia TVe. Andres learned about Catia TVe when the station's founders gave a presentation to a class he was taking as part of *Mision Ribas*, the secondary education programme the Chávez government created using oil money. The infomercial we watched finished with the slogan 'Now Venezuela is truly planting the seeds of petroleum'. Andres explained to me that that phrase *'sembrar el petroleo'* (plant or sow the petroleum) was a phrase coined by Arturo Uslar Pietri, a Venezuelan politician from the 1930s. Lighting a cigarette, Andres commented that 'politicians have used that phrase for decades but no one has really done it until Chávez'. Andres shuffled the mini-digital video tapes in his hands that he had come to the station to edit. Earlier that week he had borrowed a camera from Catia TVe to film the reconstruction of one of his neighbour's homes financed by PDVSA. 'Before, they didn't understand what harvesting the oil really meant,' he said. 'It means invest-ing in the people of Venezuela, in providing them necessities and services, not in inverting the resources in PDVSA or in the hands of the few.'

While Andres and others responded to the official PDVSA advertise-ments with a measure of pride and satisfaction, others producers ex-pressed frustration with having to play the PDVSA advertisements on Catia TVe. At a meeting held at Catia TVe that discussed the reliance of the community station on state resources, Hector, one of the Catia TVe assistant directors commented: 'Many times, publicity enters community media and spoils everything that a community media station is. This has happened with PDVSA. PDVSA sends publicity where there is an engi-neer with lipstick, all made-up with make-up, and she's opening a petro-leum valve. Well, come on, that's just a lie. It shows we have the repetition of a capitalist mode of communication.' Hector expressed his understand-ing that the overt staging of perfectly made-up individuals did not match the goals of community media, whose stated mission was to allow 'the people' to make their own voice and image.

At around the same time that Catia TVe was trying to raise funds to re-model their new facility, PDVSA Gas, a subsidiary of PDVSA dedicated to the exploration of natural gas reserves, approached Catia TVe and invited the station to apply to do video production for the company. Márquez, the director at the time, explained, 'we went and competed with professional production companies, including some international ones…. But we went and demonstrated what we could do and they tested us, and we won the contract.' Catia TVe's contract with PDVSA Gas included filming the com-pany's events, symposiums, workshops in Caracas, and projects PDVSA Gas had undertaken in different towns throughout Venezuela. From this material, Catia TVe produced promotional segments about the company. Given the relative inexperience of Catia TVe producers, it seemed likely that PDVSA's desire to work with Catia TVe involved the way in which their collaboration might legitimise PDVSA's claim that the company is truly of and for the people. Catia TVe's less polished production values and the 'community media feel' of the segments they co-produced sub-stantiate PDVSA Gas's message that the poor majority now benefit from and participate in the state company.

Arlene, Catia TVe's then administrative director, directed and pro-duced these informational commercials and short documentaries. From a middle class background, Arlene was working at a large private compa-ny when the growing alienation she felt from the attitudes of her middle class colleagues toward Chávez during the coup and the oil strike led her to find work at Catia TVe. According to Arlene, Catia TVe brought the same approach to making information segments about PDVSA Gas that they used in their own neighbourhoods. She explained:

> The idea of the informational segments is to show what's really happening in the popular zones, to show the reality. We don't want to make simple institutional publicity that has empty images and doesn't show the people participating. We don't make a script and cast people. If there is an event or activity and people express what they feel about the benefits [of PDVSA Gas's work] and the engineer explains some process – from this material we'll create an informational segment. We want people to see the reality. That's how our television station is.

Unlike the perfectly manicured people of the official PDVSA advertisements, Arlene asserted that the promotional material Catia TVe made for PDVSA Gas included interviews with 'real' people. She rejected any staging of the advertisement and instead wanted to show poor people participating in events and learning about the gas company. Arlene commented, 'People from the communities want to see what we make … . And when they see it they say wow, how beautiful. There's an appreciation and valorisation of who they are. They see it [PDVSA Gas] as their company. This is their company. It's a huge change.' Arlene emphasised that this kind of collaboration with PDVSA before Chávez took control of PDVSA would have been impossible and noted, 'Now the vision and missions of PDVSA are good; PDVSA is interested in the social development and development of communities. I can't say that everything is perfect, because one doesn't really know, and I'm not inside to see it in order to know, but I believe that yes, they have accomplished a lot.' Arlene emphasised, 'the people have appropriated something that is truly theirs.'

Arlene noted that when they first started making the promotional segments, in early 2003, Catia TVe followed a script and did not depart from what the company asked them to cover. Later they branched out from the script and started documenting what they felt was important. She asserted, however, that the public relations producers at PDVSA Gas were more interested in composing a 'perfect' picture. Jhonny, a nineteen-year-old volunteer at Catia TVe, worked as a camera person with Arlene to produce PDVSA Gas's advertisements. Jhonny's production experience consisted of several videos he had made in his poor neighbourhood in a free workshop offered by Catia TVe just a year earlier. Jhonny explained, 'One of the first differences we had with them [PDVSA Gas producers] was about *bombonas*, which they claimed were a thing of the past.' *Bombonas*, metal canisters that contain cooking gas, are still found predominantly in poor areas in Caracas without central pipe lines that deliver gas to homes. According to Freddy, PDVSA Gas producers did not want to show gas tanks in the segments they were producing. Freddy explained, 'We said, "hey, listen, *bombonas* are still used by lots of people". From there began the differences.' Freddy concluded:

> We ended up having distinct visions of what was the mission of PDVSA Gas and what should be focused on given the directives of the President [Chávez]. The people in charge of public relations in PDVSA were interested in something else. They wanted special effects stuff and weren't even interested in the Revolution or the process of putting gas lines in barrios, which was something really important.

Freddy claimed that unlike those employed at PDVSA Gas, Catia TVe truly understood Chávez's goal for the company, and sought to remake PDVSA Gas's image according to that vision. The directors of Catia TVe explained that they stopped working with PDVSA Gas when their 'distinct visions' of the company's purpose became increasingly difficult to overcome. Catia TVe's approach to making promotional segments that reflect people's experiences and lives conflicted with PDVSA Gas's expectations and ultimately led to the non-renewal of the contract.

Catia TVe's short-lived collaboration with PDVSA Gas illustrates the way in which Catia TVe sought to shape the message of oil nationalism through an audio-visual text that they felt accurately reflected the realities of Caracas's poor neighbourhoods. Catia TVe refused to ignore the ongoing deficiencies in infrastructure that still plague the *barrios*. They engaged in a struggle over the representation of daily life and the success of the gas company. Catia TVe was interested in producing publicity that went beyond the traditional script and represented the realities of barrio life. Despite the symbolic efficacy Catia TVe's production of PDVSA Gas's message might have afforded the company, the PDVSA Gas producers were ultimately inflexible. Arlene and Jhonny found that PDVSA Gas's producers were unwilling to follow their community media approach.

Arlene, Freddy and Hector resisted staging scenes they felt were fabricated and communicated a sense that Catia TVe was more true to Chávez's vision than those employed by the company to create publicity for PDVSA. Nevertheless, Catia TVe continued to broadcast the PDVSA infomercials on their airwaves in order to fund the station, despite criticisms like Hector's that official propaganda could 'spoil everything that a community televisions station is'. While the official PDVSA infomercials continued to play on Catia TVe after they stopped producing segments for PDVSA Gas and therefore to a certain extent legitimised the state message, these state-produced propaganda segments were framed in the sequence of Catia TVe's programming by community-made productions that often highlighted the problems that continued to plague poor neighbourhoods.

These barrio productions at times challenged the notion that oil resources are being delivered to the people. Arlene, Jhonny and Hector did not explore, however, Catia TVe's involvement in other moments of staging. I now turn to analyse two examples of Catia TVe involvement in producing state spectacle.

Case Two: Attending State Spectacle

A few days before the presidential recall referendum in 2004, which opposition groups hoped would cut short Chávez's mandate, I accompanied two Catia TVe producers to a press conference to which the station had been invited at PDVSA's headquarters. When we arrived at the reception area of the tall concrete and glass PDVSA building, Marianela and Gloria, both Catia TVe staff members, excitedly presented their Catia TVe press credentials. I presented my US passport and explained my project. We were quickly granted permission to enter. Passing through the cool quiet halls of PDVSA's headquarters, the women's excited tones became hushed. Marianela, who was about thirty years old, grew up in the neighbourhood where Catia TVe originated and started working at the station to help with administrative issues, particularly fundraising. Gloria, in her mid forties, had been involved in Catia TVe since its earliest days, volunteering as an actress for Catia TVe's first video productions about domestic violence. In addition to working at Catia TVe in the production department, Gloria had just started her undergraduate degree in Communications at the Universidad Bolivariana, a university created in a former PDVSA building the Chávez government gained control of after the 2003 oil strike.

We entered a long room bustling with people. Numerous television crews had already arrived. Their massive cameras were perched on tripods in an area marked off with blue velvet ropes. Streams of cable flowed towards a table crowded with microphones decorated with bright emblems of the national television networks. Each camera was surrounded by two or three large men in jeans and long-sleeved t-shirts. They chatted with each other or on their mobile phones. In the rows of metal chairs sat men and women, many dressed in suits.

Gloria and Marianela marched down the middle aisle towards where the camera crews were set up. Gloria's bright orange headband, which matched her orange t-shirt, made her visible from across the room. Finding the roped off area for the press already full, Gloria and Marianela settled for a space on the floor in front of the other camera crews and took out their camcorder. Marianela balanced the camera on her bent knee, creating a make-shift tripod. Gloria's identification card, dangling around her neck, informed on-lookers that they were from Catia TVe. A security guard monitoring the room noticed Gloria and Marianela but did not ask them to move. Although they were positioned at the feet of the profession-al press core, the layout made them more visible to the other camera crews and afforded them an unobscured camera angle. While the other women who were there representing media outlets were reporters, dressed in for-mal attire (suits with heels) and heavy make-up, Gloria and Marianela were the only women camera operators, the only non-professional media producers, and they were casually dressed.

When the press conference began it became clear that its purpose was to calm the nerves of international investors on the tense eve of the refer-endum. Rafael Ramírez, the Minister of Energy and Mines, together with Ali Rodriguez Araque, then President of PDVSA, firmly asserted that the referendum presented no risks of instability for national or international oil investors. Ramírez and Araque also took the opportunity to highlight PDVSA's commitment to social investment. In a series of complex graphs and charts, Ramírez and Araque explained that US$1.7 billion from PD-VSA's US$5 billion budget financed social programmes. The display of de-tailed statistics was part of a language of state and practice of governmen-tality (Foucault 1991), which brought 'the state' into being before our eyes. A further element of creating the 'effect of stateness' (Mitchell 1999) for the Bolivarian Revolutionary State was the presence of Catia TVe producers.

During the question and answer period towards the end, international and national reporters peppered Ramírez and Araque with questions about what would happen if Chávez were to lose the referendum. Neither of the women from Catia TVe asked a question. When it was over they approached a man they knew from PDVSA who had been involved in securing funds for Catia TVe. After a friendly chat we said goodbye. Glo-ria and Marianela decided to have lunch in the PDVSA cafeteria. Over a low-priced meal, they told me about how their lives had changed remark-ably in the preceding few years. Gloria pinched her upper arm, remarking on the extra layer she now had. 'I was so skinny back then. I mean, we were really struggling; both my husband and I were unemployed. There just wasn't enough to go around.' Looking around, Marianela asserted, 'We never would have been let in here before.' Laughing she added, 'They would have accused us of trying to *rancho*-ise (make into a poor person's house) PDVSA.'

To my surprise, in the days that followed, Gloria and Marianela never edited or broadcast the footage they had shot at the press conference. They were busy organising community media producers to film their neigh-bourhoods during the recall vote. When I asked Gloria why, she laughed uncomfortably saying, 'Well, everyone knows about that by now.' The press conference, in fact, had been broadcast live on the state channel and was covered later that same day on state and commercial television.

Gloria and Marianela's attendance at the PDVSA conference was clearly not intended to grant 'voice to the voiceless' or 'make the invisible, visible' over the airwaves of Catia TVe, which was the stated goal of the station. Rather, Gloria and Marianela were making the formerly invisible visible by their presence at the press conference. They did not create news coverage. Instead they produced a display of popular power in front of journalists from all over the world. At the same time, in the company of Venezuelan professional media producers (who come largely from middle class backgrounds) as well as international observers, Gloria and Marianela asserted themselves as media savvy modern subjects with the right and the ability to participate in the representation of the state to the people. Increasing the visibility of Catia TVe was also important to confirm that PDVSA was making a good investment in their station and to increase their future chances of raising funds. They were also substantiating a message of oil nationalism; their presence provided evidence of the process of investing oil money into social programmes. The attendance of these barrio-based producers at the state oil company's press conference on the eve of the referendum served the interests of both PDVSA and Catia TVe.

The display of the exercise of rights first granted by the 1999 Constitution for 'the people' to produce media carried much symbolic weight for the Chávez government whose legitimacy depended on displays of its commitment to social justice and the poor, and the appearance that social change was being initiated from below. Press conferences serve as one obvious practice of state spectacles; their sole purpose is to draw media attention to an issue that the conveners wish to highlight. While this scenario could be assessed as clients performing their empowerment to placate their patron, this example suggests that the mutually beneficial collusive construction of agency taking place was more complex than the traditional explanation of clientelism affords. Gloria's and Marianela's participation in producing state spectacle and discourse allowed them to contribute to the state's narrative about itself and at the same time form their own life narratives. Their participation in state spectacle such as this press conference and what it meant for their own empowerment cannot be separated from their day-to-day experiences of the state in educational programmes made possible by the Chávez government's redistribution of oil rents.

Case Three: Re-nationalising the Oil?

Late one afternoon, a woman from the Ministry for Communication and Information (MinCI) telephoned Vanessa, Head of Production at Catia TVe (a department of four people), to invite the station to an upcoming event: the celebration of the 'nationalisation' of the oil belt of Venezuela's Orinoco River. The woman from MinCI told Vanessa that they wanted a Catia TVe 'reporter' to be there to document the historic assertion of Venezuela's 'petroleum sovereignty'. On an almost weekly basis, MinCI called Catia TVe to invite them to press conferences at the presidential palace or other official state events. A special section of MinCI was dedicated to the administration of issues concerning 'Community and Alternative Media'. Most often the agendas of MinCI and Catia TVe were compatible: the station was pleased to have the opportunity to attend important press conferences, like the one described above. Nevertheless Vanessa, the head of production, expressed the concern that MinCi had little understanding of Catia TVe's limited production capacity. She wanted the production department to also be available to cover events that were directly related to community organising projects and problems in the surrounding neighbourhoods. Vanessa told me that the problem with the financial support they receive for playing MinCI advertisements was that it was accompanied by what she called 'el combo' of having to cover events at which MinCI deemed it was necessary for Catia TVe to be present. MinCI's 'invitation' to accompany the Venezuealan state press on a flight to the Orinoco River that week was thus experienced as more of an order than a request.

A few days later, Nestor, an eighteen-year-old Catia TVe producer from a poor family in Caracas, accompanied state press outlets on an aeroplane to 'cover' the celebration. That day, I tracked the news coverage carefully on television. Both state-operated and commercial networks focused on the events taking place at the Orinoco Oil Belt, which Chávez billed the 'Nationalisation of the Oil Belt of the Orinoco River'. Having heard no discussion of new agreements or changes to oil policy in the weeks leading up to that day's events, I was confused. Flicking through the television channels did little to clarify matters.

On the state-run television channels, Venezolana de Televisión (VTV) and Vive TV, I watched Chávez and Rafael Ramírez, the Minister of Popular Power for Energy and Petroleum and PDVSA's president, give speeches. They stood in front of a huge banner of Chávez, his fist raised, superimposed on a map of Venezuela, with a slogan underneath that read 'Full Petroleum Sovereignty. On the Road to Socialism!' In front of a sea of people dressed in red, Chávez asserted: 'This is truly the end of the oil opening which we have suffered too long at the hands of imperialists

and their national lackeys. Though they were born here, these Venezu-
elans don't have a fibre, not even one molecule of Venezuelan-ness. To be
Venezuelan you have to love Venezuela. That's how we are, the authentic
Venezuelans.' The crowd roared in approval.

The segment cut to an interview with a PDVSA worker, dressed in a
red hard hat and overalls, who claimed, 'We are here for the progress
of the nation, in fraternity and with humility. This is the most happy a
human being could feel.' Over shots of PDVSA workers entering buildings *en masse*, indicating they were taking over the facilities, the narrator
of VTV asserted: 'Now these fields will be the people's through PDVSA
for the socio-economic transformation of the nation.' The news segment
ended with thousands singing the Venezuelan national anthem and shots
of signs reading 'Long Live Venezuela, Free and Sovereign!'

On Globovision, a national commercial twenty-four-hour news network staunchly aligned with the government's opposition, Leopoldo
Castillo, the host of *Alo Ciudadano*, was conducting an interview about
that day's events at the Orinoco Oil Belt. The programme is a call-in talk
show established as a counter-point to Chávez's weekly marathon television programme *Alo Presidente*. The programme's guest, labelled with the
title 'Oil Expert', explained with an air of disgust that what was *actually*
happening was that the government was 'making a salad out of the terms
when they used the word *nationalisation*'. He continued, 'What took place
today was just a simple transfer of shares so that PDVSA owns 60 per cent
of the interests of the four major companies who operate in the Orinoco
Oil Belt. This is simply putting in place what was already established in
the 2001 Law of Hydrocarbons.'

With a dramatic tone, the host finished their discussion of the day's events
with the assertion, 'If the President's announcement today about oil was really important – despite the disguise, forgetting the performance [*zarzuela*],
putting aside the trumpets – the news agencies would have been bouncing
up and down excitedly to cover it. Not even CNN in Spanish, which lives
for Chávez and always immediately puts him on the air, is paying attention.
Because this is a comedy!' For Castillo the fact that there were few news
agencies at the event was proof that it was politically insignificant.

People I spoke to at Catia TVe explained to me that now PDVSA owned
the majority of interests of the companies operating in the Orinoco Belt
Basin. 'We are re-asserting our sovereignty', several people claimed, repeating the message on state television. One producer I spoke with, however, gave me a long lecture about how the government should not extract
oil at all. She had just seen Al Gore's documentary *An Inconvenient Truth*
and she explained how global warming was worsening as result of the
burning of fossil fuels. None of this made the situation I saw on television

any clearer. This moment was not unlike many others: the perspectives expressed on commercial and state television were radically contradictory. Was PDVSA asserting more control over foreign involvement in oil? Was this a move to re-nationalise gains that had been lost during the privatisation of PDVSA in the 1990s or was this a highly orchestrated publicity event meant to build support for the Chávez government?

In the early-1990s, the Venezuelan government, through the 'oil opening', allowed foreign investment in the Orinoco Oil Belt, a region widely understood to contain the world's largest reserves of extra-heavy crude oil. As a result of the 'old' PDVSA contracts, the state company was a minority stakeholder in the Orinoco Oil Belt ventures with foreign companies. Chávez's 2001 Law of Hydrocarbons created the legal figure of joint ventures (empresas mixtas) between foreign oil and PDVSA, undoing the less preferential agreements made by the previous leaders of PDVSA. In February 2007, the president decreed that all private, national and international companies operating in the Orinoco had to renegotiate, in the following four months, their transference to new joint ventures with PDVSA in the terms originally established by the 2001 Law of Hydrocarbons (Lander 2007). These changes implied significant increase in profit for PDVSA.

The event I witnessed via television that day (the first of May, a date chosen no doubt for its worldwide regard by many as a day to celebrate the achievements of the working class) marked the agreement of four international oil companies to the new terms that established PDVSA as the majority stake holder in all the joint ventures with foreign companies. While these agreements with foreign oil companies were worked out over long and hard fought negotiations between the international oil giants and PDVSA, the news propagated by PDVSA and the Ministry of Communications and relayed by the state television channels was that oil in Venezuela had finally been renationalised. Through an intricate display of oil nationalism, the new joint ventures were spectacularised as the true assertion of Venezuelan sovereignty.

Nestor, the Catia TVe producer, returned exhausted but ebullient from his trip to cover the events that day at the Orinoco Oil Belt. The sun and the crowds were intense, he told me, but he met someone from a community radio station who helped him conduct interviews. He beamed. 'It was really exciting to be there to celebrate our petroleum sovereignty.' I commented to him that I was confused about what it all meant. He explained to me, 'Now PDVSA owns the majority stakes of all those companies. It's a reversal of the policies that the old elites of PDVSA had put in place.'

Several days later, after Nestor had had the time to catch up on his sleep and the work he had missed, he sat down to edit the footage he had filmed of the 'nationalisation'. His segment began with Chávez and the minister

Ramírez asserting that the day's events signified the true completion of Venezuela's independence and sovereignty. Unlike the official state coverage, Nestor's segment included interviews with several on-lookers who did not work for PDVSA. One older woman who had travelled for several hours just to see Chávez seemed uninterested in the specifics of the day's events, commenting that 'whatever Chávez says is good'. Another on-looker noted, 'This should have been done a long time ago.' Several representatives of a *Consejo Comunal* (Community Committee, a key stone of the government's plan to allow neighbourhood groups to control local governance) commented that 'Now the petroleum is all ours, it belongs to all Venezuelans. Thanks to God, Chávez, and the Revolution.' A PDVSA worker then explained how the reforms meant that all workers could organise for their rights within a united labour union. The final interviewee, who had the last word of the segment, was positive about the 'nationalisation' but commented that there were still joint ventures with foreign companies and it '[wa]sn't one hundred percent Venezuelan, as it should be.'

The Chávez government's assertion of control over PDVSA and reversal of privatisation were indeed bold moves that promised the national oil company higher profits to be invested massively in social programmes. The way this May Day event was staged and represented – with the collaboration of Catia TVe – however, publicised the changes to reflect an even more radical departure from previous PDVSA policies than what was in fact in motion. The state footage which showed workers storming buildings, as if they were taking and occupying foreign companies to reappropriate them for the nation, was a far overblown representation of the day's events, and seemed to purposefully reference images of Fidel Castro's nationalisation of Cuban industries. While the opposition-aligned *Alo Ciudadano down*played the changes, obscuring the significance of PDVSA's majority ownership, the state television coverage *over*played the day's events.

Catia TVe participated in the spectacle, under some duress from the Ministry of Communciation. Catia TVe's presence at the state's staging of events, like Gloria's and Marianela's attendance at the PDVSA press conference, was an important exhibition of the re-investment of Venezuela's oil resource in the 'authentic' Venezuelan *pueblo*. Nestor clearly believed the message of oil sovereignty being produced by the government. Yet he also shot and edited the segment in a way that allowed people to voice their opinions in ways that went beyond the official script of the state-produced coverage. The final interviewee's critique that PDVSA still does not control 100 per cent of the Venezuelan petroleum industry provided a limited critique that the nationalisation did not go far enough. Yet, the segment overall reaffirmed the message that what is good for the state oil company is good for the people.

Nowhere on state television nor at Catia TVe, however, was there a discussion about how PDVSA's new joint venture contracts, while increasing revenues for PDVSA, still involve dealing with transnational oil companies, many of which were involved in practices across the globe that undermine the values that the Bolivarian Revolution claims to hold (for example, in Iraq, Bolivia and Nigeria). Moreover, the negotiation of joint ventures took place with little public debate about either the merits of this new policy or the broader question of how socialism can be constructed in Venezuela atop a capitalist rentier edifice, whose structure the Chávez government has left almost entirely intact.

By attending the event, Nestor co-produced state spectacle, confirmed the state's investment in social projects, and granted the importance of the day's events legitimacy by participating and by broadcasting the events on community television. From his discussion of his experience at the event, it was clear that Nestor felt privileged, energised, and more committed to the message of oil nationalism as a result of being part of the production process of this state spectacle. He expanded Catia TVe's reach from a neighbourhood community television station in Caracas, to a 'news' outlet that travelled across state borders with professional journalists. The most significant result of his being there was not the impact of the news coverage he produced, but his presence and participation at the state spectacle.

Conclusion

The ability of barrio-based leaders to influence the direction of the state and win oil-derived resources for themselves and their communities was contingent upon their constant public performance as agential and autonomous media-savvy subjects who appeared authentically to represent barrio support for the government. I have illustrated that the process of producing this appearance allowed media producers to build confidence and social capital. The accumulation of Catia TVe's participation in state spectacle secured the station's access to resources and social contacts with government actors. Arlene's and Nestor's participation and attempt to refashion the state message of oil nationalism in their co-production of PDVSA Gas advertisements and Gloria's, Marianela's and Nestor's participation at state spectacles generated the kinds of subjectivity that their participation in these oil-nationalist productions seem only to display.

Local actors and organisations like Catia TVe, which support the government and receive state funding, have been depicted as intoxicated followers of Chávez who lack the ability to form nuanced analyses of the political landscape (Duno Gottberg 2004). Chávez's popularity is commonly explained by his opposition and by scholars and critics as a result of state patronage and clientelist networks in which goods and services are exchanged for votes (Hawkins 2003). Analysing Catia TVe's relationship with government actors only through the traditional lens of clientelism obfuscates the practices of everyday state formation in which barrio subjects are engaged (Schiller 2011). The mutually reciprocal relations between the grassroots and the state were not simply co-optation of social movement agency, rather it was a dialogic production of power for both barrio-based producers and the ascendant governing elite, albeit within unequal relations of force.

Oil nationalist discourse can be used not only to maintain the status quo and legitimate the state, but also, as is explored in this chapter, as a basis to exert pressure on the state from below. In tracing how nationalist messages about oil are produced and circulated, I have argued that Chávez's policies were not simply embraced from the bottom but involve the active participation and influence of barrio-based media producers. Catia TVe's relationship with government representatives and state funding brings to the fore the 'complex issue of the relationship between autonomy and subordination' (Joseph and Nugent 1994: 23). Following Joseph and Nugent, I recognise that neither the 'state' nor 'popular' projects are autonomous; together they are 'reciprocally engaged during particular conjunctures' (ibid.). Catia TV producers attempt to challenge the historic exclusion of the poor from media and politics in order to prevent the Chávez government from recreating the magical state. Catia TVe coproduces state spectacle and embraces a discourse of oil nationalism as part of their effort to advance popular participation and leadership. Catia TVe producers collaborated with the government during this period to produce representations and realities of bottom-up social change.

Notes

1. The 'popular' in the context of Latin America refers to a collective marginalised subject that is often 'strategically produced, marked, hidden, and mediated' (Albro and Himpele forthcoming).
2. An *arepa*, a round corn cake, is a staple in the Venezuela diet. A square *arepa* indicates the failure of a common sense.
3. The third-world debt crisis was initiated and perpetuated by the transformation of US economic policy and diplomacy in the 1980s (Grandin 2006). The crisis was

a golden opportunity to achieve the structural reforms the Reagan administration sought in Latin America and beyond in order to assert the financial and geo-political interests of the United States (ibid.: 184).

4. During the strike, international businesses, like McDonald's, Burger King, and corporate chains in malls remained closed. Local markets and shops operated and patronised by the poor remained open and poorer neighbourhoods quickly returned to normality. The beer and cigarette industry came to a standstill, an inconvenience for the poor and middle classes alike. Nevertheless, a popular chant among chavistas became 'No queremos cerveza, queremos una nueva PDVSA' (We don't want beer, we want a new oil company) (Valentine and Podur 2003).

5. In February 1998, a barrel of oil cost US$11 (McCoy 2004). In late 2007, due to the interruption of flows of oil as a result of the continued US War on Iraq together with Chávez's strengthening of OPEC quotas, a barrel averaged around US$80.

6. The 'spectacularisation of politics' on television has been most visible during significant moments in Venezuela's recent history such as the 1989 urban uprising known as the Caracazo, Chávez's televised apology for his 1992 coup attempt, and most recently during the 2002 coup against Chávez (Hernández 2004).

References

Abrams, Philip. 1988. Notes on the Difficulty of Studying the State. *Journal of Historical Sociology* 1(1): 58–89.

Abu-Lughod, Lila. 2005. *Dramas of Nationhood*. Chicago: University of Chicago Press.

Albro, Robert and Jeff Himpele, nd. *Popular Publics in Latin America: Regional Variations from North to South*, unpublished.

Aretxaga, Begona. 1997. *Shattering Silence: Women, Nationalism, and Political Subjectivity in Northern Ireland*. Princeton: Princeton University Press.

Briceño-León, Roberto. 1990. *Los efectos perversos del petróleo*. Fondo Editorial Acta Científica Venezolana: Consorcio de Ediciones Capriles.

Bustillos, Lourdes Fierro and Yoston Ferrigni. 1981. El Proceso de estructuración capitalista de la formación social Venezolana. In *Formación histórico-social de América Latina*, ed. Germán Carrera Damas, 132–96. Caracas: Universidad Central de Venezuela, Ediciones de la Biblioteca/CENDES.

Coronil, Fernando. 1997. *The Magical State: Nature, Money, and Modernity in Venezuela*. Chicago: University of Chicago Press.

———. Coronil, Fernando. 2000. Toward a Critique of Globalcentrism: Speculations of Capitalism's Nature. *Public Culture* 12(2): 351–74.

Coronil, Fernando and Julie Skurski. 1991. Dismembering and Remembering the Nation: The Semantics of Political Violence in Venezuela. *Soc. Compar. Study Soc. and Hist.* 33(2): 288–337.

Dávila, Luis Ricardo. 1993. Rómulo Betancourt and the Development of Venezuelan Nationalism (1930–1950). *Bulletin of Latin American Research*: 49–63.

Duno Gottberg, Luis. 2004. Mob Outrages: Reflections on the Media Construction of the Masses in Venezuela. *Journal of Latin American Cultural Studies* 13(1): 115–35.

Ferguson, James and Akhil Gupta. 2002. Spatializing States: Toward an Ethnography of Neoliberal Governmentality. *American Ethnologist* 29(4): 981–1002.

Foucault, Michel. 1991. Governmentality. In *The Foucault Effect: Studies in Governmentality*, ed. Burchell. Graham, Colin Gordon and Peter Miller, 87–104. Chicago: University of Chicago Press.

Geertz, Clifford. 1973. *The Interpretation of Cultures*. New York: BasicBooks.

Ginsburg, Faye. 1991. Indigenous Media: Faustian Contract or Global Village? *Cultural Anthropology* 6: 92–112.

Grandin, Greg. 2006. *Empire's Workshop: Latin America, the United States, and the Rise of the New Imperialism*. New York: Owl Books.

Hansen, Thomas Blom and Finn Stepputat. 2001. Introduction. In *States of Imagination: Ethnographic Explorations of the Postcolonial State*, ed. Thomas Bloom Hansen and Finn. Stepputat, 1–38. Durham: Duke University Press.

Hawkins, Kirk. 2003. Populism in Venezuela: The Rise of Chavismo. *Third World Quarterly-Journal of Emerging Areas* 24(6): 1137–60.

Harvey, David. 2005. *A Brief History of Neoliberalism*. Oxford: Oxford University Press.

Hellinger, Daniel. 2003. Political Overview: The Breakdown of Puntofijismo and the Rise of Chavismo. In *Venezuelan Politics in the Chávez Era: Class, Polarization and Conflict*, ed. Steve Ellner and Daniel Hellinger, 27–54. Colorado: Lynne Rienner Publishers.

Hernández, Juan Antonio. 2004. Against the Comedy of Civil Society: Posthegemony, Media and the 2002 Coup d'Etat in Venezuela. *Journal of Latin American Cultural Studies* 13(1): 137–45.

Himpele, Jeff. 2007. *Circuits of Culture: Media, Politics, and Indigenous Identity in the Andes*. Minneapolis: University of Minnesota Press.

Joseph, Gilbert and David Nugent. 1994. Popular Culture and State Formation in Revolutionary Mexico. In *Everyday Forms of State Formation*, ed. Gilbert Joseph and David Nugent, 3–23. Durham: Duke University Press.

Karl, Terry. 1997. *The Paradox of Plenty: Oil Booms and Petro-states*. Berkeley: University of California Press.

Lander, Luis, ed. 2003. *Poder y petróleo en Venezuela*. Caracas: Faces-Universidad Central de Venezuela, PDVSA.

———. 2007. Venezuela: Petróleo, diplomacia e integración. *XXVII Conference of the Latin American Studies Association (LASA)*, Montreal, Canada.

Lander, Luis and Margarita López-Maya. 2002. Venezuela's Oil Reform and Chavismo. *NACLA* 36(1): 21–3.

Lomnitz, Claudio. 2001. *Deep Mexico, Silent Mexico: An Anthropology of Nationalism*. Minneapolis: University of Minnesota Press.

López-Maya, Margarita. 2005. *Del viernes negro al referendo revocatorio*. Caracas: Alfadil Ediciones.

Mankekar, Purnima. 1999. *Screening Culture, Viewing Politics: An Ethnography of Television, Womanhood, and Nation in Postcolonial India*. Durham: Duke University Press.

Marquez, Ricardo. Author interview. Caracas, Venezuela. 2003. Translated from Spanish by author.

McCoy, Jennifer L. 2004. From Representative Democracy to Participatory Democracy? In *The Unraveling of Representative Democracy in Venezuela*, ed. Jennifer L. McCoy and David.J. Myers, 263–95. Baltimore: Johns Hopkins University Press.

McDermott, R.P., and Henry Tylbor. 1995. On the Necessity of Collusion in Conversation. In *The Dialogic Emergence of Culture*, ed. Bruce Mannheim and Dennis Tedlock, 218–36. Urbana: University of Illinois Press.

Mitchell, Timothy. 1999. Society, Economy, and the State Effect. In *State/Culture: State-Formation After the Cultural Turn*, ed. George Steinmetz, 76–97. Ithaca: Cornell University Press.

Mommer, Bernard. 2003. Subversive Oil. In *Venezuelan Politics in the Chávez Era: Class, Polarization and Conflict*, ed. Steve Ellner and Daniel Hellinger, 131–46. Boulder, CA: Lynne Rienner Publishers.

Ortner, Sherry. 2005. Subjectivity and Cultural Critique. *Anthropological Theory* 5(1): 31–52.

Petras, James, and Morris Morely. 1978. The Venezuelan Development 'Model and U.S. Policy. In *Critical Perspectives on Imperialism and Social Class in the Third World.*, 228–44. New York: Monthly Review Press.

Quintero, Rodolfo. 1972. *Antropología del petróleo*. Mexico: Siglo Ventiuno Editores.

Schiller, Naomi. 2011. Catia Sees You: Community Television, Clientelism, and Participatory Statemaking in the Chávez Era. In *Venezuela's Bolivarian Democracy: Participation, Politics and Culture under Chávez*, ed. David Smilde and Daniel Hellinger. Durham: Duke University Press: 104–130.

Scott, James. 1998. *Seeing Like a State: How Certain Schemes to Improve the Human Condition Have Failed*. New Haven: Yale University Press.

Steinmetz, George. 1999. Introduction. In *State/Culture: State Formation after the Cultural Turn*, ed. George Steinmetz, 1–49. Cornell: Cornell University Press.

Taussig, Michael. 1993. Maleficium: State Fetishism. In *Fetishism as Cultural Discourse*, ed. Emily Apter and William Pietz, 217–47. Ithaca: Cornell University Press.

Trouillot, Michel-Rolph. 2001. The Anthropology of the State in the Age of Globalisation. *Current Anthropology* 42(1): 125–38.

Valentine, Diana and Justin Podur. 2003. Slow, Low Intensity (So Far Largely Bloodless), Class Warfare. http://www.zcommunications.org/slow-low-intensity-so-far-largely-bloodless-class-warfare-by-diana-valentine (accessed 30 July 2010).

Wilpert, Gregroy. 2004. The Main Obstacle Is the Administrative Structure of the Venezuelan State. http://venezuelanalysis.com/analysis/599 (accessed 20 August 2004).

Wortham, Erica. 2002. Narratives of Location: Televisual Media and the Production of Indigenous Identities in Mexico. Doctoral Dissertation, Anthropology, New York University.

———. 2004. Between the State and Indigenous Autonomy: Unpacking Video Indígena in Mexico. *American Anthropologist* 106(2): 363–69.

Chapter 9

FLASHPOINTS OF SOVEREIGNTY

Territorial Conflict and Natural Gas in Bolivia

Bret Gustafson

It was mid-May of 2006 in Camiri, a provincial city of thirty thousand in the gas- and oil-rich Chaco region of southeastern Bolivia (Figure 9.1). Several hundred Hispano-Bolivian[1] college students and indigenous Guarani schoolteachers-in-training milled about on the Parapeti River bridge north of town. The atmosphere was one of bored calm, yet they were staging a contentious blockade of the modest dual carriageway crossing the bridge. On the town side, a road grader was parked across the road. Its tyres were flattened and mounds of rocks and logs had been piled around it. On the other side of the bridge hundreds of trucks, buses and cars were lined up several miles to the north. Drivers sat idly in and under their trucks, biding their time. Hundreds more vehicles were lined up on the dual carriageway south of town, where a similar blockade point was set up. The only major road and trade route in the region that linked the economic hub of Santa Cruz in the north and Argentina to the south, was shut down. The Chaco was, in local parlance, 'mobilised' (*movilizados*).

I stood on the bridge and chatted with eighteen-year old Marcos. He was shooting rocks out over the river with a little slingshot and chatting with his friends as they took their shift manning the blockade. Several listened to small radios for reports about the negotiations that were underway in town. Backed by the town's civic committee (*comité cívico*), an assembly of local institutions who cast themselves as representatives of regional interests, the students aimed their blockade at the university rector. He was a local man accused of corruption, nepotism, sexual harassment, grade-selling, and the over-payment of his wife, cronies and even mistress, all enjoying jobs – even double salaries, said some – in the local public university. Like most of my interlocutors in Camiri, Marcos shared these accusations and laced them with invective against the rector for his

Figure 9.1. Town of Camiri in the gas- and oil-rich Chaco region of southeastern Bolivia.

abuse of power. Universities have long been contested sites for access to public monies, and were generally entangled with party politics and powerful clans. Camiri's university was a local branch of the main campus in Santa Cruz, the city to the north, where kickbacks certainly flowed out of local machinations. Natural gas had intensified the issue, since a year earlier public universities also 'mobilised' to demand a percentage of thousands of new dollars in hydrocarbon tax revenues. Ousting this fellow was only the beginning; relocating these resources into local hands also demanded the creation of a new independent university. 'That's what we want,' said Marcos, 'our own University of the Chaco.' This was not just a moral, but a geopolitical struggle underway. Disgust with the abuse of power and the motivation of regionalist sentiment also flowed through Camiri's airwaves. One disc jockey defended the students' demand for their own university because, unlike the 'Cruceños' of Santa Cruz, here the people were 'Chaqueños' (of the Chaco). 'We Chaqueños are something else! *¡Somos otra cosa!'*

Between 2000 and 2007, outbreaks of large and small-scale civil violence and collective direct action like the Camiri blockade erupted across the cities, towns and major roads of eastern Bolivia, marking a tectonic shift in the cultural and political landscape of the country. By my conservative count, 115 such events – from local attacks on indigenous or peasant activists to ritual displays of regionalist sentiment to large scale 'mobilisations' spanning several weeks – were linked directly with intensifying conflicts over territorial authority, conflicts in turn linked implicitly to the newly emerging politics of gas rents and a wider conflict between conservative elites and an array of social movements backing what would become the government of the MAS, the Movement to Socialism, under Evo Morales. Spread over eastern Bolivia and erupting every few weeks, these largely extralegal and informal political practices reflected a near permanent state of mobilisation. Normal territorial and institutional orders were frequently suspended, or at least deeply questioned, as competing actors sought to constitute new symbols, formations and relations of authority and legitimacy. In all cases, mobilisation was framed through spatialising claims to rights and legitimacy, as a deeply questioned set of norms tied to *de jure* national sovereignty confronted multiple *de facto* claims for the reconfiguration of the state's territorial order.

In what follows I draw on the interpretation of this conflictive period – and some of its key events – to examine how natural gas and political change were articulated with the intensification of spatial and spatialising modes of generating political sentiment and practice, a common effect of hydrocarbon booms in weakly institutionalised (or recently destabilised) capital-poor, resource-rich states (Watts 2001, 2004). *Spatialisation* refers to the discourses, practices and organisational forms through which social actors foreground referents of community, locality or region – over and above, or providing frames for, alternative categories of class, race, ethnicity, gender etc. – and use these to mobilise collective engagements with or against existing relations of power or formal institutional order. While the 'nation' itself is frequently the anchor of spatialising spectacle and discourse in hydrocarbon-rich states, alternative scales and spaces are frequently imagined as having privileged or subversive significance in relation to national narratives and imaginaries, in effect, bringing state-centred patterns of uniform territory, authority and sovereignty into question (Apter 2005; Coronil 1997; Karl 1997). The events discussed here are manifestations of emergent spatialising politics in post-neo-liberal Bolivia, battles for *de jure* and *de facto* territorial authority, that directly or indirectly relate to the rents – and expectations about their circulation and distribution – derived from natural gas. I suggest that the Bolivian case is more widely relevant as it is illustrative of the cultural-political potentialities that link resource struggles to struggles over the signification of space, as opposed to models which view space as given, and simply seek to outline the logics of resource-fuelled conflicts over it.

I concentrate here on two spatialising modes discernible as patterns in the wider series of multi-layered, politically complex conflict events in the eastern part of the country. The first mode is a subaltern, provincial and inter-ethnic form of territorialising practice allied with the nationalist-indigenist political agenda. I refer to this mode as a 'national-popular-indigenous' or *popular* articulation, described further below. The second is an urban-centred project tied to agro-industrial elite-backed proposals for regional 'autonomy' against the central government. This is a regionalist mode that I label *autonomist*, also described below. I distinguish these modes not only as opposing interests, but as opposing forms of struggle, with distinct implications for the cultural-political transformation of the state. Comparing forms of direct action (blockades in the first; targeted violence, spectacle and the defence of social-spatial hierarchical orders in the second), I draw a distinction between the *popular* spatialising mode based on inter- and intra-territorial *articulations* and elite *autonomist* spatialising mode based on practices of territorial *closure*. Despite differences, for both the popular and the autonomists, mobilisations are marked by the intensification of localising discourses of identity and claims to authority.

Reflections on these two modes of spatialising practice lend themselves to two wider arguments about Bolivia and petro-states. The first is that spatialising projects do not necessarily emerge in a straightforward way from ethno-territorial or communitarian claims (the most commonly assumed pattern for such conflicts (cf. Watts 2004)). The racialisation of space and the ethnicisation of territorial and rights claims are certainly part of what we see. Yet the (relatively small) demographic weight of indigenous groups in eastern Bolivia and the concatenation of indigenous and non-indigenous territorial imaginaries and geopolitical agendas generate a situation in which both popular and autonomist projects must engage indigenous claimants as components of a wider spatialising practice. By extension, indigenous peoples tactically articulate either with popular or regionalist points of power to advance their own territorial struggles.

Yet unlike crude paradigms that essentialise ethnicity and territory as primordially linked (and causally explanatory of conflict), we see complex, negotiated interactions and transformations of identity and territorial imaginaries, rather than absolutist or purist claims derived from pre-existing groups. Understanding spatial politics in this hydrocarbon context thus requires going beyond the communitarian paradigm, toward what Anna Tsing (2005) refers to as articulations and collisions between multiple, often contentious, 'scale-making projects'.

The second argument engages anthropological treatments of sovereignty and the reordering of state space in relation to transnational hydrocarbon activities. James Ferguson has suggested that oil companies, as agents of transnational capital and neo-liberalism, increasingly transcend and traverse sovereign states, often bypassing them altogether to establish 'privately secured enclaves' tied to resource extraction. Setting up their own forms of governance and violence, firms thus create territorial orders de-linked from wider national space and society (Ferguson 2005; see also Reyna 2007). These privatised territorial enclaves generate conditions similar to what Aihwa Ong (2006) calls 'graduated' or 'variegated' sovereignties, sub-national territorial spaces or 'zones' set up under the auspices of developmentalist states where regulatory frameworks are designed to attract foreign investment. Whereas Ferguson suggests the state is often bypassed altogether, Ong illustrates how state elites wilfully suspend or modify absolute claims to sovereignty to grant regions (and certain kinds of firms and subjects) particular rights. In both models, other subjects and spaces are contained through exclusionary tactics or abandoned altogether (Ong 2006: 75–120).

Colonial and contemporary export enclaves have long created such *de facto* conditions in Latin America. The neo-liberal turn, especially through the overarching discourse of decentralisation and the privileging of markets over national(ist) development projects, has pursued this in a modern form. In her study of contemporary Ecuadorian hydrocarbon politics and indigenous rights struggles, Suzana Sawyer (2004) illustrates how state elites allied with oil companies to impose a kind of graduated sovereignty in oil-rich indigenous territories. Indigenous subjects who accepted oil extraction and framed their lives around territorial scales reduced to 'communities' around oil areas of operation were deemed congenial to extractive practice and privileged with certain rights. Others labelled 'radical' or bearing supralocal territorial claims or transformative political demands were marginalised, often violently. Differentiated territorial modes of sovereignty and citizenship (or their suspension) were sustained through the conjoined interests of the state and transnational capital.

Though unlikely in the short term, Bolivia could still devolve into a scenario of detached enclaves controlled by foreign capital (and perhaps, as in Nigeria, allied with the 'national' oil company) and secured by private violence (the Ferguson model). After oil and gas were privatised in 1996, the country was certainly on its way toward the kind of variegated sovereignties described by the Ong-Sawyer model. This included the hollowing out of the state as a regulatory agent, and the marginalisation of robust indigenous and nationalist claims as incompatible with development.[2] Yet the rise of the MAS Party and the election of the indigenous leader Evo Morales to the presidency in 2005 created a watershed alliance between indigenous, progressive and nationalist agendas. Though often labelled petro-nationalism or populism (which assumes merely the centralisation rather than the transformation of state authority and territory), the MAS regime seeks to articulate agendas of multiple geographically sited social movements. This generates a complex scenario for the reconfiguration of territorial orders. Competing political actors, both regional and national, indigenous and not, for and against the nationalist turn, are all struggling over the control of *de facto* sovereignties, with expectations for their routinisation either through legal or extralegal means. Transnational capital is neither free to carve out privatised regional enclaves, nor does it enjoy full state support. To further complicate matters, the collapse of traditional hegemony tied to elite parties and the conflicts over a new constitution have created in Bolivia a state of suspended animation in which normative orders are up for grabs in much of the country. Geopolitical flashpoints of sovereignty erupted where the conflict between the nationalist turn and the elite resistance are strongest. The Chaco region (including towns like Camiri with its little two-lane bridge) became crucial geopolitical chokepoints in this transnationalised battle over the state. Before returning to describe the emergent forms of sovereignty-making practice, some background on geohistorical layers of gas, meaning and power will be useful.

Geopolitical and Cultural Faultlines

According to the panoptic vision of the 2000 World Petroleum Assessment, carried out by the United States Geological Survey, Bolivian gas is located in a 'geologic province' named the Santa Cruz-Tarija Basin (Alhbrandt 2000). Oil and gas deep underground derives from 300 million year-old marine deposits lain down when South America and Africa were one. Named for the two large cities of the region, the Santa Cruz-Tarija Basin is estimated to hold over four billion barrels of oil equivalent (BBOE). The mapping prioritises oil over sovereignty, and most geological provinces traverse national boundaries, in this case including much of the Paraguayan Chaco and a sliver of northern Argentina. It is ranked seventy-fifth among the world's seventy-six 'priority' provinces, those out of some six hundred provinces world-wide that together make up 95 per cent of the world's known and probable hydrocarbon reserves (Klett et al. 1997; Lindquist 1998).[3] In Bolivia gas deposits are found along the arc formed where the Andean 'fold and thrust belt' extruded upward into the flat lowlands of the Chaco (Lindquist 1999). Three 'megafields' at the centre of this conflictive region hold most of Bolivia's gas reserves. These include San Alberto and San Antonio, operated by Brazil's Petrobras, and Margarita, operated by Spain's Repsol-YPF, both in consortia with others. While critics of the nationalist turn warn of the coming end of Bolivian gas, the US Geological Survey (USGS) estimated that between 30 and 170 more undiscovered fields exist in the region (Lindquist 1999).

From the perspective of Bolivian geographies and histories, the gas-rich region is not known as the Santa Cruz-Tarija Basin, but as the Chaco, a cultural-ecological region that intersects parts of Santa Cruz, Tarija and Chuquisaca Departments. In national discourse, the region is invariably framed in relation to intense symbols of nationalism and threatened sovereignty tied to the War of the Chaco, fought with Paraguay between 1932 and 1935. The Chaco War was devastating, including loss of both life and a chunk of territory to Paraguay. Yet like most violences, the war was (and is) politically and ideologically productive. The Chaco War is today interpreted by nationalists as a fratricidal war provoked by the transnational oil industry. Historians argue that the war stimulated the rise of a national consciousness and claims to citizenship by Andean indigenous footsoldiers who were its main protagonists and ultimately propelled peasant and labour mobilisations that led to the Bolivian Revolution of 1952 (Klein 1982). As Bolivia saw other chunks of territory gobbled up by Chile, Brazil and Argentina, the Chaco fits into a deeper consciousness of national loss. The 'Chaco' itself is reimagined as a key space for the reconstitution of a sovereign nation through revindication of this longer historical struggle. Talk of the Chaco, contrary to the panoptic vision of the oil and science industry, is thick with nationalist and anti-imperialist discourse (Orgaz 2005). When the indigenous president Evo Morales 'nationalised' gas in 2006, he did so at a grandiose ceremonial retaking of the Petrobras-controlled San Alberto field in the eastern Chaco. The performance included heavily armed Bolivian soldiers with distinctly indigenous features with huge banners hung on gas tanks that read 'Property of all Bolivians'. Invoking the martyrs of the Chaco War, the MAS government once again rearticulated this contested region with a nationalist history, naming the state nationalisation plan the 'Heroes of the Chaco Decree'.

Beyond the nationalist frame, a deeper localising history of the Chaco also underpins current struggles over sovereignty and state space. The Chaco is one of Bolivia's distinctive cultural regions imagined largely through a national pantheon of folkloric music and dance. 'Chaqueños' are one of the country's iconic regional identities. Bolivians who call themselves 'Chaqueños' speak a distinctly accented form of Spanish, and highlight their particularities tied to the region's agrarian and cattle economy; e.g., drinking *yerba mate,* eating grilled meat, racing horses, or enjoying a milk-alcohol cocktail mixed straight from the udder (*leche de tigre*). Though framed in masculinist, cowboy-like terms much like the Argentine Gaucho, the Chaqueño is as much a city-dweller as a rural farmer or rancher. A racialised understanding of masculinity and feminine beauty, defined against the region's indigenous peoples as well as Andean outsiders, is traditionally at the core of Chaqueño self-representation.

The Chaqueño complex underpins one dimension of spatialising projects in the region, manifest through the rising demand for a new 'tenth department' (like a fifty-first state) called the Department of the Chaco. Geopolitically, this would disrupt the power of the Santa Cruz-Tarija block, the departments that currently hold most of the country's reserves. The idea of a tenth department resonates deeply with Chaqueños, who speak often of exploitation and abandonment by the more powerful urban centres of Santa Cruz and Tarija. It would also recognise a long-standing grievance since the 'Chaqueños' as an imagined collective are the only regionalist grouping without their own department. Those who express loyalty and sentiment with Santa Cruz call themselves 'Cruceños'; those of Tarija, 'Chapacos'. Though far from reality, the tenth department idea is cultivated by nationalist grassroots intellectuals (and circulated through broadsheets, radio, pamphlets and media diffusion) and has significant mobilising power.

Yet before the rise of the Bolivian nation-state, the unfolding of bloody wars tied to the transnational geopolitics of oil, and the formation of a Chaqueño symbolic complex, the indigenous Guarani were settling across the Chaco and Andean foothills from at least the 1300s (Gustafson 2009). They jousted, sometimes violently, with other indigenous peoples including the Chane, the Weenhayek and the Toba. Eventually the Guarani carved out a territorial space that extends, coincidentally, along the same arc of the Andean fold-thrust belt. For Guarani the region was attractive not for its oil, but for the fertile valleys running north and south that were rich for corn production. The Guarani were soon followed by the Spanish and several centuries of violent colonial and republican state formation that absorbed their lands as part of the 'Bolivian' national space. The Guarani territorial base shrunk into archipelago-like fragments as the agrarian frontier expanded. The Guarani were reduced to a racialised, rural underclass of semi-subsistence farmers and debt labourers largely subordinate to Spanish-speaking *mestizos* and Whites, whether Chaqueños, Cruceños or Chapacos. Today, the Guarani represent about 25 per cent of the Chaco region's 300,000 people.

During the earlier oil booms of the 1920s and 1970s, Guarani were largely silent actors as earlier waves of petro-nationalism swept over their territory, a space now criss-crossed by lines, exploration transects and wells. Yet with the global indigenous surge of the 1980s and 1990s, the Guarani began organising to demand territorial rights, political representation and economic equality. Early demands revolved around territory and bilingual education rights, both crucial for economic and political empowerment. Nationally, Bolivia's indigenous movements succeeded in gaining rights to collective landholdings called TCOs (*tierras comunitarias de orígen*, communal lands of origin) in 1995. Though bearing no formal political or economic rights, TCOs provide a conceptual and practical base from which many Bolivian indigenous organisations have begun to make more robust claims for autonomy and control over subsoil resources, both highly contentious claims, even for the indigenous-friendly nationalist regime. For the Guarani, their multiple local zones dot the wider Chaco, outlining a transterritorial project that in emergent discourse has sought a new relationship with the 'Chaqueño' complex. With the increase in gas activities in the 1990s, the Guarani began confronting foreign companies on their actual and ancestral lands. Monetary concessions were extracted through blockades and negotiation from gas pipeline projects that crossed through Guarani TCOs. Repsol's massive Margarita plant, for instance, arose practically in the midst of a Guarani community. These indigenous territorialities are distinct from Chaqueño-style regionalism, and like the possibility of a Chaco department are deeply opposed by autonomist elites. While ultimately limited by strong national sovereignty claims, the Guarani have largely allied with the nationalist state, the only guarantor of legal transformations of land tenure and control. Articulating a slowly decolonising Chaqueño regionalism and an indigenous-nurtured nationalism outlines the emergent spatialising agenda I refer to as the 'popular' territorial project.

The large regional cities of Santa Cruz and Tarija represent a third aspect of the territorial game, that of the urban-centred autonomists. In the north, Santa Cruz arose as a hub of colonial and state power in eastern Bolivia and remains so today. To the south and east, the smaller city of Tarija was another. Historically, both were launching points for colonial forays into the Chaco, first to violently pacify the Guarani 'savages' and later to transform the region into an agrarian economy that fuelled the rise of mining in the Andes. Santa Cruz today is the main gateway for transnational hydrocarbon capital, with operator and service company offices, infrastructure and contracting services concentrated there. Tarija is a relative backwater, yet over 80 per cent of Bolivia's reserves fall within its departmental boundaries, most of this out in the Chaco periphery where loyalties to the city centre are ambiguous, and increasingly fragile. The elites of both cities' civic committees propose departmental autonomies as a 'democratic' answer to the threat of the indigenous-controlled centralised regime. Autonomists have labelled their project the half-moon (*media luna*), a reflection of that same troubled oil- and gas-rich arc that curves down around the edge of the Andean Chaco, the Santa Cruz-Tarija Basin.[4]

Gas, Territory and Power

During the neo-liberal era (1985–2003), then President Gonzalo Sánchez de Lozada privatised the national oil company, YPFB (*Yacimientos Petrolíferos Fiscales de Bolivia*, roughly, Bolivian State Oil Fields). Refining and transport infrastructure as well as exploration and extraction concessions were sold to Brazil's Petrobras, Spain's Repsol, Exxon, Shell, Enron, British Petroleum, France's Total and others. Investment and exploration increased and by 2005 Bolivia's known and probable gas reserves grew to around 48.7 trillion cubic feet, second only to Venezuela in the region (Ministerio de Hidrocarburos y Energía 2006). Sánchez de Lozada was later rewarded for his actions by being ousted by a massive popular mobilisation against his plans to export gas via Chile. This movement culminated in the 'Gas War' of October 2003, which crystallised nationalist sentiment and set the stage for the rise of the MAS Party, which unified nationalist and progressive sectors across lines of identity, class and region, and took power in 2005.

Having pledged to nationalise gas, the Aymara peasant leader Evo Morales won the presidency with more than 57 per cent of the vote. Bolivia is in a difficult, if momentous time, between an unfinished, yet partial neo-liberalisation of the country, the residues of corporatist forms of the past, new indigenous demands, and reformulation of older elite-led regionalist claims and new visions of a nationalist-plurinationalist state built on indigenous and non-indigenous popular movements. The indigenous-leftist alliance is often troubled and the prospects for the return of a corrupt patronage state are high. Yet against the emergent elite-led project of regional fragmentation, the nationalisation of gas was portrayed as the only hope for maintaining the geographic integrity of the country. The sociologist, former left-wing guerilla, and now vice-president, Alvaro García Linera, saw the struggle for gas as 'the most important national mobilisation since the struggle for democracy' against military dictatorship in the 1980s (García Linera 2005: 58). Another nationalist intellectual – coincidentally from the provincial town of Camiri – declared that 'we either nationalise gas or we disappear as a country' (Orgaz 2005). Andrés Soliz Rada, another of the *criollo*, non-indigenous intellectual architects of nationalisation, expressed the leftist-indigenous articulation by associating the struggle against neo-liberalism with the struggle against racism: 'nationalisation [of gas] was the impulse for the recovery of the dignity and self-esteem of our people [that] racist and neo-liberal policies sought to crush definitively' (Solíz Rada 2006).

Conflicting ideological stances are charged with rising clamour for gas rents. Prior to nationalisation the state received between 18 and 50 per cent of hydrocarbon revenues depending on the concession block. After the 2003 Gas War, a national referendum demanded the state take at least 50 per cent of hydrocarbon revenues. After the 'nationalisation' decree of 2006 – actually a renegotiation of contracts – the state continued to take at least 50 per cent (from smaller and older fields) and would demand up to 90 per cent of revenues from mega-fields. Annual payments of royalties, taxes, and transfers to the national treasury increased from just over US$100 million in 1998 to almost US$1.3 billion in 2010 (Cámara Boliviana de Hidrocarburos y Energía 2010). Some of this money is slated to go to the rebuilding of the YPFB, although multinational oil companies still dominate extractive operations. Talk of 'industrialisation' of gas is also booming but most of Bolivia's gas still fuels industrial growth in neighbouring Brazil. As of 2010, between 30 and 42 million m^3 of gas produced each day. Though output fluctuates, about 15 per cent is for domestic consumption, around 12 per cent is exported to Argentina and the rest goes to Brazil. The megalopolis of Sao Paulo depends heavily on gas from Bolivia for domestic, vehicular, and industrial energy, as does the border state of Mato Grosso (Hidrocarburos Bolivia 2010).

As a reflection of the political power of regional elites, hydrocarbon legislation passed before the MAS victory distinguished 'producing departments' (*departamentos productores*) and 'producing municipalities' (*municipalidades productoras*) as having particular rights over hydrocarbon revenues. 'Producing departments' (Tarija, Santa Cruz, Cochabamba and Chuquisaca) receive larger proportions than other departments.

The nationalisation decree has yet to transform the spatialising logic of surplus distribution, a reflection of the power still wielded by traditional elites who are quick to mobilise regionalist sentiment against any suggestion that the 'percentages' should be adjusted to a formula based on population or poverty.[5] As such, gas wealth adds to existing biases of hydrocarbon-related growth, which concentrate wealth in urban-centred sectors of the economy (public services, transport and skilled labour) (Anderssen and Faris 2002). It also fuels the political power of elites who lost control of the centralised state, but retrenched themselves in departmental capitals like Santa Cruz and Tarija. Gas-rich, yet thinly populated Tarija receives around US$321 per capita. Poor and populous departments like Andean Potosi, which financed the rise of the nation with its silver and tin over many centuries, will receive only US$36 per capita (CEDLA 2006: 19). Whether nationalisation will be able to convert gas revenues into productive investment or will simply fuel the re-territorialisation of corruption and rentier politics remains to be seen.

Back at the Barricades

Back on the bridge in Camiri, the struggle over the transformation of national territory and spaces of authority coalesced around the convenient corruption of the local university rector. What was at stake was an intense struggle over a local source of power and patronage, a struggle through which regionalist sentiments imbued with moral righteousness could be mobilised and intensified. Yet what was also at stake was this wider national dilemma, the multi-layered process of articulatory or regionalising tactics that sought to bridge or weaken the arrangement of diverse territorial axes – the indigenous, the popular provincial and the nationalist. The battle against the rector, as it turned out, was in fact part of a wider battle between popular articulations and the territorial closure of the elite autonomists in Santa Cruz.

On the bridge the nationalist-indigenist articulatory strategy had to grapple with locally intense racism against indigenous peoples as well as latent distrust of the 'Andean' state centre. The university rector was a convenient icon through which regional sentiment could be redirected against the elites of Santa Cruz, rather than those of the Andes. This part was not difficult. Gangly teenagers like Marcos and his companions on the bridge, bolstered by the reckless energy of youth and their disgust with the rector, and their localist sentiment, seemed prepared for violent sacrifice in the name of the regional demand. Angry lorry drivers had stormed the barricade the night before in an attempt to move the tractor. Students repelled them in a flurry of rock throwing and fist shaking. Marcos showed off his little slingshot for me, which he had 'just in case' they came again. He teased his friends about who would cut and run if the lorry drivers organised another charge.

As a pressure tactic, the blockade itself was not so much against the state or the rector, as it was a means of crippling daily life in Santa Cruz, to the north. Tankers full of diesel fuel imported from Argentina and heading for the city were stalled on the main road. After two or three days, dwindling diesel supplies began to squeeze wealthy farmers and the operators of public transport, both linked to the pro-autonomy civic committee of the larger city. In this sense, locals like Marcos were not simply regional defenders, but were proxies for the national government, who sought to apply pressure on the regional elites through whatever means possible, even a convenient battle over the corrupt rector.

A sign of the state of suspended sovereignty, it was not clear who or what might be deployed to violently contest what was in effect a violent seizure of public space. In the past the central or departmental governments were quick to send riot police to break up such blockades. Now the national government kept the police in their barracks. Elite autonomists had responded to their loss of access to the instruments of legal violence by promoting urban youth gangs, deployed as enforcers against peasant or indigenous marches in the city. Yet here far to the south such a move would only exacerbate local sentiments against the urban centre. Within Camiri, those locals who opposed the blockade also considered mobilising private violence to disrupt the student blockade (as was attempted against a Guarani mobilisation the following year), yet this did not materialise. With both private and official violence temporarily suspended and regional sentiments highly animated, the philandering rector refused to budge. This was a new, gas-related form of a Bolivian territorial stand-off.

Indirectly articulated with the nationalist agenda of the MAS-led central government – though never explicitly framed in those terms – the provincial movement was also a constitutive project that sought to transform and rearticulate intra-regional relationships of power and authority. Part of the process revolved around the transformation of the local civic committee. The *comité cívico* is a fixture in most mid-sized and large Bolivian cities. Historically these civic bodies have been self-defence vehicles for self-elected notables (merchants, landowners, politicians). The committees were also platforms for waging intra-elite struggles over state patronage. As an elite instrument, civic committees elevated the *regional* to sacred status through rituals of tradition, beauty pageants, folkloric shows and commemorative events, all tactics that sought to manage challenges from subaltern sectors in the immediate or rural periphery (such as workers or the rural peasantry). In relation to indigenous peoples, 'civic' itself was marked as an 'urban' category, a space of authority that by its nature excluded the rural indigenous. As I have described elsewhere (2006), traditional civic committees like that of Santa Cruz maintain this essentially colonial expression of civil society as elite, light-skinned chambers of informal authority.

Yet in Camiri, an alliance of activist NGOs, the Guarani indigenous organisation and progressive-minded locals waged a public campaign to transform the civic committee into a popularly elected assembly. The product of a longer struggle of the indigenous Guarani to insert themselves into fields of urban power, and a reflection of the rising power of activist NGOs, the transformation of the civic committee marked a significant shift in the local political landscape. This turn was later reflected in the multi-ethnic articulation – still far from an intimate pluralist relationship – between indigenous and non-indigenous political agendas. The *regional* was being decolonised, albeit slowly, to generate a space of horizontal engagement with the Guarani as political interlocutors rather than representatives of a spatially and socially subordinate race. 'Popular regionalism' was being repositioned as an inter-ethnic, inter-cultural reality, imbued with a nationalist sentiment, rather than an expression of pure ethnoterritorial alterity.

In addition to youngsters like Marcos, the blockade at the bridge was in large part carried out by indigenous Guarani teachers and their students from a local indigenous, bilingual teacher-training school. As representatives of the Assembly of Guarani People, the local indigenous federation, these teachers and students also occupied a crucial point of articulation with the Hispano-Bolivian dominated urban institutions. This was an atypical protest for the Guarani, who were more often mobilised in relation to rural land struggles. Yet by lending their support to the blockade, a sometimes tense ethnic boundary was being rewritten as a shared, popular identity marked by a demand for participation. Members of the bilingual teachers' school formed the largest contingent from a civic institution supporting the blockade, and its staff and students were a key presence in the negotiating spaces. Marcos, who was not indigenous, marvelled at Guarani discipline. His eyes widened as he described admiringly how they had followed their 'leader' in and out of negotiating meetings *'como un solo cuerpo'*, as one body. 'We need that kind of organisation too,' he said, referring to the sometimes lackadaisical students. In addition, inside the university, several Guarani leaders had joined student hunger strikers, a frequent ritual of corporatist and labour struggles of the past, now refitted for regionalist movements. Shared sacrifice was a mode of enacting these new articulations. Pictures of Che Guevara and denunciations of the rector as a 'rat' were hung on the gates outside. Inside, the Guarani used the venue to lobby for support for the MAS slate in the upcoming constitutional assembly elections.

After several days of blockade and negotiation, the rector eventually resigned, only to be later reinstated. Yet the 'failure' of the mobilisation was in many ways insignificant. The event had mobilised emergent political actors and discourses, exerted pressure on elite autonomists during a moment of deeply contested political campaigns, and played a role in leading to a nationalist-indigenous victory in the local vote for constitutional assembly members (the MAS' Guarani candidate won).

These admittedly summary observations illustrate local forms of articulation through which a spatialising project takes shape, different from ethnocommunitarian forms that highlight essential territorial (or racial) purities of space and subjects. The event takes on further significance because of its relation to spatialising forms. Of note are the potential and real forms of violence involved. Though invoking the possibility of violence (seizing gas valves, defending the bridge), the tactics did not involve consciously planned violence against subjects as differentiated or threatening external identities. The blockade – a *de facto* form of violence that disrupts the normal order – hinges on a contestatory disruption of flows through territorial space, rather than on the defensive closure of that space. The elite 'autonomist' mode of reconfiguring territoriality takes on a quite different shape.

The Autonomist Response

During the same period (2000–2007), Santa Cruz, to the north, and Tarija, to the east, were transformed into urban anchors of the elite autonomist project. Surrounded by frequent blockades and direct actions in provincial flashpoints, city centres also became the stage for mobilisation events of various types. Elite-organised actions in defence of the department or for autonomy were not always obviously about gas, but were all part of the underlying tug-of-war between the social movements (who sought to both take control of, and transform the state) and the regional autonomists (who pursued a radical decentralisation and consolidation of traditional forms of state power). Movements like that in Camiri were spoken of by their backers as part of a popular and democratic turn. Elites viewed these movements as populist and demographic threats to the status quo emanating from the poorer Andean and rural populations. As movements sought to establish new geopolitical foci of authority, urban elites sought to recentralise control over natural resources (gas, minerals, forests and land), legitimate violence (the police) and the production of knowledge (school administration), looking to urban centres like Santa Cruz and Tarija.

I have discussed the cultural and social forms of the autonomist project elsewhere (Gustafson 2006). For purposes of comparing modes of spatialising practice, the significant distinction between the elite autonomist movements and subaltern regionalisms like Camiri is seen in differing tactics and idioms of spatial control. Many tactics are shared between autonomists and populists, for instance, the hunger strike, the street assembly, and the *cabildo*.[7] Yet at two extremes, there are clear differences. The blockade, which temporarily disrupts flows to and of power (through space), is a popular form, never utilised by the autonomists. In contrast, autonomist tactics are spatialising modes for controlling, stabilising and closing institutional and geographic spaces, distinguished most clearly by the use of violence targeted toward individuals or collectives deemed threatening 'traitors' or 'outsiders'.[8] While seizing land or gas facilities (both associated with 'power' deemed illegitimate rather than with a threatening other), subaltern violences are not targeted toward collective subjects but have been limited to the blockade and its consequences as the central mode of action.

Geopolitical Arm Wrestling

The competing tactics of urban autonomists and provincial, peasant and indigenous populists have unfolded since before and after the election of Evo Morales as a slowly intensifying and expanding tit-for-tat between nationalist and elite movements. Spectacles of the urban *cívicos* were met with blockades to shut off flows to the urban centres. The rising drama of urban support for autonomy was countered with actions, like the Camiri university blockade, designed to expose the corruption of elite power holders. Assaults on urban institutions like the departmental labour confederation were met with peasant occupations of contested lands, usually tracts held by some component of the urban elite. Mapped in space, there are clear points of conflict that reflect a long-standing movement tactic of enclosing and pressuring urban centres of power, as well as a deeply rooted form of urban spectacle and mobilisation that has its roots in the colonial schism between cities and threatening rural masses. Mapped through time, the conflicts illustrate the erosion of formal deliberative and representational channels for elites and populists alike, as formal governmental procedures are accompanied and backed, sometimes vetoed, by direct, often violent, action in the streets.

This chess game in which players are moved, sacrificed and withdrawn is in Bolivian political parlance referred to as 'measuring forces' (*midiendo fuerzas*) or 'political arm wrestling' (*pulseta política*). Despite the formal electoral and constitution-writing procedures underway, the continuation of mobilisations in streets and major roads illustrates how in a context of structural and hegemonic instability exacerbated by the rising rents and expectations tied to natural gas, sovereignty and law arise from the mosaics of street action, rather than (only) from deliberative or legislative forms. Sovereign power is not resolved by elections, as reflected in the ability to commit violence with impunity still held by autonomist elites and the limited ability of the social movement-led state to enforce the rule of law, evidenced by uncontested elite seizures of several state institutions.

Conclusions

These competing modes illustrate spatialisations of political sentiment and practice in contexts of hydrocarbon development that differ from ethnoterritorial and communitarian struggles (Watts 2004), of indigenous minorities resisting the state (Sawyer 2004; Watts 2001), or of enclosed development enclaves (Ferguson 2005; Ong 2006). I have presented an exploratory overview of the emergent dimensions of these practices here. Further research would illuminate the inter- and intra-subjective processes – and more complex local negotiations and exchanges – through which mobilising processes unfold. The alliances and articulations I have described above are quite fragile, as the lingering racism that flows through urban and rural society makes the indigenous–nationalist alliance a contentious articulation, always risking erosion into crude rentier politics. Elite-controlled media and leaders have also modified their exclusionary rhetoric into one of tactical incorporation (and division) of indigenous movements, paralleled, however paradoxically, with the intensification of racially charged discourse designed to spread fear and uncertainty among the urban middle class.

What is most interesting in the wake of neo-liberalism's collapse – seen by many as a powerfully hegemonic force – is how the vacuum of animated suspension created by the collapse of traditional institutions of rule has generated a space in which both elites and non-elites embrace collective subversions of norms, rules and routines, and do so by resuscitating prior modes of corporatist politics tied to the language of 'sectors' (groups) rather than only, or primarily citizens (individuals). Despite the language of liberal democracy voiced by elites, a corporatist logic persists across both popular and autonomist expressions. As the traditional institutional mechanisms for the mobilisation and representation of these groups have dissolved, transformations of sovereign order proceed through direct action. As Hansen and Stepputat (2006: 301), following Agamben (1998), suggest, 'the origin of sovereign power is the "state of exception" – the suspension of rules and conventions creating a conceptual and ethical zero-point from where the law, the norms, and the political order can be constituted'. Bolivian mobilisations do not begin at a 'zero-point', influenced as they are by prior forms and residues of statecraft and social struggle. Yet they do seek to reconstitute the law and political order through suspensions of existing rules and conventions. Through the cultivation of new kinds of subjects and bodies, new rituals of contention, and modes of organisation that gradually become routinised, competing actors seek to restructure a territorially grounded group politics through grassroots practice.

For elites, the tactic is made explicit in their oft-cited slogan, *'autonomía al andar'* or '[we will create] autonomy as we go along'. Autonomists seek to claim legal attributes and assure certain orders of authority through forms of de facto rule that combine fear-inducing violence with extralegal performances of state-like authority (calling referendums, naming officials, and so forth). Social movements are also in a paradigm shift, from modes of contention associated with the older form of patronage politics (largely defensive manoeuvres aimed at petitioning for state resources through pressure or patronage relations with party elites) to modes of contention, both formal and in the streets, that seek the institutionalisation and legitimisation of new bearers and forms of territorial authority. Elites boast that they will produce 'autonomy as they go along' and do so with explicit transnational (and US) assistance. On the other hand, movement tactics for reconstituting the state from the ground up are bolstered by the MAS democratic victory. For the moment, these movements do not resist the state, but seek to transform it.[9] Movement theorists and leaders like the former guerilla fighter, sociologist (and now Bolivian vice-president) Alvaro García Linera write of this historical transformation:

> To the extent which the political power over which the social movements now struggle is not only a place (the governmental palace) but a relationship of forces, capacities, and actions of effective power, the possibility of taking control of political power must come by way of the *expansive construction of political power through a territorial form ... sustained through prior processes of territorialised and growing construction of political, economic, and cultural power of social movements in their areas of influence.* This is because the issue of state power is not only an issue of resistance but of general sovereignty [*soberanía general*], not only an issue of petitioning but of the control and exercise [*mando y ejecución*] of the *res pública* and that is the historical limit that the social movements must supersede in their political, electoral, *and mobilisation actions,* if they want to conduct and transform the state structure (Linera 2005: 72–73, author's translation, emphasis added).

Though counter-intuitive, these competing modes of spatialising practice reveal not the breakdown of the state, but its recrafting through competing languages of moral, legal and geographic order. For now the game has not spiralled into large-scale civil or ethnic violence. Two trends may presage a negative turn. The MAS regime's use of social movements as proxies for confronting regional autonomists has to date been relatively non-violent.

Yet rituals demonstrating the unity between the military and indigenous and popular movements, as well as some rhetoric calling for the possibility of civil militia activity in support of the state, do not bode well for the future. On the autonomist side, the targeted assaults, organised violence in cities and rural land defence committees, all backed by the intensification of militaristic language and clear public support for violence against the 'rural' threat, echo early forms of paramilitary movement emergence elsewhere in Latin America (i.e. Colombia). Natural gas has thus created conditions for progressive transformation as well as the polarisation and racialisation of regional sentiment. While the MAS rhetorically seeks a 'democratic cultural and political revolution', the alternatives – populist autocracy tied to an essentialised notion of indigeneity, rentier politics mired in decentralised corruption, or exclusionary autonomies built on the retrenchment of race and class privilege – are also potential outcomes.

Notes

1. This local term refers to Spanish-speaking Bolivians who do not identify themselves as indigenous (native South Americans, descended from pre-colonial populations).
2 . During the neo-liberal period, NGO and indigenous activists invoked state law (which had adopted the International Labour Organisation Convention 169 on indigenous rights) and saw themselves as guarantors of state sovereignty in their struggles with oil and gas companies. The state as a regulatory regime, they argued, was largely absent (interview, Alfredo Rada, La Paz, 13 September 2005; see also Bazoberry and Heredia 2005).
3. Portions of this section draw on Gustafson (2011). There are four other 'priority provinces' in South America: the Andes-Amazonian region of south Colombia, Ecuador and Peru (already marked by violence); the off-shore Caribbean (pitting US, Venezuelan and Cuban interests); the far south of Argentina; and off-shore Brazil.
4. The USGS World Energy survey cartographically dovetails with the anti-Andean regional autonomy agenda of Santa Cruz and Tarija. In earlier maps, oil experts apparently used the label "Altiplano Basin" (see Halbouty 1999). It appears that later remappings created the Santa Cruz-Tarija Basin as a separate area.
5. Regionalists argue that departments like Potosí have privileged access to mineral taxes distributed only within the producing department (Fundación Jubileo 2006).
6. In the colonial era the *cabildo* was a municipal council that negotiated between local Spanish and *mestizo* subjects and the royal bureaucracy, and between these figures and local indigenous people. Cabildos today are public urban street gatherings convoked by civic leaders, ostensibly to make a public decision. Generally, decisions are made among a select group of leaders (the 'civic committee') and large publics then ratify them in a mass street spectacle bordering on fascism. In one I attended in Santa Cruz in 2006, autonomist leaders asked a crowd of thousands if they wanted autonomy, to which the public 'voted' by roaring 'Sí!' While choreographed to the last detail in the large urban sphere (with musical groups, fireworks and helicopters dropping pamphlets), cabildos can become unruly in more face-to-face contexts like Camiri. The public sometimes overrides (locally, *rebasar*) the leaders, as in one Camiri

blockade during which the crowd 'voted' by advancing on the gas facilities to take the valves. 'Assemblies' are similar rituals that convoke public institutions to intensify and mobilise regionalist sentiment, as in the 'Assemblies of Cruceñity' staged by the autonomists of Santa Cruz or 'Assemblies of Chaqueñity' staged by provincials.

7. These include paramilitary-style assaults on peasant land occupiers, beatings and threats of rural activists, and urban and provincial assaults on popular or pro-MAS groups. *Kollas* – Andean migrants to the eastern lowlands – are frequently explicit targets of these rural confrontations. In the city, attacks have included directed racial slurs and violence toward women wearing Andean dress (Gustafson 2006).

8. The pursuit of hegemonic sovereignty on the part of the MAS regime will surely produce future clashes between state and movement agendas given the multiplicity of movement centres and the fragility of indigenous-nationalist-progressive articulations.

References

Agamben, Giorgio. 1998. *Homo Sacer: Sovereign Power and Bare Life* (trans. D. Heller-Roazen). Stanford: Stanford University Press.

Ahlbrandt, Thomas. 2000. *U.S. Geological Survey World Petroleum Assessment 2000 Compiled PowerPoint Slides – U.S. Geological Survey Open File Report 99-50-Z* (accessed 3 May 2006).

Apter, Andrew. 2005. *The Pan-African Nation: Oil and the Spectacle of Culture in Nigeria.* Chicago: University of Chicago Press.

Bazoberry, Oscar and Fernando Heredia. 2005. Las TCOs guaranis: dilemas y desafíos. In *Territorios indígenas y empresas petroleras*, ed. Sarela Patiño Paz, 151–82. Cochabamba: CESU/CEIDIS/CENDA.

Cámara Boliviana de Hidrocarburos y Energía. 2010. Recaudaciones estatales. http://new. cbh.org.bo/documentos/RECAUDACIONES.pdf, accessed 3 March 2011.

CEDLA. 2006. Ley de Hidrocarburos: Regalías y participaciones. http://www.cedla.org/ obie/system/files/regalia-idh.pdf. Accessed 3 June 2007.

Coronil, Fernando. 1997. *The Magical State: Nature, Money, and Modernity in Venezuela.* Chicago: University of Chicago Press.

Ferguson, James. 2005. Seeing Like an Oil Company: Space, Security and Global Capital in Neoliberal Africa. *American Anthropologist* 107(3): 377–82.

Fundación Jubileo. 2006. Redistribución de regalías en la Asamblea Constituyente. La Paz: Fundación Jubileo. http://www.jubileobolivia.org.bo/recursos/files/pdfs/1_Redistribucion_de_regalias.pdf (accessed 4 May 2007).

García Linera, Alvaro. 2005. La lucha por el poder en Bolivia. In *Horizontes y límites del estado y el poder*, ed. Grupo Comuna,11–74. La Paz: Grupo Comuna and Muela del Diablo.

Gustafson, Bret. 2006. Spectacles of Autonomy and Crisis: Or, What Bulls and Beauty Queens Have to Do with Regionalism in Eastern Bolivia. *Journal of Latin American Anthropology* 11(2): 351–79.

———. 2009. *New Languages of the State: Indigenous Resurgence and the Politics of Knowledge in Bolivia.* Durham: Duke University Press.

———. 2011. Power Necessarily Comes from Below: Guarani Autonomies and their Others. In *Remapping Bolivia: Resources, Territory, and Indigeneity in a Plurinational State*, ed. Nicole Fabricant and Bret Gustafson, 166–89. Santa Fe: School for Advanced Research Press.

Halbouty, Michel T. 1999. Giant Oil and Gas Fields of the 1990s: An Introduction. In *Giant Oil and Gas Fields of the Decade 1990–1999*, ed. Michel T Halbouty. American Association of Petroleum Geologists Memoir 78. pp. 1–13.

Hansen, Thomas Blom, and Finn Stepputat. 2006. Sovereignty Revisited. *Annual Review of Anthropology* 35: 295–315.

Hidrocarburos Bolivia. 2010. Estadísticas: Promedios de Exportaciones y Consumo de Gas Natural Enero/Diciembre 2010. http://www.hidrocarburosbolivia.com/nuestro-contenido/estadisticas/37467-estadisticas-promedios-de-exportaciones-y-consumo-de-gas-natural-enerooctubre-2010.html. Accessed 3 March 2011.

Karl, Terry. 1997. *The Paradox of Plenty: Oil Booms and Petro-states*. Berkeley: University of California Press.

Klein, Herbert S. 1982. *Bolivia: The Evolution of a Multi-ethnic Society*. New York: Oxford University Press.

Klett, Timothy R., Thomas. S. Ahlbrandt, James W. Schmoker, and Gordon L. Dolton. 1997. *Ranking of the World's Oil and Gas Provinces by Known Petroleum Volumes*. http://pubs.usgs.gov/of/1997/ofr-97-463/index.html#Table (accessed 9 July 2007).

Lindquist, S. 1998. *The Santa Cruz-Tarija Province of Central South America:Los Monos-Machareti (!) Petroleum System. Open File Report 99-50-C*. http://energy.cr.usgs.gov/energy/WorldEnergy/OF99-50C/OF99-50C.pdf (accessed 10 June 2007).

———. 1999. Sub-Andean Fold and Thrust Belt Assessment Unit 60450101. In *U.S. Geological Survey World Petroleum Assessment 2000 – Description and Results*. Washington, DC: U.S. Geological Survey. http://energy.cr.usgs.gov/WEcont/regions/reg6/p6/tps/AU/au604511.pdf (accessed 10 June 2007).

Ministerio de Hidrocarburos y Energía. 2006. *Boletín Dignidad* 1(7). http://www.hidrocarburos.gov.bo/Noticias/Boletines/Dignidad/Dignidad-1-7-2006.pdf (accessed 14 May 2007).

Ong, Aihwa. 2006. *Neoliberalism as Exception: Mutations in Citizenship and Sovereignty*. Durham: Duke University Press.

Orgaz García, M. 2005. *La Nacionalización del gas*. La Paz: CEDLA/C&C Editores.

Reyna, Stephen. 2007. Waiting: The Sorcery of Modernity, Transnational Corporations, Oil and Terrorism in Chad. *Sociologus* 26(1): 1–30.

Sawyer, Suzana. 2004. *Crude Chronicles: Indigenous Politics, Multinational Oil, and Neoliberalism in Ecuador*. Durham: Duke University Press.

Solíz Rada, Andrés. 2006. Carta de renuncia. http://www.izquierdanacional.org/articulos/reproduccion/r002.html (accessed 14 June 2007).

Tsing, Anna L. 2005. *Friction: An Ethnography of Global Connection*. Princeton: Princeton University Press.

Watts, Michael. 2001. Petro-violence: Community, Extraction, and Political Ecology of a Mythic Commodity. In *Violent Environments*, ed. Nancy L. Peluso and Michael Watts, 189–212. Ithaca: Cornell University Press.

———. 2004. Antinomies of Community: Some Thoughts on Geography, Resources, and Empire. *Transactions of the Institute for British Geography* 29: 195–216.

PART IV

POST–SOCIALIST RUSSIA

Chapter 10

OIL WITHOUT CONFLICT?

The Anthropology of Industrialisation in Northern Russia

Florian Stammler

During the public hearing [with the oil company] in the tundra, we were told that losses in territory are inevitable, and herders have to accept this. Members of the brigades [herding work teams] asked questions, tried to find out more details. Only one of them, Nyadmanesia, was silent all the time, listened carefully. Not long after the consultation, Nyadmanesia hanged himself. He could not cope with all this in his soul, and decided to commit suicide, in order not to see all these things happening to his land.

> – Alexander, reindeer herder from Yamal, remembering the sad results of a consultation from 1995. Story told to author during fieldwork on 10 November 2006.

Nyadmanesia was a highly respected experienced reindeer nomad in northwest Siberia, whose migration route leads through Bovanenkovo, one of the world's largest gas deposits, on which extraction is due to start before 2013. His sad story indicates a tendency in the north of avoiding open conflicts when confronted with industrial development. Nyadmanesia chose suicide as one way of avoiding conflict, but his son continues to move with his herd on that route, and recently had to sign off a crucial area for an industrial sand quarry which effectively renders his migration to the summer pastures impossible. This chapter will review several other strategies beyond suicide connected to the same tendency of avoiding open conflicts in northern Russian hydrocarbon extraction.

Russia is the world's largest energy supplier. Its continuously growing oil sector makes the country the world's largest oil producer, with 505.193 million tons (2011)[1]. It is also the world's second largest producer, holder and exporter of natural gas, with 650,311 billion m^3 (2010). Gas consumption in the EU rose by 42 per cent from 1997 to 2007, and according to some experts will become an ever more important energy source in the EU (White 2007; European Gas Industry 2010). Russia is increasingly using gas as a political tool to force its will onto neighbours such as Belarus and Ukraine. Seventy per cent of the oil and 90 per cent of the gas in Russia is extracted in the north of the country, in the West Siberian Tyumen region. Hence, not only is Russia a key actor in future world power relations that base so much on resource control, but we might also learn from the development in the country's northern hydrocarbon industry in the last forty years, unlike Chechnya without wars. This chapter will analyse reasons for the absence of violent conflicts around oil and gas extraction in the region, paying special attention to questions of integration and isolation.

Conflicts and wars between states over mineral resources get most political and media attention, as the two Gulf wars have demonstrated. The numerous civil wars that have arisen in countries with mineral resources receive less attention, leading authors such as Karl (1997) and others to suggest that there is a relationship between mineral wealth and likelihood of civil war in a country, as corruption and the gap between poor and rich increase (see also Gashawbeza 2006). Still less attention is given to cases where oil extraction does not cost human lives, but negatively affects human livelihoods so that protests might arise, as they did in Sakhalin in recent years (Stammler and Wilson 2006; Wilson 2007). The focus of this chapter is on an even lower rank of this 'attention scale', where native communities and industrial workers coexist in oil and gas extraction regions of Siberia without open protests. However, the introductory quotation shows how problems still deeply touch people's lives. The analyses on the basis of participant observation among both parts of the population on the ground[2] can fruitfully contribute to fundamental topics in the anthropology of mineral resources, such as the determinants of collective agency, power, hierarchy and leadership.

Local Population and Hydrocarbons

The current ethnic and social composition of the population in the north of Russia is largely a result of Soviet and post–Soviet mineral resource extraction. The majority, slightly less than two million in West Siberia's hydrocarbon province, are incomers of the last forty years, attracted to move to the north by job opportunities connected to resource extraction. These people have become subjects of recent political discussion as to whether and how they can be relocated back to the south after their work in the north (Heleniak 2001; Hill and Gaddy 2003). However, recent research suggests (Bolotova and Stammler 2010; Razumova 2005; Round 2005; Thompson 2004) that many people develop intimate ties to their northern living places, which make them reluctant to leave even in times of industrial contraction or after the end of oil in the region. How the oil has made non–indigenous incomers feel at home in the north is an understudied sphere in the anthropology of mineral resources, which potentially contributes to understanding general questions of collective regional identity formation and of homeland (Stammler 2010).

On the other hand, there is a numerically less significant but better studied indigenous population in these areas. Reindeer herders, fishers and hunter–gatherers in northwest Siberia account for 7 per cent of the population and present one of the world's most vivid and active nomadic cultures that thrives even in the age of oil and gas extraction. A crucial component of their livelihood is their high mobility and the extensive use of reindeer pastures over a large territory, part of which is now affected by hydrocarbon development (Forbes et al. 2009; Stammler 2002, 2005).

Oil is a major commodity which drives the current world economy, and is of crucial importance for an anthropological understanding of power and politics. However, I suggest the whole hydrocarbon complex as a unit for anthropological analysis, rather than only oil. The strength of anthropological research is to present an analysis 'from the ground', based on the implications of people's practices. In this respect oil and gas as resources are hardly distinguishable from each other. Whether gas condensate, and Liquified Natural Gas (LNG), for example, belong to the oil or the gas part, is not always clear, and almost every oil well produces associated gas as well. Both gas and oil can be used as fuel for the same purposes (mainly cars, heating, power generation), require the same industrial development, and produce the same kind of infrastructure, causing the same social and similar ecological impacts, and both contribute to a country's economic and political power. On the ground the difference is not so much between oil and gas, but more between liquid and non–liquid hydrocarbon resources. An oil–, gas condensate– or LNG–spill in the Arctic pollutes all the surrounding areas for decades and makes the land (or sea) surface unusable for local populations. In case of a non–liquid gas 'spill' on the ground, the gas goes in the air and contributes to global warming, but does not destroy surrounding territories. But it does destroy precious fish stocks if the pipeline is under water, as recently disastrously happened in the Ob' Bay of West Siberia. While for political and economic sciences it might make sense to distinguish between oil and gas, for an anthropological research agenda focusing on local perspectives, I suggest analysing hydrocarbon resources together. Doing so makes our research results relevant for all cases of mineral resource extraction in a global perspective.[3]

The Industrialisation of Northern Russia

The whole development of the Soviet Union, as now of Russia, relied much on mastering its resources in the north. Since the independence of the southern Soviet Republics, 70 per cent of Russia's territory counts as ,regions of the far North or equivalent to them'.[4] Northern Russia has always been a resource colony of the various empires in northeastern Europe and north Asia: Tsarist Empire, the Soviet Union, and the Russian Federation (Forsyth 1992; Kappeler 1993; Lincoln 1994). From the 1950s on, minerals replaced fur as a crucial resource for the Russian state. The Soviet Union had a goal to integrate these resource colonies very early (Slezkine 1994). Under Stalin the north became a giant accumulation of prison camps, mainly for resource extraction. In the 1940s, there were 250,000 GULAG prison workers in West Siberia. Stalin made his plans of a railway running more or less parallel to the Arctic Circle, because he knew of the giant gas and oil deposits, which in the 1960s and 1970s became the Soviet pride and the world's largest deposits (Urengoi/Medvezhoe, see fig. 10.1). Relocation of southerners to the north was used to integrate these remote regions into a single Soviet territory, by building cities there, connecting them through railways to the centre, starting to dig out the coal and metal, and drilling for oil and gas (Bolotova and Stammler 2010; Mote 2003).

In the early Soviet period, the principle of mineral resource extraction in northern Russia was similar to that of other empires. Conquering the north was a colonial undertaking not much different from those of other empires, insofar as the resources should support the empire and the region should be politically subjugated. Accumulation of resources and of economic power went hand in hand, and in Stalin's case obeyed a 'violent logic of economic force constitution' (Reyna 2004). These processes are not specific for Siberia, but can be observed in many cases where the quest for resources pushes forward a particular frontier into what is perceived as a wilderness (Brightman et al. 2007: 2f). Recently, scholars have paid more attention to the similarities between colonialism of the Soviet Union and that of other empires (Kuzio 2002; Ssorin–Chaikov 2003; Verdery 2002), some going as far as stating that the Soviet and US construction of space at their eastern and western frontiers did not differ much from each other (Argounova–Low 2007: 48).

Collectivism as a Prerogative for Coexistence

In spite of the primarily economic incentives which might be similar in many regions, there was an explicit ideological factor to what was called the *osvoenie severa*, the Soviet mastering of the north. *Osvoenie* was

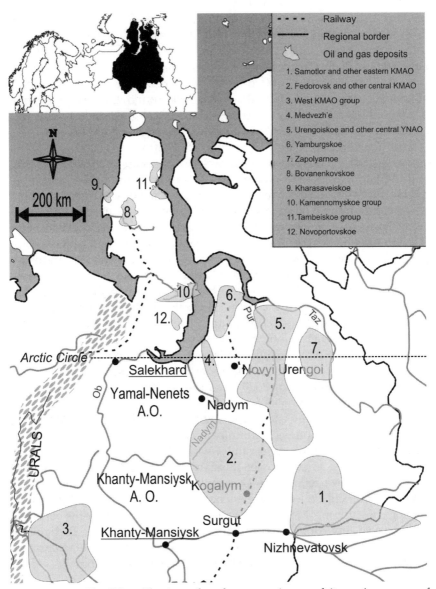

Figure 10.1. The West Siberian oil and gas province and its main groups of deposits. *Source*: Based on a map of Yamal–Nenets regional administration. Fieldwork by Florian Stammler. Drawing by Kari Viertola, Arctic Centre, Finland.

connected to a development ideology with the goal of integration. The north became an integral part of the single Soviet economy. Parallel to this, the people there were to become part of a single Soviet people (*edinyi sovetskii narod*). This functioned as a kind of super–identity, a community of the Soviet nation, a super–family uniting all the nationalities, which formed this empire with its satellites, and in which many people really believed (Hann 2002: 11). These non–economic properties of Soviet imperialism make up the difference from other empires. If we take Reyna's (this volume) description of imperialism as a background, there is no division between different kinds of dominators here. The whole undertaking was run by the officials, without the separate category of capitalists.

This giant economic and cultural transformation project brought about a new layer of the population, incoming prisoners and their descendants, and industrial workers (Bolotova and Stammler 2010). These people became 'heroes of socialist work', celebrated for making the Soviet Union what was thought to be superior to all other empires (Gurkov and Evseev 1984). Part of the Soviet integration project was also the coexistence of these industrial communities with indigenous herders and hunters, supposed to supply locally produced cheap meat for the extractive industry. As part of the same Soviet people, all children went to school, or boarding school, according to a standard curriculum, using the same books, reading the same ideology. Two pupils 8,000 km away from each other, surrounded by a different climate and different ethnic groups, studied exactly the same curriculum, regardless of its 'cultural compatibility' (cf. Anderson 2000: 192). As a result, a distinctive Soviet collective consciousness developed even in the remotest regions of the resource colonies (see Hann 2002: 8; Konstantinov 2000; Vladimirova 2006).

The integrative potential of Soviet values was powerful in the north, and continues to be after the end of the Soviet Union (Humphrey 2002: 13). A priority of benefits to one's community (*kollektiv*)[5] over individual rents was an important feature of these values, which have their roots in concepts deeply embedded in pre–Soviet Russian and indigenous ideas of collectives (Vladimirova 2006: 120f). This contributes to explaining the absence of violent conflicts. Collective experience was also strengthened through an ideology of suffering. Many individuals suffering together for the benefit of the whole society contributed to a homogenisation of values. Particularly the experience of the Second World War was a catalyst for Soviet integration against outside enemies even after these enemies ceased to exist.

Post–Soviet Collective Conscience

Even though there is no officially engineered Soviet identity fifteen years after its break up, anthropological research has shown the persistence of socialist values and common beliefs (Humphrey 2002: 13; Vladimirova 2006: 124ff), and often worldviews change less rapidly than economical or political climates (Lampland 2002: 32). Fieldwork in West Siberia among industrial workers and reindeer herders has shown that the idea of the Soviet *kollektiv* still serves as important social glue, giving a feeling of security. This is why for example reindeer herders still are reluctant to get rid of old Soviet collective institutions such as the state farm (*sovkhoz*) (Anderson 2000: 192f; Stammler 2005: 251) and enjoy with oil workers jointly the celebration of the day of victory over fascist Germany.

Alongside the collective conscience, the importance of personal continuity in social relations for the maintenance of the system has also persisted from the Soviet Union: on the ground conflicts are less likely between local populations and oil and gas workers, where there is a long personal continuity on both sides (Stammler 2002; Stammler 2005: 302f; Stammler and Wilson 2006: 30), whereas high personnel turnover is more likely to lead to dissatisfaction, stagnation in development and possibly conflicts – though not violent – as examples in the European northern Russian Nenets region have shown (Tuisku 2003; Stammler and Peskov 2008).

There is a problem with the widespread assumption that Soviet development principles were wrong and just have to be corrected to create a brighter future of the region. This assumption is at the heart of a prominent approach to restructuring the Soviet Arctic economy. Hill and Gaddy (2003) call this the 'Siberian Curse', leaning on the 'resource curse' hypothesis, which claims that the presence of mineral resources hinders instead of fosters economic growth (Karl 1997; see also Bulte et al. 2004). Reform programmes in this direction, favouring fly in/fly out shift labour instead of the Soviet permanent industrial cities, have created irritation on the ground among local people and company workers alike: with a loss of personal continuity in relations on the ground, the sense of collectivity is also lost.

Since 2004 Russia has returned to a more centralised authoritarian regime that turns the country more into an empire in the old territorial sense, whereas during Yeltsin's time, there were many traits of what Reyna (2004) calls rhizomatic empire. This re–established dominance involves, as Reyna has shown, a flow of forces from the dominated to the dominator. Therefore the governors of the regions in Russia are not elected any more, but appointed by the president. The central Russian empire accumulates capital and economic forces back from the regions. The central Russian state also reclaims economic force by acquiring oil companies. Russian gas extraction is almost entirely run by the giant state–controlled company Gazprom, and more recently the state–controlled oil company Rosneft became Russia's largest oil producer. Centralising tendencies, I suggest, can be described as a re–formalisation of the Russian empire. This restructuring is happening without any violence or open confrontation. The Kremlin exerts efficient pressure in the background. This subtle threatening leads to pre–emptive surrendering of possible competitors or enemies. Subtlety leaves space for regional authorities, which can through pre–emptive action stay loyal to the centre and still secure special benefits from the resources in their regions, as I argue below. Even where there are problems, the largely state–controlled media make sure that they do not become public, and civil society institutions hardly get the chance to use media as instruments of pressure in possible conflicts.

Factors for Integration and Conflict Resolution

The remainder of this chapter will analyse, against the general background of the situation in West Siberian mineral resource extraction, which general factors have contributed to a relatively peaceful extraction of mineral resources in the twentieth to twenty–first centuries, and what role these factors play in the region. Judging from fieldwork and comparative literature studies (Argounova–Low 2007; Brightman et al. 2007; Habeck 2002; Haller et al. 2000; High 2007; Stammler and Wilson 2006; Tuisku 2003; Wilson 2007), I suggest the following factors as significant for a comparative anthropological analysis of mineral resource extraction:

(a) social organisation and traditions of conflict resolution among the local population prior to the advent of mineral resource extraction;
(b) regional demography and geographically specific land use patterns;
(c) presence or absence of international organisations/corporations, forming civil society action; and
(d) the role of the state and its approach to economic diversification, civil society and information politics.

Social Organisation and Traditions of Conflict Resolution

Haller et al. (2000: 621–3) suggested to consider the internal systems of conflict management among residents of oil and gas regions. Nenets, Khanty and other reindeer herders and hunter–gatherers of West Siberia have a long history of conflicts among themselves prior to the advent of Russian colonisation. Like in other nomadic contexts, conflicts mostly evolved around theft of animals and women (Golovnev 1995). All these conflicts were restricted to an immediate occasion and did not result in major wars or extinction of larger parts of the population. Corresponding to the nature of these conflicts was the indigenous leadership pattern in these rather egalitarian societies. Leadership positions were not inheritable, institutionalised nor permanent in any way. Leadership was and is rather temporarily earned by character qualities of individuals that become useful and appreciated in concrete situations, where these individuals then are supported by their peers. As soon as this situation is over, the leader retreats to his previous position as a fellow reindeer herder among a group where every household lives independently (Golovnev 2000), although within a tight network of mutual assistance of relatives and neighbours (Stammler 2005: 187–203).

An ideology of defending exclusive access to territory has not played a role among these indigenous communities. They have a flexible system of using the land, which is based on their intimate knowledge of changes in the distribution and abundance of the on–surface resources such as game, reindeer, berries and fish. Access to land is therefore flexibly negotiated, although in most cases there is a clear sense of emotional and spiritual belonging (Jordan 2003; Stammler 2005: chapter 6). I have argued elsewhere that this cooperative approach includes coexistence of different users on the same land as a norm, even though indigenous politicians now use a more defensive language in talks about oil and gas development (Stammler 2005: chapter 7).

Russian and Soviet colonisation met little organised resistance. Conflicts arose about specific problems, such as extracting fur–tax from northern people, or collectivisation and the Soviet prosecution of shamans (Golovnev and Osherenko 1999; Petrova and Khariutschi 1999; Slezkine 1994; Ziker 2002). The hostilities were not about a general objection to Russian presence in the area. Along similar lines, problems with oil and gas extraction arise, related to particular behaviour of workers, pollution of resources, or infrastructure construction, but the principle of coexistence of two forms of land use in the same area, unlike in other northern areas such as Alaska or Canada, is not questioned (Flanders et al. 1998: 263f; Forbes 2008; Stammler and Forbes 2006; Stammler and Wilson 2006). Among Nenets nomads there is a tradition of avoidance instead of confrontation in cases of possible conflicts. In many cases the first choice for nomads was stepping aside to more remote territories.

Recent fieldwork among reindeer nomads has shown that there is no major resistance against industrial development of the region. Instead there is an expressed will to coexist, and the ambitious idea to turn the region into an exemplar of successful cooperation between two different land use systems. Reindeer nomads are practitioners with 365 days per year experience in using the Arctic tundra and subarctic taiga, and they have decades–long experience with industry in their areas. Therefore they have very practical suggestions on how to improve coexistence for the future. Among the most important are (Stammler et al. 2009):

- elevating pipelines to enable free movement of people and animals across the tundra. This flexibility in land use is one of the main assets that enable the nomads to react to a changing economical, political and natural climate;
- restricting access of incomers to the tundra, to minimise negative cumulative social impact, and maximise positive in terms of trading relations along the following lines: 'the gas workers would do better to buy fish from us tundra people than to fish themselves, as they don't always do the fishing properly; (Sergei Serotetto, then head of brigagde 8, sovkhoz Yar Sale, 10 July 2005);
- using tundra people's local knowledge for monitoring environmental impacts of industrial development;
- consulting tundra people at the earliest possible stages of project planning, e.g. drilling sites, infrastructure construction;
- carrying out a transparent information policy on both sides, providing knowledge about each other's activity on the ground, which leads to better understanding and coordination on site; and
- companies following a 'minimal footprint' approach in their activity.

Tundra people coexist and engage with industry in everyday life, for example when stocking up on staples such as bread, tea or butter from industrial settlements, using company helicopter or ground transport, trading meat, fish and at times reindeer antlers with industry workers, or using medical services.

This situation is arguably different from other contexts, where the social peace would be difficult even without oil extraction, such as in Chechnya (Khizriyeva and Reyna, this volume), Darfur (Behrends, this volume), or where oil projects are met with violent protests and killings such as among the Huorani in Amazonia (High 2007: 35) or in the Niger Delta (Watts 2004a and 2004b, and this volume). In those cases violence has been among the previously used means of conflict management for the local population with and without oil extraction. Supporting Haller et al. (2000) I argue for the anthropological analysis of the cultural position of violence in different communities as important for our basic understanding of conflict potentials.

Demography and Geographically Specific Land Use Patterns

I have highlighted elsewhere how specific preconditions have to be met in the area to enable a strategy of conflict avoidance (Stammler 2005: 128, and chapter 7). For the comparative context of this volume, it shall be enough to mention that the extremely low population density of the area, with 0.67 persons per km^2, and the vast area of reindeer pastures on the flat tundra

Figure 10.2. Alexei and his son passing by an oil rig on the Toravei deposit. Often herders prefer to walk instead of sitting on sledges close to the rigs to see possibly damaging iron junks before their reindeer injure themselves. *Source:* Photo by Florian Stammler.

or boreal taiga without significant physical barriers have enabled a more flexible use of land and allowed for a strategy of stepping aside, at least in the past. This is different from regions in Africa with a large population density where there is much stronger competition for resources. However, it would be wrong and dangerous to conclude from there that in scarcely populated areas people always step aside and there are no conflicts. Recent comparative research (Brightman et al. 2007) has highlighted that for example in Amazonia the human population density is also low and the area vast, and still there is a long history of resistance against oil extraction, e.g. among the Huorani (Haller et al. 2000: 318; High 2007).

This exemplifies how important it is to consider the social organisation of the communities, their history of contacts with outsiders and their land use pattern in an analysis. The latter is significantly determined by geographical climatic specifics. Amazonia is among the regions with the highest biomass production and the largest biodiversity worldwide, whereas Siberia is on the opposite end. Resources are scarcely spread over thousands of kilometres, and extensive mobile pastoralism is the best way to use them in all seasons. In order to sustain a community in Siberia, there-fore, a much larger area is needed than in the Amazon. Casimir (1992) has shown in general that with such extensive land use patterns, the cost of defending territories would be much higher than the benefits. But stepping aside in a scarcely populated area is viable only to a limited extent.

In January 2009 there were 651,100 reindeer in the Yamal region, graz-ing on roughly 50 million ha pastures[6] herded by approximately fifteen thousand nomads. This is the highest number of domestic reindeer and herders worldwide, and concerns about overgrazing (Podkorytov 1995) increase with new oil and gas development (Stammler 2005: 239–52). Rein-deer herders have already indicated during fieldwork that under these conditions their usual strategy of avoiding industrial sites is not an option any more. The suicide of Nyadmanesia mentioned above might point to a sad alternative strategy of the herders: avoiding conflict through suicide instead of violent resistance.

Distance and remoteness, which have been major resources for reindeer herders to rely on in the past, now have become a hindrance to develop-ing efficient collective agency (Stammler and Wilson 2006). Distance and space made it possible for reindeer herders to elude and avoid conflicts rather than fight. They always had their seemingly inaccessible ranges of the tundra to retreat to when threatened. This was also true for the Soviet time, when the arms of the system in many cases ended on the margins of the trading posts. Now there is the freedom and the need to develop effi-cient communication and collective action, which would be advantageous for organising herders' relations with oil companies, but space has turned from being their major asset to a major pitfall. Vitebsky (2000) has shown the consequences of this isolation for remote northern communities, and Fondahl (1998) identified it as an important factor inhibiting the claiming of land rights by indigenous communities.

The significance of distance might decrease, however, with the advent of the mobile phone into the tundra and taiga of Russia. Such techno-logical change is mainly driven by the extractive industry for communica-tion with their workers, but reindeer nomads make use of it increasingly (Stammler 2009). The above mentioned factors show that for a compara-tive study of conflict and integration in regions of mineral resource ex-traction, context analysis is essential for answering the question of why in some cases mineral resource extraction leads to war, whereas in other cases it happens peacefully.

Presence and Absence of International Attention and Globalisation

Besides factors internal to the region, there is also a whole range of exter-nal factors which ought to be considered in times of rapidly increasing global interconnectedness of resource–colonies with end users. One of those is the presence of international organisations. The international attention generated by different projects of mineral resource extraction varies. International organisations may come in to support all actors, e.g. international financing institutions granting loans for industrial companies (such as the World Bank or EBRD[7]), or multinational oil and gas companies keen to benefit from mineral resources anywhere on the globe, or environmental NGOs lobbying for the preservation of flora and fauna, or human rights organisations wishing to protect the interests of the local population in the extraction areas.

I argue that in Russia nowadays the presence of international organisations increases the likelihood of open conflicts. This does not imply, however, that these actors have a detrimental effect on the social or ecological situation in extraction areas. International support generates more confidence among all actors to stand up for their interests and not give in to agreements that they think are disadvantageous for them. There is a strong correlation between the development of institutions for collective action (such as indigenous NGOs) and mineral resource development. It was in the oil and gas regions where the post–Soviet indigenous movement started, and all three presidents of the Russian Association for the Indigenous Peoples of the North came from such regions.[8] However, this empowerment differs significantly between regions where international organisations are active, and those where business is run mainly by Russian representatives.

The case of the Russian Far Eastern oil projects on Sakhalin Island, analysed in detail by Wilson (2003, 2007; see also Stammler and Wilson 2006), exemplifies this well. The consortium of Shell, Mitsubishi and Mitsui had applied for a loan from EBRD for the largest foreign investment in Russia and the largest integrated oil and gas project in the world. It includes a LNG terminal on the shore close to fishing grounds and 800 km of pipeline crossing 1,100 rivers, 192 of them salmon–spawning rivers. The international involvement required environmental and social impact assessments according to international standards. Although most of the regulations were followed, the project came under intense scrutiny by NGOs. Animal protectors accused the consortium of endangering the world's last refuge of grey whales (Brahic 2007), environmentalists heavily criticised the river crossing strategy for the pipeline, and activists complained about ignoring the needs of the local population of fishermen (WWF 2005a: 12; WWF 2005b). The conflict was deepened by Russian indigenous peoples' organisations asking for an anthropological expert review addressing specifically indigenous issues (Roon 2006; Stammler and Wilson 2006) and by the Russian government accusing the industry of violating Russian environmental legislation (RBK 2007). Protests and accusations from all sides led to a slower implementation of the project; road blockades by activists on Sakhalin; protests in front of the EBRD headquarters in London and the UN in New York; and the loss of Shell's control over the consortium – Shell handed over the majority of its shares to Gazprom.

This is in contrast to the situation in West Siberia, where there is less international involvement and the Russian industry has much more freedom to extract mineral resources according to its own standards without protests. This is true for oil deposits in Khanty–Mansiiskii and Yamal–Nenets autonomous regions, where there has been a continuous presence of the industry since the 1960s. Gazprom, Lukoil, Surgutneftegaz, Rosneft and other major Russian companies build on the relationships that they have developed since the 1960s with local people and administrations (Novikova 1997). This has both plusses and minuses (Wiget and Balalaeva 1997). For example, companies can still afford to revive late–Soviet development plans and implement those without major alterations, if the Russian state pushes these projects forward as a priority. In the case of gas development on the Yamal Pensinsula, this meant that environmental and social impact assessments were being neglected under time pressure.[9] Infrastructure was constructed the most convenient way, by subcontractors with little concern for local needs and cutting through crucial migration routes of the world's largest reindeer herding community.

Moreover, we have argued (Stammler and Wilson 2006: 17) that the Russian system of revenue distribution has detrimental effects on the ground. Since most of the benefits of industrial developments go to the federal centre, the local administration has to rely on individual agreements with companies. Their only leverage is their entitlement for damage–compensation. For the municipal budget more damage from industry means more income. 'Minimal footprint' and damage–prevention are therefore not popular. In the worst case this may lead to municipally induced relocation of one–third of the nomadic population of the Yamal Peninsula,[11] with all of the known detrimental effects when nomads become sedentarised: loss of perspective, alcohol and drug abuse, criminality, unemployment, loss of cultural diversity. All this can happen because there is no independent media coverage of these issues, no international standards were applied, and Russian state companies do not come under scrutiny from NGOs, civil society institutions or international organisations.

On the other hand, the strong understanding of Russian collective solidarity plays an important role. For example, in 2006 road construction had blocked fish migration to an important fishing lake, as well as the migration routes for reindeer nomads and herds. The herder went to the local chief of the gas company to talk about these problems. He was offered a meal of smoked fish, beer and vodka, according to good Soviet tradition, and they spent the whole evening informally socialising and talking about life and the common Soviet past. The industry built a temporary pass–way for reindeer over the road the next day, the fish had come back to the lake by the next season, and the gas chief promised to consider the herders' needs during future constructions.

This sense of belonging to a broader collective brings herders in West Siberia and northwest Russia nearer to those oil workers with whom they have experience rather than newcomers. The 'alienness' of foreigners in Russia is very often put to contrast the idea of close relatedness of everybody and everything from Russia. The difference between *nashi* (ours) and *chuzhye* (aliens, foreigners) is the most basic categorisation for humans and things in Russia. In 2006 it was used by reindeer herders of Yamal to support *nashi gazoviki* (our gas people) and to prevent the advent of *chuzhye*. In this case, the administration had threatened to withdraw the licence for extraction from the local Gazprom subsidiary and transfer it to another Gazprom subsidiary to punish them for slow implementation of construction. Herders supported the first company vigorously, and believe this contributed to preventing the internal takeover by the more powerful Gazprom subsidiary. It is this collectivity that may count more on the ground than meticulous implementation of international standards. I argue that this sense of *nashi* contributes to appeasing conflicts in industrial development. This is also part of the reason why so many agree to the principle of sacrificing individual advantages for the sake of 'national interests'. The Russian state and industrial companies therefore exploit this rhetoric to push forward their development agenda, and a discussion of whether to give a 'yes' or a 'no' to an oil project, such as happened in Alaska recently for the ANWR[12] or the Mackenzie River Valley in Canada, would be hard to even imagine in Russia. I have therefore heard from all sides in Russia sceptical remarks about the presence of international organisations, be it industry, NGOs, politics or human rights.

However, international presence and attention such as in Sakhalin also creates more awareness about global developments, international standards and values. One important impact of globalisation is what Hoffmann–Novotny (1993) called 'Wertintegration' (value integration). I have shown that this is not new for northern Russia. Post–Soviet collective conscience is a result of Russian and Soviet value integration. International presence can lead to a confrontation with international ('Western') values, and as a result tensions like those in Sakhalin arise. In other places such as West Siberia, there is less confrontation than what I call value syncretism, when Soviet values become well adapted to previously existing indigenous worldviews.

The Role of the State and its Approach to Economic Diversification

There is no doubt that even in a globalised world states play the crucial role for development of or disasters on the planet, and as mineral resources fuel states' economies and budgets, they will always have a key role for determining industrial development. Political Science studies mainly distinguish 'weak states' from 'strong states' and democratic from undemocratic ones (Kaldor 2007; Kaldor et al. 2007; Karl 1997). The main message of such studies is about the problem of oil being extracted in weak states and consumed in strong states. Extraction leads to violent conflict, fuelled by the never–ending demand for oil among 'strong states'.

While acknowledging the principal arguments of this research, field material from northern Russia invites reflection on the basic categories. Russia's centralisation policy becomes ever more relevant in its northern resource colonies; Putin's law and order regime and Russia's behaviour in the great game for global power become a major concern for world politics (White 2007). Therefore I suggest that seeing in Russia a 'weak state' alongside Iraq and Sudan (Kaldor 2007) is somewhat misleading. Russia may be weak in democratic development, but was democracy very highly developed in the US during the regime of George W. Bush? The problems of the Russian state to control the Chechnya conflict might be seen as a sign of a weak state. However, the US is not more successful in introducing peace to Iraq or Afghanistan, and other 'strong states' with functioning democracy have similar problems, such as Northern Ireland or the Basque conflict.

The northern resource extraction in Russia, instead, supports the argument that Russia's strong control over politics, civil society and media in the region reduces conflicts. As stated above, this does not mean that it improves the situation significantly (Okotetto and Forbes 1999), but a strong state can try to prevent conflicts before they become violent, in which case no violence is needed to control the situation. Since the beginning of 2007, it has become difficult even for Russians to enter the Yamal–Nenets oil and gas region, because of its 'strategical importance' for Russia. This resembles the late–Soviet situation where strategically important regions, including the Arctic, were declared 'secret' (Flanders et al. 1998: 263).

Economic diversification has been often identified as a key strategy for avoiding the 'resource curse' that has become proverbial for oil–dependent states (Auty 1993; Gashawbeza 2006; Kaldor 2007). However, in a country such as Russia with its vast internal diversity, it is useful to go beyond state–level analysis and contribute with anthropological insights from the regions (Stammler and Wilson 2006). Without ignoring prevalent problems, there is evidence for at least some revenues 'trickling down' to the regions in West Siberia. Within the last fifteen years, it has become hard to recognise the Soviet past of the West Siberian oil and gas region. All cities and most villages have state–of–the–art modern housing, paved roads, modern health–care centres, a functioning helicopter ambulance, modern schools, computers and internet access. Much of this change is due to oil companies' social investment and regional support programmes. The standard of life of the population has increased, not only among the oil managers. However, the sad exception is the tundra population, which is too often neglected as revenue negotiations with municipalities follow a 'sedentary logic' (see above). Nonetheless, the number of herders and reindeer on Yamal has been increasing for decades now, and in the future industry revenue is planned to be invested for increasing profitability of herding, so that nomads need fewer animals to lead a decent life.[12]

For the longer–term perspective, in the Khanty–Mansiisk region a 'fund for generations' was established in 1994 with the explicit goal of stimulating economic diversification of the region to reduce the dependence from oil revenues, thus making it fit for the time after the oil age. The main capital of the fund comes from 15 per cent of the tax on mineral resource extraction in the region. Investments go primarily towards renewable resources, supporting companies not associated with mineral resource extraction, higher education programmes, support for children born after the year 2000, and pensions. This strategy resembles that in Norway, where oil revenues were used to create the world's largest pension fund.[13] A similar

Figure 10.3. Yamal's northernmost school (Northern Latitude 70 10.003, Eastern Longitude 72 30.690), built by Gazprom for children of reindeer nomads in 2001, featuring computer classes and broadband internet connection. *Source:* Photo by Florian Stammler.

investment fund for sustainable development and the future has also been established in the Yamal–Nenets Okrug, and the regional administration tries to change the economy to more than a pure resource colony.

In this respect the nation state as a unit of analysis is not suitable for assessing economic diversification. The approach of the otherwise excellent volume by Kaldor et al. (2007) of analysing the Russian case from the point of view of its history of conflicts in oil regions does not fit well to Russia's richest resource colonies. These regions have lived without significant violence for the last 350 years, and after the collapse of the Soviet Union gained considerable regional financial autonomy, which created economic and social wellbeing. 'Regional states' with their own governments, parliaments and legislation under the umbrella of the Russian Federation developed. This created stability in the region and political, social and economic development without the ruptures that we know from the Moscow centre. The Khanty–Mansiiskii and Yamal–Nenetskii regions in West Siberia were ruled up to 2010 by the same two governors for the previous 18 and 13 years respectively, at a time where it seemed that everything else in the country turned upside down. In spite of a strong centralisation policy by the Kremlin, this diversity has created a legacy in the regions likely to last for decades. Neither the central nor the regional 'states' in Russia have a strong democratic basis or a developed civil society in the Western sense, and they are dependent on oil and gas revenues. Nonetheless this did not lead to violence in mineral resource extraction, even though studies of international relations and economy see these factors as contributing to conflicts (Gashawbeza 2006; Seifert and Werner 2005).

I agree with Karl's (1997) and Kaldors et al.'s (2007) argument that the likeliness of conflicts in oil–rich countries lies in the nature of society and economy of these countries. Therefore it is worth analysing these factors, as I have started to do above, alongside with the role of the state, on the regional level too. This enables us to explain why in West Siberia mineral resource business is done rather peacefully, whereas within the same country it is accompanied by war in Chechnya (Khizriyeva and Reyna, this volume).

Conclusion: Lessons for an Anthropology of Mineral Resources?

On the basis of an introduction to Soviet and post–Soviet Arctic mineral resource development and its impacts, this chapter has attempted to find answers for the absence of significant conflicts over the whole duration of forty years' oil and gas extraction in West Siberia. Aggregating fieldwork and background studies, a number of variables have been suggested to be analysed for explaining the presence or absence of conflicts during the exploration and extraction process. This final section will ask what if anything we can learn from looking at these factors with the help of anthropological fieldwork.

None of the relevant factors discussed above alone can explain the rather peaceful process of oil and gas extraction. The relevance of traditions of conflict responses and social organisation, specifics of land use, international presence and the role of the state is also connected to the potential for collective action in hydrocarbon development (cf. Haller et al. 2000: 638–48) and the internal potential for such action among all stakeholders, which we called collective agency (Stammler and Wilson 2006). It is the combination of these factors as pieces in a mosaic that gives the answer. Therefore anthropological evidence from the ground is valuable, with deeper insights into local people's intentions and motivations for either cooperative or provocative behaviour in mineral resource extraction.

I have first argued that Nenets nomads' social structure and their extensive mobile pastoralist lifestyle facilitate peaceful coexistence of several people on one land. No permanent hierarchy and a strong idea of sharing resources, alongside a tradition of avoiding instead of provoking conflicts, is an important background for explaining the current situation. Currently, tundra people are not opposed to industrial development, but rather committed to turning the region into an exemplar for successful coexistence. More generally I argue that studying classical themes in anthropology, such as hierarchy and egalitarianism, chiefdoms and acephalous communities, local histories and cultural contacts, delivers important background data explaining why in some cases violent conflicts arise more than in others. In the case of West Siberia, the independent lifestyle of reindeer pastoralists, their remoteness from each other and their egalitarian structure may inhibit the development of efficient institutions for collective action. Haller et al. (2000: 648) argued that the homogeneity of people's interests determines the potential for resistance to mineral resource extraction. In addition, the evidence of this chapter suggests that the traditions of conflict management and collective agency within the group crucially influence the reaction of local communities to industrial development.

Second, I have argued that demographic characteristics and land use practices facilitate or inhibit peaceful coexistence. This is not only about low population density, but also about the distribution of resources, which facilitate particular patterns of land use. In the case of nomads, their main resource – the herd – is mobile. If needed, they can circumvent particular places on their seasonal migration – a practice which they applied during the last centuries. I have shown, however, that this does not change their intimate sense of belonging to the land (Stammler 2005: chapter 6). With competition for pastures and gas deposits under them increasing, the circumventing practice comes to its limits. But even then the experience from West Siberia (Stammler 2003) shows that the local population will most probably not organise resistance against industrial development. Many nomads internalised the Soviet idea of the superiority of the state's interests. The indigenous elite trained in the Soviet Union largely subscribes to a view that it is morally questionable to endanger strategic interests of the state. They appeal to the individuals' conscience as a member of the overall collective. So resistance might be negatively sanctioned by your own people. In extreme cases, suicide for some seems to become a treacherous way of escaping.

This is complemented by the situation of indigenous peoples being marginalised. As a result, the minority of indigenous people who are negatively affected have neither the tradition, nor the idea, nor the power, nor the spatial and communicative connectedness enabling them to resist. The majority of the (mostly Russian) population would not think about protesting, as they are themselves immigrants to the region doing industrial labour for hydrocarbon companies and related business.

Third, I have shown that international attention and the presence of international organisations, companies, NGOs and other actors may lead to a confrontation of values in the areas of mineral resource extraction, and tensions arise. As a result, I argue that the internationalisation of mineral resource extraction leads to division of the population in the regions into different groups of alliances with their international partners, e.g. indigenous peoples integrated into the global indigenous movement, companies integrated into the global business world, regional politicians integrated into international cooperations, e.g. the Arctic Council. This factionalism increases the likelihood of tensions around industrial projects. I have emphasised that this is not to say these actors have only a 'bad' influence. They increase collective agency among negatively affected parts of the population, and through lifting their cases to the global arena they open up other opportunities for organised action. Absence of this internationalisation, on the other hand, leads to emphasising commonalities of all those active in the region regardless of their affiliation. The uniting aspects of Russian post–Soviet identity, of Russian citizens as opposed to foreigners (*nashi* and *chuzhye*), count more in this situation.

Thus, I conclude from this material that collective action is more likely to happen across all stakeholder groups in one region, when there is no or little international integration. When there is international presence, alliances for collective action are more likely to develop across the globe but stay within stakeholder groups rather than uniting different interests. To illustrate this point with practical examples: in West Siberia indigenous people went to Gazprom to talk about a solution for the impacts of infrastructure construction. Their voices are heard regionally, but not necessarily considered during industrial development. In Sakhalin, indigenous people joined with national and international NGOs to protest against the impacts of oil development in their area and to put pressure on funding bodies. Their voices were heard globally, the relations to industrial companies became tense, and their arguments were finally used cleverly by the Russian government to nationalise the oil project.

This brings us, fourth, to the role of the state. The Russian cases described in this chapter show the importance of the state on various levels: a strong national state can overrule the impacts of globalisation, inhibit resistance to development with subtle oppressive or co–opting tactics, like in the Soviet and some post–Soviet cases. The cases analysed here also show that the state has multiple faces, which are worth investigating. The regional states (administrations) in West Siberia are different from the federal Russian state. Their long–term political stability and personal continuity, alongside careful investment into economic diversification and social programmes for the local population, contribute to appeasing the relations between different stakeholders in hydrocarbon extraction. Indigenous representatives in both the regional states and the companies may contribute to this coexistence.

Russia has returned to more authoritarian ways of governing and a *de facto* one–party system. The government openly uses mineral resources for its own interests in foreign policy, leading to irritations internationally. The process of industrialisation in northern Russia started with a violent logic of force accumulation, but this led to an integration, which over time was welcomed by most of the local population. One reason for this is that the logic of the integration was not only exploitative, but had an explicit social component, namely the creation of a single Soviet nation. This led to an embedding of oil and gas alongside reindeer herding into a broader socio–political concept. Thus, the absence of violent resistance was a result not only of the disempowered marginal position of local people in the Soviet Union, but also of their integration into the overall caring 'state–family' (Khlinovskaya–Rockhill 2011). In theoretical terms, once the force was constituted violently (Reyna 2004, and this volume), violence was not necessary any more to perpetuate it, not only because nobody dared to resist, but because people had common beliefs.

Thus, there does not have to be a correlation between freedom and democracy in a state and peaceful mineral resource extraction. In northern Russia there is no 'oil war', even without democracy. People there are used to finding their niches as part of an authoritarian state. There is no perception of political freedom and democracy as increasing the potential for human wellbeing. In Russia there is more demand for optimising the already practised coexistence of state–controlled mineral resource economy with subsistence and market production of the local population. Therefore Western–style democracy is not necessarily an all–curing medicine for the problems in mineral resource economy. It is questionable if it would make sense to restructure civil society in the area according to a Western template for making the tools of the aforementioned democracy work, including the praised international standards of community participation and co–management of resources.

Anthropological research from the ground shows that there is no universally 'right or wrong' way of organising hydrocarbon extraction, and in particular not those approaches designed in Western 'progressive' think–tanks. The criterion for evaluating a project should not be whether or not it meets particular standards ratified by particular states, companies or funding bodies. It should be whether it fits the local conditions and is the best possible compromise between meeting the needs of the global economy and being beneficial to the local population. If they do not fall victim to state–induced sedentarisation programmes that would wipe out one of the world's most vital nomadic societies, Nyadmanesia's grandchildren will continue to move through the Bovanenkovo gas deposit throughout its extraction period and thereafter.

Acknowledgements

This chapter could not have been written without the openness, trust and friendship of reindeer nomads, gas workers and administrators in West Siberia. Research was funded by numerous projects, most recently by the Finnish Academy's research projects ENSINOR (decision 208147), MOVE–INNOCOM (decision 118702) and the British Broadcasting Corporation (BBC).

Notes

1. For oil: according to Reuters, article by Vladimir Soldatkin, January 2 2011 at http://www.reuters.com/article/2011/01/02/us–russia–enrgy–idUSTRE7010DI20110102. For gas: according to Rian news service, 2 January 2011, at http://en.rian.ru/russia/20110102/162026904.html. See also the overview of the US energy administration at http://www.eia.doe.gov/cabs/Russia/Background.html (May 2008).
2. A total of 23 months between 1998–2010.

3. Thanks to Terry Lynn Karl for stimulating thoughts on this difference by a critical remark at the conference 'Oil, integration and conflict', Halle (Germany), 13 Dec. 2004.
4. This is the official term used in Russian legislation.
5. *Community* is not the ideal translation for the Russian *kollektiv*, which has many different notions, but it comes closest to what we want to refer to here. Compare David Anderson's elaborate reflection on translating this and other crucial Soviet concepts (2000: 187–94).
6. According to data by the Russian Union of Reindeer Herders in the Ministry for Agriculture, unpublished government statistics.
7. European Bank for Reconstruction and Development
8. Namely Vladimir Sangi from Sakhalin, Yeremey Aipin from Khanty–Mansiiskii, and Sergei Khariutschi from Yamal–Nenets autonomous region in West Siberia.
9. This view was expressed by reindeer nomads as well as gas industry workers during fieldwork in 2005–2008.
10. According to a plan by the Yamal municipality and Gazprom, presented in a speech in Yar–Sale, 17 March 2008. Also mentioned by A. Gubarkov in Moscow, 29 January 2008, see http://www.geobotany.uaf.edu/yamal/documents/gubarkov_2008_yamal.pdf.
11. Arctic National Wildlife refuge. See Mc Carthy (2001) and CBC (2010) for a discussion.
12. For a detailed analysis of the reasons for the recent thriving of reindeer herding see Stammler (2005).
13. As of August 2007, according to *Der Spiegel*, No. 29, 16 July, p. 60.

References

Anderson, David. 2000. *Identity and Ecology in Arctic Siberia: The Number One Reindeer Brigade*. Oxford: Oxford University Press.

Argounova–Low, Tatiana. 2007. Frontier: Reflections from the Other Side. *Cambridge Anthropology* 26(2): 47–57.

Auty, Richard 1993. *Sustaining Development in Mineral Resource Economies: The Resource Curse Thesis*. London: Routledge.

Bolotova, Alla and Florian Stammler. 2010. How the North Became Home. Attachment to Place among Industrial Migrants in Murmansk Region. In *Migration in the Circumpolar North: Issues and Contexts*, ed. Lee Huskey and Chris Southcott, 193–220. Edmonton, Alberta: Canada Canadian Circumpolar Institute Press, University of Alberta.

Brahic, Catherine. 2007. Construction of Oil Site 'Frightening Whales Away'. *New Scientist Environment*, 3 July. http://environment.newscientist.com/article/dn12187 (accessed 5 September 2007).

Brightman, Marc., Olga Ulturgasheva and Vanessa Grotti. 2007. Introduction: Rethinking the 'Frontier' in Amazonia and Siberia: Extractive Economies, Indigenous Politics and Social Transformations. *Cambridge Anthropology* 26(2): 1–13.

Bulte, Erwin, Richard Damania and Robert Deacon. 2004. Resource Abundance, Poverty and Development. *ESA Working Paper, No. 04–03*, Food and Agriculture Organisation of the UN.

Casimir, Michael 1992. The Determinants of Rights to Pasture: Territorial Organisation and Ecological Constraints. In *Mobility and Territoriality: Social and Spatial Boundaries among Foragers, Fishers, Pastoralists and Peripatetics*, ed. M. Casimir and A. Rao, 153–203. Oxford and New York: Berg.

CBC News 2010. Mackenzie Valley pipeline: 37 years of negotiation. 16 December. http://www.cbc.ca/news/business/story/2010/12/16/f–mackenzie–valley–pipeline–history.html. Accessed 03 April 2011.

European Gas Industry 2010. Report *Long term outlook for gas demand and supply 2007–2030*. http://www.eurogas.org/uploaded/Eurogas_Brochure_Outlook_LR_030510.pdf (accessed 2 April 2011)

Flanders, Nicholas E., Rex V. Brown, Elena Andreeva and Oleg Larichev. 1998. Justifying Public Decisions in Arctic Oil and Gas Development: American and Russian Approaches. *Arctic* 51: 262–79.

Fondahl, Gail. A. 1998. *Gaining Ground? Evenkis, Land, and Reform in Southeastern Siberia*. Cultural Survival Studies in Ethnicity and Change. Boston, London and Toronto: Allyn and Bacon.

Forbes, Bruce. 2008. Equity, Vulnerability and Resilience in Social–ecological Systems: A Contemporary Example from the Russian Arctic. *Equity and the Environment. Research in Social Problems and Public Policy* 15: 203–36.

Forbes, Bruce, Florian Stammler, Timo Kumpula, Nina Meschtyb, Anu Pajunen and Elina Kaarlejarvi. 2009. High Resilience in the Yamal–Nenets Social–ecological System, West Siberian Arctic, Russia. *Proceedings of the National Academy of Ssciences* 106(52): 22041–8.

Forsyth, James. 1992. *A History of the Peoples of Siberia. Russia's North Asian Colony 1581–1990*. Cambridge: Cambridge University Press.

Gashawbeza, Ewenet. 2006. Curse of Oil for African People: A Story of Plenty and Paucity. *Oil and War* 10. http://pangea.stanford.edu/~jshragge/OilWar/Ewenet.html (accessed 10 August 2007).

Golovnev, Andrei. 1995. *Govoriashchie kul'tury*. Ekaterinburg: Ural Branch, Russian Academy of Sciences.

———. 2000. Wars and Chiefs among the Samoyeds and Ugrians of Western Siberia. In *Hunters and Gatherers in the Modern World: Conflict, Resistance, and Self–determination*, ed. Peter P. Schweitzer, Megan Biesele and Robert K. Hitchcock, 125–49. New York: Berghahn Books.

Golovnev, Andrei. and Gail. Osherenko. 1999. *Siberian Survival: The Nenets and Their Story*. Ithaca and London: Cornell University Press.

Gurkov, Genrich and Valeri Evseev. 1984. *Erdgas kommt aus Urengoi*. Moscow: Progress Publishers.

Habeck, Joachim. O. 2002. How to Turn a Reindeer Pasture into an Oil Well, and Vice Versa: Transfer of Land, Compensation and Reclamation in the Komi Republic. In *People and the Land. Pathways to Reform in Post–Soviet Siberia*, ed. Erich Kasten, 125–47. Berlin: Reimer.

Haller, Tobias., Anja. Blöchlinger, Markus John, Esther Marthaler and Sabine Ziegler, eds. 2000. *Fossile Resourcen, Erdölkonzerne und indigene Völker*. Infostudie 12. Giessen: Focus–Verlag.

Hann, Chris. 2002. Farewell to the Socialist 'Other'. In *Postsocialism. Ideals, Ideologies and Practices in Eurasia*, ed. Chris Hann, 1–12. London and New York: Routledge.

Heleniak, Tim. 2001. Migration and Restructuring in Post–Soviet Russia. *Demokratizatsiia* 9(4): 531–49.

High, Casey. 2007. Oil Development, Indigenous Organisations, and the Politics of Egalitarianism. *Cambridge Anthropology* 26(2): 34–47.

Hill, Fiona and Clifford Gaddy. 2003. *The Siberian Curse: How Communist Planners Left Russia Out in the Cold*. Washington, DC: The Brookings Institution.

Hoffmann–Novotny, Hans Joachim. 1993. Weltmigration – Eine soziologische Analyse. In *Migrationen aus der Dritten Welt: Ursachen – Wirkungen – Handlungsmöglichkeiten*, ed. Walter Kälin and Rupert Moser, 57–68. Bern and Stuttgart: Paul Haupt.

Humphrey, Caroline. 2002. Does the Category 'Postsocialist' Still Make Sense? In *Postsocialism. Ideals, Ideologies and Practices in Eurasia*, ed. Chris Hann, 12–15. London and New York: Routledge.

Jordan, Peter 2003. *Material Culture and Sacred Landscape. The Anthropology of the Siberian Khanty*. Archaeology of Religion vol. 3. Oxford and Walnut Creek: Alta Mira Press.

Kaldor, Mary. 2007. Unilateral Destruction. *The Guardian China Dialogue*. London. http://www.chinadialogue.net/article/show/single/en/1181–unilateral–destruction (accessed 23 July 2007).

Kaldor, Mary, Terry Lynn Karl and Yahia Said, eds. 2007. *Oil Wars*. London: Pluto Press.

Kappeler, Alexander. 1993. *Rußland als Vielvölkerreich. Entstehung – Geschichte – Zerfall*. München: Beck.

Karl, Terry Lynn. 1997. *The Paradox of Plenty: Oil Booms and Petro–states*. Berkeley: University of California Press.

Khlinovskaya–Rockhill, Elena. 2011. *Lost to the State: Family Discontinuity Social Orphanhood and Residential Care in the Russian Far East*. Oxford, New York: Berghahn Books.

Konstantinov, Yulian. 2000. Pre–Soviet Pasts of Reindeer–herding Collectives: Ethnographies of Transition in Murmansk Region. *Acta Borealia* 17(2): 49–64.

Kuzio, Taras. 2002. History, Memory and Nation Building in the Post–Soviet Colonial Space. *Nationalities Papers* 30(2): 241–64.

Lampland, Martha. 2002. The Advantages of Being Collectivized: Cooperative Farm Managers in the Postsocialist Economy. In *Postsocialism. Ideals, Ideologies and Practices in Eurasia*, ed. Chris Hann, 31–57. London and New York: Routledge.

Lincoln, Bruce. 1994. *The Conquest of a Continent. Siberia and the Russians*. London: Jonathan Cape.

McCarthy, Terry. 2001. War over Arctic Oil. Time Magazine, 11 February 2001. file:///C:/users/my_files/Oil&Gas/McCarthy20010211_ANWR.htm. Accessed 03 April 2011.

Mote, Victor L. 2003. Stalin's Railway to Nowhere: 'The Dead Road' (1947–1953). *Sibirica* 3: 48–63.

Novikova, Natalya I. 1997. Vzaimodeistvie obshchin korennykh narodov Severa Rosii i neftedobyvaiushchikh korporacii. Vzgliad antropologa. In *Ekologija, obshchestvo i traditsia: Sotsialnye i politicheskie krizisi v SNG v kontekste rasrusheniia prirodnoi sredy (Tadschikistan i rossiiskii Sever)*, Nauchnie doklady vol. 15, ed. M. Olkott and A. Malaschenko, 42–62. Moscow: Carnegie Endowment for International Peace.

Okotetto, Mikhail N. and Bruce C. Forbes. 1999. Conflicts between Yamal–Nenets Reindeer Husbandry and Petroleum Development in the Forest Tundra and Tundra Region of Northwest Siberia. In *Sustainable Development in Timberline Forests*, ed. Sakari. Kankaanpää, Tapani Tasanen and Maria–Liisa Sutinen, 95–9. Helsinki: Finnish Forest Research Administration.

Petrova, Valentina P. and Galina P. Khariutschi. 1999. *Nentsy v istorii Yamalo–Nenetskogo avtonomnogo okruga*. Tomsk: Tomsk University Publishers.

Podkorytov, Fedor. 1995. *Olenevodstvo Yamala*. Sosnovyj Bor (Leningrad): Atomic Power Station Publishing House.

Razumova, Irina. 2005. On the Problems of Local Identity and Contemporary Russian 'Migratory Texts' (with Reference to the Northwestern Region of Russia). In *Moving in the USSR. Western Anomalies and Northern Wilderness*, ed. Pekka Hakamies, 110–29. Helsinki: Studia Fennica.

RBK. 2007. Rostekhnadzor priostanovila stroitel'stvo Truboprovoda v Ramkakh Proekta Sakhalin II. http://www.advis.ru/cgi–bin/new.pl?53D2D915–757F–0B4E–BF98–71649C42F8E4 (accessed 5 September 2007).

Reyna, Steve. 2004. Artica and the Bull: Warfare Involving Petro–states and the Aging Bull in Imperial Fields. Paper prepared for the workshop *Oil, Integration and Conflict*, MPI for Social Anthropology, 13 December 2004.

Roon, Tatiana 2006. Globalisation of Sakhalin's Oil Industry: Partnership or Conflict? A Reflection on the Etnologicheskaia Ekspertiza. *Sibirica* 5(2) (special issue on *the Oil and Gas Industry, Local Communities and the State*, ed. Emma Wilson and Florian Stammler): 95–114. Oxford: Berghahn Books.

Round, John. 2005. Rescaling Russia's Geography: The Challenges of Depopulating the Northern Periphery. *Europe Asia Studies* 57: 705–27.

Seifert, Thomas and Klaus Werner. 2005. *Schwarzbuch Öl. Eine Geschichte von Gier, Krieg, Macht und Geld*. Vienna: Zsolnay Verlag.

Slezkine, Yuri. 1994. *Arctic Mirrors: Russia and the Small Peoples of the North*. Ithaca: Cornell University Press.

Ssorin–Chaikov, Nikolai. 2003. *The Social Life of the State in the Siberian Subarctic*. Palo Alto: Stanford University Press.

Stammler, Florian. 2002. Success at the Edge of the Land: Present and Past Challenges for Reindeer Herders of the West–Siberian Yamal–Nenets Autonomous Okrug. *Nomadic Peoples* 6(2): 51–71.

———. 2003. *Überlebensstrategien im postsozialistischen Russland: Das Beispiel der rentierzüchtenden Khanty und Nenzen in Nordwestsibirien*. Kölner Ethnologische Beiträge, vol. 6. Cologne: Hundt Press.

———. 2005. *Reindeer Nomads Meet the Market: Culture, Property and Globalisation at the End of the Land*. Halle Studies in the Anthropology of Eurasia, vol. 6. Münster: Lit Publishers.

———. 2009. Mobile Phone Revolution in the Tundra? Technological Change among Russian Reindeer Nomads. In *Generation P in the Tundra*, ed. Aimar Ventsel, 47–78. Talinn: Estonian Literary Museum.

———. 2010. 'The City became the Homeland for its Inhabitants, but Nobody is Planning to die here' – Anthropological Reflections on Human Communities in the Northern City. in *Biography, Shift–labour and Socialisation in a Northern Industrial City / Биография, вахтовый труд и социализация в северном индустриальном городе* ed Florian Stammler and Gertrude Eilmsteiner–Saxinger, 33–42. Arctic Centre Rovaniemi & Tyumen State University: online edited volume (www.arcticcentre.org/anthropology), accessed 3 April 2011.

Stammler, Florian and Bruce C. Forbes. 2006. Oil and Gas Development in the Russian Arctic: West Siberia and Timan–Pechora. *Indigenous Affairs, Arctic Oil and Gas Development* 2–3(6): 48–57.

Stammler, Florian, Bruce Forbes and research partners of the ENSINOR project 2009. *Ilebts Declaration on Coexistence of Oil and Gas Activities and Indigenous Communities on Nenets and Other Territories in the Russian North*. Arctic Centre, University of Lapland, Rovaniemi, Finland. http://www.arcticcentre.org/declaration. accessed 3 April 2011.

Stammler, Florian and Vladislav Peskov. 2008. Building a 'Culture of Dialogue' among Stakeholders in North–west Russian Oil Extraction. *Europe–Asia Studies* 60(5): 831–49.

Stammler, Florian and Emma Wilson. 2006. Dialogue for Development: An Exploration of Relations between Oil and Gas Companies, Communities and the State. *Sibirica* 5(2): 1–42. Oxford: Berghahn Books.

Thompson, Niobe. 2004. Migration and Resettlement in Chukotka: A Research Note. *Eurasian Geography and Economics* 45(1): 73–81.

Tuisku, Tuula 2003. Surviving in the Oil Age. In *Social and Environmental Impacts in the North*, ed. R.O. Rasmussen and N.E. Koroleva, 449–61. NATO Series IV, *Earth and Environmental Sciences* vol. 31. Dordrecht, Boston and London: Kluwer Academic Publishers.

Verdery, Katherine. 2002. Whither Postsocialism? In *Postsocialism. Ideals, Ideologies and Practices in Eurasia,* ed. Chris Hann, 15–29. London and New York: Routledge.

Vitebsky, Piers. 2000. *Coping with Distance: Social, Economic and Environmental Change in the Sakha Republic (Yakutia), Northeast Siberia.* Scott Polar Research Institute, University of Cambridge (unpublished project report).

Vladimirova, Vladislava. 2006. *Just Labor. Labor Ethic in a Post–Soviet Reindeer Herding Community.* Uppsala Studies in Cultural Anthropology, no. 40. PhD dissertation, Department of Cultural Anthropology, University of Uppsala.

Watts, Michael. 2004a. The Sinister Political Life of the Community. Economies of Violence and Governable Spaces in the Niger Delta, Nigeria. Paper prepared for the workshop *Oil, Integration and Conflict,* MPI for Social Anthropology, 13 December 2004.

Watts, Michael. 2004b. Violent Environments: Petroleum Conflict and the Political Ecology of Rule in the Niger Delta, Nigeria. *Liberation Ecologies: Environment, Development, Social Movements,* ed. R. Peet and Michael Watts, 273–98. London: Routledge.

White, Jeffrey. 2007. Europe's Escape Route. *Transitions Online* 4(230): 13 August. http://www.tol.cz/look/TOL/article.tpl?IdLanguage=1&IdPublication=4&NrIssue=230&NrSection=4&NrArticle=18903 (accessed 4 September 2007).

Wiget, Andrew and Olga Balalaeva. 1997. National Communities, Native Land Tenure, and Self–determination among the Eastern Khanty. *Polar Geography* 21: 10–33.

Wilson, Emma. 2003. Freedom and Loss in a Human Landscape: Multinational Oil Exploitation and the Survival of Reindeer Herding in North–eastern Sakhalin, the Russian Far East. *Sibirica* 3: 21–47.

———. 2007. New Frontiers for the Oil and Gas Industry: Company–Community Relations on Sakhalin Island. *Cambridge Anthropology* 26(2): 13–34.

WWF (World Wildlife Fund). 2005a. *Risky Business – The New Shell.* Public Report, World Wildlife Fund. November. London: WWF–UK. http://www.wwf.org.uk/filelibrary/pdf/bu_riskybusiness.pdf (accessed 5 September 2007).

WWF (World Wildlife Fund). 2005b. Korennie narodi protiv bezotvetstvennih neftyannikov. Available at http://www.wwf.ru/resources/news/article/1565 (accessed 1 April 2011).

— Chapter 11 —

'AGAINST ... DOMINATION'

Oil and War in Chechnya

Galina Khizriyeva and Stephen P. Reyna

'For the entire period from 1785 to the present in the Eastern Caucasus has been essentially one long struggle by the Chechens against Russian domination'
— Lieven (1998: 304).

The Czarist Empire had been moving south into the Caucasus in fits and starts since the sixteenth century. This expansion intensified in 1783, during Catherine the Great's reign, as part of the Russo-Turkish Wars. It provoked Sheikh Mansur's uprising in 1785, that sought to drive the Russians from the Caucasus, but which had failed by 1791. Russia proclaimed the Northern Caucasus to be a part of the Russian Empire in 1817. Historians of the Caucasus have argued that Russian acquisitions in the region promised very little in terms of natural riches, and that securing of oil was not a reason of Russian invasion at the beginning of the eighteenth century. Nevertheless, the importance of natural resources was evident from the very beginning, and had imperial officials complaining of scarce labour force, roads and technical facilities to exploit them. By the late nineteenth century it was clear that Russia was one of the world's leading oil-producing regions, due to the oil found in Apsheron (Azerbaijan) and Grozny (Chechnya). This meant that the 'oil factor' played a growing role in the domestic policy of the Russian Empire. Grozny was an industrial oil giant of the Soviet economy by the 1920s. Oil was declared a 'strategic material' in the Soviet epoch. Reserves and refining problems could only be discussed in military and professional circles and not by historians or the public, which is a reason why anthropologists and historians still skirt 'the oil bogs'. Our topic is the recent Chechen Wars beginning in 1994 and officially declared over by Vladimir Putin in 2000; and to investigate these we are obliged to muck about in the 'oil bogs'.

Chechnya has been populated by Vainakhs, members of the Chechen and Ingush linguistic group, and at other times Chechens, those who are purely Chechen speakers. 'Chechnya' refers roughly to the Chechen-Ingush Autonomous Soviet Republic of the former Soviet Union. Journalistic accounts of the Chechen War were full of romantic images of Vainakhs as deeply traditional and archaic. Russian authorities, on the other hand, were portrayed as crude violators of a wild and free culture. Indeed, Chechen society was imagined as a fossil of a medieval historical reality, rather than the consequence of modernisation dynamics (Nukhaev 2002).

Our concern is to explore this modernisation which in Chechnya involved domination. In such dynamics oil played an influential role in constructing the 'new Chechnya' and 'new Chechens'. We investigate this fluctuating dynamic in local, national and global terms over three periods: Czarist Russia (1817–1917), the Soviet Union (1917–1991) and the current Russian Federation (1991–present). Most recently, post-Soviet neoliberal modernisation featuring oil privatisation transformed Soviet property in Chechnya into private property over which there has been a cruel rivalry. The Chechen elite used oil to frame a powerful secessionist ideology. Chechens were told that oil could give them personal prosperity and make Chechnya an independent part of the global world. Further, oil also influenced traditional ethics and morality as well as the religious situation in the region; and, in so doing, it contributed to constitution of a particular clientelistic network for acquiring oil, as well as other, revenues.

We will employ a 'reconstructive' approach utilising historical and anthropological evidence. This reconstruction is organised into five sections. The first section describes the imposition of Russian imperial domination in Chechnya until the middle of the nineteenth century, during which certain characteristic Vainakh institutions and identity emerged. The second section documents development of the region's oil industry, roughly in the period between 1860 until 1917. The third section examines a first period of Soviet domination roughly from 1917 until the 1940s, discussing the most spectacular act of Soviet domination, deportation of Vainakhs during the Second World War. The fourth section considers the post-Soviet era, seeking to understand the recent Chechen War in terms of the constitution of a clientelistic network that helps Chechens resist capitalist and political domination from the new Russian Federation. Empirically, the overarching object of this chapter is to interrogate the claim that post-1785 Vainakh modernisation dynamics involved centre–periphery conflict, which, from the vantage point of the Chechen periphery, was 'against … domination' (Lieven 1998).

Conceptually the chapter's objective is to warrant formulation of a notion of Hobbesian elitism. The Chechen War occurred following the break-down of the Soviet Union when Russia might be said to have been a fragile state. Hobbes wrote during a comparable period of the English Civil War (1642–1651) when there was a fragile state due to a break-down of the British monarchy. Hobbes believed such contexts to be what we have chosen to term the Hobbesian proposition. This was the view that in fragile states the nature of humanity resulted in a 'war of all against all' (*Leviathan* 1651, XIV) so that a strong central authority was required to prevent such hostilities. We believe that the Chechen War justifies re-thinking Hobbes' proposition in terms of class, which we do by proposing the concept of Hobbesian elitism in the conclusion.

Imposition of Russian Imperialism: Creation of Chechnya as a Territory and of the Vainakh Identity

Chechnya occupies the southeastern part of the North Caucasus and is bisected by the Terek River. Half of its territory is highlands suitable for agriculture and cattle breeding, and the other half belongs to the foot-hills and lowlands, rich with oil deposits. The territory is populated by the Vainakh. They speak different dialects of the Nakh language group, a branch within the Ibero-Caucasian linguistic family. The name *Vainakh* is a compound word. It consists of two words – *vain* ('our') and *nakh* ('people'). The Russian name for Vainakh highlanders is *Ichkeriytzy* (Ichkeri-ans). It stands for the 'Vainakhs of the highlands' and appears derived from a Chechen word for 'the groups of people' (*Nokhmakhkakho*), an ob-solete meaning of the compound word 'people that are bound by blood', with *makh* signifying 'bloodwealth' (Aliroev 2005). Nowadays the word *makhkakh* means 'a relative', 'a man from the same community'. The name *Ichkeria* was chosen in 1991 for the newly proclaimed state by President J. Dudayev's government.

During the 1897 census the name Vainakh was registered by Rus-sian authorities as an ethnic one to indicate the group of peoples who differed themselves from their neighbours. These were Dagestani-speak-ing Muslim groups and the groups of Christian peoples of the former Kartl-Kakheti Kingdom of eastern Georgia in the highlands; and in the foothills and lowlands, Turkic-speaking Buddhists and Muslims, and Iranian-speaking Christians and Muslims. *Vainakh* is a collective term in Russian documents and historiography indicating four big and heteroge-neous groups whom the Russians called *Chechens*, *Ingushs* (Russia), *Batsbi* and *Kists* (Georgia). Vainakh lived in the North Caucasus as acephalous peoples in lands belonging to their different clans (*teips*), living 'free and equal like wolves', as one of their proverbs has it. However, at the end of the eighteenth century, the 'wolves' were about to learn about freedom in a modernising world.

Western modernisation, whatever else it involved, featured an imperialist dynamic that involved on the periphery of empire the metamorphosis of 'equal' wolves into unequal imperial subjects. Russia and the Kartl-Kakheti Kingdom signed the Treaty of Georgievsk in 1783, in which Russia extended political and military protection to the co-religious, Transcaucasian Georgian state against Turkish and Persian invaders. Subsequently, the Russian Empire invaded the North Caucasus mountains to secure communications with its new Transcaucasian acquisitions. The first organised highlanders' resistance to Russia dates back to 1785–1791, during the reign of Catherine the Great. It was conducted under Sheikh Mansur, the leader of the Chechen Naqshabandi Sufi brotherhood. His efforts to establish a theocratic state on the basis of Islamic doctrine and Sharia practice failed because of the opposition of many Vainakh tribes who did not share his Islamic ideology but rather followed the socio-cultural heritage of their closer neighbours. This included complicated belief systems and ritual practice borrowed from the doctrines of Early Christian mysticism, Georgian Orthodoxy, Judaism, Yezidism, Tengri Cults, Zoroastrism and Muslim mysticism. Inter-group solidarity between these people was low. Mostly, they acted as separate and mutually hostile tribes, frequently changing sides during conflicts. Depending on the situation they supported or opposed immigrating Russians and Cossacks who re-settled from Volga to the Terek River. These Cossacks were to serve the Russian Empire as the 'Terek Cossack Line Host'. A Cossack 'host' was a distinct population of Cossacks. The Terek Cossacks were such a host settled by imperial commanders along a 'line' of fortified settlements on the Terek River, with the military responsibility of pacifying Vainakhs.

In the middle of the nineteenth century the Vainakhs led a long rebellion against the imperial centre that has come to be known as the Caucasian War (1834–1859). During the war, Vainakh kin-groups began to mobilise manpower to defend their lands and to continue their migration down from the mountains. A strong clan system emerged. Conceivably at this time Vainakhs came to recognise, as one Chechen proverb has it, that 'the *teip* is the fortress of *adat*' (Lieven 1998: 304), with *adat* being the term for culture. It is possible that various territorial groupings of clans (*tukum*) emerged at this time. Vainakh clans of valleys and highlands which had not yet Islamised began to convert to Islam and became warriors (Al-Karakhi 1990). In Chechen and Ingush ethnicity Islam began to play an identity-constructing and differentiating role. From that time on,

Chechens and Ingushs actively started to separate themselves from 'the Infidels'. In a word, a Vainakh identity began to emerge, which is discussed next.

Crucial in this Islamisation was the religious activity of Sheikh Kunta-haji Kishiev (1800–1866?), a charismatic Vainakh who furthered Islam among his people. On the basis of the Qadiri Sufi doctrine he separated Vainakhs from the Naqshabandi tradition that had been popular among the peoples of Dagestan. Kunta-haji's was not only a religious mission, but also an attempt to create an organisational model for Vainakh society that would be an alternative to a theocratic Imamate. According to his teaching Vainakh unity could be constructed by a 'one language, one ritual, one nation' formula. He offered a system of consolidation of numerous clans by including them within a supra-clan organisation of religious communities on the basis of the Qadiri doctrine (Khizriyeva 2005). But his efforts did not succeed in cultural and political unification of all Nakh-speaking peoples who still divided themselves into Naqshabandi and Qadiri brotherhoods (the representatives of Naqshabandi tradition were adepts of Imam Shamil and influenced by the idea of an independent Muslim state).

So Islamisation was accompanied by the simultaneous formation of a Vainakh identity, in which every Vainakh was imagined to belong to one *gar* (family), *teip* (clan) and *wird* (religious brotherhood). Vainakh clans were incorporated into a larger Muslim community, which was divided into two bigger brotherhoods, each with common rituals and ideology. The most prestigious occupation for a man in the system of values of this unity was to defend the Muslim community by being a warrior of *Jihaad* and 'a good Muslim'. The land and its riches were considered to be 'God's blessing for being a good Muslim'. The brotherhood system was not congruent to the local clan division among the Nakh-speaking peoples. This could be a reason why the system weakened after the passing of Kunta-haji. But the system survived and even strengthened during the deportation of Vainakhs to Kazakhstan in 1944, when it was temporally restored because it strengthened local and family solidarity. Vainakh Islamisation and with it identity formation continued long after Kunta-haji's death up to the events of the First Russian Revolution in 1905.

Vainakh pacification involved fundamental changes in land distribution. Vainakhs in many places were removed from their lands which were given to Cossack *stanitzas* (fortified villages). This expropriation resulted in many homeless people migrating to the vicinity of the fortress called Grozny ('the terrible'), which had been newly founded in 1818. They could not return to their lands, and they had no hope of dwelling in any of the Vainakh villages due to highland land scarcity. Their livelihoods and property were harmed; so the values and traditional norms of their life were unattainable. Some resorted to robbery, others preached against the rule of 'infidels', or lived a beggarly existence. It was in this context that Sheikh Kunta-haji Kishiev imagined the Vainakh unity. He instructed his followers not to send such people away but try to share at least small plots of land with them. In contrast, Russian imperial officials issued administrative decrees authorising regional rulers to arrest such people or to find an occupation for them. The Russian government negotiated with Turkish and Iranian authorities the *Muhajjir* movement (1856–1864), a scheme to resettle whole families and even villages of North Caucasus highlanders in Turkey. The policy failed. Most Vainakhs stayed in the Russian Empire.

People were concentrated in the lowlands during the Caucasian War. This area now experienced the sort of modernisation termed *industrialisation* involving development of the oil industry, railway construction, oil transportation and mine development. New professions appeared (oil workers, capitalists, merchants, intellectuals, engineers, professional mullahs). This led to some erosion of boundaries between social classes; although those which coincided with ethnic and land property boundaries remained rather strong. The process of Vainakh modernisation had started. They formed a new 'oil-boom' population of the region whose fate was to become an active political force for future social-political movements among Vainakhs and to form a new elite among highlanders. However, it should not be forgotten that the Vainakh institutions of family, clan and religious brotherhood were forged out of the experience of violent imperial domination and its resistance. Let us now turn to the development of oil.

'Oil goes in all directions...': 1860–1917, State versus Tradition – Cossacks versus Vainakhs – Oil versus Land

Chechnya experienced an oil boom and rapid industrialisation in 1860s, as a result of which Chechen society experienced painful changes. However, North Caucasus peoples had extracted and refined oil for several hundred years before the Russian conquest. The medieval text of *Tarik ad-Derbendi* (the History of Derbend) is the first to describe the usage of oil by the peoples of the region. From the eighth century when Islam established in the region of Derbend all income from salt and oil exploitation accumulated in this largest cultural and financial centre of the North Caucasus (Minorsky 1963). Oil and salt from seasonal trips were included as *vaquf* (property of Muslim communities among highlanders) and kept in mosques. In some cases the *vaquf* was used to financially support the community (Bobrovnikov 2006). Written sources complement oral narration on Sheikh Mansur's oil-fire war against Russian penetration into

Vainakh territories. The legend says that kerosene – or as people called it: *karasin* (etymologised by local people from Turk. *kara* – 'black' and local languages *shin* – 'water') – 'burned under the soldiers' feet'. Vainakh peoples call oil *mekhkadatta*. One interviewee told me that people in the past had extracted *mekhkadatta* for heating. They got oil from 1.5-metre holes using buckets covered with wattle to draw the oil. These exposed deposits had been found by the people in Grozny and Mamakaev valleys in the region of Staropromyslovsky, next to the contemporary villages Braguny and Samashki in Chechnya, Achaluki and Karabulak in Ingushetia, and Mikhailovskoye in the North Ossetia. Entrepreneurs began to move from the densely populated central part of the Russian Empire into newly acquired Caucasuses by the 1850s and 1860s.

The first two Russian oil men to appear – the Dubinin brothers – were serfs of the duchess Panina. In 1823 they constructed a primitive 500 litre oil-processing 'cube' in the garrison town of Mozdok. The cube was maintained inside a brick oven with an ash-pit. Oil was heated in the cube; steam went through a coiled pipe, condensed and produced kerosene. Forty buckets of oil made sixteen buckets of kerosene. This was sent to Moscow, Nizhnii Novgorod and other cities of Russia. The 'factory' worked until 1847 and produced one thousand *pud*s (121 barrels) of kerosene in all.

The oldest oil field was situated at 6 km north-west from Grozny on lands that were Vainakh communal property. But after the foundation of the Terek Cossack Line Host in 1818, it became clear that practically all oil of Grozny district was located in the newly established Terek Cossacks' territory. Although oil was on their newly acquired land, the Cossacks never actually produced oil. Remember their task was to maintain regional security. For this service they received a salary and a plot of land to feed their families. The government also attracted labour for servicing the state-owned oil pits. Local people rented the land plots from the Cossacks and paid the rent by working the land. Some of them rented small plots specifically for oil extraction. Private businessmen of different ethnic origins (their names were Chikalov, Savdigalov, Mirsoev, Nitabukh and Akhverdov) in the early 1860s produced 12,500 *pud*s (1,512 barrels) of oil per day. In 1885–1986 one oil producer, Nitabukh, rented two more plots for ten years and in 1887, his four wells produced all the oil of Terek district. Practically all his workers were of Chechen origin. He also had a 'laboratory' for oil refining. At the beginning of the 1890s Nitabukh sold his oil plots and the 'Chechen laboratory' to a lawyer, Akhverdov.

One of the region's specialists in oil refining and oil-well cleansing was a Mr Labazan from the village of Urus-Martan. In 1893 he invented the method of deepening and cleansing old oil pits, which introduced the technology of drilled oil wells. In the same year, he and his Russian colleagues – geologist A.M. Kokoshin and L.I. Baskakov – found on 6 October an oil-gusher that produced oil from the depth of 132 m with a daily output of 108,000 *puds* (13,090 barrels). This date marks the beginning of industrial oil production in Russia.

But it was Akhverdov who hit the gusher jackpot. He drilled six wells and all of them struck oil. But the seventh well drilled in May, 1895, gave him a real triumph. By 27 August, from the depth of 141 m, it gave a gusher with a daily production of 16,000 barrels. During the first three years it gave 17,095,000 barrels (according to other sources three times more) of oil. In 1895 the newspaper *Terskiye Vedomosti* (Terek Region News) informed the public: 'Oil goes in all directions ... and floods the neighbouring mines. The atmosphere is so saturated with gas, especially in the canyons, that it is difficult to breathe. The situation is extremely dangerous for possible conflagration from any careless act with fire'. The news of Akhverdov's oil-gushers immediately spread world-wide. Grozny became known for its for oil and gas riches. The same year, English businessmen established the joint stock company Petrol de Grozny in Brussels. Belgians had bought twenty-four thousand shares in the enterprise. The south of Russia became popular among Western capitalists. The area of dedicated oil plots in Tersky district (the lands around the Terek River) was 619 hectares (Ragosin 1884: 118).

Chechens and Ingush owned less than one half as much land as Terek Cossacks by 1912 (Wood 2007: 27). The Cossack Line Host had one hundred and seventy shallow wells. The Host owned 80 per cent from the regional budget in money from rent of occupied Vainakh lands. Thus, the local people (mostly Chechens), who worked at all levels of oil production on the lands that were originally their own property, were largely deprived of oil revenues. This produced interethnic tension that was complicated by the fact that the 1905 Russian Revolution took place at the time when Russia had just begun to re-construct its administrative system, rendering local management inept. In such a situation Cossack and Vainakh rivalry intensified from 1905 to 1914. On the one hand, the Vainakh population tried in all possible and impossible ways to regain their lands (together with the oil fields), an act they regarded as the 'restoration of historical justice'. Documents of the time register the escalation of mutually hostile activity of Vainakhs and Cossacks; their petitions to the authorities with pleas for help against the opposite side's violence; and petitions against violence and unpredictable actions of the Russian military and civil administration. The absence of any adequate conflict resolution led to desperation on both sides. However, gradually Cossacks began losing political leadership in the region as a result of the weakening of the Czarist Empire, because their influence was based on ties to this state and its oil rents. Vainakhs received neither help from the administration nor economic compensation for national humiliation. The First World War prevented both sides from open military conflict. In part this was due to the fact that lowland Vainakhs who joined the Russian army found themselves fighting side by side with Cossacks during the Russo-Japanese War (1905–1906) and against Germany (1914–1917). The withdrawal of manpower from the region also delayed violence.

Let us now consider Grozny oil in the first half of the twentieth century. In Russia by 1900 the non-state sector of oil-industry and expatriate capitalists collaborated with the oil companies and governments of oil-producing countries (Germany, France, the USA, Great Britain and Turkey). At this time, Western oil companies began openly competing with Russian ones. The events discussed in the previous section represent a local modification of the process of conflict over spheres of influence between industrially developed and energy-producing states on the turf of the Russian Empire. The global actors tried to eliminate businesses in the industrially underdeveloped countries, dividing their riches between enterprises of developed states. Russia was among such countries, because its ineffective economic policy and its natural riches made it a most desirable option for the global actors.

As a result of the global competition Russian oil production began to drop for several reasons. First, Standard Oil and Shell dumped cheap petrochemical products, undercutting Russian competitors. Second, the Russian government enacted an unfriendly tax policy for domestic Russian oil companies, which made modernisation of technologies impractical for Russian oil traders. Third, the continued reliance upon out-of-date Russian drilling and oil-processing technologies made competitive development of the industry impossible.

This competition occurred in the context of rising revolutionary and nationalistic movements. In the Russian Empire the epicentre of the activity became Baku (Azerbaijan) and Batumi (Abkhasia) oil districts. Here Joseph Stalin (the future leader of the Soviet state) started his revolutionary carrier as a Bolshevik. In July 1903 oil-industry workers in Baku (and afterwards in Batumi) went on strike and 225 oil derricks burned for fourteen days. The Armenian-Azeri massacre happened from 6 to 10 August 1905. Some blamed the Bolsheviks for organising this event to get money from the German government to support the Russian Communist Party. Others blamed Azeri nationalists for cooperating with Turkish nationalists against Russian interests. The disturbances in Azerbaijan increased the importance of oil from the North Caucasus to Russia.

By 1914, the Grozny oil district had become the largest centre of world oil-extraction and a centre of intersection of the economic interests of Germany, Great Britain, France, Belgium, Iran and Turkey. Turkish troops, allied with Germany, invaded the Caucasus at this time. With Russia exhausted by war and the inner instability of revolution, the fledgling Bolshevik government signed the Treaty of Brest (3 July 1918). Under one condition of the treaty, Transcaucasia was declared to be independent. Lenin denounced this condition to be 'shameful' for the Soviet state. However, by the end of July 1918, Turkish troops were welcomed to Baku by the local Public Council (*Bakinski Sovet*) where Bolsheviks were in the minority. Subsequently, Turkish troops profiting from the weakness of the nascent Soviet state continued to invade northwards to the Caspian Sea. They invaded the Dagestan city of Derbend, which remained Russian territory under the Peace of Brest. The Ottoman troops were stopped by pressure from Great Britain upon the Ottoman Empire. The Don River Valley was occupied at the same time by Germans. The general-*ataman* Krasnov came to head, with German help, the autonomous state of the Don Cossacks. German and Turkish moves were to help secure Caucasus oil, which prompted Lord Kerson to quip (at the Conference of Oil Allies on 20 November 1918) that they 'swam' to their victory 'on the oil wave' (Ragozin 1928).

The Grozny oil region was not occupied but it was encircled by occupied territories. The city of Grozny itself was blockaded. The oil industry was at a standstill. Hostile Vainakh and Terek Cossacks found themselves face to face without any overarching powerful institutions to regulate their land and oil distribution disputes. The Terek Cossacks wanted to establish an autonomous area like the Don Cossacks, and consequently they welcomed the squadrons of the white Russian army lead by General Denikin. On the other side, the Bolshevik leaders Ordzhonikidse (1886–1937) and Kirov (1886–1934) maintained a dialogue between the Vainakhs and the Soviet government, and induced the Vainakhs to fight against the Cossacks of General Denikin's army. The Soviets prevailed. It should be clear, ethnic groups in Chechnya responded to the Soviet revolution in terms of their position within the Czarist Empire. If they were subjects of the emperor without any privilege, as was the case of the Vainakhs, they supported the Bolsheviks. If they were military compradors, as was the case of the Cossacks, they continued to support a system of domination in which they enjoyed special advantage.

By 1917 and the start of the Bolshevik Revolution the interethnic North Caucasus oil rivalry turned into real war which embraced all of southern Russia. By then, the imperial administration began to realise that the state sector of the oil industry was bound to be destroyed (the private sector continued to work effectively, being under the control of local people). In March 1917, the Russian administration aggravated interethnic rivalry with its decision to give all rights for the industrial production of oil in Grozny district to the Terek Cossack Line Host, as a state structure. It was a serious blow for the private companies in the region. The decision provoked violence. Cossacks started energetically to implement the national decision, trying to restore their economic influence in the region. Rumours spread that soldiers killed some Vainakhs. To prevent the government from killing their people, the Chechens left Grozny in 1917. During the summer of 1917 they attacked oil-industry targets and railways in the region of Grozny. The national pipe-line Grozny–Port-Petrovsk (now *Makhachkala*) was destroyed. On 21 September 1917, the Conference of Producers and Factories Commission was convened by Russian oil industry workers. It proclaimed itself to be the 'strike committee' and the decision of the committee was to start a continuous strike (*bessrochnaya zabastovka*) beginning 27 September.

Vainakh oil-industry workers gathered in November 1917 in the village Starosunzhenskaya on the side of the Bolsheviks. They presented the administration with an ultimatum to remove troops from Grozny. The demands were fulfilled and the 111th and 252nd squadrons of the Samara infantry left Grozny. But after the manoeuvre the 111th squadron returned to Grozny in order to help the armed workers and Cossacks that held Starye Promysly (Old Oil Fields) district.

Then later in November so-called *abreks* (armed Chechens) besieged Grozny where the oil stocks were stored. The government demanded the closure of all state wells. The only pipe-line of the region which continued to function was Akhverdov's . This private pipe-line had been constructed at the end of the summer in 1914. It worked in spite of all the demands of the authorities. Akhverdov's own wells were run by Chechen workers. Due to the economic and political instability in the region the number of oil workers declined from 11,312 men to 3,659 men. Russians left industrial jobs. Some of them left Grozny district during 1917–1918. Some of them returned to the agricultural occupations to survive and to feed their families. The siege of Stary Promysly and Grozny continued until May 1918. Chechens destroyed pumping stations in Gudermes and Temirgoi, demolished the bridges, and with the burning wells went one-quarter of the yearly budget of the Russian Empire. Most Chechens returned to agrarian occupations.

The conflict, which started as a conflict of oil interests, ended as a conflict of values. The dearest values for Cossacks were loyalty and honest service to the imperial state. The most important value for the Muslims was battling state dishonesty and monopolistic practices, 'especially in the area of necessities of life', and illegal methods to gain property by land

and oil renting which would lead to 'the growth of unlimited fortunes and division of society into two classes', which was incompatible with their image of the world (Mitchel 1969). The land and oil rewards that the Czarist state had piled upon the Terek Cossacks for policing the Vainakh periphery had exploded into interethnic violence by the time of the Bolshevik Revolution as the power of imperial Russia to dominate imploded.

Under Soviet Domination: Grozny Oil until the Second World War

Restoration of the destroyed oil economy of Grozny district began during the first months of Soviet rule. Global competitors were permanently eliminated by the Bolsheviks. The experience of the destruction of local industry by this competition inhibited the Soviet government from seeking international development cooperation. The same memory helped the newly formed Soviet administration to secure the loyalty of the indigenous population. Specifically, Soviet rulers declared that Imam Shamil's nineteenth-century fight had been a 'just war for independence against Czarist Russia'. The Vainakh peoples were promised religious autonomy and freedom. Critically, loyalty was won by a socialist redistribution of property from Cossacks to Vainakhs. Vainakhs moved to the former Cossack villages (*stanitzy*). Most of the local population celebrated the event. Within the limits of the socialist doctrine, all lands and riches belonged to 'people'. In lowland Vainakhs' popular understanding, they were the 'people', and the restoration was regarded as an act of historical and social justice. It was a reversal of land tenure fortune. For the first time, the state backed Chechens and Ingushs against Cossacks. Peaceful life was restored to 'Red Ingushetia' and the Chechen valleys.

Grozny became the capital of what eventually would be termed the Chechen-Ingush Autonomous Soviet Socialist Republic (1934). Grozny district, then, embraced five hundred thousand people with six thousand members of the Communist Party and ten thousand Comsomol members (a youth organisation in the USSR – Young Communist League). Soviet authorities fostered the Grozny proletariat and gave the city the status of a capital, believing that the urban working class would influence the agrarian population that was fragmented into different parties organised according to principles of kinship (Sulaev 2003).

The cities of Grozny and Vladikavkas (the Soviet name was Ordzhonikidze), with a mixed Chechen-Ingush-Russian-Ossetian population, began to restore the industry of the regional and national economy. Rehabilitation was not possible without the support of the local people, which is why the economy was declared 'people's property' (*narodnaya sobstven-nost*). However, to Vainakhs, land and its riches were *their* clandestine property.

All oil revenues went to state institutions. Oil was now 'the property of the socialist state'. Grozneft (Grozny Oil), the Soviet oil company, was established in 1920. This state corporation (*proizvodstevennoye ob'edinenie*) is still working in Grozny. Now half-destroyed, it used to comprise six oil-extracting units (*upravlenia*), six drilling units, one academic institute, nineteen multi-facets, and one gas-condensing layer (*Neftianaya entsiklopedia* 2002). The fact that it was declared the property of the Soviet Socialist state did not mean much to Vainakhs. Profits 'from oil extraction and refineries went directly to the USSR central budget' (Tishkov 2004: 41).

Additionally, it was largely Russians who worked in the oil industry. Grozneft and Orgsynthez, the two largest oil companies, employed a total of fifty thousand workers by the late 1980s, only a few hundred of whom were Chechen (ibid.: 41). The people's mode of life changed rapidly. It is possible to speak of a veritable 'cultural revolution' due to the industrialisation associated with the development of oil, especially during the first five-year plan of economic development (*pervaya piatiletka*) from 1928 to 1932. One change was an exponential transformation of an agrarian into an urbanised population. Social groups came to be based less on kinship and more on an urban, modern culture. Everything had the adjective 'the first'. There were 'the first' Ingush writers and poets, 'the first' Chechen historians, 'the first' meeting of a North Caucasus women's group, etc. Social life acquired new values. Prestige was to be achieved through secular and women's education. Textbooks were to be written in the newly invented national alphabet. A widespread propaganda insisted upon the worth of atheist views and of collective labour for the social benefit. Existing, deeply rooted values were preserved in the kinship sphere. However, these were now disparaged as 'traditional' and 'obsolete'. Holidays, rituals and crafts were outmoded 'survivals' of the pre-socialist epoch. Religious rituals and customary norms (*adat*) were forbidden. The state introduced the 'new values of modernity' by cruel methods. The Bolsheviks fought violently against 'survivals'. Many people who dared to maintain a traditional mode of life were prosecuted and died in concentration camps and prisons (Avtorkhanov 1996).

The politics of the new Soviet state began to resemble the repressive practices of the Russian Empire. Disturbances broke out in 1929 in protest against agricultural collectivisation. These were followed by a small-scale insurgency that lasted until 1935, and flared up again in 1937 following a NKVD (secret police) security operation in which thousands of Chechens were arrested and executed (Lieven 1998: 318). Khasan Israilov, a Chechen journalist and poet, decided to organise rebellion against 'Red imperialism'. The uprising he organised occurred between 1940 and 1944, during the darkest days of German invasion. The Germans sought an alliance with Israilov, but this proved impossible. Further, the vast majority of Vainakhs supported their country during the Second World War, joining the Red Army and fighting fiercely all the way to Berlin. However, Israilov's rebellion would have its repercussions.

One can say, then, that the Grozny oil industry went through an early twentieth century period when there was competition with international oil cartels over who would dominate the oil. This struggle ended with Soviet victory, so that just as during the nineteenth century the Russian centre dominated over the Vainakh periphery. It is time now to consider a still greater threat to Soviet domination in the Caucasus.

Oil and Deportation: 1941–1989

It is often supposed that the German attack of the Soviet Union in 1941 was the result of a megalomaniac's decision; a decision that opened a second eastern front and vastly overstretched German armies, an overstretch that considerably contributed to the Third Reich's defeat. Consider the following. Germany had no oil. Oil was the *sine qua non* of German military might. Russia was a huge oil producer in the Caucasus and Caspian regions. So there was an oily method in the Nazi madness. Let us now consider the oil situation in the Grozny area and other regions of the Soviet Union.

War-time industrial demands required more and more oil revenues to run the Soviet Union. But in the early 1940s the USSR's leaders learned that Grozny's oil reserves were nearly exhausted. However, oil deposits had been discovered in Tatarstan in 1943. Additionally, West Siberian oil prospecting gave hopeful results. So the USSR's leaders knew there was oil in two other Muslim regions – Tatarstan (in the Volga River region) as well as West Siberia. Then in 1944 catastrophe occurred for Vainakhs. Chechens, Ingushs and Kists were deported to Kazakhstan.

Although the oil discoveries and the deportations are not normally connected, the two events might be linked. Some of Khizriyeva's interviewees posited such links using the following logic. The underground location of oil deposits in Grozny demanded expensive, deep, vertical and horizontal drilling. The USSR fought on a number of fronts during the Second World War, and had neither the manpower nor money for such drilling technologies. Further, the bulk of what capital was available for oil industry infrastructure would have to be invested in developing the

Tatarstan and Siberian oil fields. So a decision was made to change the specialisations of Soviet oil regions. Tatarstan was to be an oil producing area. The Grozny area was to be the centre of oil refining and distribution.

This new specialisation increased the security requirements of the Vainakh region for the USSR. This is because crude oil would now be transported by pipe-line from producing regions to Grozny, where it would be refined and turned into different petroleum products, and then further distributed for consumption. Now if an enemy captured the Grozny region, almost all the oil of the USSR would be lost. Consequently, maintaining the region's security was even more imperative to the central government, where officials remembered that only a few years earlier Vainakhs had been involved in Israilov's rebellion. So Stalin classified Vainakhs as 'enemies of the Soviet people'; Beria, head of the NKVD, deported them; and in so doing totally destroyed their existing social life.

Soviet propaganda could not mention that the making of Grozny into an oil refining and distribution centre was a real cause of the events because of the secrecy that accompanied any industrial project in the USSR. The regime could not declare that it sacrificed peoples' lives for oil because it could destroy the main ideal principle of Soviet rule: 'everything for a human being, everything for wellbeing'. So the only way Moscow could act was to blame the local population whom it mistrusted anyway. In a similar way, Stalin mistrusted the Muslim population who lived along the new Tatarstan pipe-lines. Some former members of the Tatarstan Communist Party insist that they have read documents which discuss plans to deport the Tatar population. But the only territory in the former Soviet Union which was subjected to total deportation was that of Grozny's Vainakhs. Deportation was accompanied by massacres. In the village of Khaibakh all people were burnt in the mosque. It might be noted that the practice of deportation was commonplace in other imperial countries as a way of solving problems of security and economic development.

A consequence of the deportations was that the urban Vainakhs intermingled with rural members of their ethnic group and, as a result, became rural again. It was a painful process. The urban population was new to the highlanders. The roots of this alienation and conflict of interests between the two big segments of the Vainakhs can be traced back to the days of the beginning of industrialisation and it stands in close connection to oil production. In the lowland industrial region such as Grozny, it was not prestigious to be a *kolkhosnik* (a member of a rural agricultural commune). The highlanders for many years had not played an active political role in Vainakh society. But the agrarian population adapted better to the new rural conditions in Kazakhstan, so they played a leading role in the nation's survival. They restored 'traditional and obsolete' forms of communal support, and religious life that helped people to overcome their psychological trauma, their cultural shock, fears and frustrations. The trinity of family, clan and religious brotherhood, invented in the nineteenth century, was reinvented in the twentieth and, as such, might be termed a re-imagined imaginary. Khrushchev, during the time of de-Stalinisation, permitted the Vainakhs to return home in 1957, when it became clear that the 'traditionalist' imaginary had one important quality: it worked. It worked in the sense that the number of returned Vainakhs was higher than that of the deported population, in spite of high rates of child mortality and the lack of males.

Partly due to their low level of education and partly due to prevailing public prejudices, according to which they were still the Soviet people's enemies (*vragi naroda*), even after their return to their homelands, Vainakhs were excluded from leadership in the Soviet state. Despite the fact that Chechnya and Ingushetia were formally 'title nations' (*titulnaya natsia*) in the Soviet Republic, their populations were denied work in important sectors of Chechen economy. Only a few could work in oil refineries and industrial enterprises, where jobs were filled by Russians, Cossacks, Armenians, Ossets or Ukrainians.

When the Vainakh highlanders returned to their destroyed villages in the late 1950s they initially withdrew from any political role, because it was most important to them to normalise their life. According to Khizriyeva's informants it was easier to return to lands and homes in the highlands than in the valley. But to stay there without state support was practically impossible, and Vainakhs soon had to leave again. After thirteen years of deportation and official rehabilitation, their civil rights continued to be violated because of their exclusion from the most profitable branches of industry. So bitter disappointment arose over the national politics of the Soviet state, which was expressed in the uprisings and was aggravated by the fact that all the efforts to oblige the Soviet state to pay compensation for their sufferings had failed by the mid 1970s. There were several mass demonstrations in the USSR in the early 1970s. The people demanded that the state compensate their losses. The organisers of these were branded as nationalists and prosecuted. But the organisation of these demonstrations increasingly showed that a Soviet Vainakh national elite had re-emerged and returned to the political stage after many years of national deprivation and humiliation with a will to fight for the economic and political interests of their republic. It is time now to investigate that fight.

The Chechen War: Warlords, Oil Barons and Oligarchs, 1989–2000

The centre/periphery conflict started anew after the declaration of *perestroika* in 1989, quickly followed by the USSR's dissolution, and its replacement by the Russian Federation in 1991. This conflict was in some measure because the demise of the old Soviet Union led to a triple crisis: in part of legitimacy (by what right did the Russian Federation govern?); in part of authority (what were the rules of that governance?); in part of power; and in large part because there was no money for the military. Nevertheless, throughout the turmoil a firm policy of the new Russian Federation was for privatisation, designed partially by neo-liberal US economists, which transferred public enterprises into the private hand of elites at bargain prices. Such a policy delighted elites both in the centre, at Moscow, and on the peripheries of the republics. Vainakh elites were motivated to enter political and economic activity to acquire some of the privatised assets. However, their particular take on the new neo-liberalism included a demand that Russia must restore historical and social justice that had been violated by the deportations. This claim was at least in part satisfied by passage of the Federal Law on Rehabilitation, which was adopted by the Supreme Soviet on 26 April 1991.

Local politicians insisted that it gave Chechens a chance to achieve historical justice and define their own politics towards their neighbours. Chechens were especially eager to reacquire their traditional oil-bearing lowlands. In an editorial of the Chechen-Ingush government newspaper concerning the Rehabilitation Law, the chairman of the Supreme Soviet of the Chechen-Ingush Republic, Doku Zavgayev, did not mention the oil industry. Rather, he said:

> The Supreme Soviet of Russia, in adopting this historical document, took into consideration literally all corrections and offerings of the Chechen-Ingush delegation …. Big efforts were made to exclude from the law an article according to which the territorial question could be regulated only by negotiation between parties (that is North Ossetia, Dagestan and even Georgia) because such an article could block the possibility of the full restoration of violated justice' (*Golos Checheno-Ingushetii* 1991: 1).

Immediately after the Rehabilitation Law was adopted, Chechnya was covered by a network of rehabilitation committees. These identified and calculated the property lost under deportation. It became evident that the state would fail to compensate the loss of all people. The ensuing war in Chechnya is often explained as a result of botched negotiations over these and other claims between corrupt officials and oil barons in Moscow and

Chechen leaders. In some sense this is correct. But any war is partially a result of bad negotiations. In Chechnya the oil question was politicised and became an instrument of 'negative mobilisation', in the sense of becoming a rallying cry to mobilise rejection of the post-Soviet state in favour of Chechnya's independence. Added to this were the unsolved grievances – especially deportation – of previous periods. Let us discuss the framing of this negative mobilisation and, then, the structural form that implemented its policies.

Doku Zavgayev, who since 1989 had been First Secretary of the Chechen-Ingush Autonomous Soviet Socialist Republic (ASSR), was a moderate in respect of the implementation of the law. But he was ousted by the charismatic and aggressive General Johar Dudayev (1944–1996), who insisted upon nation-state building of a Chechen sovereign state that was economically secure due to the attractiveness of its oil resources to Western investments. Chechnya's independence was declared on 1 November 1991 at Dudayev's inauguration. In 1992 Dudayev began to use the oil industry as an instrument of political pressure on the government of the Russian Federation. From that moment on, the propaganda machine of the Chechen revolution began negatively mobilising the population, using the nationalistic discourse that played on memories of deportation. The propaganda was soon to be even more negative and to attack other nations. There were cries of, 'Russians go to Riazan, Ingushs go to Nazran!' (Riazan is a town in central Russia, Nazran is the largest town of Ingushetia). These cries were evocative of the Soviet slogans of the time of deportation.

Chechen revolutionaries – revolutionary in the sense that with their negative mobilisation they struggled for an independent Chechen state – did not want to waste time in talks with Moscow. Self-styled 'President' Dudayev and his 'ministers' began to force the situation. A Bolshevik spirit infused the tone and style of their speeches. On 29 February 1992, Dudayev accused Yeltsin's government of organising an economic blockade of the 'young Chechen national state'; to defend against this a Chechen revolution was required.

To culturally frame this revolution, Dudayev and his counsellors employed old and new 'friends of Russia' (American experts, new Russian capitalists, religious propagandists from Turkey, Saudi Arabia and Kuwait, and different non-governmental organisations from many European states), who became the ideological sponsors of the Chechen revolution, which was to include a process of globalisation of the oil. In every issue of the Chechen newspapers of 1992 one read about meetings and consultations between Dudayev and representatives of some Western country or with liberal Russian capitalists who helped to globalise the Chechens.

It was understandable that the Chechen elite wanted to enter the global economic world. Certainly, it would help their desire to boost their own economy. This depended upon them acquiring valuable resources, especially access to oil revenues – resources largely controlled by Moscow's political or economic oligarchs. However, getting ordinary Vainakhs to support their elites had its problems. After all, Chechnya was a small half-agrarian republic, whose agrarian sector had been subsidised for more than seventy years by the central state budget, which in reality still suffered from inner fragmentation, and whose oil industry was deeply dependent on Russia. So let us describe how the Vainakh elite framed the need for revolution in historical and cultural terms to those Vainakhs who would actually have to fight for it.

A first framing of the Chechen revolutionary propaganda was to ideologically focus upon the nineteenth century Caucasian War during which the Vainakhs were incorporated into the Russian Empire. Memories were evoked of heroic rebellion against imperial aggressors. Young highlanders were the target group of this propaganda and they became the main source of mobilised manpower. A second cultural frame and 'tool' of mobilisation built up an ideology around 'pure' Islam. The target group for this kind of rhetoric was the young people in lowland villages leading an urban life. The existing form of Islam was not adequate for the mobilisation of this group, because the social status of a religious leader prevented him from directing a follower into revolutionary activities. However, religious leaders of the Wahhabi sect, who claimed they practised a 'pure' Islam, laboured under no such compunctions. In addition to financial support provided by Wahhabis, there was moral code supportive of violent revolution that played a major role during a period of ideological vacuum. So, Wahhabi structures were introduced into the republic. The competition over young followers became a real battlefield between Quadiri Islamic leaders and the new militant Wahhabi communities. Wahhabi discourse constituted a cultural frame that made it easy for the young men to rebel against the authority of the elders and to leave home in order to join 'the true Muslims' in *jihaad* against impure infidels.

One result of Dudayev's politics was severe industrial decline. This was in a situation where the majority of the urban population could not leave Chechnya, and so were obliged to return to agrarian occupations. Further mobilising newly agrarian people for their revolution, Chechen ideologists framed their appeals for revolution in terms of fulfilling archaic cultural ideals of traditional farming folk; ideals that had been re-invented during the deportation period and had maintained solidarity and social support. Some of the 'traditional' values of this third framing of revolution included so-called Sharia courts ordaining the cutting off of hands and legs, stoning, feuding, slave trade, hostages, car stealing and kidnapping. Among the wider Russian public, all these practices were regarded as rejecting of modernity. They created a new image of the cruel and criminal highlander. Actually, this revival of 'archaic' social practices, a most striking result of Dudayev's times, was not at all popular among Chechens.

It was discovered soon after the Chechen national revolution began that oil stocks in Chechnya were insufficient to provide for every Chechen family. However, propagandists promised vast oil wealth if the revolution occurred. This promise of something that did not exist was a fourth frame of the revolution, and is considered by many to have been what really snared Vainakhs into revolution. Curiously, its propaganda resembled the slogans of the early Soviet epoch: 'Oil and riches of the land belong to the Chechen People!' or 'Homelands to Chechen and Ingush Peoples!'

Such cultural framing cannot fully explain the causes of the Chechen War, if only because it brackets out of consideration what was occurring in the centre with Yeltsin's government. Nevertheless, the framing does show how Chechen elites constructed a Vainakh consciousness that favoured war with the centre. This war came in two phases – an initial one (1994–1996) that resulted in de facto acceptance by Moscow of the Chechen Republic of Ichkeria; and a subsequent one (1999–2000) that witnessed shaky reestablishment of Moscow's rule in Chechnya. It is time to consider the role of oil in this conflict.

The Chechen War has been imagined by some as a drama peopled by oligarchs, oil barons and warlords acting their parts in a Homeric, moral struggle between heroic Chechen warriors and Russian monsters, or vice versa if you happen to be on the other side. Regardless of how the war is subjectively framed, it is our claim that it involved a rivalry to dominate valuable assets, especially oil revenues; and that in order to accomplish this struggle there needed to be some organisation to do it. We argue that a centre/periphery clientelistic network was that structure.

We shall begin to understand this network by discussing its clan component. Remember the Vainakh clan is a *teip*. Now, as Lieven notes, 'The exact role of the *teip* in present Chechen society is extremely difficult to establish' (1998: 341), so it should be clear that the nature of the Chechen clans at this time requires further study. It is uncertain whether the teips were actually composed of lineal descendants of apical ancestors and would, thus, be classified as clans or lineages in the formal terminology of anthropologists; or whether they were composed of persons who simply asserted 'clanship' and who, thus, would be classified as some sort of fictive clans, but were actually looser coalitions gathered around elite figures, be they officials, oligarchs or warlords. Nor is it clear what powers such clans, however organised, actually possessed.

Nevertheless, teips appear to have had a role in organising the clientelistic network at the local level in Chechnya to provide both military assistance and political support to revolutionary leaders. To begin with let us note that the distinguished ethnographer Valery Tishkov believes that the Chechen military was not organised on the basis of clans. Rather, he argues, it was organised territorially, with people from the same village or settlement forming the 'core of each battle group' (2004: 94). However, one of his own interrogators refutes him stating,

> It is true that armed groups were formed along territorial lines, but *teip* membership also played a part. For example, the Galaizhoishaya brigade in Yermolovka were practically all from the Galai *teip*. In Zakan-Urt the Chaberloy special regiment, headed by Kurdi Bazhiyev, consisted mainly of Chaberloy *teip* members (Tishkov 2004: 235).

Our sense is that Tishkov and his interlocutor are both correct. Villages and settlements formed 'brigades' or 'regiments', which were actually informal military squads of fifteen or so people headed by a leader, the so-called 'warlord'. But many residential places tended to be dominated by a particular teip, which meant that the members of their fighting squads would come from that teip. The point here is that when Chechen 'brigades' fought it was likely that the fighters came from common places of residence where they were actual or clan brothers, motivated to fight for each other by long term physical propinquity strengthened by agnatic kinship.

In principle, these different 'brigades' were all unified into the National Guard which was loyal to the president of Chechnya. However, especially after the first Chechen War these units were organised into forces loyal to a particular warlord, who tended to be independent of presidential authority, as is described by Syed Adnan Ali Shah:

> Post Russo-Chechen war of 1994–96, four field commanders transformed into 'warlords' by building various strongholds on the basis of clan or teip solidarity, over which Grozny had almost no control. Each 'warlord' imposed his particular discipline, introduced and enforced his rule, and ensured the 'protection' of the population under his control. The 'warlords' became a main political force in the Chechen politics. These influential field commanders-cum-'warlords' were Salman Raduev, Shamyl Bassaev, Ruslan Gelaev, and Arbi Baraev. Shamyl Bassaev's territory comprised of a large part of the areas of Vedeno, Shali, Shatoy, Achkhoy-Martan, and part of Urus-Martan districts of Chechnya. Salman Raduev controlled a territory that included the Nozhay-Iurt District and the villages of Samashki and Iandyrka, and Gekhi-Chu in the district of Urus-Martan. Ruslan Gelaev based himself mostly in the Grozny

area and in the Argun District. Baraev was limited to the district of Urus-Martan (Ali Shah 2004).

Clans were also involved in political alliances with peripheral political officials, and these alliances had implications for access to valuable assets, especially oil. For example, the Terekhskoi clan was reported allied with Zavgayev, who was himself Terekhskoi, and this alliance facilitated its 'domination of the oil industry' (Lieven 1998: 336); in no small part because Zavgayev 'placed in all of the Republic's key posts men of his *teip*' (Avioutskii 2002: 2–3). This provoked 'burning resentment among other groups' (Lieven 1998: 337). Such antipathy, in turn, is reported to have motivated the formation of 'a new *teip* coalition' dominated by the Myalkhi teip, under Dudayev (Lieven 1998: 337). One well-placed informant reported that after Dudayev replaced Zavgayev, Dudayev 'and others like him ... [were] bound together .... With the pension and oil [money] that his circle has gobbled up, you could build a republic like Kuwait. Even if 5% of the sale of oil were given to the needs of the population, how we would live. ... They've swallowed up the oil together: he gobbled it, Gantemirov gobbled it, Mamodayev gobbled it' (in Tishkov 2004: 66).

The clan alliances, among other things, operated to allocate oil wealth, and because everybody wanted as much wealth as possible they could be fragile. For example, Gantemirov, the Mayor of Grozny, and Mamodayev, the head of the Chechen government during Dudayev's time, were early allies of Dudayev. However, this alliance would come apart in 1992–1993 over oil, as described by the geographer Viatcheslav Avioutskii (in a grammatically rather adventurous manner):

> In 1992–1993, a struggle for oil opposed on one hand, the President Jokhar Dudayev, the oil minister Sultan Albakov, and the state security minister Sultan Gueliskhanov (Yalkhoroy teype (taip, clan)), and on the other, the chief of the Chechen government Yaragui Mamodayev and the mayor of Grozny Beslan Gantemirov (Tchonkhoy teype (taip, clan)). In the same time, Dudayevites opposed to members of the Nijaloy teype (taip, clan) of the former speaker of the Chechen-Ingush parliament Zavgayev, based in the Nadterechny District and directed by its mayor Umar Avturkhanov. The conflict for the oil profits' sharing drove to uniting members of two teypes (clans), opposed to Dudayev (Nijaloy and Yalkhoroy teypes (clans)). In summer 1994, they were rejoined by the former speaker of the Russian parliament and his Chonkhoy (Chinkho) teype (taip, clan). During the summer-fall 1994, the sporadic clashes between Dudayev fighters and the Chechen opposition increase and change gradually in a civil war. The opposition call Moscow to intensify its military help. Implied in the conflict, in December 1994, the federal troops are introduced in Chechnya (2002: 4).

In effect, Avioutskii is arguing that the first Chechen War started as part of a struggle between competing clan alliances, with one alliance, that of the Opposition, calling upon the Russian Federation to help it in its struggle.

These networks equally extended to the centre in Moscow, where there were deals between peripheral and central oligarchs. 'Deals' involved a generalised reciprocity: central oligarchs helped their peripheral counterparts acquire something of value, and vice versa. Deals were not always about oil. They could be about drugs, any sort of valuable commodity, protection money, kidnapping ransoms, etc. However, many deals were about division of oil revenues, and could have military consequences. Tishkov observes that Dudayev 'and his immediate circle had an undisclosed agreement with Russian oil industry barons and top leaders … to transfer to Moscow only 80% of the money from Grozny oil and keep the remaining 20%' (2004: 89). Further, Tishkov asserts, referring to the start of the 1994–1996 war, 'The real conflict became unavoidable when Dudayev violated the rule and established a 50–50 split between Moscow and Grozny' (ibid.: 89).

Consider the case of one central baron, Boris Berezovsky. He became in the early 1990s the richest and most powerful of the new Moscow elite, with vast holdings in the motor industry, finance, aluminium and the media. He entered the oil industry founding a company called Sibneft, with its holdings largely in Siberia. Consider how he became an oil baron:

> From aviation, Berezovsky moved on to the really big money in Russia – oil. His entry into the oil business was facilitated by the most egregious of all the great ripoffs that have characterised post-Soviet Russia, the 'loans for shares' scheme by which our hero and his fellow oligarchs helped themselves to priceless chunks of the country's resources, for pennies on the dollar, in return for financing Yeltsin's re-election in 1996. Following that free, but hardly fair, election, the godfather increased his political profile, taking various high-level government posts (without of course ceasing his business operations for a second). It was at this time that his interest in Chechen matters re-emerged, in the form of lavish ransom payments to kidnappers in Chechnya for the retrieval of their victims. Khlebnikov points out that this flow of money to the gangs in the devastated territory effectively made it impossible for the elected Chechen leader to stabilise his country. The consequent anarchy, culminating in the invasion of Dagestan in the summer of 1999 by fundamentalist Islamist Chechens, provided the backdrop for the second Chechen war (Beyond the Fringe 2006).

Throughout the Chechen Wars Berezovsky maintained cordial relations with certain Chechen leaders, including Salam Raduiev and Shamil Basaev. The former tied Berezovsky to oil in the Caucasus, commenting, 'He is personally interested in this oil (the pipeline Bakú-Novorossisk)' (Voltairenet 2004: 1). Then,

> The year was 1999. Berezovsky had extensive contacts with Chechen rebels, negotiating several hostage releases. Seemingly out of nowhere, Chechen rebel commanders invaded neighbouring Dagestan. This shut off Caspian oil supplies from the south, vastly increasing the Siberian holdings of Berezovsky and a number of other oligarchs. It also moved the region from a delicate peace to almost inevitable conflict (*New Internationalist* 2003: 1).

Basaev was the main Chechen warlord who led the attack upon Dagestan. The conflict that became 'inevitable' because of this attack was the second phase of the Chechen War. The *New Internationalist* implies that the conflict may have been a result of one set of peripheral actors in the clientelistic network returning a favour to another central actor in the network, a favour that had to do with the value of oil revenues. Next, we think a bit more abstractly about the situations we have been describing.

These situations may be described as those exhibited by a 'centre/periphery clientelistic network' that had three sorts of structural actors: the first of these are ordinary Vainakhs; the second are largely Chechen capitalist or political elites; and the third are Moscow capitalist or political elites. Capitalist elites will be understood as the network's various 'barons'. Political elites were its 'oligarchs' or 'warlords'. An oligarch occupied a political position. A warlord commanded troops that were quasi-independent of any political position. What this network did was to regulate the production and allocation of value in, among other places, the Chechen oil sector. These operations were often illegal, so that by and large the network could be characterised as corrupt and criminal.

Individuals in the network did one of two things. Ordinary Chechens provided much of the network's physical labour. This involved the actual fighting and running the various activities involved in the oil industry (pumping oil from wells, siphoning it from pipelines, refining it, and transporting it to market). Oligarchs, warlords and barons in both Moscow and Chechnya performed the managerial chores, directing the fighting, managing the working in the oil industry or, for that matter, in any other revenue-producing enterprise. It was they, as we have already heard, that enjoyed the lion's share of the oil revenues. The networks were competitive in the sense that there was usually more than one network in existence at any one time, and different networks sought to increase their share of the oil, and other, values at the expense of other networks.

The networks were clientelistic in that they involved patron–client relationships: (1) in which richer and more powerful elite patrons in Chechnya provided ordinary Chechen clients with the salary or protection that allowed them to work the oil industry; and (2) in which still richer and more powerful elite patrons in Moscow provided Chechen counterparts with the services they required in order for them to operate their patron–client network in Chechnya. It is difficult to know just how much of Grozny oil revenues went into this clientelistic network. However, Tishkov writes, 'Beginning in 1998, the illegal pillaging of oil revenues reached unprecedented proportions. … Most oil wells were seized by armed groups, and the state's industrial oil production dropped to 400 tons daily in 1999, compared to 4,200 tons in 1998' (2004: 188). Such figures suggest that the clientelistic network received in 1999 ten times the oil that the government received.

A striking characteristic of the clientelistic network we have identified is that it developed in a context where centre/periphery relations had become unregulated because of a sharp decline in the legitimacy, authority and power of the central state. In this context the network of allied patron–client linkages that emerges is able to perform the labour involved in, as well as the management of, military and economic practices required for the production and allocation of value, which value in the case of Chechnya was especially that of oil revenues. If a mode of domination is a situation where one category of actors is able to regulate the flow of substantial amounts value to itself, at the expense of other categories of actors, the clientelistic network we have just described for Chechnya in the 1990s appears to be a third mode of domination that has occurred in Chechnya. Let us close this section with a few words on the ability of the clientelistic network to facilitate state-building and authoritarian systems of governance.

Although, theoretically, Chechen oil might have been a source of integration for the state-building process – as happened in Azerbaijan, Bashkortostan, Tatarstan, Turkmenistan etc. – no Chechen political force so used it. It disintegrated Chechnya, Ingushetia, Dagestan and Abkhasia. Let us explain why. During the last fifteen years, the clientelistic networks organised by Chechen oligarchs, oil barons and warlords, devoted to enhancing their own value-accumulating powers, were indifferent to state-building. Rather, elites struggled against each other to acquire and market oil. The state, whoever happened to govern it, turned out to be an annoying obstacle for their predatory activities. Thus, even though elites subjectively framed their activities in terms of state-building, they objectively organised them for state-wrecking.

Finally, an observation should be made concerning the possibility of authoritarian rule in Chechnya. A strong dictatorial leader like Aliev or Turkmenbashi (a 'Soviet' type of leader) could hardly improve the situation in the Chechen Republic. First, such a person would be very threatening to the war-based economic structures and would provoke open (violent) opposition. Even if this model seems to work in Azerbaijan, Byelorussia, Turkmenistan, Bashkortostan or Tatarstan, it does not mean that it would function for the Caucasus. This view is supported if one considers the cases of Qadirov and Ziazikov. Qadirov was a strong president of the Chechen Republic from 2000 to 2003. Ziazikov was assassinated on 9 May 2003. Ziazikov was president of Ingushetia. He escaped a number of assassination attempts. Chechen and Ingush public opinion regard authoritarian rule as a return to Stalin's times. It reminds them of deportation. The possibility of an authoritarian regime horrifies them even more than terrorists with whom they can speak the same language and at least negotiate because of their similar socio-cultural background. Thus, the people prefer terrorists because they help them to escape authoritarian rule, and justify their violence as opposition to all external domination. 'European peacemakers', 'American observers', 'Federal forces' or 'Moscow pocket presidents' such as Qadirov and Ziazikov all represent such forces. The attempts to assassinate the representatives of such forces are regarded as unavoidable (not to say 'proper'). One of Khizriyeva's interviewees in Ingushetia put the matter thus:

> People from the government [*liudi v pravitelstve*] should understand – in my view – that they have to abandon Stalin's national policy and Soviet state politics. They must do away with everything the Soviet times have brought to us. But who can force them to think about another way out? It is a great task. We are paying now for the legacy of Stalinism. And every small political individual today imagines himself to be a Stalin.

Conclusion

This chapter has proposed an understanding of the function of oil and violence in recent Chechen history. It has stressed the role of domination in reaching this understanding. Three periods of Vainakh history with different modes of domination were distinguished: a first era when Chechnya was subjected to the domination of the Russian Empire; a second era when it experienced Soviet domination; and a third era when it has struggled over the domination with the Russian Federation. The first period when Chechnya was incorporated into the Russian Empire was marked by the long Caucasian War. This helped forge a common identity among Vainakh speakers and, at the same time, developed severe conflict between Vainakhs and Cossacks brought in by imperial officials to police their southern frontier. Oil was discovered and developed around

Grozny in the final half of the nineteenth century and the beginning of the twentieth under a regime involving competition between local and transnational capitalist interests.

The Bolshevik Revolution ended this competition in favour of a Soviet mode of domination in which the oil industry became state property and from which transnational oil companies were excluded. Soviet domination was experienced by Vainakhs as not dissimilar to that of the Czars and provoked in the interwar years a number of rebellions. The Grozny area became a key petroleum production and distribution centre for the entire USSR during the Soviet era. This elevated Grozny's strategic importance. It is proposed that the enhanced strategic value of the Grozny region, in conjunction with the Vainakh record of rebellion, played a role in Stalin's decision to deport Vainakhs from their homeland to Kazakhstan during the Second World War.

A third mode of domination began with the 1989 collapse of the USSR and the assumption of neo-liberal economic policies in the newly formed Russian Federation. During this period, the Chechen War developed and with it what we have chosen to term the centre/periphery clientelistic network. This war, like the earlier Caucasian War and the different rebellions of the Soviet era, involved resistance of the Vainakh periphery to a Russian centre trying to dominate its periphery. The struggle against domination was, among other matters, over who would get how much of the oil revenues. Further, the clientelistic network is suggested to be a structure that, by integrating both the oil industry and military means into a single organisation, gave the Chechen elite the capacity both to produce oil revenues and to fight to hold on to them. Given the existence of these three modes of domination, it seems warranted to assert that the history of Chechnya since 1785 has been, as Lieven (1998) put it, 'against … domination'.

Finally, as promised, let us introduce the notion of Hobbesian elitism. Remember the Hobbesian proposition that 'a strong central authority is required, given the nature of humanity, to prevent the "war of all against all"'. This chapter suggests that the situation in Chechnya does support the Hobbesian view that in the absence of a strong central authority violent and grim warfare can occur. However, in the instance we have examined, warfare is not a matter of human nature. Rather, it is a matter of class. It is the elite classes of both the periphery and the centre in the weakened Russian Federation who organise a clientelistic network that will fight for their interests. This observation justifies the proposition, 'Hobbesian situations of violent and grim warfare in weakened states may occur due to the inability of such states to regulate the accumulative appetites of their elite classes'. We term such a proposition 'Hobbesian elitism' and have shown that events of the Chechen War warrant it.

References

Aliroev, Ibragim. 2005. Orsiin-Nokhchiin Slovar. Moscow: Akademia, 314, 321, 346.

Ali Shah, Syed Adnan. 2004. Genesis of the Chechen Resistance Movement. http://www.issi.org.pk/journal/2004_files/no_/article/4a.htm (accessed 26 March 2008).

Al-Karakhi, Muhammed-Tahir. 1990. *Tri Imama*. Makhachkala: Daguchpedgis, 10.

Avioutskii, Viatcheslav. 2002. Chechnya: Towards Partition? http://www.amina.com/article/partition2.html (accessed 20 March 2008).

Avtorkhanov, Abdurakhman. 1996. The Chechen and Ingush during the Soviet Period and Its Antecedents. In *The North Caucasus Barrier (the Russian Advance towards the Muslim World)*, ed. Marie Bennigsen-Broxup, 161–92. London.

Beyond the Fringe. 2006. Luguvoy and the Timeline Change. http://www.kadjitcha.com/2006/12/10/luguvoy=&-the-timeline-change/ (accessed 26 March 2008).

Bobrovnikov, Vladimir. 2006. Sud'by vakfa na Vostochnom Kavkaze. In *Islam v sovremennom mire*, ed. Damir Muhketdinov, Aidar Khabutdinov and Galina Khizriyeva. Nizhnii Novgorod: Makhinur, no. 3–4, vyp. 5–6, 21.

Golos Checheno-Ingushetii. 1991. September, 25. Grozny: Groznensky rabochiy.

Hobbes, Thomas. 1651 [1982]. *The Leviathan*. Harmondsworth: Penguin.

Khizriyeva, Galina. 2005. Virdovye bratsva na severo-vostochnom Kavkase. *Etnograficheskoye obozrenie* 1: 121–35.

Lieven, Anatol. 1998. *Chechnya: Tombstone of Russia's Power*. New Haven: Yale University Press.

Minorsky, Vladimir. 1963. *Istoriya Schirvana i Derbenta*. Moscow: Nauka.

Neftianaya entsiklopedia. 2002. Moscow: MAI, 249.

New Internationalist. 2003. Boris Berezovsky – Worldbeaters. http://findarticles.com/p/articles/mi_mOJQP/is_363/ai_1116127808/print (accessed 25 March 2008).

Nukhaev, Khozh-Akhmed. 2002. Prilozhenie. *Adat*, St.Petersburg: Tekhicheskaya kniga, 247.

Ragosin, Viktor. 1884. Neft' I neftianaia promyshlennost' (s prilozheniem issledovania kavkazskoi nefti gospod Markovnikova i Ogloblina). – St.Petersburg: Tipografia 'obshestvennaia polza', 118.

Ratgauser, Yakov. 1928. *Kistorii grazhdanskoi voiny na Tereke*. Baku: Isdatelstvo Bakinskogo otdela narodnogo obrazovania, 145.

Sulaev, Magomet. 2003. A nuzhen li nam novyi Mekh-khel? *Molodezhnaya smena* 1, April. Grozny: Groznensky rabochiy.

Terskie Vedomosti. 1895.Vladikavkas: Electropechatnia Terskogo oblastnogo pravlenia.

Tishkov, Valery. 2004. *Chechnya: Life in a War-torn Society*. Berkeley: University of California Press.

Voltairenet. 2004. Boris Berezovski, the Smuggler. http://www.voltairenet.org/article30030.html (accessed 25 March 2008).

Wood, Tony. 2004. The Case for Chechnya. *New Left Review*. http://www.newleftreview.org/?page=article&view=2533 (accessed 18 March 2008).

———. 2007. *Chechnya: The Case for Independence*. London: Verso.

Yushkin, Evgenyi. 1928 [2005]. *Ocherki o nachale grazhdanskoi voiny na Tereke*. Moscow: MGIMO, 107, 110, 143.

SUGGESTIONS FOR A SECOND READING

An Alternative Perspective on Contested Resources
as an Explanation for Conflict

Günther Schlee

Crude Domination proposes an anthropological perspective on the analysis of oil. As a number of scholars have suggested, oil has been a curse in developing countries, most of whom have found their economies more fragile, their political regimes more authoritarian, and their conflicts increased. Stephen Reyna and Andrea Behrends, in the volume's introduction, go one step further and suggest that this curse is 'crazy' because oil brings wealth, which would seem to be the means to bring harmony and affluence, but which turns out to be the means to bring trials and tribulation. The different articles in this volume richly, and from an ethnographic perspective, analyse oil's crazy curse. Reyna and Behrends in the volume's introduction suggest a 'crude domination' anthropological approach to the study of oil, which is concerned with groups' struggle to dominate other groups by regulating the distribution of value created by the production of oil. The pun 'crude' domination, which alludes to crude oil, suggests a relationship between the kind of resource and the social relations – the forms of alliance, competition and conflict – which develop around it. This relationship needs to be discussed.

I have tried to propagate the view that there is no such thing as a 're-source-based conflict' or 'identity-based conflict' for over ten years now, since long before these terms became so fashionable. My recent book on the topic (Schlee 2008) is mainly a summary and systematisation of earlier publications. I have always maintained that there is a resource aspect to all conflicts but also that identification plays an equally important role in all conflicts. In fact, the two can never compete with each other on the same scale of importance, because they address quite different questions. The resource question is: What do people fight about? The identity questions are: Who fights whom? and Who fights with whom? or, to combine the two, Who takes whose side against whom? One can say that one kind of question is about the objects of a conflict, the other one about the subjects.

The resource question (whether a conflict is about oil, water, employment opportunities or power – which can be an aim in itself or an indirect resource for the acquisition of other resources – comprising political representation) never determines the identification processes of friend and foe. There is no 'commodity determinism', as Watts (this volume) puts it. I say 'determines'; there may be subtle influences between the kind of resource contested and the identification processes leading to the choice (or affirmation) of persons as group members or allies or excluded from participation or even fought as enemies. Whatever such influences we find, they are never strong enough to predict in a strict sense, who is going to side with whom. The world of conflict is full of unexpected alliances and of new fissions occurring where people who just look only at the resource map least anticipated them. In the ascription of enemy stereotypes on the one hand and the reasons given for the inclusion of people into groups and alliances on the other, we mostly find dimensions of identification like ethnicity, religion, nationality, historical affiliation or language. None of these are universal or eternal; all of them are constructs of the human mind. But these are the categories that happen to have evolved as dominant in the present political discourses, globally, regionally and locally.

For the research programme of my department (Department 1, *Integration and Conflict*, of the Max Planck Institute for Social Anthropology at Halle) I decided to give priority to the *who* question over the *what* question. Not that I found the resource question unimportant, but it was already addressed by many competent people, while I found the question of identification under-researched. Of course, a lot has been written about identity and identification, but much of it appeared a bit loose to me. It was not the systematic description of categories, the logic of possible and impossible combination of such categories, the modelling of decisions between them and the analysis of the forms of identity change which I envisaged and still envisage (the task has not been completed). So identity and difference, not oil and water, have become key concepts in our theoretical work and in the empirical fieldwork meant to feed into it.

Still, I had two active and very eloquent colleagues, Stephen Reyna and Andrea Behrends, who chose a resource as the defining feature of their field of research. They wanted to hold a big conference about oil. Stephen and Andrea also had ideas about doing research in Chad, establishing a research station in its capital, N'Djamena, and many other things. So I decided to allow this one exception to the rule in our general research programme and to let them go ahead with oil. I wanted to see how far they would get with it.

How far have they got? They have not done too badly, I must admit. For their theory of 'crude domination', they postulate the necessity of an 'anthropology of oil'. They postulate the 'crazy curse' of oil and OMOD (oil modes of domination). All this suggests that the forms that conflicts take are indeed determined or at least strongly influenced by the physical nature of the contested resource, at least if the resource in question is oil. Still, the rich ethnography in Andrea Behrends' individual contribution about two wars in the area on either side of the Chad/Sudan border shows that reality cannot be squeezed into such a framework. She does not even attempt to do so, and rather looks at resources from an identity perspective, foregrounding social relations. Still, the physical nature of the resource in question cannot be ignored. Some of Behrends' findings show the impact that the presence or the expectation of the discovery of oil has had on the course of these conflicts, but other findings suggest that the relationship between the nature of the resource and the form of the conflict is very indirect or entirely absent. She applies the theorem of 'lootability', which is based on the distinction between locally fixed resources and removable resources and which, in this sense, has implications for the corresponding types of conflicts. Evidently, however, there are limits to the possibility of predicting features of conflicts with reference to the physical nature of the contested resource on which the conflicts are based. Behrends wisely does not even attempt to relate the 'transient constellations [of the fighters] which can easily regroup' to the fact that there is oil around.

For Behrends' case study, an observation that has often been made with regard to ethnic conflicts – namely, that ethnicity cannot be the 'cause' of a conflict, because it often becomes a factor only after the conflict has escalated and processes of identification have become more rigid and exclusive – can also be made with reference to oil (or, tentatively, even with reference to resources in general). In this case, it also appears that the role played by resources can change in the course of a conflict. The conflicts in the Chad/Sudan borderlands had been going on for quite some time, beginning well before the topic of oil entered into the 'hate talk' of the various protagonists, who only much later began accusing one another of just being after the oil. Typically, as pointed out above, the resource question comes into the analysis of a conflict when one addresses the question of what the conflict is all about. In contrast, questions concerning whom to support and whom to fight are posed in terms of ethnic or religious discourses, often of a racialised variety. Here, in an interesting reversal, oil has been introduced into the discourse accompanying the conflict in order to discredit those who were already established adversaries – a phenomenon not easily subsumed under the 'crazy curse' idea or OMOD.

Oil has not yet been found in Darfur; rather, a long-standing conflict is just receiving additional fuel, to take up a phrase by Kok (1992), by oil found elsewhere and by the expectation of future oil production in Darfur. But the role of such expectations is not determined by the nature of the resource in question. Behrends' statements about Chad and Darfur remind me very much of the situation in Southern Ethiopia in 1991, when the members of the Mengistu government had escaped from the country, and the country was left without a government for a period. Life went on peacefully, at least in comparison to the situation before and after the interregnum. No state services where missed, because the state had not been much of a service institution anyhow. The new powers were still busy establishing themselves in distant Addis Ababa. It took months before different militias began to fight for a share in the new order. The fighting was not about available resources but about future resources. Sooner or later, statehood of a kind would be re-established throughout the country, and it was this anticipation of statehood that fuelled the conflict. In this case the contested resources consisted only in government posts and administrative positions which had not even been created yet. But the perceptions of the conflict – and this resonates with Behrends' findings as well – were not uniform. For the ordinary fighters, the war was between tribes seeking access to scarce pasture and water; but, for their leaders, war was being waged between the members of rival political movements – materially, over pieces of the national cake and, on the level of discourse, over political programmes. Under these conditions, it often seemed as if two or more different wars were going on in the same place at the same time (Schlee and Shongolo 1995).

Schiller's account (in this volume) of popular media in Venezuela starts with a young woman from a poor neighbourhood claiming emphatically on television that the state-run oil company belongs to the people. She regarded it as an asset belonging to her and others like her. Schiller found the government and the oil industry in Venezuela to be in alliance with the popular media movement. All of this is identification politics – President Chávez and the Venezuelan oil industry are good at it, and they have co-opted the people. In contrast to the violent oppression in other oil states, this is an interesting finding; but it is primarily about identification, not about oil. Letting the people participate is not a bad idea, irrespective of the kind of resource involved. Elsewhere, such a policy has turned hunters (criminalised as poachers) into game wardens by giving them jobs and their communities a share in the profits from tourism. Similarly, separatists may become fervent supporters of the wider nation they initially wanted to leave, if you give them a say and a share of the jobs in it.

By privileging the question of identification – e.g., with the nation or with other possible identities – over the question about the kind of resource being shared or contested, I am not taking the side of culture or ideology over economics. Narrower or wider identification is not just a question of culture. It is a key concern of economists (or it should be). It involves the referent of any cost/benefit analysis – the answer to the question of for whom one economises. Any given actor's economic decisions may differ, depending on whether he or she calculates costs and benefits on a strictly individual basis or takes his or her narrower or wider family, clan, community, parish, nation or other social affiliations into consideration.

These points cannot be subsumed, at least not entirely, under a 'crazy curse' theory and OMOD, and the same is true of the materials presented in other contributions to this volume. All of the contributions are ethnographically rich, containing plenty of food for thought, also along other lines. They start with oil, but they are not just about oil. My recommendation to the reader is, therefore, to read this book twice. First, in the way the authors of the introduction want us to read it, focussing on oil; and then a second time with a spotlight on questions about how particular identifications and alliances have come about.

References

Kok, Peter Nyot. 1992. Adding Fuel to the Conflict: Oil, War and Peace in the Sudan. In *Beyond Conflict in the Horn: The Prospects for Peace, Recovery and Development in Ethiopia, Somalia, Eritrea, and Sudan*, ed. Martin Doornboos, Lionel Cliffe, Abdel Ghaffar M. Ahmed and John Markakis, 104–13. London: James Currey.

Schlee, Günther. 2008. *How Enemies Are Made: Towards a Theory of Ethnic and Religious Conflicts*. Oxford and New York: Berghahn Books.

Schlee, Günther and Abdullahi A. Shongolo. 1995. Local War and Its Impact on Ethnic and Religious Identification in Southern Ethiopia. *Geo-Journal* 36(1): 7–17.

NOTES ON CONTRIBUTORS

Andrea Behrends graduated from the Free University Berlin and conducts anthropological research in Chad on conflict, displacement, aid and resilience and oil production. She coordinated an interdisciplinary research project on conflict management with PhD candidates from several sub-Saharan countries. She teaches at the Institute for Anthropology and Philosophy, Martin Luther University of Halle-Wittenberg, and at the Institute for Anthropology, Georg August University Göttingen. She is presently co-editing a book on *Travelling Models in African Conflict Management* and is completing a monograph on biographies, resources, conflict and resilience in eastern Chad.

Jonathan Friedman is Directeur d'études at the Ecole des Hautes Etudes en Sciences Sociales in Paris, and Distinguished Professor of Anthropology at the University of California, San Diego. He has carried out research on the anthropology of global systems and processes, on Marxist theory in anthropology, the study of crises, social and cultural movements as products of global systemic crisis. He has done regional research on southeast Asia and field research in Hawai'i, Europe and central Africa. Among his most recent works are the two-volume publication on the *Anthropology of Global Systems* with Kajsa Ekholm Friedman, 2008 (Vol. I: *Historical Transformations* and Vol. II: *Modernities, Class, and the Contradictions of Globalization*), and the chapter 'Holism and the Transformation of the Contemporary Global Order' in Ton Otto and Nils Bubandt (eds), *Experiments in Holism: Theory and Practice in Contemporary Anthropology* (New York: Wiley-Blackwell, 2010), 260–83.

Kajsa Ekholm Friedman is Professor Emerita in Social Anthropology at Lund University, where she founded the department and worked from 1974 to 2003. She has carried out field and historical research on the Congo, northeast Madagascar, Hawai'i, Sweden and more recently on the Bronze Age in the Middle East and the Mediterranean. Among her recent publications are the two volumes on the *Anthropology of Global Systems*, 2008 (with Jonathan Friedman), and *Trubbel I Paradiset: hawaiianers återkomst (Trouble in Paradise: The Return of the Hawaiian)*, 1998, as well as numerous articles on the political disintegration of the Republic of Congo and its social and cultural consequences. Furthermore, she has published several articles and book chapters on the expansion and collapse of the Bronze Age world system. She is currently finishing a larger book, *Bronze Age Worlds*, which is destined for publication in 2011.

John Gledhill is Max Gluckman Professor of Social Anthropology at the University of Manchester, UK. He is a Vice-President of the International Union of Anthropological and Ethnological Sciences, a member of the Academy of Social Sciences and a Fellow of the British Academy. He has carried out fieldwork in Mexico and Brazil. His publications include the books *Casi Nada: Agrarian Reform in the Homeland of Cardenismo* (also published in Spanish), *Neoliberalism, Transnationalization and Rural Poverty, Power and Its Disguises: Anthropological Perspectives on Politics* (also published in Spanish, Greek and Chinese), and *Cultura y Desafío en Ostula: Cuatro Siglos de Autonomía Indígena en la Costa-Sierra Nahua de Michoacán.*

Bret Gustafson is an Assistant Professor of Anthropology at Washington University in St. Louis. He received his PhD in Social Anthropology from Harvard University (2002), based on his study of the politics of indigenous language education in Bolivia (*New Languages of the State: Indigenous Resurgence and the Politics of Knowledge in Bolivia*, Duke University, 2009). He is currently researching the relationship between nationalist state-led development regimes, energy geopolitics, and indigenous territorial rights in Bolivia and Brazil.

Galina Khizriyeva graduated from Moscow State University and works as a researcher at the Institute for Cultural Studies and the Institute of Oriental Studies of Moscow State University (RAS). She also is a lecturer at the Russian State University for Humanities. From 1995 to 2010 she periodically conducted her fieldwork in the oil regions of the Russian Federation such as West Siberia and the northern Caucasus. In 2003 she was invited by the Max Planck Institute for Social Anthropology (Halle, Germany) to take part in a project on the religious situation in the post-Soviet space. She published more than one hundred articles on the subject. Her recent publications include 2008, 'Siberian Oil and Muslim Mobilisation', *Etnograficheskoye obosrenie*; 2009, 'The Role of the Islamic Factor in Russo-Chechen Conflict and the Formation of New International Ties between the Russian Federation and the Muslim World' and 'Oil against Tradition in Chechnya and Ingushetia' in the IOS Working Papers *Caucasus and Central Asia*.

Stephen P. Reyna is a Senior Research Fellow at the Humanitarian and Conflict Response Institute at the University of Manchester (UK) as well as a Research Associate at the Max Planck Institute of Social Anthropology (Germany). He was the founder and first Editor of *Anthropological Theory*. His publications include: *Wars without End: The Political Economy of a Precolonial African State* (1990); *Connections: Brain, Mind and Culture in a Social Anthropology* (2002); 'The Traveling Model that Wouldn't Travel, or Developing Dystopia: Oil, Empire, and Patrimonialism in Contemporary Chad', *Social Analysis* (2007); and 'Taking Place: "New Wars" versus Global Wars', *Social Anthropology* (2009).

Naomi Schiller is an Assistant Professor in the Department of Anthropology at Temple University in Philadelphia. She earned her PhD in Anthropology from New York University in 2009. Her research and teaching focuses on the anthropology of media, ethnographic film, the state and social movements in Latin America. Dr Schiller is completing a manuscript on community media and the state in Venezuela.

Günther Schlee (PhD Hamburg, 1977, Habilitation Bayreuth 1986) was Professor at the Faculty of Sociology at Bielefeld from 1986 to 1999. Since 1999 he has been the director of Department I, 'Integration and Conflict', at the Max Planck Institute for Social Anthropology at Halle/Saale, Germany. His book publications include *Identities on the Move: Clanship and Pastoralism in Northern Kenya* (International African Institute, 1989), *Rendille Proverbs in their Social and Legal Context* (with Karaba Sahado, 2002), *Boran Proverbs in their Cultural Context* (with Abdullahi Shongolo, 2007) (both: Cologne: Rüdiger Köppe), *How Enemies Are Made* (Berghahn Books, 2008) and *Changing Identifications and Alliances in North-east Africa* (two volumes, with Elizabeth Watson, Berghahn Books, 2009).

Florian Stammler has worked on the anthropology of extractive industry and pastoral nomadism since 1995, mostly on northern Russia. He is the Coordinator of Anthropology at the Arctic Centre, University of Lapland, Finland, an Associate at Scott Polar Research Institute, University of Cambridge, UK, and Coordinator of the Extractive Industries Working Group of the International Arctic Social Sciences Association (IASSA). He published *Reindeer Nomads Meet the Market* (Lit Verlag, 2005), 'High Resilience in the Yamal-Nenets Socio-ecological System' (with B. Forbes, *PNAS* 2009) and collaborated in the making of several films on the Arctic, e.g. with BBC 2.

Michael Watts is director of the Center for African Studies, University of California, Berkeley. He has taught development studies at the University of California for three decades and has published on agrarian change, famine and rural development in Africa and Asia. He is currently completing a book on oil and violence in Nigeria.

INDEX